Department of Health

Framework for the Assessment of Children in Need and their Families

Guidance Notes and Glossary for:

Referral and Initial Information Record,

Initial Assessment Record and

Core Assessment Records

London: TSO

Social Care Group

The Social Care Group is one of the four business groups in the Department of Health. It is jointly headed by the Chief Social Services Inspector and the Head of Social Care Policy. It supports Ministers in promoting high quality, cost effective services through

- national policies
- support to external social care agencies
- inspection

The Social Services Inspectorate is a part of the Social Care Group. It is headed by the Chief Social Services Inspector who is the principal professional advisor to Ministers on social services and related matters.

First published 2000

Fifth impression 2008

Published with permission of the Department of Health on behalf of the Controller of Her Majesty's Stationery Office.

ISBN 9780113224241

Published by The Stationery Office Ltd

Printed in the United Kingdom for The Stationery Office
ID5913501 C2 9/08

Contents

1 REFERRAL AND INITIAL INFORMATION RECORD

Background

The Referral and Initial Information Record has been developed in response to the *Framework for the Assessment of Children in Need and their Families* (2000) and *Working Together to Safeguard Children* (1999). The Referral and Initial Information record begins the process of systematic information gathering about children in need and their families. This process is continued in the Initial Assessment and Core Assessment Records. The records have been designed to provide an integrated framework for the process of recording and analysing information in line with the Guidance in the *Framework for the Assessment of Children in Need and their Families* (2000).

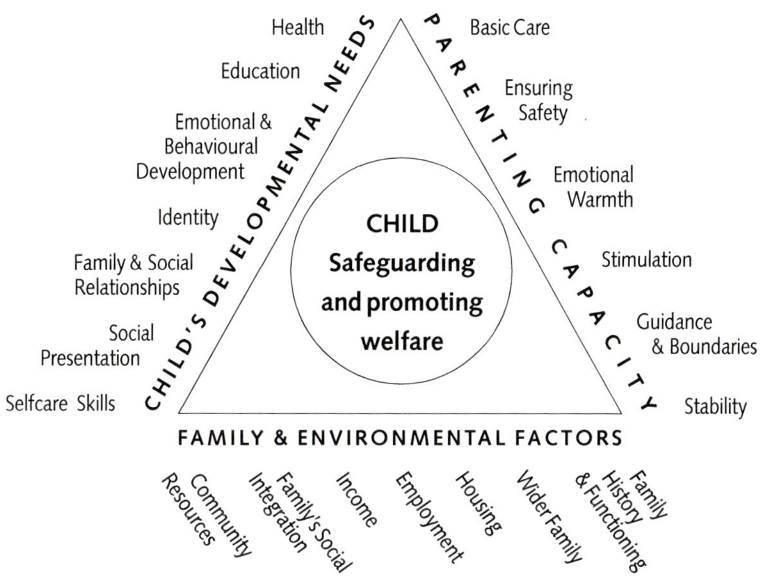

Referral and Initial Information Record

The Referral and Initial Information Record gathers together the essential information about the child including ethnicity, household composition, parental responsibility and agencies currently involved with the child and family.

In order to meet the assessment time scales set out in *The Governments Objectives for Children's Social Services* (1999) a decision should be is made on what the response will be to a referral within one working day of it being received.

The Referral and Initial Information Record records the reason the referral or request for services was made and how it was responded to by the SSD. For example, some referrals can be dealt with by the provision of information and advice, or by a referral to another agency. When referrals require a response from a social services department then an initial assessment should be carried out.

The Referral and Initial Information Record therefore has two purposes: to record basic information on the child and family; and to record the SSD and other relevant agencies response to the referral. The Initial Information Record can therefore be used by social services departments to process referrals and to record essential information gathered at the point of referral.

GLOSSARY

1. SSD Case No.

This is the index number given to the referral by the Social Services Department.

2. Is the Parent/Carer aware of the referral?

This refers to awareness at the point in time the referral is being made.

3. Re-referral

A re-referral is defined as a referral about the same child received within a twelve month period, where the child's case has been closed.

4. Address

This is the child's usual or home address. Where parents have shared care, the child may have two addresses.

5. Current Address if different from above

This should be used in situations where the child is not living at their usual or home address. For example, if a child is living temporarily with a relative or is a hospital patient.

6. Principal Carers

This should record the main carers of the child at their usual or home address.

7. Responsible Local Authority

This section should be completed if a referral is being made regarding a child who is the responsibility of an authority other than your own. For example, a child on another authority's Child Protection Register, or a child in the care of another authority who is residing in your local authority area.

8. Agency/Rel to child

This records the relationship of the referrer to the child. If the referrer is making the referral on behalf of their agency then this should be recorded i.e. if a teacher made a referral then 'school' would be recorded. A family member would have their relationship to the child recorded. A neighbour would be recorded as such.

9. Address

This is the referrer's agency address, where appropriate, i.e. St John's School, or home address in the case of a relative or neighbour. If the referral is made anonymously this information should be recorded.

10. Ethnicity

The categories listed are those used by the Government. They will assist authorities in the completion of statistical returns.

11. Other Household members

This section is used to record all those people (children and adults) living at the child's usual or home address.

12. Significant family members not members of child's household

This section is used to record significant family members not living in the child's household. For example, a birth parent or relative who provides care for the child on a shared basis or has a lot of contact with him or her.

- **SSD case number if appropriate.** This is used if a family member is already a Social Services Department service user. This should include the parent or carer if they are known to adult social services, for example the Community Mental Health Team.
- **Tick if also referred to SSD**. This should be completed if another household member is being referred to your social services department, at the same time. **A separate Initial Information Record should be completed for each child referred. Following the Data Protection Act 1998 it is recommended that each child has a separate file.**

13. SSD cases associated with the referred child

In some cases it is important to record links to other social services department cases. For example where half or stepsiblings are looked after by an authority or have had their names placed on an authority's Child Protection Register or are receiving family support services. This section may also be used in situations where there are concerns about, for example, sexual abuse which involve a number of different families.

14. Key Agencies

The name of the key professional from all agencies currently involved with the child and family should be recorded. This includes agencies working with parents. Agencies should be consulted/involved as appropriate as part of the initial assessment and this should be indicated by a tick. Parental permission to contact other agencies should be obtained from parents except in cases where by doing so the safety of the child would be jeopardised (*Working Together to Safeguard Children* (1999)). It will have to be made clear at this point whether other professionals agree to information they provide being shared with the child and/or family.

15. Reason for referral/request for services

In this section brief details are recorded about the reason for the referral, or services requested by, or on behalf of, the family. It is important to note these details, even when the services requested cannot be provided, or can not be provided immediately.

16. Further Action

It is important to indicate what action has been taken and what action is planned, by whom and from which agency. This includes no further action. The referral should be collated with previous referrals and/or files, which should be consulted and information in them drawn upon as part of the analysis and decision making processes.

The worker who has completed the referral should always sign and date the record. The record should then be passed to the relevant manager to confirm the action recommended, in accordance with the Social Services Department's policy.

2 INITIAL ASSESSMENT RECORD

Background

The Initial Assessment Record has been developed in response to the *Framework for the Assessment of Children in Need and their Families* (2000) and *Working Together to Safeguard Children* (1999).

The full title of the record, *Initial Assessment of children's needs and issues which impact on parents' capacities to respond to them appropriately*, emphasises the link between the Initial Assessment record and the Core Assessment Record, *Core Assessment record of children's needs and issues which impact on parents' capacities to respond to them appropriately.* The content of both the initial Assessment and Core Assessment Records have been informed by relevant research findings.

The Initial Assessment Record continues the process of systematic information gathering, commenced in the Referral and Initial Information record, and the analysis of this material. This process of assessment is continued if a core assessment is undertaken. The main headings of both records are organised according to the Assessment Framework domains and dimensions.

Initial Assessment

In order to meet the time scales set out in *The Governments Objectives for Children's Social Services* (1999) an initial assessment should be completed within 7 working days of the referral **being received**.

The Initial Assessment covers:

- **The Child's Developmental Needs.** These are set out under the seven dimensions in the *Framework for the Assessment of Children in Need and their Families.*
  As it is an initial assessment of the child's needs, some dimensions which are inter-related have been placed together, for example, Identity and Social Presentation.
- **Parents'/Carers' Capacities to Respond Appropriately to the Child's Needs.** It is important that parent's strengths as well as weaknesses are recorded. Key issues which research has shown to affect parent's ability to respond appropriately to their child's needs have been included.
- **Family and Environmental Factors which have an Impact on the Family.** The environment within which children and families live can play an important role in reducing or increasing the stresses on families, depending on the support available to them.

The purpose of the Initial Assessment is to decide whether the child is a child in need, the nature of any services required, from where and within what times scales, and whether a more detailed core assessment should be carried out. The fact that a decision is made to carry out a core assessment should not prevent a child or family receiving services which are necessary to support them.

Agencies contacted/involved during Initial Assessment

Agencies should be consulted and involved as appropriate as part of the initial assessment. Parental permission to contact other agencies should be obtained from parents except in cases where the safety of the child would be jeopardised. It will have to be made clear at this point whether other professionals agree to information they provide being shared with the family. Agencies contacted or involved in the Initial Assessment should be recorded by a tick. The name and address of any agency contacted or involved in the Initial Assessment not already recorded on the Referral and Initial Information Record should be added to the Initial Information Record.

Reason for Initial Assessment

Brief details of why an Initial Assessment is being undertaken should be recorded in this section.

Child's Developmental Needs

The child's strengths and current needs should be recorded under each of the developmental dimensions listed. For example, in the case of Daniel Williams aged eighteen months:

Health	Daniel was born profoundly deaf. In areas other than speech, Daniel's development is at the expected level.

Parents'/Carers' Capacities to Respond Appropriately to the Child's Needs

It is important to record the strengths of all parents/carers as well as any areas of difficulty they are experiencing. In relation to the issues affecting parent's capacity to respond to the child's needs, research has shown that problems with mental health, domestic violence, drug and alcohol misuse, a history of childhood abuse or being a child abuser are likely to affect parenting. It is important to record not simply that an issue is present but to whom it refers and its effect on parenting capacity. For example:

Basic Care	Mrs Williams is at times unable to care for Daniel. However Mr Williams is able to respond to Daniel's needs.

Physical/ mental illness	Mrs Williams has suffered from post natal depression since the birth of Daniel earlier this year. Mrs Williams is receiving medication for this.

It is also important to record in this section any adult who poses a risk of significant harm to the child. For example, if the grand father is a schedule one offender or a parent is extremely violent to their partner. The social worker should select the most appropriate category(ies) in which to record the information.

Family and Environmental Factors

It is important to record factors that support families as well as those that increase stress. For example, extended family may offer a great deal of support to a young lone parent, alternatively they may compound their difficulties. It is also important to note how family and environmental factors have impact on the child and family. For example:

Housing	The family lives on the 10th floor of a block of flats. The exterior of the building is in poor condition. However Mr and Mrs Williams keep the flat in good condition.

Immediate Action

This section is used to record any actions taken during or on completion of the initial assessment. More than one box may be completed. For example, a family may be allocated a specific service, such as sponsored day care in addition to a referral being made to another agency and a strategy discussion. It is important to remember that if a core assessment is planned, during the process a family should receive services as appropriate. When deciding which services to offer, it is important to take account of the family's likelihood of being able to access or choosing to access these services.

Strategy Discussion If at any stage during the process there are suspicions or allegations about child maltreatment and concern that the child may be suffering, or is likely to suffer, significant harm there must be **strategy discussions** and interagency action in accordance with the guidance in *Working Together to Safeguard Children* (1999).

Immediate legal action to protect the child includes court orders applied for by the local authority, Police Protection and orders applied for by parents to protect a child, such as an injunction.

Further Action

Professional judgement is required to determine whether a **Core Assessment** is appropriate. In some cases more specialist assessment(s) may be commissioned and this should be recorded. For example, a psychiatric assessment of a parent.

The worker who has completed the Initial Assessment should always sign and date the form. The form should then be passed to the relevant manager to confirm the action recommended. A copy of the completed Initial Assessment should usually be sent to appropriate family members. All decisions will have to take account of the child's safety and whether permission has to be obtained from other agencies to share information. In some cases it will not be appropriate to include all the initial information. For example where a neighbour made a referral but wished to remain anonymous.

3 CORE ASSESSMENT RECORDS

The **Core assessment record of children's needs and issues which impact on parents' capacities to respond to them appropriately (Core Assessment Record)** is one of series of tools commissioned by the Department of Health to support the implementation of the *Framework for the Assessment of Children in Need and their Families* (2000).

Background

The Core Assessment Records were developed over a two-year period. Following a feasibility study in three local authorities, the Core Assessment Records have been revised to take account of the feedback from service users, social work practitioners and managers, and other professionals.

The records have their basis in relevant research findings, which were used to identify the essential information that should be recorded in each dimension. Key research findings have also been included on the left-hand side of each page to act as a sign-post to key areas and to assist practitioners in evaluating the importance of information gathered during the assessment.

Relationship to other Assessment Processes and Tools

A core assessment will typically follow a referral and initial assessment but it may also be used for a re-assessment of a family already known to social services. The Core Assessment Record has been developed to build on the information gathered in the initial information-gathering stages to avoid unnecessary duplication of work. As families report not liking to have to repeat the same information several times to different professionals, it is important to avoid this.

The Core Assessment Record recognises that in order to obtain a clear understanding of the inter-relationship between a child's needs, parents' capacities and the impact of family and environmental factors it is necessary to collect and analyse information from a variety of sources, using a number of different methods.

In many cases a number of professionals and agencies will know the family. Although it is the responsibility of the social services staff member to complete the Core Assessment Record, it has been designed to be inter-disciplinary in its approach. Typically the social services staff member will be collecting and analysing information from a number of agencies. Where detailed and up to date assessments about a family or child are available from another agency, for example a Statement of Educational Needs or hospital assessment on a disabled child, these should be incorporated into the Core Assessment Record (having obtained the necessary consents). This can be done in two ways; Either by using the information from a specialist assessment to complete the relevant area of the core Assessment Record, or by attaching the specialist assessment as an appendix to the Core Assessment Record. **In every case the summary section at**

the end of the relevant area of the Core Assessment Record should be completed by the social services staff member. So, for, example in the case of a child with a recent statement of Special Educational Needs, the statement could be attached but the social services staff member should complete the social worker's summary at the end of the Education dimension.

The use of Questionnaires and Scales can make a valuable contribution to specific areas of a core assessment. The Core Assessment Record indicates when it may be appropriate to use particular questionnaires and scales. Eight questionnaires and scales are contained in *The Family Assessment Pack of Questionnaires and Scales* (Department of Health, Cox and Bentovim, 2000).

Purpose of the Core Assessment Record

The Core Assessment Record is intended to aid social workers undertaking a core assessment by providing a framework to record information systematically and in a manner which facilities analysis and planning.

The Core Assessment Records have been structured to ensure that information is recorded in each of the three systems or domains of the *Framework for the Assessment of Children in Need and their Families* (2000):

- the developmental needs of children;
- the capacity of parents or care givers to respond appropriately to those needs;
- the impact of wider family and environmental factors on parenting capacity and the child.

The core Assessment Record is underpinned by the same principles as **are in** the *Framework for the Assessment of Children in Need and their Families* and therefore may be viewed as making a major contribution to the operationalisation of the Framework.

It is important to remember that the Core Assessment Record is a tool, and requires the skills, knowledge and professional judgement of practitioners and their managers to use it effectively. **Good tools cannot substitute for good practice, but good practice and good tools can achieve excellence.**

The Core Assessment Records

There are five age related Core Assessment Records. With the exception of children under 2, the age bands are congruent with those used in the **Looking After Children Assessment and Action Records**. The age bands for the Core Assessment Records are: 0–2; 3–4; 5–9; 10–14; 15 and over.

Structure of Core Assessment Records

The structure of each Core Assessment Record is the same. Each record can be considered to have two parts; **information gathering, and analysis and planning**.

Information gathering

- Sources of Information

This section is used to record the sources of information and methods used to gather information during the core assessment. This includes agencies involved, meetings with family members, questionnaires and scaled used. It is recommended that this page is completed as the assessment progresses.

- Details Concerning Core Assessment

This records the background details to the core assessment. The reason(s) the assessment is being undertaken and details of any specific matters, including disability, affecting the child. This section should be completed prior the beginning of the core assessment and will draw on information already known about the child and family from the initial assessment or existing records.

- Child's Developmental Needs/Parenting Capacity

This section records information about the child's developmental needs and the parents' capacities to respond to these needs appropriately. There are two pages for each developmental need of the child; health, education, emotional and behavioural development, identity, family and social relationships, social presentation (for children under five this is combined with identity) selfcare skills (for children under five this is combined with emotional and behavioural development).

The first part of each section records key needs for each child. A Yes/No box is included next to each of the key needs. The purpose of these boxes should be understood clearly. **The Core Assessment Record is not a questionnaire**. The Yes/No boxes are included to ensure that information identified from research as significant for the child's development or wellbeing is recorded.

They will assist practitioners and supervisors to quickly identify the key factors in an assessment. However ticking the boxes alone is not enough. It is important that further information is included to provide the context for information which is recorded. The space to record this information is limited. This is not to encourage practitioners to be brief, but to be relevant. Practitioners should consider the significance of information before it is entered into the record.

For Example – From Education Dimension, Child Aged 5 –9

Stimulation	Yes	No	
Parent regularly reads, tells stories, plays counting games, watches TV with child	✔	☐	Mrs Foli's depression means that at times she has no energy to play games with Kwane. However Mr Foli regularly plays with him and reads to him each evening
Other	☐	☐	

Following information about the child's needs, information about the parents' capacities to respond appropriately to those needs is recorded. Parents' capacities are detailed across the six areas identified in the parenting capacity domain of the *Framework for the Assessment of Children in Need and their Families*: basic care; ensuring safety; emotional warmth; stimulation; guidance and boundaries; and stability. Key parenting responses, identified from research, are included for each area. It is important to record the strengths as well as weaknesses of parents.

If any of the key areas identified are not appropriate for the child or parents, they can be marked N/A. In addition, it is important that the reason the issue is not considered to be relevant is recorded.

At the end of each of the child's developmental dimensions is a summary section. This is to enable practitioners to summarise the child's needs and parents' capacities to respond to them appropriately. In completing this section practitioners should consider the impact on the child's health and development of any needs which are not responded to appropriately. The research information on the left-hand side of the page is intended to help with this process.

- Family and Environmental Factors

The final section of the information gathering part of the Core Assessment Record is concerned with the Family and Environmental Factors domain of the Assessment Framework. The layout of this area is similar to those covering the child's developmental needs.

Summary, Analysis and Plan

Research, the findings of Inquiry reports and Social Services Inspectorate inspections have frequently highlighted weaknesses in this area of assessment. A great deal of time and effort goes into the information gathering stage. This results in an assessment that focuses on describing what is happening. However, often less attention is given to the analysis of the information gathered. Analysis takes the assessment process beyond surface considerations and explores why particular strengths and difficulties are present, the relationship between these and the implications of them for the child and other family members, as well as considering what types of services would best help the child and family members. The second part of the Core Assessment Record therefore is concerned with analysis and planning.

- Summary

The second part of the record starts with a summary of the needs, strengths and difficulties identified in each of the domains. Young people and parents are asked for their views. This provides an opportunity for them to contribute to the assessment summary. If possible they should be encouraged to write their views themselves or to indicate them in some other form of communication, which can then be recorded.

- Analysis

The next section is for practitioners to analyse the significance and consequences of the needs, strengths and difficulties identified in the assessment. This is a key stage in the assessment process. Practitioners should consider the inter-relationship between each of the domains of the *Framework for the Assessment of Children in Need and their*

Families. For example, a child's difficult and demanding behaviour may be a major contributory factor to a parent's depression, which may in turn lead to the home environment being neglected. It will be helpful to list key protective and stress factors in each domain and indicate how they relate to those identified in the other domains. It is important that strengths as well as difficulties are identified. Parental and family strengths should be built on and used to inform the plan. When analysing the information gathered, practitioners should also evaluate the impact on the child and family of any services already provided.

- Objectives and Plans

This section records the objectives and the actions which are to be achieved to ensure that all the child's identified needs are responded to appropriately. The objectives of the plan should be specific, measurable and have clear time scales. The actions should include those to be taken by the child and family members, social services and all other relevant agencies. It is important that the child, as appropriate, and family members are involved in agreeing the objectives and actions to be taken and that they are able to comment on the plan. This will enable the plan to serve as a written agreement.

The review of care plans and child protection plans are set out in Volume 3 of the Children Act 1989 and Guidance and Regulations (paragraphs 2.59 to 2.62) and in paragraphs 5.90 to 5.95 in *Working Together to Safeguard Children* (1999) respectively. It is good practice for children in need plans to be received regularly, at least every six months (see paragraph 4.36 in *Framework for the Assessment of Children in Need and their Families* (2000)). There is an outcome section for each objective which should be completed at the review. This enables progress to be monitored and any necessary changes made to the plan.

4 COMPLETING A CORE ASSESSMENT RECORD WITH A DISABLED CHILD – ADDITIONAL GUIDANCE

Introduction

This guidance supplements the **Core Assessment Record guidance** and is intended to support social work staff completing a Core Assessment Record with a disabled child and their family.

The Core Assessment Records have been developed in consultation with specialists working with disabled children and young people. They are underpinned by the principle that children are children first: however, each child is unique.

The Framework for the Assessment of Children in Need and their Families (2000) sets out the inter-related systems or domains that any assessment of a child should consider to achieve a clear understanding of the child's needs. These are:

- the child's developmental needs;
- the parents' or carers' capacities to respond appropriately to these needs;
- the impact of wider family and environmental factors on parenting capacity and the child.

The Core Assessment Records are intended to assist social workers undertaking a core assessment by providing a framework to record information systematically across all domains and dimensions in a manner that facilitates analysis and planning.

An assessment of a disabled child should consider the same domains and dimensions as an assessment of a non-disabled child. The needs of disabled children, however, may be very complex in one dimension: it is important that all areas of their needs receive attention during an assessment.

Using the Core Assessment Record with a Disabled Child

General Principles

The Core Assessment Records are informed by the principles which underpin the *Framework for the Assessment of Children in Need and their Families* (2000). Social work staff undertaking assessments of children in need are expected to be familiar with this Guidance. The accompanying practice guidance *Assessing Children in Need and their Families* (Department of Health, 2000) has a chapter on assessing the needs of disabled children and the Reader which accompanies the training pack, *The Child's World: Assessing Children in Need* includes a chapter on assessing the needs of children with complex needs.

Using Age-related Records

The Core Assessment Records are age related. As with the Looking After Children Assessment and Action Records, social work staff should use the record which relates to the child or young person's chronological age.

It is recognised that for some children this may result in some sections of the record being inappropriate to their needs. For example, the section of the Education Dimension which records GCSE results may be inappropriate for a young person with profound learning disabilities. However, the preceding question, **Young person's educational progress is at expected level** provides the practitioner with an opportunity to record the young person's achievements.

It will also be important to record how the parents respond to the identified needs of the child.

It must be remembered that the Core Assessment Record is only a tool and requires the skills, knowledge and professional judgement of the practitioner to use it effectively.

Links Between the Core Assessment Record and other Assessments

A key concern for many parents of disabled children is the number of assessment processes their child is involved in. These may include general and specific health assessments, psychological assessments, Special Educational Needs and other educational assessments. However, each of these assessments consider a specific area of the child's needs. They do not provide a picture of all the child's needs or of the interrelationships between the needs of the child, capacities of parents', and family and environmental factors.

The Core Assessment Record is a tool for undertaking a holistic assessment. In order to complete a Core Assessment Record a social work practitioner will draw on information from a variety of sources including the child, parent or carers and other professionals. However a Core Assessment should also draw upon existing reports and specialist assessments concerning the child and family, having obtained the necessary consents to use this information. In some situations basic details from a specialist assessment can be recorded in the Core Assessment Record and the specialist assessment attached to the Core Assessment Record as an appendix. This should mean that disabled children, their parents or carers, do not feel that they are repeatedly covering the same issues.

For some children, the Child in Need Plan in the Core Assessment Record may be used to draw together the objectives from a number of different assessments into one interagency plan for the child. It may be useful in some situations to arrange for the review of the Core Assessment to coincide with the reviews of other assessments in relation to the child and family.

One consequence of completing a Core Assessment Record may be that the need for a more specialist assessment may be identified. It is important that any further assessment is fully discussed with the child or young person and their parents or carers.

It may be necessary to undertake a more specific assessment of some areas of the disabled child's abilities in order to access particular services. For example, a more detailed analysis of a disabled child's mobility and selfcare skills may be required to identify the most appropriate day care or respite care resource for the child.

Where a child or young person is receiving respite care for periods exceeding 24 hours at a time, they are looked after under S20 of the Children Act 1989.

The Core Assessment Record and other Children in the Family

The Core Assessment Record is designed to be completed for each child in need in a family. A disabled child may have an impact on other children in a family, and this may result in siblings requiring support in their own right. In such situations a professional judgement will have to be made about whether a Core Assessment Record should be completed for other children in the family to ensure that support provided is based on a clear understanding of all the children's needs.

Recording Specific Issues regarding Disabled Children

The following section provides guidance for social work staff on recording some of the specific issues that may arise because of a child's impairment(s).

Details Concerning a Core Assessment

It is recommended that an outline of the nature and extent of the child's impairment is recorded in this section, along with details of routine hospital and outpatient appointments. More specific details about the child's health needs should be recorded in the Health dimension of the child's developmental needs.

Child's Developmental Needs

Health

This section should include details of the child's medication regime.

Education

The type of educational provision attended by the child should be recorded in this dimension. If the child has a statement of Special Educational Needs brief details of the main provisions should be recorded. Full details of the Statement can be included, if necessary, by attaching the full statement as an appendix to the Core Assessment Record.

A summary of the nature and extent of any communication difficulties experienced by the child should be recorded in this dimension. The ability of parents or carers to communicate with the child should be recorded under Basic Care in the Parenting Capacity section of the dimension.

Emotional and Behavioural Development

The nature of any challenging behaviour exhibited by the child, including whether it affects the child's safety, should be recorded under this heading. The amount of supervision the child requires should be also recorded in this dimension. How parents or carers respond to the child's challenging behaviour should be recorded under Ensuring Safety in the Parenting Capacity Section.

Identify

This dimension is important for disabled children as they may have picked up messages that to be disabled is 'wrong', 'bad' or a burden on others. They, therefore, may reject who they are and lack confidence and self-esteem. Having determined how the child perceives him or herself, it is important to record how they view their identity as a disabled person.

Family and Social Relationships

This dimension is concerned with the child's relationships with their family, peers and others; how the child relates to others and how they respond to him or her.

The impact that the child's impairment has on siblings and parents or carers is considered later in the record.

Social Presentation

In addition to how the child or young person presents socially, the way in which others, particularly outside the family, respond to the child or young person's impairment should be recorded in this dimension. This will help to develop an understanding of the barriers that the child and family may have to overcome when accessing and using community resources.

Selfcare Skills

Some of the questions in this dimension may not be appropriate for some disabled children and young people. However the first question, **Child has age appropriate selfcare skills** can be completed for all children and young people. This section can be used to record a summary of the child's abilities, including washing and dressing, eating and drinking, continence, and to go out alone.

The capacity of parents to provide the level of supervision and support required by the child, can be recorded in the parental capacity section of this dimension.

A more detailed assessment of some areas of the child or young person's abilities may be necessary to identify or access the resources which are most appropriate to the child or young person's needs.

Family and Environmental Factors which may impact on the Child and on Parenting Capacity

Family Functioning

The impact of the child's impairment on other family members is recorded in this section. When recording the impact of the child's impairment on siblings (FE4), practitioners should consider whether siblings are themselves 'children in need' and require a core assessment. Consideration will also have to be given to whether a separate 'Carer's assessment' should be carried out in respect of parents or carers (FE6).

Family's Social Integration

This is often a major issue for families with a disabled child. Any discrimination experienced by the family as a consequence of the child's impairment should be recorded. Support to the family through membership of support groups for disabled children should also be noted.

- ### Community Resources

Any difficulties experienced by the child and family in accessing resources in the community as a consequence of the child's impairment should be recorded. This would include difficulties in physically accessing resources, discrimination, or issues arising from the child's behaviour.

Plan for a Child in Need

The plan for the child should take account of the child or young person's wishes and feelings, the views of parents or carers, and any existing specialist assessments of the child. The Child in Need Plan provides an opportunity to draw together into one document individual agency plans and to produce a single inter-agency plan for the child.

REFERENCES

Department of Health (1999) *The Government's Objectives for Children's Social Services.* Department of Health, London.

Department of Health (2000) *Assessing Children in Need and their Families.* The Stationery Office, London.

Department of Health, Cox A and Bentovim A (2000) *The Family Assessment Pack of Questionnaires and Scales.* The Stationery Office, London.

Department of Health, Home Office, Department for Education and Employment (1999) *Working Together to Safeguard Children: A guide to inter-agency working to safeguard and promote the welfare of children.* The Stationery Office, London.

Department of Health, Department for Education and Employment and Home Office (2000) *Framework for the Assessment of Children in Need and their Families.* The Stationery Office, London.

The NSPCC and the University of Sheffield (2000) *The Child's World: Assessing Children in Need.* The NSPCC, London.

Assessing Children in Need and their Families:

Practice Guidance

Department of Health

Assessing Children in Need and their Families:

Practice Guidance

London

TSO

TSO
information & publishing solutions

Published by TSO (The Stationery Office) and available from:

Online
www.tsoshop.co.uk

Mail, Telephone, Fax & E-mail
TSO
PO Box 29, Norwich, NR3 1GN
Telephone orders/General enquiries: 0870 600 5522
Fax orders: 0870 600 5533
E-mail: customer.services@tso.co.uk
Textphone: 0870 240 3701

TSO Shops
16 Arthur Street, Belfast BT1 4GD
028 9023 8451 Fax 028 9023 5401
71 Lothian Road, Edinburgh EH3 9AZ
0870 606 5566 Fax 0870 606 5588

TSO@Blackwell and other Accredited Agents

Social Care Group

The Social Care Group is one of the four business groups in the Department of Health. It is jointly headed by the Chief Social Services Inspector and the Head of Social Care Policy. It supports Ministers in promoting high quality, cost effective services through

- national policies
- support to external social care agencies
- inspection

The Social Services Inspectorate is part of the Social Care Group. It is headed by the Chief Social Services Inspector who is the principal professional advisor to Ministers on social services and related matters.

Published for the Department of Health under licence from the Controller of Her Majesty's Stationery Office.

First published 2000
Sixth impression 2008
ISBN 978 0 11 3224180
Printed in the United Kingdom for The Stationery Office.
5913501 C2 9/08

Contents

Foreword

This publication is a companion volume to the Guidance on the *Framework for the Assessment of Children in Need and their Families*. It is a significant contribution to a major programme of work led by the Department of Health to provide guidance, practice materials and training resources on assessing children in need and their families. This is to assist in the achievement of one of the government's key policy objectives in children's services, delivered through the Quality Protects Programme, to ensure that referral and assessment processes discriminate effectively between different types and level of need, and produce a timely response.

Whilst government policy objectives may be clear, effective implementation requires detailed knowledge and understanding. The practice guidance has been produced to help policy makers, managers and practitioners who have responsibility for responding to the needs of some of our most disadvantaged and vulnerable children. The needs of some children require particular knowledge and sensitivity to ensure they do not suffer further disadvantage. These include children from black and minority ethnic families and disabled children. The issues involved in assessing their needs within the context of their families and communities are discussed by leading professionals in their field. The steering and advisory groups, which were set up to develop the Guidance on the Assessment Framework, have contributed to these perspectives.

It is hoped this publication will be a valuable resource for use in promoting evidence-based practice, not only in direct work with children and families but also in training and continuing staff development.

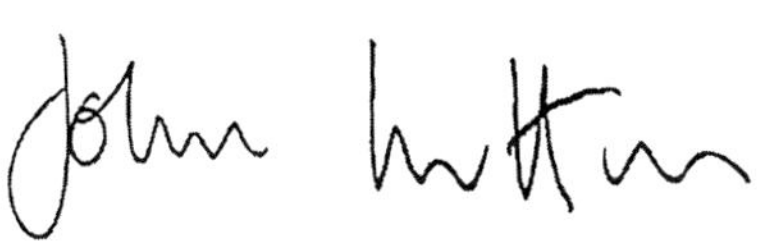

John Hutton
MINISTER OF STATE FOR SOCIAL SERVICES

March 2000

Introduction

> The body of knowledge available to those who struggle with today's problems of child care is still rudimentary compared with the physical sciences; but it is by far and away greater than what could called upon in the past… Indeed, social work today is expected to be 'evidence-based', something that would have been an unrealistic aspiration in, say, the 1950s, when there was virtually no evidence upon which to draw (Parker, 1999, pp.54-55).

Understanding what is happening to a child when there are concerns that the child's health and development are being impaired remains a core professional activity for those working with children and families. The knowledge which is available to assist them has expanded dramatically over the last two decades. However, it has not always been easily available to practitioners and their managers. The development of the *Framework for the Assessment of Children in Need and their Families* (jointly issued by the Department of Health, the Department for Education and Employment and the Home Office, 2000) has drawn heavily, from many disciplines, on the wealth of research and accumulated practice experience about the developmental needs of children. The aim of the practice guidance in this accompanying publication is to make transparent the evidence base for the Assessment Framework, thereby assisting professionals in their tasks of analysis, judgement and decision making.

Chapter 1 highlights some of the key theories, research findings and practice wisdom which have underpinned the development of the Assessment Framework and in which confidence can be placed. Staff who are working with children and families may find further exploration of the texts referenced in this chapter helpful in informing their practice. Chapter 2 provides more specific knowledge and guidance about working with black children and their families and points to useful sources of information. Chapter 3 similarly provides knowledge and guidance about assessing the needs of disabled children and their families. These two chapters address issues of major importance which must be integral to policy, planning, management and practice in work with children and families. However, the messages which can be drawn from these two chapters can be used in work with **all** children.

The Department of Health is grateful to the authors of the chapters:

Chapter 1: Wendy Rose, Senior Research Fellow and lane Aldgate, Professor of Social Care, The Open University

Chapter 2: Ratna Dutt OBE, Director, REV and Melanie Phillips, Researcher, Trainer and Consultant to REV

Chapter 3: Ruth Marchant and Mary Jones, Directors of Triangle

The concluding chapter, Chapter 4, outlines a significant package of Department of Health commissioned resources which can be used to support staff in their practice and in their professional development. These resources include texts summarising key messages from relevant research findings, questionnaires and scales to assist work with children and families, training materials and other work under development.

These are only a selection of what is available. Knowledge is continually being updated and important developments will take place over the next few years. It is, therefore, incumbent on all professionals involved in training, management and practice to be continually alert to new resources, to ensure that work with children and families is firmly evidence-based. Through the Department of Health's Quality Protects Programme, an important process of change is underway aimed at improving the outcomes for children in need. The development of the *Framework for the Assessment of Children in Need and their Families* and its associated materials forms a significant part of this programme.

Jenny Gray

SOCIAL CARE GROUP
DEPARTMENT OF HEALTH

REFERENCES

Department of Health, Department for Education and Employment and Home Office (2000) *Framework for the Assessment of Children in Need and their Families*. Stationery Office, London.

Holman B, Parker Rand Utting W (1999) *Reshaping Child Care Practice*. NISW; London.

1

Knowledge underpinning the Assessment Framework

What is meant by knowledge in this chapter

1.1 Throughout the *Framework for the Assessment of Children in Need and their Families* (Department of Health et al, 2000) to which this practice guidance relates, it has been emphasised that the framework is grounded in knowledge. Knowledge is defined as theory, research findings and practice experience in which confidence can be placed to assist in the gathering of information, its analysis and the choice of intervention in formulating the child's plan.

1.2 This chapter explores how theory, research and practice assist in understanding each of the three domains or systems of the framework and their interaction, the roles and tasks of the child and family worker, the processes of planning and decision making and the importance of evidence based work.

1.3 There are many theories from a range of disciplines which contribute to the understanding of human growth and development and the interaction between internal and external factors which have an impact on the lives of individuals. Schofield (1998, p.57) summarises the importance of the interplay of these factors which can be applied to the Assessment Framework:

> Social workers need a framework for understanding and helping children and families which takes into account the inner world of the self and the outer world of the environment, both in terms of relationships and in terms of practicalities such as housing. It is the capacity of social workers to be aware of and integrate in their practice these different areas of concern which defines the distinctive nature of their professional identity.

In Chapter 2 of the Guidance on the Assessment Framework (Department of Health et al, 2000), the three domains of child's developmental needs, parenting capacity and family and environmental factors are described (Figure 1). These domains and their interrelationship take account of 'the inner world of the self and the outer world of the environment' (Schofield, 1998).

Child development

1.4 It has long been recognised that children develop along several dimensions, often simultaneously, and that they need to reach a series of milestones along each dimension if optimal outcomes are to be achieved. It is acknowledged that there will be differential development across the dimensions for some children, for instance,

Figure 1 **The Assessment Framework**

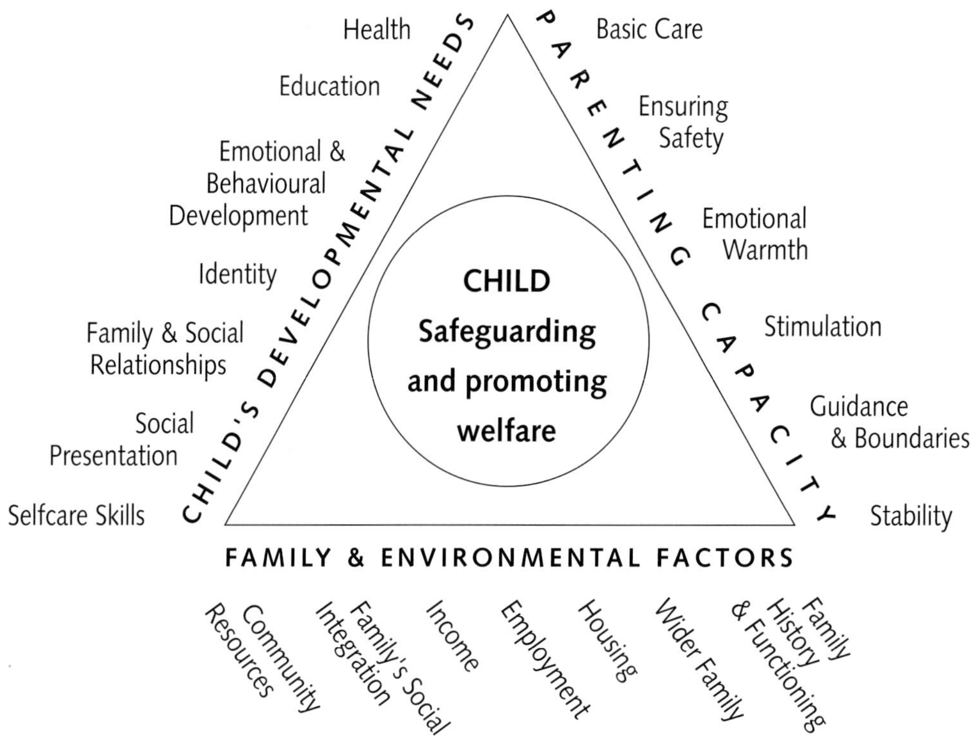

those with impairments. Different aspects of development will have more or less weight at different stages of a child's life. For example, in the early years, there is an emphasis on achieving physical milestones. Sheridan's charts on development in the early years, from one month to five years are a valuable source of reference here (Appendix 1). In middle childhood, social and academic capacity becomes more prominent although the physical development continues (for example Rushton et al, 1988), while the adolescent strives to reconcile social and emotional dependence and independence (Department of Health, 1996). Some examples of developmental tasks to be achieved at different stages are summarised by Masten and Coatsworth (1998) in Figure 2.

Figure 2 **Examples of Developmental Tasks**

Age Period	**Task**
Infancy to preschool	Attachment to caregiver(s)
	Language
	Differentiation of self from environment
	Self control & compliance
Middle childhood	School adjustment (attendance, appropriate conduct)
	Academic achievement (e.g. learning to read, do arithmetic)
	Getting along with peers (acceptance, making friends)
	Rule-governed conduct (following rules of society for moral behaviour and prosocial conduct)
Adolescence	Successful transition to secondary schooling
	Academic achievement (learning skills needed for higher education & work)
	Involvement in extracurricular activities (e.g. athletics, clubs)
	Forming close friendships within & across gender
	Forming a cohesive sense of self-identity

Masten and Coatsworth (1998)

1.5 What happens to children in the first years of life is the foundation of later development and will affect their outcomes. The significance of this must be taken into account in the assessment process. This is why secure attachments are so important in the early years. Where these attachments are absent or broken, decisions to provide children with new attachment figures must be taken as quickly as possible to avoid developmental damage. Careful distinction has to be drawn between delay which is harmful to a child's development and taking appropriate time to make good plans.

1.6 The seven dimensions along which children develop, discussed by Ward (Horwath (ed) 2000), are influenced by many factors. Recent empirical research, for example, has suggested connections between biological and other areas of development. The development of the infant brain mirrors developmental experience in general. It is argued by Perry (1993) that the brains of developing infants react to the quality and nature of sensory information. For example, children raised with little or no experience of verbal language may have difficulties in attaining the neurodevelopment required for optimal speech or language. As the result of research findings, Pugh (1999) makes the point strongly:

> Environmental stress has a negative effect not only on how the brain develops, but how it functions, and underlies our capacity to make and sustain relationships.

Additionally, as Schofield (1998) suggests, it is important to take account of the psycho-social influences on children. Clare Winnicot described in the 1960s (quoted by Schofield) how these influences relate to what takes place in children's inner and outer worlds.

The importance of attachment

1.8 Two major concepts critical to the interrelationship between the inner and outer worlds are attachment and self esteem. As Schofield suggests, these are interactive. One of the most influential writers on attachment has been John Bowlby whose work is still highly relevant (1958; 1969; 1973; 1980). His work has been taken forward by others such as Rutter, Ainsworth, Fahlberg, Jones and Howe. However, the process of attachment is far from simple, as Crittenden and Ainsworth (1989, p.432) suggest:

> Attachment theory is a relatively new, open-ended theory with eclectic underpinning. ... Although it began with an attempt to understand disturbed functioning of individuals who had experienced traumatic losses or early separations, it is a theory of normal development that offers explanations for some types of atypical development (Bowlby, 1969; 1973; 1980).

Pugh (1999) argues that 'attachment theory makes an important contribution to our growing understanding of the importance of social and emotional competence as the basis of self-esteem, and a key ingredient in the concept of resilience' (which is discussed later in this chapter).

1.9 Children who are securely attached to significant adults in early childhood have been shown to be able to develop appropriate peer relationships, and cope well with problems that confront them. It is also known that children who have had good attachment experiences will be able to use these in their relationships with their own children in later life. It is because of the importance of good attachment experiences that practice concerned with helping children who have lost attachment figures places so much emphasis on providing these children with continuity of good alternative parenting experiences. Bentovim (1998) reminds practitioners that there is strong association between significant harm and insecure attachments, citing Carlson et al (1989) who found that more than 80% of significantly harmed infants had disorganised attachments compared to less that 20% in a non-maltreated comparison group.

1.10 The central place of attachment disturbance in cases of child maltreatment is also noted by Jones et al (1999) and the relationship with parents' own experiences:

> Attachment difficulties are linked with parental childhood histories of abuse and deprivation, parental personality difficulties, as well as functional illnesses such as depression. The identification of parent/child attachment difficulties has important implications for intervention, particularly in view of the outcome literature in child maltreatment, where persisting parent/child attachment difficulties combined with evidence of psychological maltreatment on follow-up is a consistent finding (Jones, 1998).

1.11 The wealth of research on attachment reinforces the importance of paying attention to attachment in assessments of all children, irrespective of their age. Teenagers who have had poor attachment experiences in their early years are particularly vulnerable, especially if they have experienced many separations and a childhood of discontinuity. Teenagers are also vulnerable if they lose good attachments in their adolescent years. Children who are joining new families, therefore, need special attention, as BAAF (1999) suggests:

> Many children will in time build positive healthy attachments in their new family, integrate their past and present experiences, and enter adulthood with a sense of stability and belonging. Yet the experience of adult adoptees reminds us that the interruption of primary connections has consequences which are potentially lifelong, and may result in a deep sense of personal loss and rejection.

1.12 Practitioners will need to integrate multi-faceted knowledge of child development into their assessments and, in particular, what is relevant from psychodynamic theory and learning theory (Seden, 2000). The development of children's inner and outer worlds can be understood within general principles of psychodynamic theory which focuses on the importance of the psychological processes at work in three key relationships: 'between self and significant other people, past and present experience, and inner and outer reality' (Brearley, 1991, pp.49-50). These ideas are important in understanding what is happening to a child.

1.13 Children's cognitive, emotional and social development go hand in hand. Children's behaviour, both adaptive and maladaptive may be learned from their experiences. Learning theory suggests behaviour that is learned can also be unlearned, with the possibilities of maladaptive behaviours being replaced with positive, pro-social behaviours. Key exponents include Skinner (1974) on operant learning, Bandura (1977) on observational learning and Seligman (1975) on learned helplessness, and Hudson (1991) among many others. Caution has to be exercised here. The results of intervention will depend on the level and scope of children's positive and negative developmental experiences and other factors.

Protective factors and resilience

1.14 Not only are children's experiences germane to their development but other factors within individual children, such as temperament, personality and gender all influence the way they are likely to react to experiences of their families and the environment in which they are growing up. A number of writers have summarised the factors which may protect children and those which may make them more vulnerable (Rutter in Haggerty et al, 1996; Jones in Adcock and White (eds), 1998; Masten and Coatsworth, 1998). An example (Table 1) is included in this chapter from *Crossing Bridges* (Falkov (ed),1998, p.72).

1.15 Children vary widely in the way they may respond to a set of circumstances. Some children may do well even in the most adverse circumstances while others appear to have little capacity to cope with small amounts of stress. It is therefore important to understand what may act as protective factors in children's lives and what may be stressors or vulnerabilities. Increasingly, interest is being shown in the concept of resilience in children (discussed by Gilligan, 2000). Rutter (1999, pp.119-120) describes resilience as:

> The phenomenon of overcoming stress or adversity. That is, put in more operational terms, there has been a relatively good outcome for someone despite their experience of situations that have been shown to carry a major risk for the development of psychopathology.

1.16 As with attachment, resilience is a broadly based concept of some complexity. This means there must be a careful analysis which focuses not just on the individual or the family but on 'the relevant stresses and adversities in their social context' (Rutter 1999, p.159) . The importance of taking a broadly based approach to the assessment of children is highlighted by current ideas on protective factors. The evidence suggests strongly that children vary considerably in their responses to positive and negative experiences. Multiple protective and adverse factors may be involved at the same time. Rutter (1999, p.119) therefore suggests in summary that:

> Children vary in their vulnerability to psycho-social stress and adversity as a result of both genetic and environmental influences; that family-wide experiences tend to impinge on individual children in quite different ways; that the reduction of negative, and increase of positive, chain reactions influences the extent to which the effects of adversity persist over time; that new experiences which open up opportunities, can provide beneficial 'turning-point' effects; that although positive experiences in themselves do not exert much of a protective effect, they can be helpful if they serve to neutralise some risk factors; and that the cognitive and affective processing of experiences is likely to influence whether or not resilience develops.

1.17 These findings have led writers such as Buchanan (1999) to talk about the importance of mobilising clusters of protective factors for children even in the most unpromising situations. This constitutes an important consideration in assessment and intervention. One of the key protective factors identified by researchers is successful school experience. Furthermore, having a parent who promotes the importance of education is another vital factor (Utting, 1996) .

> One of the most significant protective factors found in the backgrounds of children from disadvantaged homes whose attainment is above average is having a parent who displays a keen interest in their education.

Writers such as Jackson (1987), Cleaver (1991), Katz et al (1997), Buchanan and Hudson (1998) and Sinclair (1998) provide ample evidence of why 'any consideration of how to meet the needs of a child must include their education' (Sinclair, 1998, p.5).

Table 1[1] Risks/stressors and protectors/resources relevant to children

Risk/stressor	Factor	Protector
Intrinsic		
Younger	Age	Older
Male	Gender	Female
General or specific learning disabilities, developmental disorder, lack of educational skills	Development (language and cognitive abilities)	Good cognitive and language abilities and edcation skills
Chronic physical illness/disability	Physical health	Healthy
Predisposition to mental disorder, or inreased risk	Genetics	No adverse predisposition
Difficult	Temperament	Easy
Belonging to minority – being 'different' experience of oppression, discrimination, racism	Ethnicity	elonging to majority group
Immediate circumstances		
Discordant/distant	parent-child relationship	Warm/mutual
Lax/hostile/no control	Parenting	Positive, e.g. co-operation and good control, age-appropriate interactions
Distant/discordant/violent	Inter-parental relationship	Mutually supportive/co-operative
Comorbidity, both parents ill, single parent ill	Parental mental health	Partner well
Absent/discordant/oppressive	Sibling and peer relationships	Warm/supportive
Material hardship	Socio-economic resources	Financially secure
Crowded, unhygenic	Housing	Good, spacious
Poor ethos, low support, bullying, punitive	School	good ethos, supportive
Life events		
Loss and other negative life events and experiences	Life events and experiences	Positive life events, acknowledgement of achievements

1. Reproduced with kind permission of the authors. From: Falkov A (ed) (1998) *Crossing Bridges. Training resources for working with mentally ill parents and their children. Reader – for managers, practitioners and trainers.* p.72. Pavilion Publishing, Brighton.

1.18 The ability to differentiate the vulnerabilities and strengths of children at different ages and stages of development is critical in assessment. The neglect of some of these issues for adolescents is increasingly being remedied. Cleaver (2000a) provides summaries of research findings of the relevant factors for different age groups, including children over 10 (Table 2).

Table 2[2] Vulnerabilities and strengths for children aged 10-14 years and teenagers 15 years and over

Vulnerabilities	Strengths
Coping with puberty without support.	Factual information about puberty, sex and contraception.
Denying own needs and feelings.	A mutual friend. Unstigmatised support of relevant professionals.
An increased risk of psychological problems, behavioural disorders, suicidal behaviours and offending. Low self-esteem.	The ability to separate themselves either psychologically or physically from stressful situations.
Poor school attainment due to: difficulties in concentration, poor attendance in order to look after parents or younger children, unacceptable behaviour esulting in a pattern of school exclusion.	Regular school attendance. Sympathetic, emphatic and vigilant teachers. A champion who acts vigorously on behalf of the child. For those no longer in school, a job.
The fear thatrevealing family problems will lead to the family being broken up. This may result in increased isolation from friends and adults outside the family.	A mentor or trusted adult with whom the child can discuss sensitive issues. Practical and domestic help.
Increased risk of abuse. Innappropriate role models.	An alternative, safe supportive residence for children and young people subjected to violence or the threat of violence.

2. Reproduced with kind permission of the author. From: Cleaver H (2000a) *When parents' issues influence their ability to respond to children's needs*. In Horwath J (ed) *The Child s World: Assessing Children in Need. The Reader*. The NSPCC, London.

Children's perspectives

1.19 Finally, children's own perspectives on their experiences are an important source of knowledge. Increasingly, the validity of children's views on their lives is acknowledged in research. Children have views about what is happening to them. They attach meaning to events. They have wishes and feelings which must be taken into account and they will have ideas about the direction of decisions and the way in which those decisions are executed (for example, Butler and Williamson, 1994; Shaw, 1998;

Brandon et al, 1999; Department of Health, forthcoming) . Thomas and Beckford (1999), in their study of adopted children speaking, emphasise the importance of work with children being 'underpinned by good adult-child and child-adult communication'. The responsibility for trying to establish effective communication lies firmly with the adults. They identify the following imperatives for the adults involved (pp.131-132):

- Express themselves simply and clearly and use concepts which are familiar to children;
- Match their explanations of new ideas to the children's age and levels of understanding;
- Be aware of the possible impact of emotional distress on children's understanding;
- Elicit children's fears and offer reassurances;
- Allow children plenty of opportunities for asking questions;
- Ask children for feedback to see if information and explanations have been remembered and understood;
- Repeat, simplify, expand and build on explanations if appropriate;
- Use communication tools such as games, prompt cards, books and videos.

Innovative materials for use with children and young peoples of different ages and in different circumstances have been developed which assist good communication. Examples are included in Chapter 4.

Parental capacity

1.20 Optimal child development is dependent on the positive role of parents or caregivers from children' s birth to adulthood. However, it is recognised that there can be a diversity of family styles (Department of Health, 1989, p.7):

> Although some basic needs are universal, there can be a variety of ways of meeting them. Patterns of family life differ according to culture, class and community and these differences should be respected and accepted. There is no one perfect way to bring up children and care must be taken to avoid value judgements and stereotyping.

1.21 Rosenfeld et al (1986) add a note of caution about understanding parents' behaviours. They emphasise that just because a behaviour is normative does not necessarily mean it is optimal for child development.

1.22 However, children's chances of achieving optimal outcomes will depend on their parents' capacities to respond appropriately to their needs at different stages of their lives. There are many factors in parents that may inhibit their responses to their children and prevent their providing parenting to a level necessary to promote optimal outcomes in children. The number of parents who set out to cause harm to their children is very small. The majority of parents, including most of those who neglect or maltreat their children, want to do the best for their children and have their best interests at heart. However, as Rutter (1974) (quoted by Utting (1995)) suggests:

> Good parenting requires certain permitting circumstances. There must be the necessary life opportunities and facilities. Where these are lacking even the best parents may find it difficult to exercise these skills.

Most of the parents interviewed by Thoburn et al (2000) were well aware that their standard of parenting at times failed to meet their children's needs.

1.23 Belsky and Vondra (1989) identify the multiple determinants of parenting. They can be summarised as follows:

- **Individual**
  (parental personality, child characteristics)
- **Historical**
  (parental developmental history)
- **Social**
  (partner satisfaction, social support network)
- **Circumstantial**
  (poverty; job dissatisfaction; ignorance about child development)

1.24 There are, therefore, many factors that may inhibit parenting responses, including parents' life experiences as adults and in childhood. Reder and Duncan (1999) suggest that parents' own childhood experiences may spill over into adult life. For instance, experiences of rejection, abandonment, neglect and feeling unloved as a child may be associated with excessive reliance on others and fear of being left, or excessive distancing from others and fear of dependency in adulthood. As with children, it is important to understand both the nature of the adversity parents have experienced and the level of any protective factors which can build resilience in adult life to help overcome adversity. For example, the important research of Rutter and colleagues on intergenerational factors showed that the presence of a supportive partner in adulthood could help counteract negative experiences of growing up in care (Rutter and Rutter, 1992).

1.25 Some parents may have serious health problems or impairments which may place upon children responsibilities inappropriate to their years unless informal support and appropriate services are provided for the family, in consultation with the child (Aldridge and Becker, 1999; Tucker et al, 1999). It is therefore necessary for social workers to understand what may inhibit parental responses to children and what the consequences of that inappropriate response may be for children of different ages.

1.26 Research studies (Department of Health, 1995; Department of Health, forthcoming) have suggested that, among problems likely to affect parenting are mental illness, problem alcohol and drug use and domestic violence (Buchanan (ed) , 1994; Cleaver and Freeman, 1995; Reder and Lucey, 1995; Falkov, 1996; Brandon et al, 1999; Cleaver et al, 1999; Thoburn et al, 2000; Department of Health, forthcoming) . A study for the Department of Health by Falkov of local reviews of deaths and serious injuries to children revealed that in a significant proportion, mothers were suffering from identifiable mental illnesses (Falkov, 1996). Cleaver et al (1999) particularly emphasise the damaging effects for a child of living with and witnessing domestic violence between adult members of the household.

1.27 It is important, therefore, that practitioners understand the impact of parental responses on the particular child. A two year old may be at risk of significant harm from a parent whose practical caring skills are diminished by a misuse of drugs or alcohol but a sixteen year old in a similar situation may be able to remain relatively unharmed. Understanding the interaction between parents' responses and capabilities and children's needs is a key principle underpinning effective assessment and intervention. As Cleaver (2000a) points out, not all children are equally vulnerable to the adverse consequences of parental problems.

1.28 Research suggests (Cleaver et al, 1999) children are less likely to be adversely affected when parental problems are:

- Mild and of short duration;
- Not associated with family violence, conflict and disorganisation;
- Do not result in the family breaking up.

Children may also be protected when other responsible adults are involved in child care, or assume the role of the child's champion or mentor. Careful account should be taken, therefore, of the context within which the parent or parents may be experiencing problems and the impact of parental behaviour on the child.

1.29 Some parents may be directly responsible for maltreating their children. Bentovim (1998, p.57) argues that 'significant harm represents a major symptom of failure of adaptation by parents to their role':

> It may be useful to think of significant harm generally as a compilation of significant events, both acute and long-standing, which interact with the child's ongoing development, and interrupt, alter, or impair physical and psychological development. Being the victim of significant harm is likely to have a profound effect on a child's view of themself as a person, and on their future lives. Significant harm represents a major symptom of failure of adaptation by parents to their role, and also involves both the family and society.

1.30 Writers such as Adcock (1998) and Brandon et al (1999) draw an important distinction between significant harm and abuse. Adcock (1998, p.35) argues that:

> Significant harm needs to be understood separately from child abuse or neglect, although the two may coexist. The two can be differentiated by the idea that child abuse describes *acts* and *omissions*, significant harm describes *effects*... Ill Treatment may lead to the impairment or likely impairment of health and development... Some children may need protection to prevent the recurrence (of ill treatment); any child whose health or development has been impaired may need services to deal with consequences of this.

1.31 Not only parent figures or caregivers maltreat children. Additionally, children may be abused by siblings. Outside their families, children may also be at risk of encountering perpetrators. Utting (Department of Health and Welsh Office, 1997) has drawn attention to the particular dangers of child sexual abuse for children living away from home. It is important to understand why adults or other children maltreat children. Social workers should inform themselves about the characteristics of personality and behaviour, profiles and methods of perpetrators of different forms of child maltreatment, including physical, sexual and emotional abuse, both where children are living with their families and elsewhere (Department of Health, 2000a).

Parents' Perspectives

1.32 Parents' views about their contact with child welfare and other statutory services have been well documented, particularly when there have been child protection concerns (for example, Cleaver and Freeman, 1995; Farmer and Owen, 1995; Jones and Ramchandani, 1999; Thoburn et al, 2000). Aldgate and Bradley (1999) in their study of short-term accommodation found how these experiences influenced parental worries about asking for help from social services when they needed assistance. Parents' worries were about:

- being vulnerable to child protection enquiries and being afraid of losing their children;
- being perceived as failed parents;
- the impact of using short term accommodation on their children and being detrimental to their future relationship with them.

1.33 The sense of losing control once child welfare agencies are involved is keenly felt by parents. They want help but not at the cost of forfeiting their parenting responsibilities. Ghate and Hazel (forthcoming) found in a national study of parenting in poor environments that parents' wish to stay in control of the delivery of support services was an overriding theme.

1.34 What parents value from child welfare agencies is clearly detailed in studies of family support services (see Butt and Box, 1998; McAuley, 1999; Social Services Inspectorate, 1999; Tunstill and Aldgate, 2000), in studies of contact (Cleaver, 2000b) and of court processes (Hunt et a1 1999) and includes:

- communication which is open, honest, timely and informative;
- social work time with someone who listens, gives feedback, information, reassurance and advice, and is reliable;
- services which are practical, tailored to particular needs and accessible;
- an approach which re-inforces and does not undermine their parenting capacity.

These issues are explored further in later chapters in this practice guidance.

Theories and myths of the individual in society

1.35 Alongside the theories concerned with the development of individuals are those related to the individual in society. There is a wealth of knowledge from sociological and psychological research which provides important background material for understanding the impact of negative factors such as social exclusion, racial and other discrimination, deviancy and unsafe communities on the children and families with whom practitioners will come in contact. Of particular relevance in assessment are sociological theories concerned with the issues of social exclusion and use or misuse of power, such as social constructionism and stereotyping. Writing on the identification of child abuse, for example, Parton (1987) discusses how the parameters of child abuse have changed over time.

1.36 Good outcomes for children have sometimes been blocked by assumptions which tend to stereotype families. This is especially pertinent in relation to black children. Ahmed et al (1986), for example, were among the first black British writers in social work to emphasise the negative impact of institutional racism on service provision for black children and their families. The picture from recent research is complex. Some research suggests that black and other minority ethnic groups are under-represented as service users receiving preventive and supportive social services (Tunstill and Aldgate, 2000). However, when black and minority ethnic families are referred to social services, it is less likely to be about concerns of maltreatment but more likely to be with a request for a specific service (Thoburn et al, 2000). The following chapter by Dutt and Phillips provides a helpful comparison of black and white families in relation to the assessment of children's needs. They draw attention to factors such as family structures, cultural values, and discuss the myths and realities of black family networks. Accurate information of this type helps to remove confusion and uncertainty and avoids stereotyping of children and families.

1.37 It is also important not to confuse theory with ideology. Work with children and families has sometimes been subject to fashionable ideologies which may dictate the style of work adopted. Ideological approaches, for example, 'all children should be in family based care because residential care is bad for them' or 'siblings should be kept together at all costs' should never get in the way of ethical and professional practice which discriminates effectively in relation to the developmental needs of a particular child.

Wider family, community and environmental factors

1.38 The role of the wider family can be a significant source of support. Conversely, extended families may not always be supportive. Sometimes, even when families live nearby, links are not maintained (Aldgate and Bradley, 1999). Thoburn et al (2000) found that, at times, the stresses within the whole family were such that grandparents and other relatives could not find away to help, or were too caught up in their own problems. Some parents do not always wish to acknowledge to their wider kin that they are not coping with a burgeoning problem. However, Brandon et al (1999) found that when problems became serious, extended family members are likely to rally round to provide protection and care.

1.39 Similarly, the contribution of the community in providing practical and emotional support to the immediate family also needs to be understood. Living in a supportive community may offer considerable help to parents. It may be important to chart both families' interrelationships over time and their current wider connections in the communities in which they live. Genograms and Ecomaps may be useful means of doing this with families (Appendices 2 and 3 respectively).

1.40 Social isolation, through an absence of both physical and emotional support, is an important factor in limiting adults' sense of wellbeing and control over their lives (see Argyle, 1992; Coohey, 1996; Aldgate and Bradley, 1999). Research from HomeStart has also suggested that social isolation is one of the major reasons for referral for befriending support (McAuley, 1999). A two year survey of referrals to HomeStart (Northern Ireland) indicated that the predominant referrers were health visitors and that the five main reasons for referrals were:

- Mother's mental health (with postnatal depression being most prevalent);
- Mother's physical health;
- Multiple births/multiple young children;
- Child/ren's special needs eg. health problems;
- Mother's isolation/loneliness.

1.41 Where social isolation is combined with fears for personal safety because of a hostile neighbourhood, cumulative negative factors can have an impact on parents' mental and physical health. Additionally, the part the wider family and others may play in organised abuse needs to be understood (Cleaver, 1996). This includes the threats to children from dangerous individuals in unsafe communities.

1.42 Finally, there is considerable evidence which catalogues the impact of the environment on parental capacity. The impact on families' health and wellbeing is well known (for example, Bradshaw, 1990; Utting, 1995; Acheson, 1998). The day to day meaning of living on a low income is summarised by Amin and Oppenheim (1992, p.36), who describe material disadvantage as:

> ... a kind of partial citizenship, since the effects of material deprivation make it very difficult to participate in society as a full member...

1.43 The importance of recognising the interface between families and the communities in which they live has recently been identified by the Social Exclusion Unit (1998, p.9): While most areas have benefited from rising living standards, the poorest neighbourhoods have tended to become more rundown, more prone to crime and more cut off from the labour market.

1.44 Writers such as Jack (1997) and Stevenson (1998) have been concerned at the omission of environmental considerations from the social work process. Research studies have shown the strong association between economic disadvantage and living conditions and the chances that children will fail to thrive (Utting, 1995; Iwaniec, 1996) . Differences are clearly apparent in the health and educational development of children growing up in areas of deprivation. This has its impact both on young adults' ability to succeed as effective parents and directly on children themselves, through the standards of school available to them, the sub-culture of peer groups with whom they relate and the community facilities provided.

1.45 Holman at a conference in 1998 put it starkly: 'Poverty undermines parenting'. The meaning of living in continuing poverty is exemplified by Anita in her account of bringing up her children in an environment of social deprivation, in Holman's *Faith in the Poor* (1998, pp.96-98):

> Poverty is a terrible thing. I just cannot cope with what I am getting on income support. I just wish I could feed and clothe my children but it is impossible with what I receive... I am really worried about the kids growing up in Easterhouse... I know in my heart they will either turn to drugs or end up in prison. My kids keep asking to move. They are lovely kids and intelligent and I would dearly love to see

them make something of themselves... but what can I do with no money? My children don't stand a chance.

1.46 Bebbington and Miles (1989) have demonstrated how the cumulative effect of disadvantage can dramatically increase a child's chances of coming into the care system:

Table 3 The cumulate effect of disadvantage

Child A	**Child B**
Age 5-9	Age 5-9
No dependence on social security benefits	Household head receives income support
Two parent family	Single adult household
Three or fewer children	Four or more children
White	Mixed ethnic origin
Owner occupied home	Privately rented home
More rooms than people	One or more persons per room
Odds are 1 in 7,000	**Odds are 1 in 10**

1.47 The relationship between disability and disadvantage is also important and has not always been well understood. This is well evidenced in the study by Lawton (1998) of families with more than one disabled child (of which there are some 17,000 in the United Kingdom). Such families are:

- more likely to be single parents;
- less likely to be in work;
- more likely to be in semi-skilled or unskilled jobs;
- more likely to be dependent on income support;
- less likely to own their own home;
- more likely to report housing as unsuitable;
- more likely to have extra costs

This study serves to reinforce the importance of considering the wider context in which families are caring for and bringing up disabled children (issues which are discussed more fully in Chapter 3).

1.48 The evidence suggests that the families of many children in need who are most disadvantaged are those living in poverty, in poor housing, without adequate social supports and in the poorest, hostile neighbourhoods. These families face multiple stresses which are interlinked. McAuley (1999) includes the following example in her study.

Example of interplay of factors causing stress

The parents had two children under five years of age. The mother had had a medical condition for some time, but her health suddenly deteriorated, leaving her unable to walk. She had been admitted to hospital immediately. On her return home, she fell whilst attempting to walk in her home and broke her arm. Her husband had been off work with ill health. She went on to describe her predicament when the HomeStart Organiser first came to see her:

> I was completely useless. I couldn't even, obviously with a plaster on, I couldn't do something as simple as wash myself. I could just about feed myself and no more. P (her husband) had to basically cut up my meals for me. I couldn't change S's nappies or wash and iron. Those were things I had always done and P was having to do that. And he couldn't do that and look after the kids. It just really .... everything sort of went to pot... It was every kind of stress and with him being off for two years with no wages, we couldn't pay someone to come in and help us... My kids have never been separated from me before... When I came home (from hospital) they were extremely insecure... they really took my hospitalisation majorly badly... Any kind of disappearance at all, be it only for a few seconds to the back garden, you know, the kids panicked and were in hysterics and had to be completely reassured.

Mc Auley (1999, pp.33–34

Overarching theories and approaches that inform practice

1.49 Practitioners have the arduous task of making sense of the wealth of theory and knowledge informing their assessments. Psychodynamic and learning theories help to understand the inner and outer worlds of children and families, while eco-systems theory provides a very helpful framework to analyse the interconnections between personal and environmental factors which have an impact upon the lives of children and families. These are more fully discussed in Seden's review of the literature on assessment of children and their families (Department of Health, 2000b).

1.50 The ecological approach takes the view that individuals are connected to and interact with the environment in which they live. The approach is well established in the social sciences (Siporin, 1975; Maluccio, 1981; Garbarino, 1982). A key exponent of this theory, Bronfenbrenner (1979) outlines its relevance to social work with children and families. He places children's lives in the context of a series of systems: the immediate settings of home, school, friendship group and their interrelationship; local social structures which influence those settings; and the larger institutional patterns of economic, social, educational, legal and political systems. Updated applications of ecological theory are to be found in the paper by Jack (1997), in Stevenson's study of neglected children (1998), and in relation to child maltreatment by Jones and Ramchandani (1999).

1.51 Workers have at their disposal knowledge of human growth and development in children and families, knowledge of the environment and community and of the interaction between all these elements. A concrete example of how different and interconnecting knowledge and systems may be translated into practice in relation to child maltreatment comes from Jones and Ramchandani (1999) in Figure 3. Similarly helpful examples can be found in Crossing Bridges (Falkov (ed), 1998, p.75) and the work of Capaldi and Eddy (in press) in relation to children with conduct disorders.

1.52 As Cox (1993) and others have pointed out, what is significant for a family may be the processes generated by an event or events which may interact with the child's needs and the surrounding vulnerabilities and protective factors. The event or events may set off a cycle or chain of interaction. In assessing what is happening to a child and family, thought is required about the process which has been generated and the maintenance of momentum. The importance of **context** is therefore critical in understanding the relationship between outcomes and those events which act as stressors. Reder and Duncan (1999) provide a useful summary of the key issues which should be kept in mind during the assessment process:

Key issues for assessment

- Context gives meaning to behaviour
- Individuals exist in relationships to others
- Relationship and communication are a function of each other
- Current relationships arise out of historical influences
- Interactions revolve around the meaning of one person to another
- There is circularity between a person's inner and outer world

Reder and Duncan (1999)

1.53 Another way of understanding what is happening in family functioning draws from the systemic approach which has evolved from cybernetic theory or the study of communication. The theory focuses on people in their current social and economic context and the beliefs underpinning their behaviour. It seeks to explain human problems in terms of relationships rather than individual characteristics or pathology. Problems in systems often arise from attempts to adjust to life events and are linked to notions of circular and reciprocal cause and effect. The systemic practitioner, therefore, seeks to identify repetitive sequences of interaction which maintain and are maintained by the original or subsequent problems. Accounts of the development and use of the theory are found, for example, in Gorrell-Barnes (1994) and White and Epston (1990). 93

1.54 Both systems and ecological models consider how the support services, including social workers and other professionals, add to or detract from the family's coping mechanisms.

Methods of intervention

1.55 During the process of assessment, workers will be thinking about interventions that will best help children and families. The choice of intervention will be governed by many factors. Among these will be the appropriate application of social work methods. These methods have been developed from a range of psychosocial theories.

Figure 3 **A developmental and ecological perspective on child maltreatment**

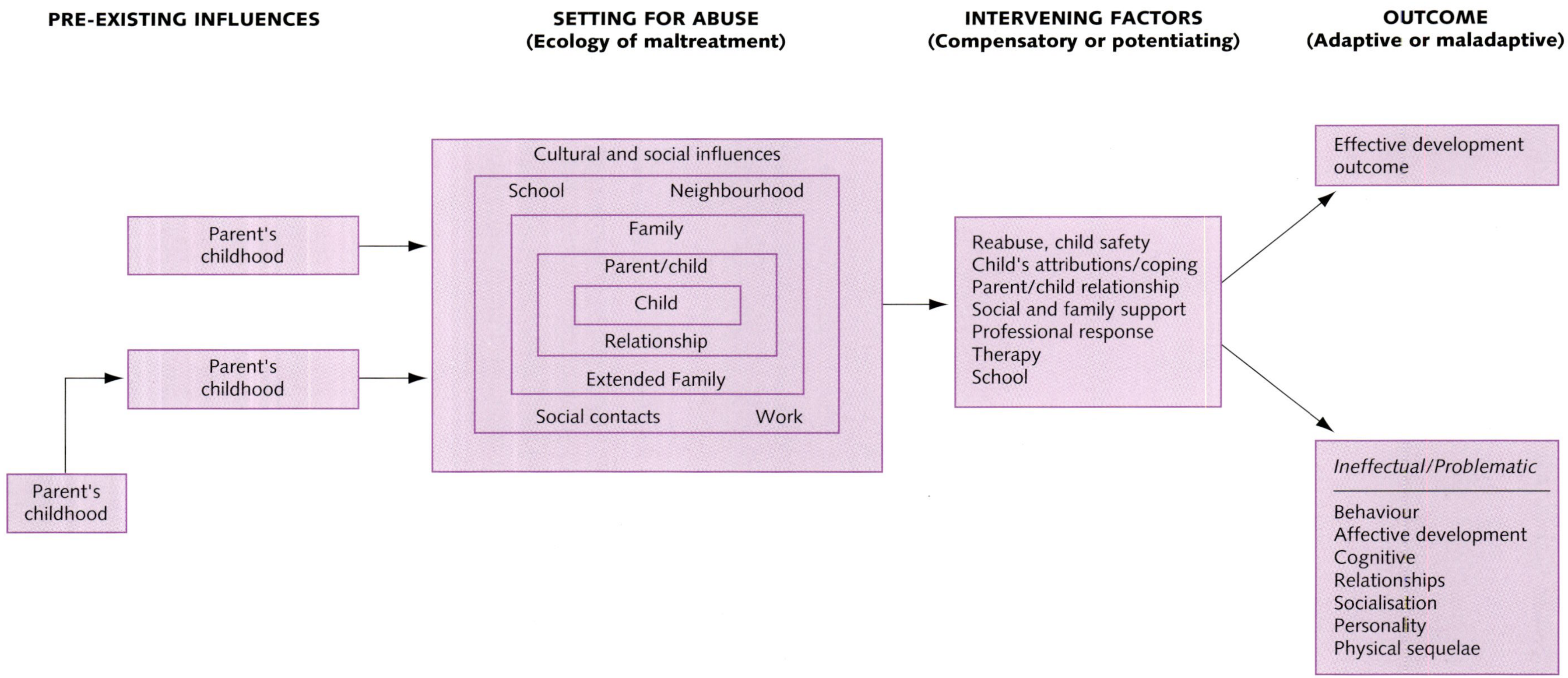

Reproduced with kind permission of the authors.
From: Jones D and Ramchandani P (1999) Child Sexual Abuse. Informing Practice from Research. Radcliffe Medical Press, Abingdon.

The methods include psychosocial casework, cognitive behavioural work, counselling, family therapy, task-centred casework, crisis intervention and so forth. Part of the assessment will be to think about which particular method will be best suited to the needs of individual children and their families. The approach must be eclectic. Workers may have their favoured approaches but it is not appropriate to use one method in all circumstances to the exclusion of all others. Choice of method should also be influenced by knowledge of what works in particular circumstances. For example, Jones and Ramchandani (1999), in writing about child sexual abuse, conclude that the 'best available evidence points to the use of focused therapies based on a cognitive-behavioural model being the most effective way of treating these symptoms'. However, they warn that 'no single therapy has demonstrable benefits for all children who have been sexually abused' (Jones and Ramchandani,1999, p.72). Texts based on clinical work like that of Jewett (1982) on helping children manage separation and loss, Fahlberg's (1991) work on children in transitions, and examples of clinical practice in direct work with children from Aldgate and Simmonds (1988) all have a major contribution to play in building up a repertoire of methods of intervention rooted in theory, research and good practice.

Roles and tasks of child and family workers

1.56 Of course in practice it is very difficult to separate the boundaries between assessment and intervention. Having established what is happening to a child within the context of his or her family and environment and the impact on the child, the purpose of assessment will change (Jones, 1998, p.111):

> Later on, the process develops into an assessment of the likelihood of change, followed by whether such change is achieved. Looked at this way, assessment continues throughout intervention.

1.57 Another important dimension of assessing the appropriate intervention is the decision whether the child remains at home or is looked after away from home, and whether this should be on a short term or permanent basis. Where a child is looked after, it will be important to consider all the factors surrounding placement choice, including plans for reunification and adoption (Thoburn et al, 1986; Department of Health, 1989; Department of Health, 1991b; Department of Health, 1999). Any decisions which involve changes for children must take account of their developmental needs. Principles of stability and continuity are important for children at any level of intervention, as are principles of safeguarding and promoting children's welfare.

1.58 Furthermore, the communication skills and interactions required to gather information will inevitably trigger in some children and families the beginning of problem solving processes. Recent research on family support has suggested that a short encounter between a social worker and a family to assess difficulties may be in itself a problem solving experience. The exchange and synthesis of information between family members and the worker may be enough to help the family without further social work intervention. At the other end of the continuum, long-term help will be necessary for a significant number of families (Department of Health, forthcoming). Schofield and Brown (1999) and Thoburn et al (2000) urge that workers remember the importance of the professional relationship between worker and children and families in any direct encounter with families.

1.59 Methods of intervention are only part of the knowledge base that practitioners need for assessment. They are important because good assessments are built on an integration of theory and practice. Knowledge is being continually developed by research findings and the evolution of new and existing theories. These include knowledge about child development, parenting and the impact of parental difficulties, and the significance of environmental factors. Work with children and families does not take place within a vacuum but in an organisational and legislative context. Understanding the roles and tasks of a worker, not only within the context of his or her own agency but also taking account of the roles and tasks of other workers and the contexts of agencies which are likely to be contributing to the promotion of the welfare of the child, is another area of knowledge essential to the assessment process. In this respect, it is also important to take account of the impact of agency factors on outcomes for children.

1.60 Effective collaboration between workers in different agencies is notoriously difficult to achieve. Recognition that inter-agency co-operation is required is not new. Hallett and Stevenson (1980) cite 'a government circular (Home Office, 1950) on ill-treated children which recommended the establishment of children's co-ordinating committees' (p.1). However, the difficulties and 'failures' in inter-agency working have been well documented in reviews of individual cases of child maltreatment and in more broadly based research studies (Department of Health and Social Security, 1982; Department of Health, 1991a; Department of Health, 1995; Hallett, 1995) . Hudson (2000) helpfully explores these issues, noting that governments have again and again exhorted public sector services to work more closely together (p.235):

> There is a paradox here, with 'collaboration' seen as both problem *and* solution failure to work together is the problem, therefore the solution is to work together!

1.61 He gives a salutory reminder that the literature constantly focuses on the barriers to collaboration including structural, professional, financial, status and legitimacy factors, but that 'inter-organisational relationships are largely built upon *human* relationships' (p.254). Some of the important messages for collaborative working which practitioners should understand are summarised below:

Collaborative Working: General Messages

- Reciprocity is the basis of collaboration
- Collaboration is a continuum with choices
- Collaboration requires a concensus of stakeholders
- Collaboration requires an expression of purpose
- Trust is essential to collaborative success

Hudson et al (1999)

The challenge of evidence based work

1.62 The Introduction to this practice guidance emphasised the importance placed on evidence based practice. This is a marked shift from thinking about evidence only as part of judicial processes. Rowe drew this out succinctly in *Patterns and Outcomes in Child Placement* (Department of Health, 1991b, pp.77-78):

> Social workers tend to think of evidence in terms of court hearings and reports, but evidence in the sense of 'facts which lead to conclusions' must be at the heart of every decision. The whole child care service, from strategic planning to monitoring of individual outcomes, is permeated by questions of evidence. Gathering, testing, recording and weighing evidence are tasks basic to professional competence, but are seldom addressed in these terms... Decisions can only be as good as the evidence on which they are based...

1.63 Throughout the *Framework for the Assessment of Children in Need and their Families* (Department of Health et al, 2000) and the materials produced to accompany the guidance, the sources of knowledge which have been used have been referenced and discussed to assist practitioners to develop their own knowledge base. However, evidence based practice also refers to the **process** whereby practitioners gather relevant information about what is happening to a child and use their knowledge from research findings, theoretical ideas and practical experience to arrive at a greater understanding of a particular child and family's experiences. Reder and Duncan (1999) provide a helpful discussion of this process, emphasising the importance of the application of knowledge at each stage of work with children and families. They refer to this as the development of a 'dialetic' mindset (p.98):

> Put at its simplest, assessment comes before action and the impact of actions needs to be monitored. Therefore, assessment should be an evolving process in which thought and action are reciprocal. Actions are guided by thought and the consequences of action are noted, considered and fed back to influence further action.

1.64 Thus, evidence based work also requires the careful use of knowledge gained during work with a child and family to undertake the task of determining what is most relevant in a family's situation, what is most significant for the child, the impact intervention is having and the judgement about when more or less action is required in the child's best interests.

1.65 Hunt et al (1999), in their study of the use of courts following the implementation of the Children Act 1989, explore the challenge of an evidence based approach for practitioners in that context (p.391):

> The new criteria for statutory intervention, for instance, and the emphasis on partnership with parents, place a premium on the capacity of social workers and their managers to evaluate evidence and manage risk, to develop skills at working with families in a voluntary framework and judging the point at which it is not viable. Once a case comes to court the social worker is expected to present coherent written evidence on what may well now be a more complex involvement with the family, be au fait with court procedures and be a competent witness even though the opportunities to accumulate court experiences are less frequent.

1.66 Although the principle of evidence based practice applies to all professionals who work with children and families, it is perhaps social work practitioners who are experiencing the challenge most keenly. It is essential for effective assessment of children in need and their families that social work is a confident profession, particularly in the context of inter-agency collaboration with other professionals. This requires social workers to be sure of their professional expertise and the knowledge on which they draw to form their professional judgements. Higham (Community Care, 1999) sums up this challenge:

> If social work is to develop further in the twenty-first century, practitioners must not rely solely on practice wisdom for decision making but use evidence based knowledge… Social work beyond the millennium needs to come of age. This will happen when social workers find an effective voice, develop new roles and establish a better knowledge base for their practice.

APPENDIX 1

Chart illustrating the developmental progress of infants and young children

MARY SHERIDAN	1 MONTH	3 MONTHS
Posture and large movements	Lies back with head to one side; arm and leg on same side outstretched, or both arms flexed; knees apart, soles of feet turned inwards. Large jerky movements of limbs, arms more active than legs. At rest, hands closed and thumb turned in. Fingers and toes fan out during extenor movements of limbs. When cheek touched, turns to same side; ear gently rubbed, turns head away. When lifted or pulled to sit head falls loosely backwards. Held sitting, head falls forward, with back in one complete curve. Placed downwards on face, head immediately turns to side; arms and legs flexed under body, buttocks humped up. Held standing on hard surface, presses down feet, straightens body and often makes reflex 'stepping' movements.	Now prefers to lie on back with head in mid-line. Limbs more pliable, movements smoother and more continuous. Waves arms symmetrically. Hands now loosely open. Brings hands together from side into mid-line over chest or chin. Kicks vigorously, legs alternating or occasionally together. Held sitting, holds back straight, except in lumbar region, with head erect and steady for several seconds before bobbing forwards. Placed downwards on face lifts head and upper chest well up in mid-line, using forearms as support, and often scratching at table surface; legs straight, buttocks flat. Held standing with feet on hard surface, sags at knees.
Vision and fine movements	Turns head and eyes towards light. Stares expressionlessly at brightness of window or blank wall. Follows pencil flash-lamp briefly with eyes at 1 foot. Shuts eyes tightly when pencil light shone directly into them at 1-2 inches. Notices silent dangling toy shaken in line of vision at 6-8 inches and follows its slow movement with eyes from side towards mid-line on level with face through approximately quarter circle, before head falls back to side. Gazes at mother's nearby face when she feeds or talks to him with increasingly alert facial expression.	Visually very alert, particularly interested in nearby human faces. Moves head deliberately to look around him. Follows adult's movements near cot. Follows dangling toy at 6-10 inches above face through half circle from side to side, and usually also vertically from chest to brow. Watches movements of own hands before face and beginning to clasp and unclasp hands together in finger play. Recognises feeding bottle and makes eager welcoming movements as it approaches his face. Regards still objects within 6-10 inches for more than a second or two, but seldom fixates continuously. Comerges eyes as dangling toy is moved towards face. Defensive blink shown.
Hearing and speech	Startled by sudden loud noises, stiffens, quivers, blinks, screws eyes up, extends limbs, fans out fingers and toes, and may cry. Movements momentarily 'frozen', when small bell rung gently 3-5 inches from ear for 3-5 seconds, with 5 second pauses; may 'corner' eyes towards sound. Stops whimpering to sound of nearby soothing human voice, but not when screaming or feeding. Cries lustily when hungry or uncomfortable. Utters little gutteral noises when content. (*Note:* Deaf babies also cry and vocalise in this reflex way, but if very deaf do not usually show startle reflex to sudden noises. Blind babies may also move eyes towards a sound-making toy. Vision should always be checked separately.)	Sudden loud noises still distress, provoking blinking, screwing up of eyes, crying and turning away. Definite quietening or smiling to sound of mother's voice before she touches him, but not when screaming. Vocalises freely when spoken to or pleased. Cries when uncomfortable or annoyed. Quietens to tinkle of spoon in cup or to bell rung gently out of sight for 3-5 seconds at 6-12 inches from ear. May turn eyes and head towards sound; brows may wrinkle and eyes dilate. Often licks lips in response to sounds of preparation for feeding. Shows excitement at sound of approaching footsteps, running bath water, voices, etc., (*Note:* Deaf baby, instead, may be obviously startled by mother's sudden appearance beside cot.)
Social behaviour and play	Sucks well. Sleeps much of the time when not being fed or handled. Expression still vague, but becoming more alert, progressing to social smiling about 5-6 weeks. Hands normally closed, but if opened, grasps examiner's finger when palm is touched. Stops crying when picked up and spoken to. Mother supports head when carrying, dressing and bathing.	Fixes eyes unblinkingly on mother's face when feeding. Beginning to react to familiar situations – showing by smiles, coos, and excited movements that he recognises preparation for feeds, baths, etc. Responds with obvious pleasure to friendly handling, especially when accompanied by playful tickling and vocal sounds. Holds rattle for few moments when placed in hand, but seldom capable of regarding it at same time. Mother supports at shoulders when dressing and bathing.

Chart illustrating the developmental progress of infants and young children – continued

	6 MONTHS	9 MONTHS
Posture and large movements	Lying on back, raises head from pillow. Lifts legs into vertical and grasps foot. Sits with support in cot or pram and turns head from side to look around him. Moves arms in brisk and purposeful fashion and holds them upto be lifted. When hands grasped braces shoulders and pulls himself up. Kicks strongly, legs alternating. Can roll over, front to back. Held sitting, head is firmly erect, and back straight. May sit alone momentarily. Placed downwards on face lifts head and chest well up, supporting himselfon extended arms. Held standing with feet touching hard surface bears weight on feet and bounces up and down actively.	Sits alone for 10-15 minutes on floor. Can turn body to look sideways while stretching out to grasp dangling toy or to pick up toy from floor. Arms and legs very active in cot, pram and bath. Progresses on floor by rolling or squirming. Attempts to crawl on all fours. Pulls self to stand with support. Can stand holding on to support for a few moments, but cannot lower himself. Held standing, steps purposefully on alternate feet.
Vision and fine movements	Visually insatiable: moves head and eyes eagerly in every direction. Eyes move in unison. squint now abnormal. Follows adult's movements across room. Immediately fixates interesting small objects within 6-12 inches (eg, toy, bell, wooden cube, spoon, sweet) and stretches out both hands to grasp them. Uses whole hand in palmar grasp. When toys fall from hand over edge of cot forgets them. (Watches rolling balls of 2 to ¼ inch diameter at 10 feet).	Very observant. Stretches out, one hand leading, to grasp small objects immediately on catching sight of them. Manipulates objects with lively interest, passing from hand to hand, turning over, etc. Pokes at small sweet with index finger. Grasps sweets, string, etc., between finger and thumb in scissor fashion. Can release toy by pressing against firm surface, but cannot yet put down precisely. Searches in correct place for toys dropped within reach of hands. Looks after toys falling over edge of pram or table. Watches activities of adults, children and animals within 10-12 feet with eager interest for several seconds at a time. (Watches rolling balls 2⅛ inches at 10 feet.)
Hearing and speech	Turns immediately to mother's voice across room. Vocalises tunefully and often, using single and double syllables, eg. ka, muh, goo, der, adah, er-lah. Laughs, chuckles and squeals aloud in play. Screams with annoyance. Shows evidence of response to different emotional tones of mother's voice. Responds to baby hearing test at 1½ feet from each ear by correct visual localisation , but may show slightly brisker response on one side. (Tests employed – voice, rattle, cup and spoons, paper, bell; 2 seconds with 2 seconds pause.)	Vocalises deliberately as means of interpersonal communication. Shouts to attract attention, listens, then shouts again. Babbles tunefully, repeating syllables in long strings (mam-man, bab-bab, dad-dad, etc.) Understands 'No-No' and 'Bye-Bye'. Tries to imitate adults' playful vocal sounds, eg. smacking lips, cough, brr, etc. (Immediate localising response to baby hearing tests at 3 feet from ear and above and below ear level.)
Social behaviour and play	Hands competent to reach for and grasp small toys. Most often uses a two-handed, scooping-in approach, but occasionally a single hand. Takes everything to mouth. Beginning to find feet interesting and even useful in grasping. Puts hands to bottle and pats it when feeding. Shakes rattle deliberately to make it sound, often regarding it closely at same time. Still friendly with strangers but occasionally shows some shyness or even slight anxiety, especially if mother is out of sight.	Holds, bites and chews biscuits. Puts hands round bottle or cup when feeding. Tries to grasp spoon when being fed . Throws body back and stiffens in annoyance or resistance. Clearly distinguishes strangers from familiars, and requires reassurance before accepting their advances. Clings to known adult and hides face. Still takes everything to mouth. Seizes bell in one hand, imitates ringing action, waving or banging it on table, pokes clapper or 'drinks' from bowl. Plays peek-a-boo. Holds out toy held in hand to adult, but cannot yet give. Finds partially hidden toy. May find toy hidden under cup. Mother supports at lower spine when dressing.

Chart illustrating the developmental progress of infants and young children – continued

	12 MONTHS	15 MONTHS
Posture and large movements	Sits well and for indefinite time. Can rise to sitting position from lying down. Crawls rapidly, usually on all fours. Pulls to standing and lets himself down again holding on to furniture. Walks round furniture stepping sideways. Walks with one or both hands held. May stand alone for a few moments. May walk alone.	Walks unevenly with feet wide apart, arms slightly flexed and held above head or at shoulder level to balance. Starts alone, but frequently stopped by falling or bumping into furniture. Lets himself down from standing to sitting by collapsing backwards with bump, or occasionally by falling forward on hands and then back to sitting. Can get to feet alone. Crawls upstairs. Kneels unaided or with slight support on floor and in pram, cot and bath. May be able to stoop to pick up toys from floor.
Vision and fine movements	Picks up small objects, eg blocks, string, sweets and crumbs, with precise pincer grasp of thumb and index finger. Throws toys deliberately and watches them fall to ground. Looks in correct place for toys which roll out of sight. Points with index finger at objects he wants to handle or which interest him. Watches small toy pulled along floor across room 10 feet away. Out of doors watches movements of people, animals, motor cars, etc., with prolonged intent regard. Recognises familiars approaching from 20 feet or more away. Uses both hands freely, but may show preference for one. Clicks two bricks together in imitation. (Watches rolling balls 2⅛ inches at 10 feet.)	Picks up string, small sweets and crumbs neatly between thumb and finger. Builds tower of two cubes after demonstration. Grasps crayon and imitates scribble after demonstration. Looks with interest at pictures in book and pats page. Follows with eyes path of cube or small toy swept vigorously from table. Watches small toy pulled across floor up to 12 feet. Points imperiously to objects he wishes to be given. Stands at window and watches events outside intently for several minutes. (Watches and retrieves rolling balls of 2⅛ inches at 10 feet.)
Hearing and speech	Knows and immediately turns to own name. Babbles loudly, tunefully and incessantly. Shows by suitable movements and behaviour that he understands several words in usual context (eg. own and family names, walk, dinner, pussy, cup, spoon, ball, car). Comprehends simple commands associated with gesture (give it to daddy, come to mummy, say bye-bye, clap hands, etc.) Imitates adult's playful vocalisations with gleeful enthusiasm. May hand examine common objects on request, eg. spoon, cup, ball, shoe. (Immediate response to baby tests at 3-4½ feet but rapidly habituates.)	Jabbers loudly and freely, using wide range of inflections and phonetic units. Speaks 2-6 recognisable words and understands many more. Vocalises wishes and needs at table. Points to familiar persons, animals, toys, etc., when requested. Understands and obeys simple commands (eg. shut the door, give me the ball, get your shoes). (Baby test 4½-6 feet.)
Social behaviour and play	Drinks from cup with little assistance. Chews. Holds spoon but usually cannot use it alone. Helps with dressing by holding out arm for sleeve and foot for shoe. Takes objects to mouth less often. Puts wooden cubes in and out of cup or box. Rattles spoon in cup in imitation. Seizes bell by handle and rings briskly in imitation, etc. Listens with obvious pleasure to percussion sounds. Repeats activities to reproduce effects. Gives toys to adult on request and sometimes spontaneously. Finds hidden toy quickly. Likes to be constantly within sight and hearing of adult. Demonstrates affection to familiars. Waves 'bye-bye' and claps hands in imitation or spontaneously. Child sits, or sometimes stands without support, while mother dresses.	Holds cup when adult gives and takes back. Holds spoon, brings it to mouth and licks it, but cannot prevent its turning over. Chews well. Helps more constructively with dressing. Indicates when he has wet pants. Pushes large wheeled toy with handle on level ground. Seldom takes toy to mouth. Repeatedly casts objects to floor in play or rejection, usually without watching fall. Physically restless and intensely curious. Handles everything within reach. Emotionally labile. Closely dependent upon adult's reassuring presence. Needs constant supervision to protect child from dangers of extended exploration and exploitation of environment.

Chart illustrating the developmental progress of infants and young children – continued

	18 MONTHS	2 YEARS
Posture and large movements	Walks well with feet only slightly apart, starts and stops safely. Runs stifly upright, eyes fixed on ground 1-2 yards ahead, but cannot continue to run round obstacles. Pushes and pulls large toys, boxes, etc., round floor. Can carry large doll or teddy-bear while walking and sometimes two. Backs into small chair or slides in sideways. Climbs forward into adult's chair then turns round and sits. Walks upstairs with helping hand. Creeps backwards down stairs. Occasionally bumps down a few steps on buttocks facing forwards. Picks up toy from floor without falling.	Runs safely on whole foot, stopping and starting with ease and avoiding obstacles. Squats to rest or to play with object on ground and rises to feet without using hands. Walks backwards pulling large toy. Pulls wheeled toy by cord. Climbs on furniture to look out of window or open doors, etc., and can get down again. Walks upstairs and down holding on to rail and wall; two feet to a step. Throws small ball without falling. Walks into large ball when trying to kick it. Sits astride large wheeled toy and propels forward with feet on ground .
Vision and fine movements	Picks up small sweets, beads, pins, threads, etc., immediately on sight, with delicate pincer grasp. Spontaneous scribble when given crayon arld paper, using preferred hand. Builds tower of three cubes after demonstration. Enjoys simple picture book, often recognising and putting finger on coloured items on page. Turns pages 2 or 3 at a time. Fixes eyes on a small dangling toy up to 10 feet. (May tolerate this test with each eye separately.) Points to distant interesting objects out of doors. (Watches and retrieves rolling balls 2–½ inches at 10 feet.) (Possibly recognises special miniature toys at 10 feet.)	Picks up pins and thread, etc., neatly and quickly. Removes paper wrapping from small sweet. Builds lower of six cubes (or 6+). Spontaneous circular scribble and dots when given paper and pencil. Imitates vertical line (and sometimes V). Enjoys picture books, recognising fine details in favourite pictures. Turns pages singly. Recognises familiar adults in photograph after once shown. Hand preference becoming evident. (Immediately catches sight of, and names special miniature toys at 10 feet distance. Will now usually tolerate this test with each eye separately.) (Watches and retrieves rolling balls 2–⅛ inches at 10 feet.)
Hearing and speech	Continues to jabber tunefully to himself at play. Uses 6-20 recognisable words and understands many more. Echoes prominent or last word addressed to him. Demands desired objects by pointing accompanied by loud, urgent vocalisation or single words. Enjoys nursery rhymes and tries to join in. Attempts to sing. Shows his own or doll's hair, shoe, nose (Possibly special 5 toy test. Possibly 4 animals picture test.)	Uses 50 or more recognisable words and understands many more. Puts 2 or more words together to form simple sentences. Refers to himself by name. Talks to himself continually as he plays. Echo(s) a almost constant, with one or more stressed words repeated. Constantly asking names of objects. Joins in nursery rhymes and songs. Shows correctly and repeats words for hair, hand, feet, nose, eyes, mouth, shoe on request. (6 toy test, 4 animals picture test.)
Social behaviour and play	Lifts and holds cup between both hands. Drinks without spilling. Hands cup back to adult. Choose well. Holds spoon and gets food to mouth. Takes off shoes, socks, hat. Indicates toilet needs by restlessness and vocalisation. Bowel control usually attained. Explores environment energetically. No longer takes toys to mouth. Remembers where objects belong. Casts objects to floor in play or anger less often. Briefly imitates simple activities, e.g. reading book, kissing doll, brushing floor. Plays contentedly alone, but likes to be near adult. Emotionally still very dependent upon familiar adult, especially mother. Alternates between clinging and resistance.	Lifts and drinks from cup and replaces on table. Spoon-feeds without spilling. Asks for food and drink. Chews competently. Puts on hat and shoes. Verbalises toilet needs in reasonable time. Dry during day. Turns door handles. Often runs outside to explore. Follows mother round house and copies domestic activities in simultaneous play. Engages in simple make-believe activities. Constantly demanding mother's attention. Clings lightly in affection, fatigue or fear. Tantrums when frustrated but attention readily distracted. Defends own possessions with determination. As yet no idea of sharing. Plays near other children but not with them. Resentful of attention shown to other children.

Chart illustrating the developmental progress of infants and young children – continued

	2½ YEARS	3 YEARS
Posture and large movements	Walks upstairs alone but downstairs holding rail, two feet to a step. Runs well straight forward and climbs easy nursery apparatus. Pushes and pulls large toys skillfully, but has difficulty in steering them round obstacles. Jumps with two feet together. Can stand on tiptoe if shown. Kicks large ball. Sits on tricycle and steers with hands, but still usually propels with feet on ground.	Walks alone upstairs with alternating feet and downstairs with two feet to step. Usually jumps from bottom step. Climbs nursery apparatus with agility. Can turn round obstacles and corners while running and also while pushing and pulling large toys. Rides tricycle and can turn wide corners on it. Can walk on tiptoe. Stands momentarily on one foot when shown. Sits with feet crossed at ankles.
Vision and fine movements	Picks up pins, threads, etc., with each eye covered separately. Builds tower of seven (or 7+) cubes and lines blocks to form 'train'. Recognises minute details in picture books. Imitates horizontal line and circle (also usually T and V). Paints strokes, dots and circular shapes on easel. Recognises himself in photographs when once shown. Recognises miniature toys and retrieves balls 2⅛ inches at 10 feet, each eye separately. (May also match special single letter-cards V, 0, T, H at 10 feet.)	Picks up pins, threads, etc., with each eye covered separately. Builds tower of nine cubes, also (3½) bridge of three from model. Can close fist and wiggle thumb in imitation. R and L. Copies circle (also V, H, T). Imitates cross. Draws man with head and usually indication of features or one other part. Matches two or three primary colours (usually red and yellow correct, but may confuse blue and green). Paints 'pictures' with large brush on easel. Cuts with scissors. (Recognises special miniature toys at 10 feet. Performs single-letter vision test at 10 feet. Five letters.)
Hearing and speech	Uses 200 or more recognisable words but speech shows numerous infantilisms. Knows full name. Talks intelligibly to himself at play concerning events happening here and now. Echolalia persists. Continually asking questions beginning 'What?', 'Where?'. Uses pronouns, I, me and you. Stuttering in eagerness common. Says a few nursery rhymes. Enjoys simple familiar stories read from picture book. (6 toy test, 4 animal picture test, 1 st cube test. Full doll vocabulary.)	Large intelligible vocabulary but speech still shows many infantile phonetic substitutions. Gives full name and sex, and (sometimes) age. Uses plurals and pronouns. Still talks to himself in long monologues mostly concerned with the immediate present, including make-believe activities. Carries on simple conversations, and verbalises past experiences. Asks many questions beginning 'What?', 'Where?', 'Who?'. Listens eagerly to stories and demands favourites over and over again. Knows several nursery rhymes. (7 toy test, 4 animals picture test. 1 st or 2nd cube test, 6 'high frequency' word pictures.)
Social behaviour and play	Eats skilfully with spoon and may use fork. Pulls down pants or knickers at toilet, but seldom able to replace. Dry through night if lifted. Very active, restless and rebellious. Throws violent tantrums and when thwarted or unable to express urgent need and less easily distracted. Emotionally still very dependent upon adults. Prolonged domestic make-believe play (putting dolls to bed, washing clothes, driving motor cars, etc.) but with frequent reference to friendly adult. Watches other children at play interestedly and occasionally joins in for a few minutes, but little notion of sharing playthings or adult's attention.	Eats with fork and spoon. Washes hands, but needs supervision in drying. Can pull pants and knickers down and up, but needs help with buttons. Dry through night. General behaviour more amenable. Affectionate and confiding. Likes to help with adult's activities in house and garden. Makes effort to keep his surroundings tidy. Vividly realised make-believe play including invented people and objects. Enjoys floor play with bricks, boxes, toy trains and cars, alone or with siblings. Joins in play with other children in and outdoors. Understands sharing playthings, sweets, etc. Shows affection for younger siblings. Shows some appreciation of past and present.

Chart illustrating the developmental progress of infants and young children – continued

	4 YEARS	5 YEARS
Posture and large movements	Turns sharp corners running, pushing and pulling. Walks alone up and downstairs, one foot per step. Climbs ladders and trees. Can run on tiptoe. Expert rider of tricycle. Hops on one foot. Stands on one foot 3-5 seconds. Arranges or picks up objects from floor by bending from waist with knees extended.	Runs lightly on toes. Active and skilful in climbing, sliding, swinging, digging and various 'stunts'. Skips on alternative feet. Dances to music. Can stand on one foot 8-10 seconds. Can hop 2-3 yards forwards on each foot separately. Grips strongly with either hand.
Vision and fine movements	Picks up pins, thread, crumbs, etc., with each eye covered separately. Builds tower of 10 or more cubes and several 'bridges' of three on request. Builds three steps with six cubes after demonstration . Imitates spreading of hand and bringing thumb into opposition with each finger in turn, R and L. Copies cross (also V, H, T and O). Draws man with head, legs, features, trunk and (often) arms. Draws very simple house. Matches and names four primary colours correctly. (single-letter vision test at 10 feet, seven letters: also near chart to bottom).	Picks up minute objects when each eye is covered separately. Builds three steps with six cubes from model. Copies square and triangle (also letters; V, T, H, O, X,L,A,C,U,Y). Writes a few letters spontaneously. Draws recognisable man with head, trunk, legs, arms and features. Draws simple house with door, windows, roof and chimney. Counts fingers on one hand with index finger of other. Names four primary colours and matches 10 or 12 colours. (Full nine-letter vision chart at 20 feet and near test to bottom.)
Hearing and speech	Speech completely intelligible. Shows only a few infantile substitutions usually k/t/th/f/s and r/l/w/y groups). Gives connected account of recent events and experiences. Gives name, sex, home address and (usually) age. Eternally asking questions 'Why?' 'When?', 'How?' and meanings of words. Listens to and tells long stories sometimes confusing fact and fantasy. (7 toy test, 1 st picture vocabulary test, 2nd cube test. 6 'high frequency' word pictures.)	Speech fluent and grammatical. Articulation correct except for residual confusions of s/f/th and r/l/w/y groups. Loves stories and acts them out in detail later. Gives full name, age and home address. Gives age and (usually) birthday. Defines concrete nouns by use. Asks meaning of abstract words. (12 'high frequency' picture vocabulary or word lists. 3rd cube test, 6 sentences.)
Social behaviour and play	Eats skilfully with spoon and fork. Washes and dries hands. Brushes teeth. Can undress and dress except for back buttons, laces and ties. General behaviour markedly self-willed. Inclined to verbal impertinence when wishes crossed but can be affectionate and compliant. Strongly dramatic play and dressing-up favoured. Constructive out-of-doors building with any large material to hand. Needs other children to play with and is alternately co-operative and aggressive with them as with adults. Understands taking turns. Shows concern for younger siblings and sympathy for playmates in distress. Appreciates past, present and future.	Uses knife and fork. Washes and dries face and hands, but needs help and supervision for rest. Undresses and dresses alone. General behaviour more sensible, controlled and responsibly independent. Domestic and dramatic play continued from day to day. Plans and builds constructively. Floor games very complicated. Chooses own friends. Co-operative with companions and understands need for rules and fair play. Appreciates meaning of clock time in relation to daily programme. Tender and protective towards younger children and pets. Comforts playmates in distress.

Reprinted from *Reports on Public Health and Medical Subjects* No 102.
HMSO 1960, revised 1975. In Department of Health (1988) Protecting Children.
A Guide for Social Workers undertaking a Comprehensive Assessment, pp.88-93.
HMSO, London.

APPENDIX 2 Genogram

Genogram symbols

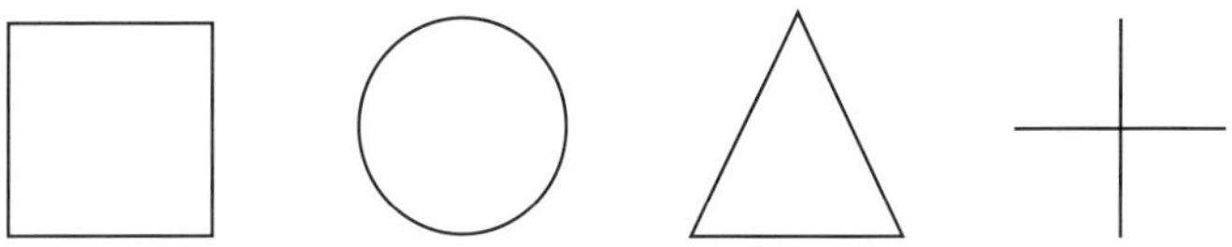

Male | Female | Gender unknown (e.g. pregnancy) | Death

Genogram symbols

Enduring relationship (marriage or cohabitation)

Transitory relationship

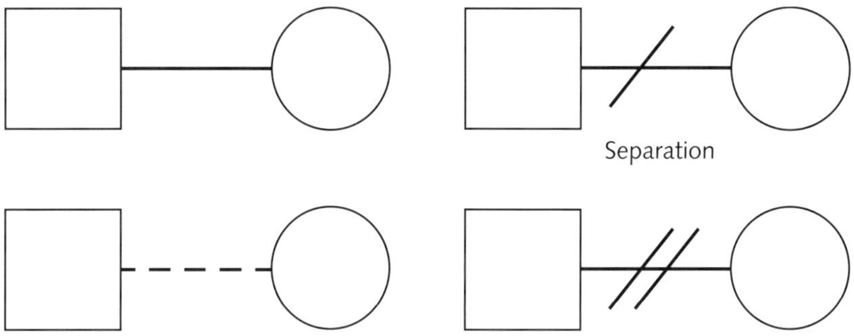

Separation

Divorce

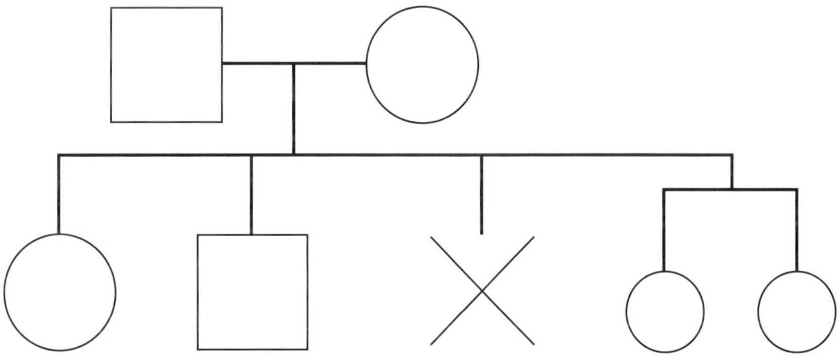

First child | Second child | Miscarriage or abortion | Twins

A dotted line should be drawn around the people who currently live in the same house.

Compiling a genogram

A genogram of family tree covering three or more generations may be compiled using these symbols. Other relatives in addition to parents and children can be involved in compiling the genogram. More than one session may be needed if the exercise is used to discuss the family's history in detail and to enter significant dates and other information. Working on a genogram also provides the practitioner with an opportunity to observe family relationships, for example how open family members are with each other, how well they respond to each other's needs, how flexible they are and how much they know about each other.

APPENDIX 3 Ecomap

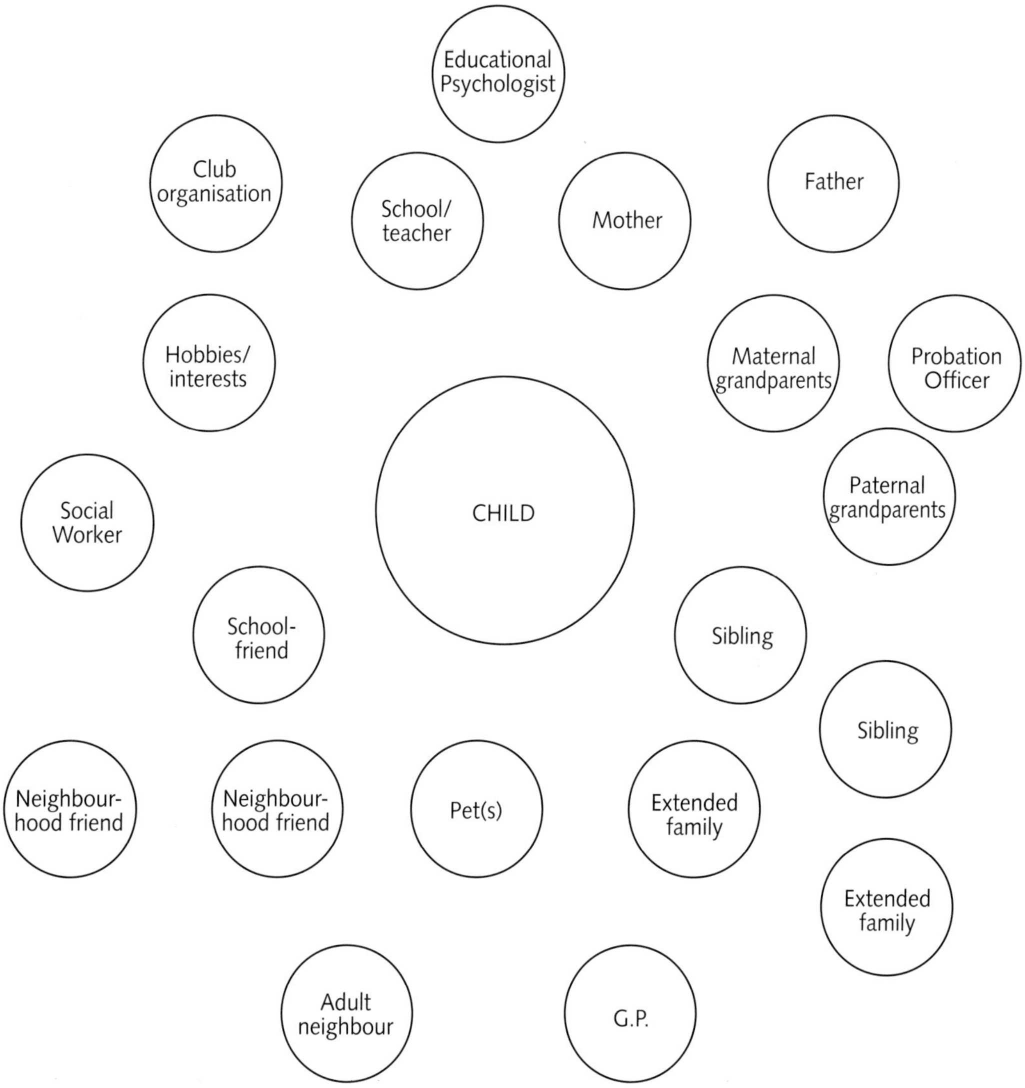

- Place child or couple or family in central circle
- Identify important people or organisations and draw circles as needed
- Draw lines between circles where connections exist
- Use different types of lines to indicate the nature of the link or relationship

——— = strong

- - - - - = weak

• • • • • = stressful

References – Chapter 1

Acheson D (1998) *Independent Inquiry into Inequalities in Health.* The Stationery Office, London.

Adcock M (1998) *Significant harm: implications for local authorities.* In Adcock M and White R (eds) (1998) *Significant Harm: its management and outcome.* pp.33-56. Significant Publications, Croydon.

Ahmed S, Cheetham J and Small J (ed) (1986) *Social Work with Black Children and their Families.* Batsford Ltd, London.

Aldgate J and Bradley M (1999) *Supporting Families through Short Term Fostering.* The Stationery Office, London.

Aldgate J and Simmonds J (eds) (1988) *Direct Work with Children: a Guide for Social Work Practitioners.* Batsford, London.

Aldridge J and Becker S (1999) Children as carers: the impact of parental illness on children's caring roles. Journal of Family Therapy. **21**: 303-320.

Amin K and Oppenheim C (1992) *Poverty in Black and White: Deprivation in Ethnic Minorities.* Child Poverty Action Group, London.

Argyle M (1992) *The Social Psychology of Everyday Life.* Routledge, London.

British Agencies for Adoption and Fostering (1999) *Making Good Assessments. Preparing for Permanence – A Practical Resource Guide.* BAAF, London.

Bandura A (1997) *Social Learning Theory.* Prentice- Hall, Englewood, NJ.

Bebbington A and Miles J (1989) The Background of Children who enter Local Authority Care. *British Journal of Social Work* **19**: 5, pp.349-368.

Belsky Y J and Vondra J (1989) *Lessons from child abuse: The determinants of parenting.* In Cicchetti D and Carlson V (eds) (1989) *Child Maltreatment: Theory and Research on the Causes and Consequences of Child Abuse and Neglect.* Cambridge University Press, New York.

Bentovim A (1998) *Significant Harm in Context.* In Adcock M and White R (eds) (1998) *Significant Harm: its Management and Outcome.* pp.57-89. Significant Publications, Croydon.

Bowlby J (1969) *Attachment and Loss, Vol I Attachment.* Hogarth Press, London

Bowlby J (1973) *Attachment and Loss, Vol II Separation: Anxiety and Anger.* Basic Books, New York.

Bowlby J (1980) *Attachment and Loss, Vol 111 Loss: Sadness and Depressions.* Basic Books, New York.

Bradshaw J (1990) *Child Poverty an d Deprivation in the UK.* NCB, London.

Brandon M, Lewis A, Thoburn J and Way A (1999) *Safeguarding Children with the Children Act 1989.* The Stationery Office, London.

Brearley J (1991) *Counselling and Social Work.* Open University Press, Buckingham.

Bronfonbrenner U (1979) *The Ecology ofHuman Development: Experiments by Nature and Design.* Harvard University Press, Cambridge.

Buchanan A (1999) *What works for Troubled Children. Family support for children with emotional and behavioural problems.* Barnardo's, London.

Buchanan A (ed) (1994) *Partnership in Practice.* Avebury, Aldershot.

Buchanan A and Hudson B L (1998) *Parenting, Schooling and Childrens Behaviour interdisciplinary approaches.* Ashgate, Hampshire.

Butler I and Williamson H (1994) *Children Speak: children, trauma and social work.* Longman, Essex. In NSPCC in association with Chailey Heritage and Department of Health (1997) *Turning Points: A Resource Pack for Communicating with Children. Introduction.* pp.1-2. The NSPCC, London.

Butt J and Box C (1998) *Family Centred. A study of the use of family centres by black families.* REU, London.

Capaldi D and Eddy M (in press) *Improving Childrens Long Term Well-being by Preventing Anti-Social Behaviour.* In Buchannan A and Hudson B L (in press) *Promoting the Emotional Well-being of Children. Messages from Research.* Oxford University Press, Oxford.

Carlson V, Cicchetti D, Barnett D and Braunwald K (1989) Disorganised/ Disoriented attachment relationships in maltreatment infants. *Developmental Psychology.* **25**: 525-531.

Cleaver H (1991) *Vulnerable Children in Schools.* Dartmouth, Aldershot.

Cleaver H (1996) *Child Abuse which involved wider kin and family .friends.* In Bibby P (ed) *Organised Abuse: The Current Debate.* Ashgate, Aldershot.

Cleaver H (2000a) *When parents' issues influence their ability to respond to childrens needs.* In Horwath J (ed) *The Childs World: Assessing Children in Need. The Reade*r. The NSPCC, London.

Cleaver H (2000b) *Fostering Family Contact: a study of children, parents and foster carers.* The Stationery Office, London.

Cleaver H and Freeman P (1995) *Parental Perspectives in Cases of Suspected Child Abuse.* HMSO, London.

Cleaver H, Unell I and Aldgate J (1999) *Childrens Needs – Parenting Capacity: The impact of parental mental illness, problem alcohol and drug use, and domestic violence on childrens development.* The Stationery Office, London.

Coohey C (1996) Child Maltreatment: Testing the social isolation hypothesis. *Child Abuse and Neglect.* **20**: 241-254.

Cox A (1993) Preventive aspects of child psychiatry. *Archives of Disease in Childhood.* **63**: 691-701.

Crittehden PM and Ainsworth M D S (1989) *Child Maltreatment and Attachment.* In Cicchetti D and Carlson V (eds) *Handbook of Child Maltreatment: Clinical and Theoretical Perspectives.* pp.432-463. Cambridge, New York.

Department of Health (1989) *The Care of Children: Principles and Practice in Regulations and Guidance.* HMSO, London.

Department of Health (1991a) *Child Abuse. A Study of Inquiry Reports 1980-1989.* HMSO, London.

Department of Health (1991b) *Patterns and Outcomes in Child Placement. Messages from current research and their implications.* HMSO, London.

Department of Health (1995) *Child Protection: Messages from Research.* HMSO, London.

Department of Health (1996) *Focus on Teenagers: Research into Practice.* HMSO, London.

Department of Health (1999) *Adoption Now: Messages from Inspection.* Wiley, Chichester.

Department of Health (2000a) *towards safer care. Training and Resource Pack.* The Department of Health, London.

Department of Health (2000b) *Studies which inform the development of the Framework for the Assessment of Children in Need and their Families.* The Stationery Office, London.

Department of Health (forthcoming) *The Children Act 1989 Now: Messages from Research.* The Stationery Office, London.

Department of Health, the Department of Education and Employment and the Home Office (2000) *Framework for the Assessment of Children in Need and their Families.* The Stationery Office, London.

Department of Health and Social Security (1982) *Child Abuse: A Study of Inquiry Reports.* HMSO, London.

Department of Health and the Welsh Office (1997) *People Like Us. Report of the Review of the Safeguards for Children Living Away from Home.* The Stationery Office, London.

Fahlberg V I (1981) *Attachment and Separation.* BAAF, London.

Fahlberg V I (1991) *A Childs Journey through Placement.* BAAF, London

Falkov A (1996) *A Study of Working Together "Part 8" Reports: Fatal child abuse and parental psychiatric disorder.* Department of Health – ACPC Series I. Department of Health, London.

Falkov A (ed) (1998) *Crossing Bridges – Training resources for working with mentally ill parents and their children. Reader – for managers, practitioners and trainers.* Pavilion Publishing, Brighton.

Farmer E and Owen M (1995) *Child Protection Practice: Private Risks and Public Remedies.* HMSO, London.

Garbarino J (1982) *Children and Families in the Social Environment.* Aldine, New York.

Ghate D and Hazel N (forthcoming) *Parenting in poor environments: A national study of parents and stress.*

Gilligan R (2000) *Promoting Positive Outcomes for Children in Need: The Assessment of Protective Factors.* In Horwath J (ed) (2000) *The Childs World: Assessing Children in Need. The Reader.* The NSPCC, London.

Gorrell-Barnes G (1994) *Family Therapy.* In Rutter M, Taylor E and Hersov L (eds) *Child and Adolescent Psychiatry: Modern Approaches.* pp.946-967. Blackwell, London.

Haggerty R J , Sherrod L R, Garmezy Nand Rutter M (1996) *Stress, Risk and Resilience in Children and Adolescents.* Cambridge University Press, Cambridge.

Hallett C (1995) *Inter-agency Co-ordination in Child Protection.* HMSO, London.

Hallett C and Stevenson O (1980) *Child Abuse: aspects of inter-professional co-operation.* Allen and Unwin, London.

Higham P (1999) *Reach Out–But will we be there?* In Community Care 29 April- 5 May 1999. pp.24-25.

Hill M, Laybourn A and Brown J (1996) Children whose parents misuse alcohol: a study of services and needs. *Child and Family Social Work.* 1: 159-167.

Holman B (1998) *Faith in the Poor.* Lion Publishing, Oxford.

Home Office (1950) *Children neglected or ill-treated in their own homes.* Joint Circular with Ministry of Health and Ministry of Education.

Horwath J (ed) (2000) *The Childs World: Assessing Children in Need. The Reader.* The NSPCC, London.

Hudson B L (1991) *Behavioural Social Work.* In Lishman J (ed) *Handbook of Theory for Practice teachers in Social Work.* Jessica Kingsley, London.

Hudson B, Hardy B, Henwood M and Wistow G (1999) In Pursuit of Inter-Agency Collaboration: What is the contribution of theory and research? *Public Management: an international journal of research and theory.* **1** (2): 235-260.

Hudson B (2000) *Inter-agency collaboration – a sceptical view.* In Brechin A, Brown H and E by M A (eds) (2000) *Critical Practice in Health and Social Care.* The Open University/Sage, London.

Hunt J, McLeod A and Thomas C (1999) *The Last Resort.* The Stationery Office, London.

Iwaniec D (1996) *The Emotionally Abused and Neglected Child.* Wiley, Chichester.

Jack G (1997) An Ecological Approach to Social Work with Children and Families. *Child and Family Social Work.* **2**: 109-120.

Jackson S (1987) *The Education of Children in Care.* University of Bristol, School of Applied Social Studies, Bristol.

Jewitt C (1984) *Helping Children Cope with Separation and Loss.* Batsford/BAAF, London.

Jones D P H (1998) *The effectiveness of of intervention.* In Adcock M and White R (eds) (1998) *Significant Harm: its Management and Outcome.* pp.91-119. Significant Publications, Croydon.

Jones D and Ramchandani P (1999) *Child Sexual Abuse: Informing Practice from Research.* Radcliffe Medical Press. Abingdon.

Jones DPH, Newbold C and Byrne G (1999) *Management, Treatment and Outcomes.* In Eminson M and Posslethwaite R (eds) (1999) *Munchausen Syndrome by Proxy Handbook.* Butterworth/Heineman.

Katz A, Buchanan A and Ten Brinke J-A (1997) *The Can Do Girls – A Barometer of Change.* Department of Applied Social Studies and Research, Oxford.

Lawton D (1998) *The Number and Characteristics of Families with More than One Disabled Child.* Social Policy Research Unit, University of York.

Masten A and Coatsworth D (1998) Development of Competence in Favourable and Unfavourable Environments. *American Psychologist,* February 1998.

McAuley C (1999) *The Family Support Outcomes Study.* Home Start UK/Northern Health and Social Services Board, Northern Ireland.

Maluccio A (ed) (1991) *Promoting Competence in Clients: a New/Old Approach to Social Work Practice.* The Free Press, New York.

Parton N (1987) *The Politics of Child Abuse.* Routledge, London.

Perry BD (1993) Neuro-development and the neuro-physiology of trauma. *The Advisor* **6(1)**: 1,14-18; **6(2)**: 1,14-20.

Pugh G (1999) *Parents under Stress.* Community Care, 2 -8 September 1999.

Reder P and Duncan S (1999) *Lost Innocents.* Routledge, London.

Reder P and Lucey C (1995) *Assessment of Parenting: Psychiatric and Psychological Contributions.* Routledge, London.

Rosenfeld A A, Bailey R, Siegal B and Bailey G (1986) Determining incestuous contact between parent and child: frequency of children touching parents' genitals in a non clinical population. *Journal of American Academy of Child Psychiatry.* **25**: 481-484.

Rushton A, Treseder J and Quinton D (1988) *New Parents for Older Children.* BAAF, London

Rutter M (1974) *Dimensions of Parenthood: some myths and some suggestions.* In Department of Health and Social Security (1974) *The Family in Society: dimensions of parenthood.* HMSO, London.

Rutter M and Rutter M (1992) *Developing Minds: Challenging and Continuity across the Life Span.* Penguin, Harmondsworth.

Rutter M (1996) Stress Research: Accomplishments and tasks ahead. In Haggerty RJ et al (1996) *Stress, Risk and Resilience in Children and Adolescents.* pp.354-386. Cambridge University Press, Cambridge.

Rutter M (1999) Resilience concepts and findings: implications for family therapy. *Journal of Family Therapy.* **21**: 119-144, 159-160.

Schofield G (1998) Inner and outer worlds: a psychosocial framework for child and family social work. *Child and Family Social Work.* **3:** 57-67.

Schofield G and Brown K (1999) Being there: a family centre worker's role as a secure base for adolescent girls in crisis. *Child and Family Social Work.* **4**: 21-31.

Seden J (2000) *A Review of the Literature: Assessment in Social Work.* In Department of Health (2000b) *Studies which inform the development of the Framework for the Assessment of Children in Need and their Families.* The Stationery Office, London.

Seligman ME P (1975) *Helplessness: On Depression, Development and Death.* W H Freeman, San Francisco.

Shaw C (1998) *Remember my messages...* The Who Cares? Trust, London.

Sinclair R (1998) *The education of children in need.* Research in Practice/NCB, Dartington.

Siporin M (1975) *Introduction to Social Work Practice.* Macmillan, New York.

Skinner B R (1974) *About Behaviourism.* Cape, London.

Social Exclusion Unit (1998) *Bringing Britain Together: A National Strategy for Neighbourhood Renewal.* The Stationery Office, London.

Social Services Inspectorate (1999) *Getting Family Support Right. Inspection of the Delivery of Family Support Services.* Department of Health, London.

Stevenson O (1998) *Neglected Children: Issues and Dilemmas.* Blackwell Science, Oxford.

Thoburn J, Murdoch A and O'Brien A (1986) *Permanence in Child Care.* Basil Blackwell, Oxford.

Thoburn J, Wilding J and Watson J (2000) *Family Support in Cases of Emotional Maltreatment and Neglect.* The Stationery Office, London.

Thomas C and Beckford V (1999) *Adopted Children Speaking.* BAAF, London.

Tucker S, Tatum C and Frank J (1999) *The Experiences of Former Young Carers.* The Children's Society, London.

Tunstill J and Aldgate J (2000) *Services for Children In Need: From Policy to Practice.* The Stationery Office, London.

Utting D (1995) *Family and Parenthood: Supporting Families, Preventing Breakdown.* Joseph Rowntree Foundation, York.

Utting D (1996) *Reducing criminality among young people: A sample of relevant programmes in the United Kingdom.* Home Office, London.

Ward H (2000) *The Developmental Needs of Children: implications for assessment.* In Horwath J (ed) (2000) *The Childs World: Assessing Children in Need. The Reader.* The NSPCC, London.

White M and Epston D (1990) *Narrative Means to Therapeutic Ends.* Norton, New York.

2

Assessing black children in need and their families

Introduction

2.1 The population of England is comprised of many white minority ethnic groups as well as black minority ethnic groups and the differences in culture, religion, language and traditions for white minority ethnic groups have to be accounted for just as they do for black minority ethnic groups.

2.2 There are also a number of white minority ethnic groups who experience oppression on the basis of their ethnic, cultural or religious identity. In assessing families these experiences should be acknowledged and addressed.

2.3 This chapter focuses specifically on the needs of black children and families. Black here refers to children and families of Asian, African and Caribbean origin including children of dual heritage.

2.4 Whilst there are some similarities and parallels in the experiences of black and white minorities in Britain there is also a fundamental difference. Institutional racism has resulted in the significant impairment of the life opportunities of black people in this country (MacPherson, 1999).

2.5 Institutional racism operates within the field of child welfare. Over the last thirty years concern has been expressed about the number of black children in care (Batta, McCulloch and Smith, 1979; Adams, 1981;Rowe et al, 1989; Barn, 1993; 1997), the lack of take up of family support services (Butt and Box, 1998), and the lack of potential for some black children (London Borough of Lambeth, 1997; The Bridge Child Care Consultancy Services, 1991).

2.6 Assessing the developmental needs of children is a complex process which requires all relevant aspects of a child's life experience to be addressed. For black children assessments should address the impact that racism has on a particular child and family and ensure that the assessment process itself does not reinforce racism through racial or cultural stereotyping.

2.7 This chapter aims to assist child welfare professionals in undertaking assessments of black children in need and their families.

Assessing black children in need and their families

2.8 Within the current context of practice, professionals charged with responsibilities for promoting the welfare of children and their families often struggle with how best to address the needs of black children and their families. Although many professionals are aware that it is essential to take account of race and culture, and in particular to be culturally sensitive in their practice, they are often at a loss to translate this into practical terms. In assessing the developmental needs of black children and their families practitioners should address two key questions: .

- **What are the developmental needs of black children and their families, and in what ways are these similar, and in what ways do they differ from the developmental needs of white children and families?**
- **How can these developmental needs be responded to in work with black children and families?**

2.9 Both black and white children require their parents or carers to respond to their same fundamental care needs. They all need basic care, warmth, stimulation, guidance, boundaries and stability. Any child who grows up without access to these basic life blocks (as a result of poor parental care) will suffer to a greater or lesser extent.

2.10 The base lines for assessing parenting capacity and the child's developmental needs should be the same irrespective of whether a black or a white child is being assessed.

2.11 Later in this chapter, we look in detail at the similarities in and differences between the needs of black children and their families compared with white children and their families when using the Assessment Framework dimensions. Each of the three domains of the Assessment Framework will be addressed with respect to each of its dimensions.

2.12 Firstly, the context will be set for assessing black children and families. This includes their demographic and socio-economic situation and the changing nature of culture, as well as some key issues in professional practice.

Demography

2.13 According to the 1991 census the total black and minority ethnic population of Britain is over 3 million people (5.5%). Of this 2.9 million black and minority ethnic people live in England, 59.5 thousand live in Scotland and 40.5 thousand live in Wales.

2.14 There are considerable regional variations in the ethnic composition of the population with the largest composition being in London at 44.8% and West Midlands, especially in Birmingham at 14% (Owen, 1992). Although there are regional variations in ethnic composition of the population, there are few areas where black people do not have a presence (Butt and Mirza, 1996).

2.15 One important feature of the black community is its relative youth compared to the white community. For instance adults aged over 45 constitute 39% of the white community compared to 18% of the black and minority ethnic community, and adults aged over 65 account for 16.9% of the white community and only 3.2% of the black and minority ethnic communities Oones, 1993).

2.16 More importantly children under 15 constitute 33% of black and minority ethnic communities compared to 19 % in the white communities. In certain parts of the country such as the London Boroughs of Newham and Tower Hamlets children make up the majority of the population. Other important features of the population include:

- A very diverse black population with wide variations in class, countries of origin, socio-economic conditions, religion and languages;
- An increasing number of adult mixed relationships with 40% of M rican Caribbean men and 20% of M rican Caribbean women in mixed relationships (Berrington, 1996; Haskey, 1997). Importantly, 80% of black adults in mixed relationships are UK born and over half the children of mixed relationships are under the age of 15 (Haskey, 1997) .

Socio economic conditions

2.17 Evidence suggests that many of Britain's black population are experiencing economic hardship. According to the Social Exclusion Unit (1998) 'Ethnic minority groups are more likely than the rest of the population to live in poor areas, be unemployed, have low incomes, live in poor housing, have poor health and be the victims of crime'.

2.18 The important point about the socio-economic conditions of black communities from an assessment perspective is, as Butt and Mirza (1998) observe 'black communities are at greater risk of experiencing some of the stress so often associated with people who need the services of social care agencies'.

The changing nature of culture for England's black population

2.19 The impact of social and economic forces, the effects of racism and racial harassment, changing family structures, access to suitable housing, the interaction between cultures, particularly in respect of children and young people and the experience of growing up in England are amongst a number of factors which have led to the changing nature of culture for black communities in this country. However, this has not led to an erosion of culture, as has sometimes been portrayed, but to the emergence of new cultural frameworks (Donald and Rattansi, 1992).

2.20 In some cases there has been a return to traditional values, exhibited by an increased interest in religious observance; in others, particularly among teenagers, there has been a mixing of cultures to create a street based culture strongly influenced by black, and in particular, black American and Caribbean culture.

2.21 Dosanjh and Ghuman (1998) describe the cross-fertilisation of cultures as 'enculturation' meaning:

> This dynamic of enculturation. . .can be summarised as comprising a continuity with some traditional norms alongside the adopting of some of the norms of British lifestyles.

2.22 Despite these significant changes, culture remains a central part of the lives of black communities, for it is the primary way in which black communities can give meaning and continuity to their own distinct identities, rites, traditions, values, beliefs and customs. For many black people, it is their culture which gives them the strength to survive in a hostile environment.

Key Issues in current child welfare practice

Numbers of black children in care

2.23 There are no current available figures on the number of black children in care in England. There are a number of small scale and local studies which have indicated an over-representation of black children in care particularly of dual heritage and African Caribbean origin. Although there are difficulties in drawing conclusions from these studies on a national basis, their findings cannot be ignored.

2.24 Local authorities should analyse their population of children looked after to ascertain the extent to which the number of black children who are looked after reflects the local profile of the black population. If there is an under or an over representation of black children, the local authority should take active steps to identify the reasons for this situation and address it.

Family Support

2.25 There is evidence also that black families are not gaining access to family support services. In a study of black families' use of family centres Butt and Box (1998) found that 13 out of the 84 centres had no black and minority ethnic users and 25 centres had black and minority ethnic users in equal proportion to their presence in the population. The authors conclude:

> Our study suggests that black communities do not always have access to family centres and rarely access the full range of services that are available. This is not merely an outcome of black families choosing which service they access (although there is an element of that) but that the services only rarely get black families through the front door and some black users appeared to be unaware of the range of services that were available.

Inquiry Reports

2.26 At the same time, several Inquiry Reports into the deaths of black children provide evidence of a lack of intervention in situations where black children were at obvious risk of suffering significant harm from their parents. Two specific reports, *Whose Child? The Report of the Panel of Inquiry into the Death of Tyra Henry 1987* (London Borough of Lambeth, 1987) and *Sukina; An evaluation report of the circumstances leading to her death* (The Bridge Child Care Consultancy Services, 1991) make a direct link between racism and the practice of professionals when responding to the children and families concerned. Both reports identify that stereotyping of black families and a reluctance on the part of white professionals to intervene for fear of being accused of racism influenced practice.

2.27 It is clear that a more informed approach to the issue of race and culture within professional assessments is required. The remainder of this chapter will discuss ways in which professional practice could be developed to improve the assessment of and planning for black children and their families through an evidence-based, systematic and holistic approach to assessments with black families.

Domain: Children's Developmental Needs

Health

2.28 The following are some of the issues to be considered regarding health and black children and families:

- Research has shown the link between poverty and ill-health. Although this is as true for the white community as it is for the black community there is evidence to suggest that black and minority ethnic people experience poorer health. There are, however, differences amongst the different ethnic groups. A study by Nazroo (1997) found that on the whole Pakistanis and Bangladeshis reported the poorest health during assessments of general health, with Caribbeans having the next worst state of health;
- There is a very strong correlation between the physical health of children of all ages and adverse social and economic conditions. This is particularly apparent in the infant mortality rate, which is directly affected by factors such as economic status, type of accommodation, access to basic amenities and access to preventative and supportive health care. A number of studies have shown a higher infant mortality rate amongst poorer black communities, particularly within families from Bangladesh, Pakistan and the Caribbean (Smaje, 1999);
- There are some diseases which are more common amongst black and minority ethnic people and some which are particular to black communities only. In relation to the latter sickle cell disorder is one such illness, affecting mainly children from the African Caribbean community but may occur in people from India and Pakistan. For those affected by it, the most difficult aspect of the disorder is the pain experienced during the crisis. Symptoms can include infections such as meningitis as well as strokes (NHS Executive, 1998). Professionals working with black children affected by sickle cell can get more information about the disorder from the Sickle Cell Society;
- Particular groups of children such as refugee children can suffer post-traumatic stress syndrome. This can be directly attributed to the past experiences of many of the children. They may have witnessed death, violence and war prior to their arrival in the U.K.

Pointers for Practice

Pointers for Practice

Assessments of black families should take account of the specific health needs of different black communities and address: .

- The extent to which the physical health of the child may be affected by adverse social conditions; .
- The extent to which the child and family have direct access to appropriate advice support and services in relation to their health care needs;

- Whether the child or family members may be likely to suffer from sickle cell disorder;
- Whether past life experiences or trauma has had any affect on the physical health of the child.

Education

2.29 From a psychological perspective, there is no difference in the cognitive or educational capacity or development of black children as compared to white. However, in social terms, there is no aspect of child development in which racism has had a greater impact in this country than that of educational and cognitive development.

2.30 Today, whilst there is an acknowledgement that there is no biological or genetic difference between black children's intelligence or educational ability as compared to white children, race continues to make a difference in the educational experience and achievements of black children. There is a great deal of evidence to suggest that black pupils in England under-achieve educationally and are more likely to be excluded from school than their white counterparts:

- The data on permanent school exclusions for 1996/97 show that African Caribbean pupils are more than four times as likely to face permanent exclusions compared to white pupils. Kundnani (1998) summaries evidence which suggests the 'profile of African Caribbean children who are excluded differs from that of excluded children generally; they are usually higher than average ability, exhibit less evidence of deep seated trauma and are less likely to have shown disruptive behaviour from early in their school career'. Kundnani (1998) suggests that there is a problem 'between teachers and black children and that teachers' perceptions of black children (and vice versa) do, somehow play a crucial role';
- The over-representation of black children excluded from school has also been identified as an important issue by the Social Exclusion Unit;
- The most recent data on achievements in school show that African Caribbean, Pakistani and Bangladeshi children continue to under-achieve;
- Black parents consistently express concern about being undermined by the school system.

Pointers for Practice

Assessment of black children's educational and cognitive development should take account of racism as it may manifest itself within the educational system and address:

- Whether the child has had the opportunity to realise their educational potential without the limitations imposed upon them by negative stereotyping;
- For an excluded child, the extent to which the exclusion is appropriate in relation to the child's behaviour;
- The extent to which the child's parents are consulted about and involved in the child's education.

Identity and Emotional and Behavioural Development

2.31 Identity is important for all children: there are close links between the development of a child's identity and their emotional and behavioural development. Children who have emotional and behavioural difficulties often have a poor self-image and low self-esteem.

2.32 There is still considerable misunderstanding about the nature of identity and its central importance to all children. One of the reasons for this, is that identity is most often spoken about in relation to black children in situations where the child is perceived to be exhibiting identity problems. In fact, many children about whom there are professional concerns have problems with their identity, self-esteem and self-worth. These issues have been shown to be particularly significant for many children in the care system, both black and white. In their recent study of the effectiveness of care in childrens homes, Sinclair and Gibbs (1998) found that over 70% of children and young people had low self-esteem.

The nature of Identity

2.33 Identity is difficult to define, yet it is central to every person's sense of their own individuality and place in society. Definitions range from spiritual or religious, through to psychodynamic, behavioural, social and structural interpretations. We will draw on the literature to propose a model of understanding identity in relation to black children and their families which is inclusive of all the elements of which it is comprised.

2.34 Within most societies, identity fulfils two useful functions. It allows individuals to understand and conceptualise themselves as distinct from others and it allows individuals to form group identities with other individuals who have similar characteristics to their own.

Group identification

2.35 Group identification allows individuals to categorise each other in social interactions. Race, gender, class, disability, age, sexual identity, are all features of group identity which have an outcome for group members in terms of institutional discrimination and disadvantage. For black children and their families, being black in a white society is not just about personal or group identity, it is about a lived experience of discrimination on the grounds of colour and physical characteristics.

2.36 For children and young people who are both black and disabled, the experience of discrimination on the basis of their disability is compounded by the effects of racism. Despite this, many black and disabled children find that only one aspect of their experience is addressed at anyone time.

Individual and personal identity

2.37 Individual identity is the internal model which allows each person to have a perception of themselves as an individual and social being. We are all members of numerous social groupings, but we are also distinct in our own individuality from any other member of a given group to which we belong, despite some areas of commonality (See Erikson, 1968).

2.38 There is a complex interaction which takes place between the elements of one's personality to form an individual identity. Although each child is born with a specific genetic blueprint, inherited from their parents, each is unique. This is because each individual interaction between a child, his or her family, relationships, social context and environment, will be processed into an individual experience. These sets of individual experiences contribute towards the development of a whole personality.

2.39 Identity, therefore, has to be defined and assessed in terms of a holistic model of children's development which incorporates other facets of his or her developmental needs. The diagram below sets out how these key elements interact to form a child's identity (Figure 4).

2.40 From the time a child is born, he or she begins to develop an individual identity. First interactions with their carers, siblings and social contacts become part of the child's internal model of identity. These experiences also locate the child within a social world in which group identities begin to influence identity formation.

2.41 For black children and their families, racism affects both individual and group identities. Although there is no biological or genetic basis for the concept of a racial group, race has a social significance in that it affects the way in which a child him or herself and is perceived by others. A black child growing up within a predominantly white society will receive negative messages about being black, and needs a positive internal model of black identity to counteract negative stereotypes. A black child who is also disabled will be affected by their own and others perception of both their disability and their race, and will need to be given the opportunity to develop a positive sense of themselves which helps them to counteract negative messages about both.

The Development of a racial identity

2.42 Racial identity is relevant to all children whether black or white. Being white is a racial identity, just as being black is one. However, because being white in England is often perceived as normative, being black becomes defined in terms of its difference to white norms. In fact, all children go through a developmental process of acquiring a racial identity, although many white adults and children along with a percentage of black adults and children are not aware they are doing so. Black children do not universally acquire a negative sense of self despite the effects of racism (Milner, 1983; Owusu-Bempah and Howitt, 1999).

2.43 The preconditions for identity formation for a secure black child growing up in a loving environment with racially aware black carers will be very different to the preconditions for a black child who has an insecure base, a poor caregiving environment and unaware or even hostile black or white carers.

2.44 For black children who do not have a positive sense of their racial identity, Cross (1971) provides one model for understanding and assessing racial identity. He explains the acquisition of their racial identity in terms of a five stage process:

- **Pre-encounter stage**
  This is before a child's has encountered racism, where their world view is influenced by a white perspective.

Figure 4 **A model of identity**

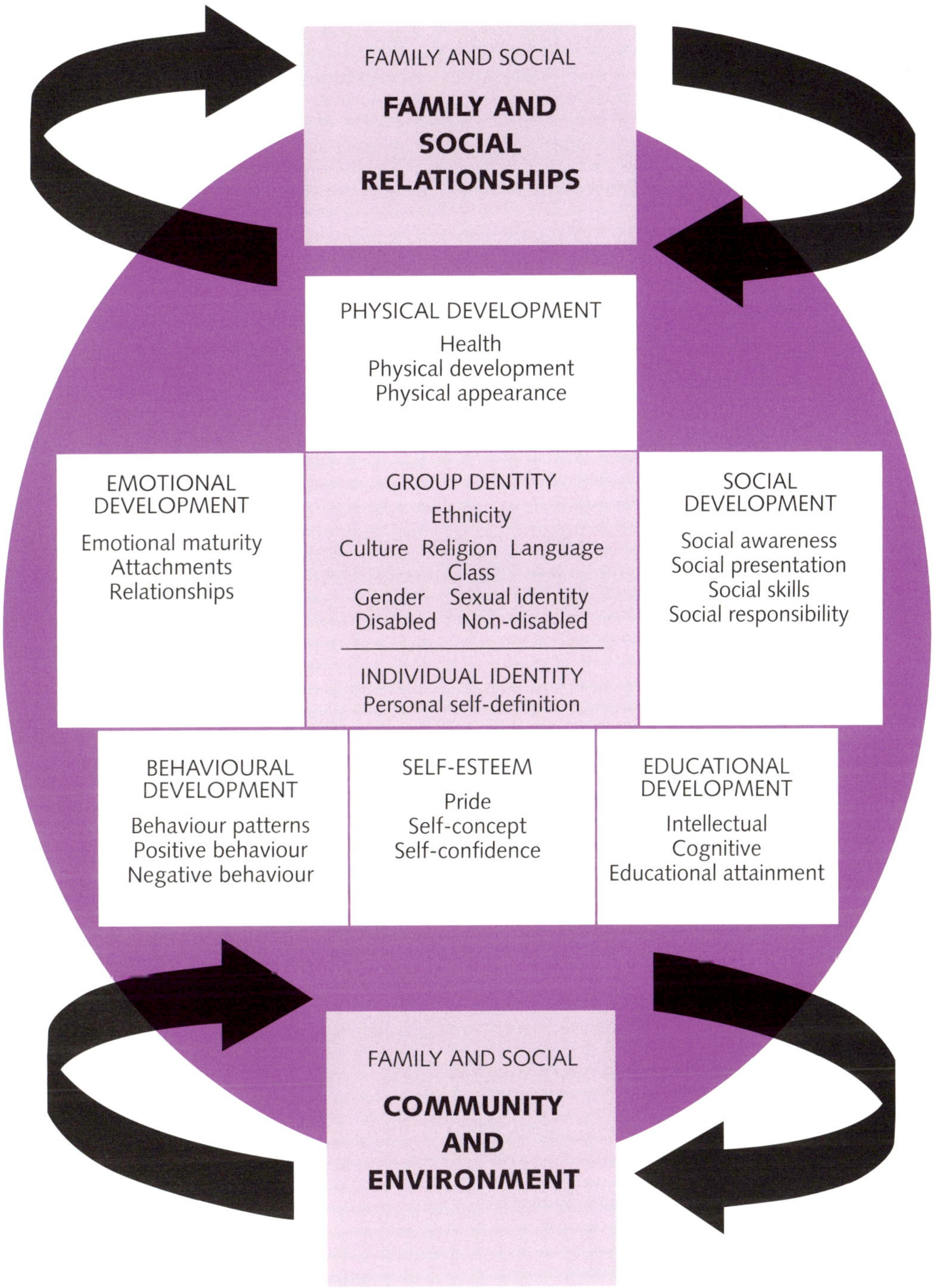

- **Encounter stage**
  This coincides with the child's first real encounter with racism. The significance of this experience forces the child to reconsider their previous world view and to reinterpret their experiences.

- **Immersion-emersion stage**
  This is where the child seeks to reject all previous aspects of their identity, and to become immersed in their blackness. However, this is only a superficial and reactive concept of black identity, which is more connected with the semblance of blackness, than with an integrated working model of a black identity. Individuals at this stage are often, wrongly perceived to have a positive black identity.

- **Internalisation stage**
  This is a move towards a more positive and integrated model of identity, in which an internal working model of black identity begins to take shape.

- **Internalisation-commitment stage**
  This is where the internal model links to aspects of a group identity, in that the child commits themselves to active participation in and commitment to the black community.

2.45 Cross' model also helps provide some insight into the links between personal racial identity and racial group identification. It helps us to understand the connections between personal racial identity, racial group identification and emotional and behavioural development. For instance a black person who group identifies as black, but is unable to internalise that identification will show in the way they behave the disconnections between their external and internal worlds. Similarly, a black child who has an integrated sense of their racial identity will exhibit this in their interactions and relationships with others.

2.46 For black children with one white parent (children of dual heritage) the connections between personal self-definition and group identification can hold particular significance. Although a number of recent studies have focused on the identity of children of dual heritage (Banks, 1992; Tizard and Phoenix, 1994; Katz, 1996), it should be stressed that these children should not be pathologised as having identity problems or identity conflicts. Many children of dual heritage have a very positive and integrated racial identity.

2.47 However, for some children of dual heritage, the dynamics of racial group identification are very complex. It is often stated that such children "want to be white" or are "denying their blackness". This is an over-simplification of their position.

2.48 For some of these children, particularly those who live with their white parent and have little or no contact with their black parent or the black parent's family, black self-definition means more than a journey towards self-recognition. For them there are emotional consequences to black racial group identification. If they perceive their white parent as caring and supportive, they may not wish to hurt a loved person by rejecting the white racial identity of their main carer, or white people in their main caregiving envIrOnment.

2.49 For these children it is important to understand the context in which the process of identity development is taking place. Working with these children and their white carers to strengthen the child's internal working model of racial identity is crucial to helping them feel positive about their racial identity and to deal with the racism which they will inevitably experience.

2.50 Whilst Cross' model was developed to help understand black racial identity, it is also applicable to the assessment of white racial identity. Just as the acquisition of an integrated sense of self in relation to race is a process for black people, so it is for white people. White children's attitudes to race reflect this. In their study of mainly white primary schools Troyna and Hatcher (1992) found that white children exhibited inconsistent attitudes towards race, ranging from overtly racist frameworks of interpretation through to well developed notions of race equality.

2.51 An interesting aspect of their research findings is the inconsistency between expressed values and behaviour:

> … a number of combinations of attitudes is possible, ranging from children who hold overtly racist beliefs but do not express them in behaviour, to children who hold racially egalitarian beliefs but use racist name calling in certain situations.

2.52 This demonstrates the need for dialogue about race and racism with white children and young people, as away of exploring and integrating their notions of race. An awareness of the impact of racism and an understanding of their white cultural heritage are **also** important parts of positive identity development for white children in a multi-racial and multi-cultural society.

Ethnicity

2.53 Whilst race is defined by heritage, colour, physical appearance, and physical characteristics, ethnicity is defined by geographic, political, historical, religious and cultural factors. Cashmore (1984) describes an ethnic group as:

> a group possessing some degree of coherence and solidarity composed of people who are, at least latently aware of having common origins and interests.

2.54 There are white ethnic groups as well as black ethnic groups. Minority status is related simply to being in the minority within a given population. Both black and white people continue to be oppressed and discriminated against on the basis of their ethnicity.

2.55 As an aspect of individual and group identity, ethnicity is significant in that it gives individuals a sense of community, heritage and belonging. Ethnicity, like race, cannot be acquired through lifestyle or association. As such, ethnicity is an important aspect of identity in both individual and group terms.

2.56 For children, the acquisition of an ethnic identity is an important process which helps them to connect their personal and family history to that of a community or social grouping. As such it gives them a sense of heritage.

Cultural, religious and linguistic identity

2.57 Culture, religion and language are three distinct parts of identity which interconnect with racial and ethnic identity. However, they are distinct from both in that they can be acquired through the process of socialisation. A child can be born into a family from one cultural background, speak one language and be brought up with a particular set of religious beliefs. With a change of lifestyle, a new parental partnership, or a geographical move some or all of these aspects of the child's life may change, whilst their racial and ethnic identity remain the same.

2.58 However, culture, religion and language are very important aspects of group and individual identity. Whilst racial identity forms one important aspect of identity, individuals from the same racial group may have differences in terms of their cultural background, religious observance and linguistic identity.

Culture

2.59 Much has been written about the concept of culture. We will not revisit old ground, but will summarise the following key points which are crucial to an understanding of the nature of culture and acquiring a cultural identity.

- Both black and white people have cultural identities;
- Culture is dynamic, not monolithic;
- Culture is acquired through live experiences; . Culture is not static, but changes and develops over time;
- There are differences between families who have the same cultural background;
- Views of black cultures are influenced by cultural and racial stereotyping.

The acquisition of cultural identity

2.60 Just as for racial identity, cultural identity functions at both a group and an individual level. It is acquired from live experiences. From birth, the child's senses are attuned to the specifics of their environment:

> Individuation begins with the environment and evolves largely through sensory and perceptual experiences (Prohansky and Gottlieb, 1989).

2.61 The particular music young children hear, the language spoken or type of regional accent or dialect, the colours of clothing and fabrics seen, distinct household and cooking smells all provide a particular and distinct environment which contributes towards the formation of their cultural identity.

2.62 As a child grows older, interacts more with their family, community and the world at large, these interactions become more complex and multi-faceted. At the same time as developing capabilities for self-reflection and self-definition, the child acquires an individual cultural identity which has been shaped both by the particular context in which it has been developed and the child's own contribution to the process.

2.63 During this developmental process, the child will act and react in relation to a host of cultural information. Some of this will be specific to their own family traditions, some will be shared with individuals and families who come from a similar cultural background to the child. Through these interactions the child learns about individual family values and norms as well as about those norms and values which may be shared as group values.

2.64 For black disabled children there may also be other cultural connections which are important to them in addition to their family connections. For example, a black child who is deaf will also have experiences of deaf culture, where they may share commonalities with children and young people who have different ethnicities and family backgrounds to themselves. Whilst these commonalities will influence aspects of group-identification with other deaf children and young people, family culture will also be significant in defining identity. In this way, the acquisition of cultural identity can only be understood by taking account of the whole experience of each child or young person.

2.65 For some children, who do not grow up in an environment where they experience their own culture, perhaps because of being in substitute care, or because they do not have contact with any black family members, the acquisition of cultural identity is a more difficult process. For some of these children the only access to such experiences is through books or television programmes.

2.66 These sources of information can provide the child with information about cultural practices and traditions, but they cannot provide the child with alive and interactive experience in which the child has the opportunity to participate in and even shape events. Although useful if used appropriately, such information can also reinforce stereotypical and monolithic notions of culture because of its essentially static nature.

Religion

2.67 Section 22(5) (c) of the Children Act 1989, requires local authorities to:

give due consideration to… the childs religious persuasion…

2.68 There is some evidence to suggest that information about the child's or family's religion is not always recorded in case files. Unpublished research undertaken by the authors in a city and county authority indicate that religion was not routinely recorded for black children.

2.69 Religion or spirituality is an issue for all families whether white or black. A family who do not practise a religion, or who are agnostic or atheists, may still have particular views about the spiritual upbringing and welfare of their children. For families where religion plays an important role in their lives, the significance of their religion will also be a vital part of their cultural traditions and beliefs (see CCETSW (1996) for a helpful training pack on Spirituality and Religion) .

2.70 In research undertaken by Carl Hylton for the Moyenda Project in 1997, an issue that emerged strongly was the importance of spirituality as a survival strategy for black families living in England. The report says:

> It is our intention to register strongly the concept of spirituality that came from all the respondents interviewed. Here, we are not particularly referring to religious adherence that forms a major aspect of the lives of many visual minority people. Spirituality as used here refers to wider feelings that include religious adherence, but is also concerned with a particular way of life encompassing strength, perseverance, forgiveness and the ability to build and concentrate on self-knowledge without posing the destruction of other ethnic groups.

Language

2.71 The acquisition of language is central to any child's development. It is also a feature of the child's individual and group identity. The particular language, dialect or accent which the child learns and speaks will help them to define themselves, and others to define the child in relation to themselves.

2.72 For children and adults, language represents more than the ability to communicate. It also helps a child to access and be accessed by groups of people who share the same language, and to reinforce the child's sense of their own cultural group identity.

2.73 Dosanjh and Ghuman (1998) in their *Study of Child-rearing Practices of Two Generations of Punjabis* found that the mothers were keen to maintain religious rites and customs:

> Likewise, they are eager to teach their children their mother tongue, despite the lack of support from infant and primary schools.

2.74 It is vital that children have the opportunity to learn and maintain family languages. Although actual figures are not available, many children placed in long term substitute care have little or no opportunity to practise and develop their language skills apart from speaking English. For these children there can be no more poignant reminder of the loss of opportunity than the inability to communicate with other members of their own family and community in their own language.

2.75 This opportunity is particularly important for disabled children whose acquisition of language may be affected by their impairment.

Social Presentation and Selfcare Skills

2.76 A child's social presentation and self care skills will reflect their own personal identity, their group affiliations and their upbringing and environment.

2.77 One of the indicators that a black child has an integrated sense of self as a black person is that they can define themselves in terms of their racial and cultural identity, as well as being self-confident about their physical appearance and characteristics.

2.78 However, some children do not grow up with any access to other black people. These children do not have the opportunity to naturally gain that support, strength and guidance in their everyday contact with black people.

2.79 For some black children who live with a black and a white parent their home is a very difficult environment in which to acquire a positive racial and cultural identity, because they experience racism from within their home or family. Some of these children internalise these negative feelings, and have very low self-esteem, whilst others may externalise their negative experiences into various forms of anti-social behaviour.

Pointers for Practice

Identity allows individuals to understand and conceptualise themselves as distinct from others and allows individuals to form group identities with other individuals who have similar characteristics to their own. Race, culture, religion and language are central to group and individual identity. Assessments should to address identity holistically by considering:

- Any difficulties which the child may be having in acquiring a positive racial identity, and what help the child requires to enable them do so;
- The child's awareness of their own ethnicity and personal, family and community history. Where this is not available, what steps can be taken to obtain such information;
- The child's access to a lived experience of their culture, for example, attendance at a wedding, or participation in celebrations which include music, food and traditional rituals will give a child a far more profound and effective sense of their cultural identity than any amount of visual or written material;
- The religious and spiritual needs of black children and their families – this will require professionals to discuss the family's belief systems religion, rites and traditions and record them routinely;
- The identity of disabled black children holistically and not as a hierarchy of need, in that being black gives the child a specific perspective on their disability;
- The extent to which the child has the opportunity to learn about and maintain family languages. Where the child has not had this opportunity, what steps can be taken to address this deficiency;
- The extent to which a black disabled child has the opportunity to learn their first language. As some disabled children rely upon other forms of communication apart from the written or spoken word, it is vital that communication with their families is facilitated in away that accounts for their own modes of communication as well as the family's first language. For example, the basis of British Sign Language is English. Translating BSL into English will facilitate the understanding of English speakers, but for those who speak other languages, further translation is required. Although the provision of interpreters is seen sometimes as a logistical nightmare for social welfare agencies, the ability to communicate and to be understood has to be promoted as a basic human right, without which any attempt at assessment would be impossible.

Family and Social Relationships

2.80 Family and social relationships are central to all children's lives, whether they are black or white. For both white and black children their early experiences of parenting and social relationships can construct a blueprint for later social interactions.

2.81 When assessing parenting capacity and social relationships, practitioners often raise questions about the extent to which eurocentric models of child development are relevant to black families. Some think that using eurocentric theories such as attachment is not appropriate to the assessment of black families.

2.82 Attachments are central to all human societies, and there are no differences between black and white families in terms of the need for adults and children to form strong and positive relationships.

2.83 Children in all communities depend upon the specific care and attention of at least one significant adult who is able and willing to respond to the child's needs for both physical and emotional care. Children are vulnerable, particularly in their early years, and attachment to a significant adult fulfils a basic function to ensure their survival and wellbeing.

2.84 In the western world these parent-child relationships are explained by the theory of attachment, but in the popular culture of all societies the central importance of loving and protective relationships is represented in stories, folklore, poetry and music.

2.85 There is no difference in the preconditions for the formation of good attachments between black and white families. In both cases, attachments develop out of a relationship which is worked at by both baby and adult over a time. This relationship requires the participation of both parties, in that secure attachments are formed out of reciprocal relationships, in which there is a high degree of communication, matched responsiveness and consistency (Klaus and Kennel, 1976; Bowlby, 1988).

2.86 The third area of similarity is the importance of attachment to the internal working model which forms the basis for developing children's self-esteem, self-confidence and self-perception, as well as acting as a model for future social relationships and interactions (Bowlby, 1973). The theory is that through the care, responsiveness and affection that children receive from their attachment figures, they learn to see themselves as valued people who have aright to care and affection and who have self-worth. Children who grow up in environments where adult carers are not responsive to their needs, and are not caring or affectionate do not learn to see themselves as worthy of such love, and adapt their behaviour accordingly.

2.87 The basic concepts on which attachment theory is based are clearly applicable to all human relationships, and are important to our understanding of the human condition. However, there are aspects of attachment theory that require more discussion in relation to their applicability to black families.

2.88 The first of these is in relation to the identity of attachment figures. Much of the literature on attachment emphasises the importance of either the mother (Bowlby, 1969) and/or parents (Schaffer and Emerson, 1964; Rutter, 1972) as the main attachment figure for a child. It is here that there may be differences for some black families. Differences to family structures, communities and networks will play an important role in determining who the child will form key attachments with.

2.89 For many black families, family structures and interactions between family members are very different in nature and character to those of white nuclear families. Within this context a child may have strong attachments with a number of family members and adults who are not blood relatives of the family. Thomas (1995) refers to this as 'multiple attachments'. He says:

> Friends and colleagues have talked about their experiences of being raised in

Bangladesh, Northern India and the Caribbean. They have talked about different cultural experiences of attachment. These have been varied, from having multiple mothering by grandmothers, mothers, aunts. . . This behaviour is thought to enable the small child to establish strong bonds with the extended family or clan which will be important for his or her future socialisation or welfare.

2.90 For many black families living in England, wider family networks and connections are important not just to the individual family, but to the survival of the whole community.

2.91 Social and economic circumstances have led to long term adult-child separations as a result of migration. Arnold (1975) highlighted particular issues of loss and separation for children who were parted from their parents as a result of migration to England, and the subsequent effects on attachments and relationships when family members were reunited having had little or no contact during the intervening years.

> The earlier the separation between mother and child in the Caribbean, the more problematic it became to re-establish bonds in the UK.

2.92 The impact of separation and loss is particularly acute for unaccompanied children and young people who are seeking asylum in this country. For these children, the losses, separations and traumas which they have experienced need to be understood within the context of attachments, separations and losses.

> These children have inevitably experienced significant disruption to their normal lives. All, whatever, their social background, will have suffered the trauma of losing familiar social landmarks, status and expectations (Social Services Inspectorate et al, 1995).

2.93 In such circumstances the existence of any family networks and connections are vital to the continued survival of individuals and communities. Owusu-Bempah and Howitt (1997) highlight the importance these connections have for children, citing the theory of socio-genealogical connectedness as a useful adjunct to attachment theory in understanding the nature of children's individual and group identities.

> The notion of socio-genealogical connectedness refers to the extent to which children identify with their natural parents' biological and social background. A basic tenet of this theory is that the degree to which children identify with their natural parent's backgrounds is dependent upon the amount and quality of information that they possess about their parents.

2.94 This echoes an earlier premise in this chapter, namely that children require positive information about their personal history and heritage in order to develop a sense of personal and group identity. For many black people, this connectedness also extends beyond individual families and into communities. Owusu-Bempah and Howitt (1997) explain:

> In a small-scale collective community where linkage may be with the whole group rather than to one's individual family, the information needed to achieve a sense of connectedness is readily available throughout the community, the child's sense of continuity is provided by the whole community rather than the individual parent of family.

Pointers for Practice

Information about family history and cultural heritage are vital not only to the child's sense of personal identity and wellbeing, but also to their sense of group identification. In assessing the child's relationships it is important to consider:

- The child's relationships within the context of their wider social networks and connections;
- The extent of quality and quantity of information the child has about their own roots and heritage, and how deficiencies in this information can be addressed;
- The specific family structure in which the child lives, and the patterns of attachment which operate within this particular black family including any attachment figures who may not be blood relatives;
- The impact of migration, separation and trauma on the child and wider family network.

Domain: Parenting Capacity

Basic Care

2.95 As stated earlier in this chapter, there are no differences in the basic care needs of black children compared to white children. For all children, their healthy development requires that basic care needs are responded to appropriately by the child's main caregivers.

Ensuring Safety

2.96 Both black and white children have the same right and the same need to be protected from abuse, whether by acts of commission or omission. However, evidence cited at the beginning of this chapter, indicates that race plays apart in the protection of black children.

2.97 Whilst research studies have indicated that there is an over-representation of black children within the care system (see paragraph 2.23), there is also evidence that some black children are not being protected out of a fear on the part of white workers of being accused of racist practice.

2.98 *Whose Child? The Report of the Panel of Inquiry into the death of Tyra Henry 1987* (London Borough of Lambeth, 1987), a black child, suggested that the lack of support provided by the Social Services Department to help the child's grandmother care for her was influenced by gender based racial stereotyping. An over-idealised view of African-Caribbean women was cited as influencing social work practice with the family. As a result of this lack of support, Tyra returned home to her parents where she was subsequently killed by her step-father.

> There is a "positive", but nevertheless false stereotype in white British society of the Afro-Caribbean mother figure as endlessly resourceful... essentially unsinkable. It may have been an unarticulated and unconscious sense that a woman like Beatrice

Henry would find a way to cope no matter what, that underlay the neglect of social services to make adequate provision for her taking responsibility for T yra (London Borough of Lambeth, 1987).

2.99 In the case of Sukina Hammond, a child of mixed parentage who was killed by her father, the report of the circumstances leading to her death (The Bridge Child Care Consultancy, 1991) states:

> We know that agencies that are moving towards trying to be more sensitive and understanding to the racial and cultural needs of their client group, do risk failing to recognise the particular needs of an individual child. In addition, white professionals who have undergone anti-racist training can sometimes over-compensate out of fear of being accused of racism.

2.100 Studies (see Finkelhor, 1986; Jones and McCurdy, 1992) have shown little difference in rates of physical abuse, sexual abuse and neglect across different ethnic and racial groups. Despite this, there is evidence of differences in referral rates in relation to specific types of abuse for particular black ethnic groups.

2.101 In their study, *Operating the child protection system*, Gibbons, Conroy and Bell (1995) state that Black and Asian families were over-represented among referrals for physical injury (58% versus 42%) and under-represented referrals for sexual abuse (20% versus 31%) compared to white families. They conclude that:

> This illustrates cultural differences in child rearing and the difficulty of deciding what forms of physical punishment are "acceptable" in Britain.

2.102 Thoburn et al (1995) echo this concern in their research on family involvement in the child protection process:

> Disagreements about the appropriateness of physical punishment features in a disproportionate number of cases involving black families.

2.103 Farmer and Owen (1995) also refer to this dilemma in *Private Risks and Public Remedies*:

> In spite of (or perhaps because of) considerable sensitivity in their perceptions, a few workers were somewhat overwhelmed by the number of factors which appeared to be relevant in minority ethnic cases and they had difficulty in combining them, especially if culture, race and ethnicity were seen not as the total context for intervention but to be added at the end of a lengthening list.

2.104 It is evident that race features at every stage of intervention, from the point of referral onwards. An example of this is the differential referral rate for black families in relation to physical injury and sexual abuse in Gibbons, Conroy and Bell's study. The referral rate is not illustrative of the actual incidence of abuse within a given community, but it is indicative of which cases are referred to statutory agencies. It is erroneous to assume that there is less sexual abuse within the black community, as this perpetuates myths which results in sexual abuse being unrecognised and undetected within black communities.

2.105 It is equally inaccurate to assume that the referral rates for physical injury of children are based on different levels of physical chastisement within black communities, and it perpetuates another myth that physical abuse is cultural within black communities.

2.106 Whilst physical injury and physical punishment are often discussed as interchangeable terms there is a distinction between physically injuring a child and using forms of physical disciplines – such as smacking.

2.107 Within current debates on parenting the acceptability of smacking is a hotly debated topic. There are very different views held by parents about this both within and across cultural boundaries. Just as many black families may strongly support the use of smacking as a form of discipline so do many white families. Equally there are black as well as white families who are strongly opposed to smacking children.

2.108 Physical injury to children occurs in black families just as it does within white families, but it is not more or less apart of black culture than of white culture. Physical abuse is unacceptable whatever the context. If physical abuse was apart of black culture then all black children would be unsafe within black communities.

2.109 When a child is abused in a family, it is important to establish the circumstances in which the abuse took place, as a means of targeting areas for intervention to change patterns of behaviour. If it is assumed that the abuse occurs as a result of cultural patterns of behaviour, then the focus for intervention may be the culture itself.

2.110 Culture does not explain abuse. A parent who has injured a child may say "It is my culture to punish my child in this way". However, this does not explain why many other parents from the same culture do not punish their child using this level of physical chastisement, and some parents from the same culture use no physical punishment at all.

2.111 Culture can explain the context in which abuse takes place, it can explain the values, beliefs or attitudes of a parent at the time when an abusive incident took place, but it cannot provide an explanation for the parent's action in response to those values, beliefs or attitudes.

Pointers for Practice

Issues of race and culture cannot simply be added to a list for separate consideration during an assessment. They are integral to the assessment process. In undertaking assessments of black families professionals should be mindful that:

- From referral through to core assessment, intervention and planning, race and culture have to be addressed using the Assessment Framework;
- Culture can explain the context in which an abusive incident took place, but not the behaviour or action of an individual parent. For example, a parent who injures their child with a belt may say that this form of punishment is "cultural ". Their cultural context may explain the parents anger within the expectations that he or she has of the child, but will not explain why the parent acted upon this anger by using a belt to hit the child. Other parents from the same culture in a similar context may choose to punish the child without recourse to any physical punishment at all;
- Racial and cultural stereotyping of black families can led to inappropriate interventions in families as well as a failure to protect black children from abuse.

Racial abuse and harassment

2.112 An area of abuse of black children, not generally addressed by the social work profession, is racial abuse and harassment. According to Dutt and Phillips (1996):

> Racial abuse and harassment on the whole received a 'no-reaction' response from social work professionals. Although many social services departments have developed policies on racial attacks and harassment, there is little evidence to suggest that the issue of racial abuse is a priority for departments or that practice is beginning to take into account the reality of racial abuse.

2.113 A review of research on racism and racial abuse undertaken by the NSPCC (Barter, 1999) highlighted a dearth of research on racial abuse of children and young people. It identified some important issues in this area namely:

- Racism and racial bullying are commonplace in the lives of minority ethnic children and young people, and in the lives of white children who will frequently witness racial bullying as bystanders;
- Studies focusing on racial bullying show that, compared to overall bullying figures, children from ethnic minorities are more likely to experience bullying than their white counterparts;
- The most common expression of racism is through racist name-calling, which research shows is often viewed by adults as trivial, although studies indicate that its impact on children can be profound;
- Although research evidence is limited, that available suggests racial bullying frequently involves the use of violence.

2.114 Although this review highlights the lack of material on the racial abuse and its impact on black disabled children, it quotes some studies specifically looking at racial abuse and black disabled people. One example is a small study undertaken by Begum (1992) on Asian disabled people and their carers. Her study shows that 'overall about half of the total sample reported that they had experienced racial harassment. Half of the disabled people had experienced some form of verbal abuse, and 14% reported racial violence'.

2.115 Whatever form racial abuse takes, the impact of the abuse is devastating for the child/young person, as well as for their family. The Childline study (1996) *Children and Racism* highlights some of the impact of racial abuse on children. The study states that 'racist bullying causes real suffering, effects children's self-esteem and confidence and renders some children and young people so despondent that they feel suicidal and attempt suicide'. The report concludes 'youngsters cannot deal with bullying on their own, they need adult help'.

2.116 Racial abuse may be a feature of the lives of black children of dual heritage living in predominantly white families. In their study of race and racism in the lives of young people of mixed heritage, Tizzard and Phoenix (1994) found that half the young people in the sample 'perceived either a parent or a sibling as being to some degree racially prejudiced'.

2.117 The Childline study also highlighted racism experienced by children in their own families. Comments from children calling Childline include:

Mum has left because dad was hitting her. Now he's hitting me and calling me 'half breed' and 'nigger' because my mum is black.

I am black and my mum is white... she has a new boyfriend who is completely racist... He is not nice to me. When we are alone... He says things like "you need a bath". This 12 year old girl felt she could not tell her mother because she wouldn't believe her

2.118 The Childline report concludes that 'perhaps the most unhappy children we hear from are those where racism is part of their family life. They are being excluded or abused by the people they love'.

Pointers for Practice

Racial abuse damages children both physically and emotionally and as such warrants professional intervention to address the effects of this form of abuse whether it comes from within or outside the family. Assessments should consider:

- Whether racial abuse, racial bullying or racial violence impacts on the child or on the wider family;
- The extent of support, advice and intervention offered to the family, or the family require, and how this can be provided.

Emotional Warmth

2.119 For all children emotional warmth is an essential prerequisite for healthy emotional development. But how is emotional warmth demonstrated, and to what extent do cultural variations exist in relation to demonstrating it?

2.120 Much of the literature on emotional abuse and neglect emphasises the absence of emotional warmth as one indicator of emotional abuse. Hoghhughi and Speight (1998) emphasise the importance of love, care and commitment to healthy emotional development: , Children need to feel they are loved consistently and unconditionally.

2.121 In *Beyond Blame, Child Abuse Tragedies Revisited*, Reder et al (1993) state: The child must be wanted and treated as a person in his/her own right, whose feelings are respected and of concern to the parent. In order to provide such care, the parents must be able to put the child's needs above their own and tolerate the child's dependency and immaturity.

2.122 This represents an important base line for the assessment of emotional warmth. Parents or carers who are unable or unwilling to respond to the child's need for unconditional love and affection will not be able to meet one of the child's basic developmental needs.

2.123 All cultures recognise the need for affectionate relationships between adults and children, just as all cultures create social structures in which these relationships can develop. There are no differences between cultural groupings in this respect. But where differences do emerge is in the way in which this emotional warmth is demonstrated.

2.124 The demonstration of emotional warmth is also dependent upon rules in a family or community about physical contact. In some communities, there are more structured rules about male-female contact than in white English families, but this does not mean that everyone from that community will behave in exactly the same way in relation to demonstrating physical affection to children.

2.125 Differences in what constitutes valued social behaviour also creates variations. For example, in western societies emphasis is placed upon children learning the distinction between social time with family members and time alone such as at bedtime. As a result, western bedtime routines encourage children to sleep alone from quite early ages (Swanick, 1996) .

2.126 If separate sleeping is not considered to be such a desired form of child behaviour, attempts by parents to impose such a pattern onto a child would be considered rigid and inflexible parenting. On the other hand, for parents who value the independence of separate sleeping arrangements, shared sleeping may be perceived as inappropriate and lacking boundaries.

2.127 Over time variations also occur within and between cultures. Fashions in child rearing practices have a strong influence in the way in which parents are expected to relate to children. At one time in England within certain white communities it was common practice to leave babies outside in prams during the day. Today this practice would be seen as neglectful. The practice of baby massaging, common in many black societies, was for many years considered to be undesirable and even abusive to children; now there are classes run by health professionals on baby massage.

2.128 The rise of the child care expert in western societies has exacerbated trends in parenting. Whereas parents traditionally learnt parenting skills from their own experience of being parented, today's parents are required to have a greater level of knowledge and skills in parenting.

Pointers for Practice

There are differences in the way in which affection and love are shown to children by adults. Some of these will be based on established cultural patterns of behaviour whilst some will be related more to individual, family or social influences. In assessing emotional warmth:

- Assessments should take account of such variations, whilst still maintaining consistency in the application of minimum standards of child care;
- Professionals need to ensure that base lines are consistent across cultures. It is not acceptable that parents who demonstrate cold and unloving responses to children are able to justify their behaviour on the grounds of cultural differences;
- In an extended family or clan family structure the whole family may participate in the parenting of the child, including providing emotional warmth for the child. The parent-child interaction will only be one of many adult-child, child-child interactions which should be addressed in an assessment.

Stimulation

2.129 Just as for emotional warmth, all children require stimulation, and just as for emotional warmth, the indicators for the presence of appropriate stimulation in an adult-child relationship have to be understood within a social and cultural context.

2.130 There are a number of myths about stimulation in black families which still have an impact on professionals today. The two key myths are:

- That Asian parents do not have toys to stimulate children;
- That black parents expect children to behave as mini-adults, and take on inappropriate responsibilities for household tasks.

2.131 The myth that Asian parents do not have toys for children seems to have been based upon the observations of some child care professionals that certain Asian families did not have play equipment in their homes.

2.132 For some Asian and Caribbean families in past generations, purchased toys were in evidence, but were not the main focus of play activity. Particularly for those families who came from rural parts of India or the Caribbean, game playing took place outdoors, and play equipment consisted of whatever was available in the fields and woods where the play took place. The same was true for many white families who grew up in similar environments in England. In a move to a colder, urban environment, the opportunity for outdoor play was severely curtailed. Children were unable to create their own games and exploration became supervised and controlled. Play thus became a more organised and contained activity. Within this context families also adapted to their changed environment, and toys have become the main focus for play for all children whether black or white.

Pointers for Practice

- In assessing stimulation in black families it is important to recognise that children's learning may be encouraged in a range of ways, and that the trappings of a stimulating environment, such as toys and play equipment are not guarantors of a stimulating environment for children. In assessing families workers should make sense of different practices.
- In western societies the concept of childhood is underpinned by the desire to be free of adult responsibilities and to have opportunities for explanation, learning and play. In many black families children are not expected to take on adult responsibilities, but they are expected to learn certain skills that will prepare them for adult life. Whilst western values encourage pretend play, many black families take pride in teaching children the basics of cooking and child care at quite young ages.

Guidance, Boundaries and Stability

2.133 Currently, guidance and boundaries is perhaps the most conflictual area of parenting for many black parents. It is also the area in which many black families seek stability in a changing world, through the maintenance of traditional values.

2.134 There are inherent tensions created by trying to maintain a strong sense of black culture and heritage, whilst at the same time living in an industrialised western and racist environment with very different values from the traditions of Africa, the Caribbean or Asia.

2.135 Black parents recognise and worry about these tensions:

> Along with trends in the wider UK population, there appears to be a trend among black families towards an emphasis on co-operation rather than the discipline of physical controL. This has been assisted by changes to UK statutes, which some Black parents view as very child-centred, and also as a double-edged sword (Hylton, 1997) .

2.136 Black parents wish to imbue their children with the values which they hope will help their children to survive in a hostile environment, but they are concerned that their values do not have the support of many professionals.

> Black parents often find that what is being reinforced at home varies greatly from at school, so both child and parent are in a dilemma regarding support for what they value within their culture (Grant, 1996).

2.137 At the heart of the value conflict between black and white western values lies different perspectives on independence.

> In non- Western European extended families, autonomy and competence are differently defined. There is more likely to be an emphasis on parents raising children to be "dependable" – that is to take on a role within the extended family, rather than be independent. This can cause much friction in the home for children who have grown up within western society (Grant, 1996) .

2.138 Dosanjh and Ghuman's study (1998) confirms the desire of many Asian parents to maintain traditional values:

> From the responses of the Punjabi mothers of both generations we infer that they are in favour of encouraging their children to be conscious of, and to appreciate, the custom of familial interdependence rather than to follow and absorb the Euro-American style of rugged individualism.

2.139 This is essential if professionals are to gain the support of black families as partners in the protection of black children. Black families at present perceive child welfare professionals as undermining of black communities. In Hylton's study, one black parent speaks for many:

> (UK) society is destroying the black family in the sense that the very same society that said to you, you cannot scold your children, you cannot speak too roughly to your children, will take your child away from you and put your child in asocial environment... so that the values that they pass down to your children are worse than what you would give... and it's the same society that would pick up your child that they took away from you in the first place, and put your child behind bars, and say he's a criminal.

Pointers for Practice

In assessing guidance and boundaries, professionals should understand the context in which these are developed. In undertaking assessments:

- Professionals should be aware that black families at present perceive child welfare professionals as undermining of black communities, particularly in relation to the guidance of and boundaries for young people;
- The imposition of a western and individualised model of autonomy and independence is at variance with the values of many black families, and it's application in assessment and intervention can destabilise families and family support networks;
- Where intergenerational or family conflicts arise in relation to guidance and boundaries, negotiations are necessary to reconcile differences.

Domain: Family And Environmental Factors

2.140 Social work with children and families is, as Macdonald (1991) acknowledges 'rooted in the pain and suffering of people who are struggling against odds which are sometimes too great, whether that is due to illness, poverty, racism, homelessness or other strains and pressures'.

2.141 Any assessment that ignores the wider context of social and economic factors and its impact on family life, is incomplete as is one which further ignores racism and its impact on the social and economic context of black families.

2.142 This section draws on research and other evidence to highlight some of the issues pertinent to black families regarding family and environmental factors. This information sets out the wider socio-economic context of black families. The general issues mayor may not all be relevant to each family and even where it is relevant will not affect all families in the same way.

Pointers for Practice

- Each of the dimensions identified should not be seen in isolation from each other. For instance, having a large family may not in itself be a problem for anyone family but if the family are also experiencing overcrowding and low income it may result in family members experiencing additional stress. Any assessment process should take account of the impact on the family of the various factors interacting with each other.

Family History and Functioning

Family size

2.143 An analysis of the 1991 census shows (Haskey, 1997) :

- of every thousand Black Caribbean families, 540 are families with children;

- for the Pakistani community this figure is 810 per thousand families;
- and 840 out of every thousand families for the Bangladeshi community;
- The comparative figure for white communities is 417 per thousand families.

2.144 There are some differences in the family sizes of different black communities. A recent survey (PSI, 1997) shows, for instance, that Pakistani and Bangladeshi people have larger families with 33% and 42% of them respectively having four or more children. In comparison, in Caribbean communities the percentage of families with four or more children is 7%, in Indian families 11% and in Chinese and African-Asian families 3%.

2.145 As Butt and Mizra (1996) conclude 'For the vast majority of black communities, family units with children under the age of 16 are a common experience. Furthermore, these families are likely to have more children under the age of 16 than their white counterparts'.

Family structure and arrangements

2.146 Butt and Box (1998) observe that public debate on families 'often conflates marital status and the actual living arrangements of families, and on occasion unmarried mothers and lone parents are seen as interchangeable'. The 1991 census has allowed both issues to be explored. In relation to marital status, the data shows that whilst over 66% of India, Pakistani and Bangladeshi men over 16 are married, over 47% of Caribbean men over the age of 16 are single. In relation to different family types, the census analysis also shows that whilst 55% of Caribbean families with children under 16 are lone parents, 92% of Indian families with children under 16 are married couple families (Haskey, 1997) .

2.147 The ONS (1996) suggests:

- around 54% of black Caribbean children are brought up in lone mother households and 3% in lone father households;
- for children of Indian origin around 7% are in lone mother households and around 1% in lone father households;
- for Pakistani and Bangladeshi communities the figures are 8% in lone mother and 1% in lone father households;
- for the Chinese community 11% of children are being brought up on lone mother and 1% in lone father households.

2.148 Regarding family structures for children in the 'Black other' category, the ONS (1996) figures suggest that 49% of children categorised as 'Black other' live in lone mother households and 2% live in lone father households. Two separate studies (Barn, 1993; Barn et al, 1997) also show that the majority of looked after children of dual heritage in these studies had a white mother and the majority of their parents had never married.

Pointers for Practice

- In assessing black families it is important to take account of family size and structure. For instance, a family with three or more children with a low income and poor housing is a family likely to experience hardship. Any assessment process should address the implications of this for families;
- Although the fact of alone parent household in itself may not be an issue for an individual family, alone parent household with no support networks may impact on family functioning. Furthermore, lone parenthood can have an impact on income and wealth, and in turn can impact on the material wellbeing of children. This should be taken account of in an assessment.
- In relation to a child of dual heritage assessments should consider the implications of family arrangements on the child and family. For instance how does living in a white only household impact on the child's position within the family, or how does a single white mother's isolation from her community affect her relationship with her child?
- It is important for assessors to understand that the evidence of a higher incidence of lone parenthood amongst Caribbean people does not rule out exploration of the issue of 'visiting' relationships, where the responsibility for care of the children may be shared although the parents may not live together.

Parenting strengths and difficulties

2.149 Despite the social and economic impact of racism on families and the detrimental impact of immigration laws and racial violence on families and communities, over many generations black families have demonstrated strengths and resilience in the face of adversity. Unfortunately social work practice with black families has often failed to work with the strengths of black families and has relied instead on a problem oriented approach to black families.

2.150 A deficit model which views families as dysfunctional can preclude adequate support being provided to families. For instance, evidence shows that where professionals fail to provide adequate support in the early stages of intervention there is an increased likelihood of the child becoming looked after (Barn, 1993).

2.151 It is also apparent that race is a factor in the support offered to black families. Many black families do not access family support services (Butt and Box, 1998) and the Tyra Henry and Sukina Hammond Inquiry Reports demonstrate that racism and gender based stereotyping can impact on the amount and timing of the support which is offered.

Pointers for Practice

- Assessments should inform interventions which build on the strengths of black families, whilst ensuring that areas of difficulty or potential risk to the child's safety are identified and addressed appropriately;
- An empowerment model of assessment should recognise the life experiences of black families, particularly the ability of families to survive and resist a system that is disadvantaging;

- Targeted support to address family problems should be based on an understanding of a family's circumstances as the result of the assessment process rather than on the basis of assumptions underpinned by stereotypical beliefs of black families.

Wider Family

2.152 The wider family, often referred to as the extended family, has been an important feature of the lives of many black and minority ethnic people. Hylton (1997) notes, in his study of the survival strategies used by black families, that the majority of black people 'rarely made a disconnection between the unit of mother, father and child – the so called nuclear family – and relatives such as grandparents, sisters, brothers, aunts and uncles. They were all collectively known as the "family" '.

2.153 For many, the wider family is not restricted to aunts, uncles and grandparents, but as has already been highlighted earlier, includes family friends and other non-blood relatives.

2.154 However, not all individual black families will have this wide family network. This is of particular relevance for many refugee and asylum seeking individuals and families who have left their homeland alone or with their immediate family. For these people, in common with other black people, the family in the wider sense is central. Family in this context could be other refugees and asylum seekers, and links will therefore be made with individuals and families coming from the same geographical regions.

2.155 For some families with no close family members in this country, links with family and friends living either in their country of origin or other parts of the world, will be important.

Pointers for Practice

- In assessing black families, practitioners should ascertain from children and family members their perception of who constitutes their wider family and tap into the strengths that may be present in that wider family network.

Housing

2.156 Butt and Mirza (1996) in reviewing the research data on housing and tenure for black communities conclude 'Though a large proportion of black people own their own accommodation there is evidence to suggest that the black community occupy older inner city accommodation which lacks basic amenities. Furthermore, black households are more likely to experience overcrowding compared to the white population'.

2.157 There is some evidence to suggest black people live in neighbourhoods that are rundown. A survey (PSI, 1997) found:

> Ethnic minorities tended to live in areas with higher than average levels of unemployment, they were more likely than whites to mention environmental problems such as graffiti, vandalism and vermin infestation, and they were more likely than whites to report problems of personal and property crime and nuisance trouble from some young people.

Overall, whites were the most likely to say they were very satisfied with the current neighbourhoods and housing: Caribbean, Bangladeshi's and the Chinese were the most likely to be dissatisfied with their local neighbourhoods, and Caribbeans and Bangladeshi's were the most dissatisfied with their neighbourhoods.

Employment

2.158 The same PSI Survey (1997) found also that unemployment rates amongst men under retirement age was the highest amongst Caribbean (31%) Bangladeshi (42%) and Pakistani men (38%) . The unemployment rates amongst Chinese, M rican Asians and Indians was 9, 14 and 19 % respectively. In relation to the white community the percentage is 15.

2.159 For women the Chinese had the lowest rates of unemployment at 6% followed by whites at 9%, M rican Asians and Indians 12% and Caribbeans at 18 %. For Pakistani and Bangladeshi women it was 39% and 40% respectively.

Income

Poverty is more than simply economic deprivation, it means being completely isolated from the means to change one's circumstances (Carter, 1998).

2.160 The extent of poverty in black communities is now well documented. Berthoud, in analysing data from the fourth national survey of ethnic minorities in Britain which was conducted by PSI/SCPR in 1994, notes that 82% of Pakistani, 84% of Bangladeshi, 45% of Indians, 41% of Caribbean and 39% of 'M rican Asian' households had incomes that were below half the average income, in comparison to 28% of white households.

2.161 The PSI survey (1997) notes that although there were wide variations in the extent of poverty in the various black communities, 'all minorities included in this survey, with the exception of people of Chinese origin, were disadvantaged with respect to the white majority'.

2.162 The survey found also that:

- the extent of poverty among both Pakistani and Bangladeshi households was outstanding;
- Caribbean, Indian and African Asian households were more likely to be in poverty, and less likely to have relatively high family incomes than white households;
- where financial problems such as arrears and money worries were concerned, Caribbeans had exceptionally high levels of rent arrears and were much more likely to report money worries than any other group.

2.163 No specific information exists about the level and extent of poverty and its impact on black disabled children and their families. Evidence suggests, however, that families with a disabled child are generally affected significantly by poverty. A national survey

(Beresford, 1995) exploring the needs and circumstances of families caring for a severely disabled child found that families in the survey chad substantially lower incomes than the general population...'. The survey also shows that employment levels for mothers of disabled children were much lower than for mothers with non-disabled children and that 'nine out of ten lone parent families, and a third of two parent families, had no income other than benefits'.

2.164 Although there are no data available on black children who are disabled the incidence and prevalence of disability amongst black communities is likely to be either the same rate and certainly no less than in the white population (Butt and Mirza, 1996) . Given that family units with children are the rule rather than the exception and the disproportionate levels of poverty in the black communities, it could be safely concluded that black disabled children are as likely to experience poverty as white disabled children.

Pointers for Practice

- In assessing the needs of children and their families it is important to understand the implications of social and economic context within which families live and more importantly how fears and worries about money, health, education and employment impact on family life;
- In assessing black families any attempts to disregard the impact of racism on the social and economic context in which black families live will result in an assessment which is incomplete.

Families Social Integration

2.165 The extent to which individual black families feel integrated and part of their local neighbourhood will vary. The following factors might have an impact on the social integration of black family's into their neighbourhoods:

- Black families tend to live in areas of higher than average black population. This is as much to do with individuals and families choosing to be in surroundings and with people who appear familiar, as it is to do with people feeling 'safe in numbers'. For many black people living amongst a majority of black people gives them a sense of belonging and provides them with a certain level of support and security;
- Black communities are not homogeneous. Some black families, although living in predominantly black areas, may be in cultural or religious minorities in those communities. This will not, in itself, be problematic but individual families from those minority groups may find their support network is located outside their locality. For instance, refugee families may consider support from other refugee families more appropriate. Their social integration into their locality may be less important than their social and emotional links with other refugees;

- Many black families live in hostile communities where racial abuse and harassment are a daily feature of their lives. There are some areas where black families are frightened to allow their children to play outside home and where adults feel under siege.

Pointers for Practice

- Any assessment with individual black families should recognise that although many black families gain strength from living amongst their own community, there are individual black families whose experience of living amongst black people may not necessarily be a positive one. As with the white community, the reasons for any black family feeling either isolated or ostracised from the majority community will vary. Whatever the reason it is important to think of the support networks for such families; .
- Alongside the individual impact which racial abuse and bullying has on children, it is important to consider the impact of racial violence on communities. Fear of abuse or attacks can affect whole ways of life in particular communities which are targeted for such treatment by reducing the freedom of movement of women, children and older people in both the hours of daylight and at night. In such cases local authorities should plan for community safety in a more pro-active and co-ordinated way, using the auspices of children's planning processes and area child protection committees, alongside initiatives to reduce crime and improve safety in the locality.

Community Resources

2.166 The anomalous situation regarding community resources for black communities is that on one hand black individuals have access to some very positive support from black voluntary organisations and on the other have little access to resources provided by the statutory sector and some white voluntary sector organisations.

2.167 In relation to preventative services for children and families provided by statutory organisations, evidence suggests that black families have less access to those services than white families. For instance in relation to child protection a study by Farmer and Owen (1995) found that 'many black families did not have access to much needed services. Even after registration this situation often continues, partly because of lack of appropriate resources .

2.168 Equally, a study of family centres and their use by black families also found that 'family centres are not intrinsically providers of accessible and appropriate services to black families' (Butt and Box, 1998).

2.169 Although services from mainstream organisations have been inaccessible black communities have had some very positive support from black voluntary organisations. The role of the black voluntary sector in providing much of needed services to black people is well recognised (Phaure, 1991; Atkin, 1996; Butt and Box, 1998). Apart from providing much needed services, involvement in black organisations has also been one of the survival strategies used by many in the black communities (Hylton,1997).

Pointers for Practice

- During the assessment process professionals should ascertain from families what are their perceptions of available community resources what kinds of services would be most helpful to them and how to make statutory sector services appropriate and accessible to them.

References – Chapter 2

Adams N (1981) *Lambeth Directorate of Social Services*. London Borough of Lambeth.

Arnold E (1975) *Out of sight not out of mind*. M.Phil, University of Sussex.

Atkin K (1996) An opportunity for change, voluntary sector provision in a mixed economy of care. *Race and Community Care*. Open University Press.

Banks N (1992) Some considerations of racial identification when working with mixed ethnicity children and their mothers as social services clients. *Child Development*. 41: 49-67.

Barn R (1990) Black children in local authority care; admission patterns. *New Community*. 16(2): 229-246.

Barn R (1993) *Black Children in the Public Care System*. Batsford, London.

Barn R (1999) White Mothers, Mixed Parentage Children and Child Welfare. *British Journal of Social Work*. 29: 269-284.

Barn R, Sinclair R and Ferdinand D (1997) *Acting on principle, an examination of race and ethnicity in social services provision for children and families*. BAAF, London.

Barter C (1999) *Protecting children from racism and racial abuse. A research review.* The NSPCC, London.

Batta I, Mc Culloch J and Smith N (1979) Colour as a variable in Childrens' Sections of Local Authority Social Services Departments. *New Community*. 7: 78-84.

Begum N (1992). *Something to be proud of The lives of Asian Disabled people and carers in Waltham Forest*. Race Relations Unit, London Borough of Waltham Forest.

Beresford B (1995) The needs of disabled children and their families. *Findings from social care research. No.76.* Joseph Rowntree Foundation, York.

Berrington A (1996) Marriage patterns and inter-ethnic unions. In Coleman D and Salt J (eds) *Ethnicity in the 1991 census. Vol1*, HMSO, London.

Bowlby J (1969) *Attachment and Loss, Vol I, Attachment*. Hogarth, London

Bowlby J (1973) *Attachment and Loss, Vol II, Separation: Anxiety and Anger*: Hogarth, London.

Bowlby J (1988) *A Secure Base: Clinical Applications of Attachment Theory*. Routledge, London.

The Bridge Child Care Consultancy Services (1991) *Sukina,. An evaluation report of the circumstances leading to her death*. The Bridge, London.

Butt J and Box L (1998) *Family Centred. A study of the use of family centres by black families*. REU, London.

Butt J and Mirza K (1996) *Social care and black communities A review of recent research studies*. HMSO, London.

Carter H (1998) A joined-up solution to poverty. *Voluntary Voice No.129*. London Voluntary Services Council (LVSC), London.

Cashmore E (1984) *Dictionary of Race and Ethnic Relations*. Routledge, London.

CCETSW (1996) *Children, Spirituality and Religion. A Training Pack*. Central Council for Education and Training in Social Work, London.

Childline (1996) *Children and racism*. Childline, London.

Cross WE (1971) The Negro-to-Black Conversion Experience: Towards a Psychology of Black Liberation. *Black World. Volume 2.*

Donald J and Rattansi A (1992) *Race, Culture and Difference*. Sage, Bristol.

Dosanjh J S and Ghuman PAS (1997) Child Rearing Practices of Two Generations of Punjabi Parents. *Children and Society*. **11**: 29-43.

Dosanjh J S and Ghuman PAS (1998) Child Rearing Practices of Two Generations of Punjabi Parents: Development of Personality and Independence. *Children and Society*. **12**: 25-37.

Dutt R and Phillips M (1996) *Report of the National Commission of Inquiry into the Prevention of Child Abuse. Volume 2, Background Papers*. The Stationery Office, London.

Erikson E (1968) *Identity, Youth and Crisis*. Norton, New York.

Farmer E and Owen M (1995) *Child Protection Practice. Private Risks and Public Remedies*. HMSO, London.

Finkelhor D (1986) *A sourcebook on child sexual abuse*. Sage, London.

Gibbons J, Conroy S and Bell C (1995) *Operating the child protection system*. HMSO, London.

Grant L (1996) Parenting in Black Families. *The Parenting Forum Newsletter No.5*.

Haskey J (1997) Population Review (8). The ethnic minority and overseas-born population of Great Britain, Population Trends No.88. Office of National Statistics, London.

Hoghhughi M and Speight A (1998) Good enough parenting for all children – a strategy for a healthier society. *Archives of Diseases in Childhood*. **78**: 293-300.

Hylton C (1997) *Family survival strategies*. Exploring Parenthood.

Jones T (1993) *Britain's Ethnic Minorities*. Policy Studies Institute, London.

Jones E and McCurdy K (1992) The links between child maltreatment and demographic characteristics of children. *Child Abuse and Neglect*, Vol l6.

Katz I (1996) *The Construction of Racial Identity in Children of Mixed Parentage. Mixed Metaphors*. Jessica Kingsley, London.

Klaus Hand Kennel J (1976) *Maternal Infant Bonding*. Mosby, St Louis.

Kundnani H (1998) The sanction of last resort. *Voluntary Voice. No.129.* London Voluntary Services Council, London.

London Borough of Lambeth (1987) *Whose Child? The Report of the Panel of Inquiry into the Death of Tyra Henry 1987*. London Borough of Lambeth.

Macdonald S (1991) *All Equal Under the Act?* National Institute for Social Work, London.

MacPherson W (1999) *The Stephen Lawrence Inquiry. Report of an Inquiry.* The Stationery Office, London.

Milner D (1983) *Children and Race Ten Years On*. Ward Lock Educational, London.

Nazroo J Y (1997) *The Health of Britain's ethnic minorities. Findings from a national survey*. Policy Studies Institute, London.

NHS Executive (1998) *Sickle Cell Anaemia*. Department of Health, London.

Office for National Statistics (1996) *Social Focus on Ethnic Minorities*. HMSO, London.

Owen (1992) Ethnic Minorities in Great Britain: Settlement Patterns, 1999. Census Statistical Paper No 1. Centre for Research in Ethnic Relations, University of Warwick.

Owusu-Bempah J and Howitt D (1997) Socio-genealogical connectedness, attachment theory and child care practice. *Child and Family Social Work*. **2**: 199-207.

Owusu-Bempah K and Howitt D (1999) Even their soul is defective. *The Psychologist*. **12**: 3.

Phaure S (1991) *Who really cares? Models of voluntary sector community care and black communities*. London Voluntary Services Council, London.

Prohansky Hand Gottleib N (1989) The development of place identity in the child. *Zero to Three*. **X**: 2, pp.18-25 .

PSI (1997) *The Fourth National Survey of Ethnic Minorities in Britain, Diversity and Disadvantage*. PSI, London.

Reder P, Duncan S and Gray M (1993) *Beyond Blame, Child Abuse Tragedies Revisited*. Routledge, London.

Rowe J, Hundleby M and Garnet L (1989) *Child Care Now*. British Agency for Adoption and Fostering. Research Series 6.

Rutter M (1972) *Maternal Deprivation Reassessed*. Penguin, Harmondsworth.

Schaffer Hand Emerson P (1964) The Development of Social Attachments in Infancy. *Monographs of Social Research in Child Development*. **29**: 94.

Sinclair I and Gibbs I (1998) *Children's Homes: A study in Diversity*. Wiley, Chichester.

Smaje C (1999) *Health, Race and Ethnicity. Making sense of the evidence*. Kings Fund Institute, London.

Social Exclusion Unit (1998) *Bringing Britain Together: A National Strategy for Neighbourhood Renewal*. The Stationary Office, London.

Social Services Inspectorate and Surrey County Council (1995) Unaccompanied Asylum-Seeking Children: A Training Pack. Department of Health, London.

Swanick M (1996) Child Rearing across Cultures. *Paediatric Nursing*. **8**(7): 13-17.

Thomas L (1995) *Multi-cultural Aspects of Attachment*. Internet.

Thoburn J, Lewis A and Shemmings D (1995) *Paternalism or partnership? Family involvement in the child protection process*. HMSO, London.

Tizard B and Phoenix A (1994) *Black, White or Mixed Race; Race and Racism in the Lives of Young People of Mixed Parentage*. Routledge, London.

Troyna Band Hatcher R (1992) *Racism in Childrens' Lives; A Study of Mainly White Primary Schools*. National Childrens Bureau/Routledge, New York.

3

Assessing the needs of disabled children and their families

Introduction

3.1 The Assessment Framework is designed to be inclusive of all children in need. Social Services Departments have a duty to ensure that every child is assessed in a way which recognises the child's individuality and particular needs. For many reasons, disabled children are more likely to come to the attention of health, education and social services and are far more likely to be assessed than other children. This guidance is therefore aimed at everyone involved in assessments, not just at those who have a specialist role with disabled children.

3.2 An assessment is a positive opportunity to identify and respond to the needs of children and families. It is most likely to be helpful to a child and family if it draws together multi-disciplinary expertise. Serious concerns have been raised about the quality of assessments of disabled children (Audit Commission, 1994; Department of Health, 1994; 1998a; 1998b; Morris, 1998b; Kagan et al,1998; Middleton,1999). The process of assessment and the likelihood of multiple assessment arrangements may compound the difficulties facing disabled children and their families and result in conflicting messages about the needs and the most effective types of intervention/or support. As stated in the Guidance (Department of Health et al, 2000, paragraph 1.42):

> ... since discrimination of all kinds is an everyday reality in many children's lives, every effort must be made to ensure that agencies responses do not reflect or reinforce that experience and indeed, should counteract it.

3.3 In the past, disabled children have often been excluded from or marginalised within mainstream services, and many standard assessment frameworks and approaches have been developed with only non-disabled children in mind. The Children Act 1989 emphasises disabled children are 'children first' and the Assessment Framework is based on this principle of inclusion. However, recognising disabled children as children first does not imply denial of a child's particular needs: 'Ensuring equality of opportunity does not mean that all children are treated the same. It does mean understanding and working sensitively and knowledgeably with diversity...' (Department of Health et al, 2000, paragraph 1.43).

3.4 This practice guidance aims to assist those undertaking assessments of need, by enabling practitioners and managers to understand and work more sensitively with disabled children and their families. It is intended that the use of the Assessment Framework will mark a radical departure in assessment, moving from single agency service led assessments to assessments of the whole child by a co-ordinated group of professionals.

3.5 In preparation for this chapter Triangle consulted with disabled children through aMaze, a Brighton based project providing advice, information and support to assist parents to obtain the best for their disabled children. Quotes referenced as personal communication are from these groups and we are grateful for the children's consent to use their words.

Disabled children and the Assessment Framework

3.6 The basic needs of disabled children are no different to those of any other child. The domains and dimensions of the Assessment Framework are relevant for all children. 'Professionals working with children need not and should not start from a different position when the children are disabled' (Middleton, 1999 p.92). While disabled children's basic needs are the same as all children's needs, impairments may create additional needs. Disabled children are also likely to face additional disabling barriers which inhibit or prevent their inclusion in society. The assessment of a disabled child must address the needs of the parent carers. Recognising the needs of parent carers is a core component in agreeing services which will promote the welfare of the disabled child. The main part of this chapter considers the needs and barriers in relation to each of the dimensions of the Assessment Framework.

3.7 The Assessment Framework is highly relevant for disabled children, for example the emphasis on responding to a child's individual needs; the expectation of children's involvement in the process; the commitment to working with parents and children; the emphasis on inter-agency working and the underlying ecological and empowerment models. A careful assessment that involves the child should be a helpful experience and result in real improvements in a child's life. Information from assessments can result in changes in the nature of service provision, especially if unmet need is recorded and used to inform children's services planning processes. Good quality assessments will also encourage active partnerships between mainstream and specialist services; working together to maximise disabled children's inclusion in family life, education and community services.

3.8 Depending on the definitions and methodology used, between 3% and 5% of children in the United Kingdom are classified as disabled (OPC5, 1986; Department of Health, 1998a). Different definitions of disability and a summary of the legislation are in Appendix 4.

3.9 Childhood disability arouses very strong feelings and touches on some of our most fundamental beliefs and assumptions. The cultural context in which assessments of disabled children take place is not a neutral one: disabled children and adults face major barriers to participating as equal members of our society. There are different ways of defining and understanding disability. Within the disabled people's movement, and within some services and some professional groups, there has been a move from an individual to a social model of disability. 'The individual model locates the 'problem' of disability within the individual and sees the causes as functional limitations or psychological losses assumed to arise from disability'(Oliver, 1999, p.33).

3.10 This guidance is informed by an understanding of the 'social model' of disability, which uses the term disability not to refer to impairment (functional limitations) but rather to describe the effects of prejudice and discrimination: the social factors which create barriers, deny opportunities, and thereby dis-able people (Morris, 1998c; Oliver, 1999). Children's impairments can of course create genuine difficulties in their lives. However, many of the problems faced by disabled children are not caused by their conditions or impairments, but by societal values, service structures, or adult behaviour (Shakespeare and Watson, 1998):

> a major problem for disabled children is that they live in a society which views childhood impairment as deeply problematic (p.20) .

3.11 Effective assessment of a disabled child must consider:

- the direct impact of a child's impairment;
- any disabling barriers that the child faces; and
- how to overcome such barriers.

Disabled Children and assessment

3.12 Disabled children are far more likely than non-disabled children to be subject to multiple assessments by health, education and social services. There are several reasons for this:

- **There are more disabled children in groups already socially disadvantaged**. Whatever system is used to classify disability, there are twice the number of disabled children in social class 5 households as in social class 1 and there is a strong relationship between childhood disability and poverty/household income (Department of Health, 1998a; Dobson and Middleton,1999). The increased prevalence of certain impairments in some minority ethnic groups has also been linked to social disadvantage (Murphy et al, 1998).
- **Disabled children are more likely to have a number of experiences that may trigger assessment**. Disabled children face an increased risk of abuse (Westcott, 1993; Westcott and Cross, 1996; Westcott and Jones, 1999); and of school exclusion and social exclusion in its widest sense (Middleton, 1999). Disabled children are more likely to live away from home: to be accommodated on a short or long-term basis and/or to be in state-funded residential education.
- **Assessment has become the route to ordinary entitlements for many disabled children and their families**. Disabled children often have to be assessed to access the same basic provisions as non-disabled children, for example education, housing, play and leisure opportunities.
- **Assessment of special educational needs.** Many disabled children are assessed before they reach statutory school age because it is likely they will have special educational needs (SEN).

Using assessments positively with disabled children and young people

3.13 When planning an assessment involving a disabled child it is important to:

- **think about your own understanding of disability;**
- **take into account the child's experience and understanding of assessment;**
- **take into account the family's experience and understanding of assessment;**
- **be clear about the focus of an assessment;**
- **find out who else is currently involved with the child;**
- **gather information from existing assessments;**
- **access helpful information on specific childhood impairments.**

Each of these areas will be addressed in turn.

3.14 **Think about your own understanding of disability**. Our perceptions of what it means to be disabled will affect our work. It is essential to actively explore our own attitudes and understanding, and to be aware of our own prejudices, fears and stereotypes about disability and about particular impairments. The inclusive approach of the Assessment Framework should be reflected in all areas of practice. Are disabled children made to feel welcome by your services? Is your building fully accessible? Do you employ disabled workers? Are your toys, books and resources suitable for all children? Are there positive images of disabled children around? Do you have a clear policy on anti-discriminatory practice? Are staff offered information, training and support on the inclusion of disabled children within the service? Is disability equality training offered to staff? Can facilities and approaches be adapted for the communication needs of disabled children, for example loop systems and/or use of signing for deaf children?

3.15 **Take into account the child's experience and understanding of assessment**. Disabled children are likely to have been assessed, often frequently, and often within a pathologising, deficit model where the child was tested against some concept of normality. For some disabled children, the very word assessment may have unhelpful connotations:

> *Its always about what's wrong with me ... they're only interested in the bits of me that don't work. They want to see what I can't do (11 year old disabled girl personal communication).*

Disabled children and young people may not be used to active involvement in assessment processes. Children are entitled to an explanation of the assessment which is appropriate to their age and understanding. As far as is possible, the purpose should be agreed with the child as an assessment of their situation rather than of the child him or herself. This enables the child to become an essential part of the assessment team, contributing to information gathering and decision making, rather than being the passive focus of the exercise.

3.16 **Take into account the family's experience and understanding of assessment.** Families of disabled children will also have experienced many assessments. Some families describe dealing with service providers as the most difficult aspect of caring for their disabled children (Department of Health, 1998b, p.32). In one study, only 25% of parents of disabled children felt that assessment arrangements were well coordinated (Audit Commission, 1994). Assessments can undoubtedly be traumatic and difficult for some families:

> *I found assessment meetings a nightmare. I felt I was listening to people talk about somebody other than the child I lived with. After the first assessment at the child development centre I went home and cried for four days...* (Parent of disabled child, quoted in Murray and Penman, 1996) .

3.17 Families require clear information about the focus of any assessment and about available services providing support. Parents should be clearly informed that their views and priorities are important and they should be encouraged to contribute to the process. The process should include recognition of the parent carers needs in bringing up their children.

3.18 Some families would like friends, advocates or relatives to support them during assessments and this should be facilitated. Experience with named persons in education indicates that discussions can be more positive and open when families who wish for support are accompanied by their own adviser or friend (Russell, 1999).

3.19 Parents of disabled children can be assigned multiple and sometimes contradictory roles by professionals. Twigg and Atkin (1993) describe the range of ways that professionals in social and health care systems conceptualise and respond to parents: they are perceived, simultaneously, as resources for the statutory services, co-workers and service recipients in their own right, while their children mayor may not be also perceived as service recipients. This can create an ambiguous and confused relationship.

3.20 **Be clear about the focus of an assessment**. The Assessment Guidance states:

> However difficult the circumstances, the **purpose** of assessing the particular child and the family should always be kept in mind (paragraph 3.37).

3.21 Assessments should focus on the circumstances of the child and family and not just on an individual and whether a particular service is available. For disabled children in particular, there is a concern that assessments may be focused around assessing the child's problems, or assessing the child for specific services, rather than assessing the child's overall situation and needs. The most recent Department of Health inspection of services to disabled children found that 'There were very few needs-led assessments ...more frequently families were subject to a number of parallel assessments, often trawling through the same information but with a different service in mind' (Department of Health, 1998b, p.23).

3.22 Clarity of focus will also enable parents and children to contribute more effectively to an assessment. As an example, parents may perceive a broad assessment of a child's social integration that considers the possibility of using inclusive play and leisure facilities as an attempt to remove existing respite care arrangements. Clarity about the focus of the assessment is likely to diminish such anxieties.

3.23 In many cases practical help is most effective for a family with a disabled child, for example advice about benefits or the timely provision of aids and adaptations in the home. The needs of disabled children and their families for specialist disability equipment and assistive technology should be included in the assessment process. Equipment could range from a wheelchair and communication aid for the disabled child to special beds and lifting equipment to help parents or other carers. Assessment for equipment may need to involve several professionals on a multi-disciplinary basis and collaboration across agencies, particularly where different types of equipment have to be integrated. Where the relevant expertise is not available at local level, specialist centres such as communications aids centres may need to become involved. The views and wishes of the child and parents should be taken into account. A choice of equipment and the opportunity to try it out, for example by visiting a disabled living centre, should be offered as far as possible.

3.24 **Find out who else is involved currently with the child.** Assessment processes 'should be co-ordinated at all stages' (Department of Health, 1998b, p.57) and assessments of disabled children may be undertaken jointly with shared responsibility across agency boundaries (Department of Health et al, 2000).

3.25 Services for disabled children are often fragmented between different agencies. Different perspectives, values and professional languages can complicate working together across agency and discipline boundaries. Young disabled children often come sequentially to the attention of health, then education and then social services. Children who acquire their impairments may come suddenly into contact with all three agencies. Children with progressive conditions may have to switch between services and agencies as their needs change.

3.26 Within agencies, responsibilities for assessments of disabled children may also be located in different teams. For example, specialist social work teams for the deaf are often in either the disability or adult divisions, yet families obtain services from child care social workers or workers located in children with disabilities teams. Working across these boundaries can be facilitated by the development of a culture of co-working to harness all available expertise when assessing disabled children.

3.27 **Gather information from existing assessments.** Disabled children are likely to have already been assessed, and information already gathered should be accessed, having obtained consents as appropriate. Parents find it hard to tell their story again and again (Department of Health,1998b, p.22). Both children and family members often assume that agencies will share information with each other and may be surprised to find that they do not. Parents and children can be asked who they think has the most relevant knowledge – many have reported thinking the wrong professionals were consulted (Russell, 1999).

3.28 Integrated inter-agency assessment processes are in place in some areas and being developed in others (Russell, 1995; McConahie, 1997; Khan and Russell, 1999). Cross-agency key working can also enable effective information sharing (Mukherjee et al, 1999). Even where these mechanisms are not yet in place, information from other assessments should be available. For example, the *Code of Practice on the Identification and Assessment of Special Educational Needs* (Department for Education and Employment, 1994) requires local educational authorities to send a copy of the final statement of a child's special educational needs and accompanying advice to the social services department, whether or not social services have provided advice during the assessment process. It is good practice to seek parent's permission to send information to other agencies but where there are concerns about a child's safety local authorities may transfer information in the best interests of children without formal permission (see *Working Together to Safeguard Children* 1999, paragraphs 7.27 to 7.46).

3.29 **Access helpful information on specific childhood impairments.** It may be important to learn in general about the likely effects of an impairment or condition before meeting a child and his or her family. As a disabled teenager reported in Cross (1998) said:

> *I wish they knew more about disability, I mean, its sort of embarrassing to have to explain yourself (p.102).*

3.30 Learning about a child's condition does not mean becoming an expert. There are organisations of and for people with almost all impairments and conditions, and for parents. These are often good sources of accessible and up-to-date information [1]. It is important however to remember that every child experiences their condition differently. It will be important to understand the impact of an impairment on this child in this family as part of an assessment. Usually the best source of information will be the child and their family.

3.31 Given that disabled children will have had many experiences of having things done to them, it is important also to be careful about issues of consent and clarity of explanations. In particular 'pretend' choices should be avoided, where the child's consent is apparently sought but in reality the child has no choice: 'shall we take your coat off?', 'do you want this injection?', 'would you like to talk to me?'. Repeatedly being offered pretend choices can distort a child's experience and may contribute to disabled children's vulnerability to abuse. A good general rule is only to ask a question if you will go along with a refusal as well as acceptance.

Domain: Child's Developmental Needs

3.32 All children need to be loved and valued for who they are, and all children have developmental needs. A disabled child's impairment(s) will affect a child's growth, development and physical or mental wellbeing to a greater or lesser degree. Some children will have many areas of development not affected by their impairments. Other impairments have more of a global impact. Like their non-disabled peers, the developmental needs of disabled children are formed by the interactions between their unique physiological and psychological characteristics, their social and emotional experiences within their families and their environment which includes prejudice and disabling barriers. Differentiating the impact of a child's impairment(s) from the impact of the child's experiences is important. Assessing concerns about a child's development requires particular clarity where a child is disabled.

3.33 ' There must be a clear understanding of what a particular child is capable of achieving successfully at each stage of development, in order to ensure that he or she has the opportunity to achieve his or her full potential' (Department of Health et al, 2000,

1. Contact a Family provides help and advice for professional workers and families caring for disabled children through CONTACT LINE. Tel: 01713833555. Fax: 0171 3830259. The British Council of Disabled People is Britain's national umbrella organisation for groups controlled by disabled people. Tel: 01332295551. Fax: 01332295580. Minicom: 01332295581.

paragraph 2.3). Assessment standards around developmental milestones should be used with great care. For example, early assessment of deaf children will enable access to language development, whether spoken or manual, as soon as possible following diagnosis.

3.34 A useful question in assessment is: 'Would I consider that option if the child were not disabled?'. Clear reasons are necessary if the answer is 'no' (Middleton, 1996) .

Pointers for Practice

CHILD'S DEVELOPMENTAL NEEDS

- Is the child loved and valued for who they are?
- Does the child's impairment directly affect his or her growth, development and physical or mental wellbeing?
- Are there disabling barriers which limit the child or otherwise hinder his or her development?
- What action can be taken to ensure that the child has maximum access to family, education and community life?
- What action can be taken to safeguard or support the child's development?

Health

3.35 All children have the right to good health care. Disabled children have the same entitlements as other children to appropriate health care when ill, and to opportUnities to maximise their wellbeing, including health and education. Additionally, disabled children's health, development and wellbeing, and sometimes their lives, may depend on specialist medical intervention. Health care in its wider sense can also reduce, prevent or sometimes cure functional impairments for some disabled children. Medical professionals are often the first to have contact with a disabled child and their family and can be major providers of information, advice and support throughout childhood. Child development centres can enable effective, holistic assessments of children by combining the skills of different professionals in one team.

3.36 The medical treatment of disabled children has led to some criticism. First, some children have been prescribed intrusive and quite vigorous treatments and therapies when the efficacy of the treatment is not known. These programmes may involve new, alternative or unorthodox approaches and concerns have been raised about the lack of safeguards: In the words of one critic, 'in the lives of disabled children... anything goes as long as you call it therapeutic' (Oliver, 1999, p.1 07).

3.37 Second, therapy and treatment can imply deficiency (i.e. something wrong or bad that needs to be made better or put right), which can interfere with the development of a positive identity. Some disabled adults are now writing very critically about the unintended consequences of childhood medical experiences for the development of children's self-esteem (see French, 1993; 1996; Cross, 1998).

3.38 An unhelpful polarisation about the benefits of medical interventions has arisen where people argue in favour of the medical model or the social model without a case by case analysis of the likely benefits and possible disadvantages of specific treatments for individual children.

3.39 Most parents want what is best for their disabled child. However, there is not always consensus among parents, children and different professionals about the treatment or therapy that is best for a child. This is sometimes the case within orthodox medicine and there is less agreement about alternative or complementary medicine. Sometimes there is strong support from parents for a particular new treatment or therapy while psychologists and physicians may remain unconvinced of the efficacy of such innovations.

3.40 Consideration of the impact of both conventional and alternative treatments may thus be an important element of assessments involving disabled children. This does not only mean a clinical assessment of the efficacy of a particular treatment, but a holistic look at the impact of treatment or therapy on a child's life. Some therapies and treatments for disabled children can be disruptive, controversial and sometimes painful or distressing. The child may have to spend long periods of time in therapy, or away from home and therefore family. The longer term benefits of treatment will have to be considered alongside any short-term social and emotional costs to the child. Denying access to appropriate treatments and therapies could be neglectful or even abusive if the child's health or development is further impaired as a result.

3.41 A balanced approach to each child's individual needs is essential. The following guiding principle is useful: services should always meet a child's particular needs in ways that least disrupt the needs they have in common with all children, and treatments and therapies should be delivered in ways that least disrupt children's lives.

3.42 It is helpful to have ways assessing the validity and risk of new treatments. Some recent attempts have been made to give guidance on decisions about alternative treatments for particular conditions, specifically in relation to autism (Howlin, 1998) and cerebral palsy (McCarthy, 1999).

Pointers for Practice

DECISION-MAKING ABOUT TREATMENTS AND THERAPIES

- How has the decision been made that this therapy is appropriate for this child?
- Can the decision wait until the child is of an age and understanding to be consulted?
- What can the child and family expect to gain or lose from the treatment?
- How long has the approach been used?
- What research is available on the treatment? What alternative interventions might be tried?
- Have the parents and/or the child had the opportunity to talk with others who have direct experience of the treatment?

Issues of consent

3.43 In the light of the above, issues of consent are crucial. As noted in Volume 4 of the Guidance to the Children Act 1989 (Department of Health, 1991), disabled children's 'ability to give consent or refusal to any action, including assessment, examination or treatment is only limited by the general conditions relating to sufficient understanding which apply to other children under the Children Act' (p.14).

3.44 When children have learning or communication impairments it can be more difficult for professionals to address questions of consent, but it is arguably even more important that they do so. If a child resists or is distressed by a treatment or therapy, it is essential that treatment is reviewed urgently taking into account the child's perspective (for further discussion of consent to treatment and disabled children see Alderson, 1993; Chailey Heritage, 1997) .

Basic health care

3.45 Although disabled children generally have more contact with the medical world than other children, they may have more difficulty than non-disabled children in getting their basic health care needs met.

3.46 Disabled children can face barriers in accessing routine dental, optical, GP or hospital care. These barriers may include inaccessibility of buildings, inflexibility of systems, or attitudes of professionals. For example, one parent of a nine year old disabled boy commented:

> *I just can't take him to the surgery any more. He doesn't understand about waiting and he never sits down. The receptionists freeze i/we walk in the door. Basically we wait until things are bad enough to call someone out or to go to the hospital* (Personal communication).

3.47 Discriminatory practice may need to be challenged: Disabled children may be given lower priority for scarce or expensive resources (Rutter and Seyman, 1999).

Pointers for Practice

HEALTH

- Is the child getting access to basic health care?
- If not, what are the barriers?
- Is the child getting access to appropriate healthcare and treatment to maximise his or her quality of life?
- How does the child experience treatment or therapy?
- Are decisions about treatment and therapy being made on the basis of c/ear information?
- Has the child been consulted, and the child's views taken into account?
- If a child has been judged unable to give or withhold informed consent and is resisting treatment, is this being acknowledged and addressed?

- Does treatment or therapy disrupt the meeting of needs that the child shares with all children (for example, family life, friends, play)?
- Does treatment or therapy lead to unnecessary segregation or exclusion?
- If yes, can the treatment or therapy be managed differently, or are there other ways of helping the child?

Education

3.48 Education is a key service for all children. Disabled children have the same entitlement to education as their peers. The *Framework for the Assessment of Children in Need and their Families* (Department of Health et al, 2000) emphasises the importance of taking 'account of a child's starting point and any special educational needs' (page 19).

3.49 Education legislation does not distinguish between disability and special educational needs. Under the Education Act 1996 a child is said to have special educational needs if (s)he has 'a learning difficulty which calls for special educational provisional to be made for him' , and a child has a learning difficulty if:

> a. *he has a significantly greater difficulty in learning than the majority of children his age,*
>
> b. *he has a disability which either prevents or hinders him from making use of educational facilities of a kind generally provided for children of his age.*
>
> Education Act 1996

3.50 Thus not all children with special educational needs are disabled, and some disabled children do not have special educational needs. However, there is significant overlap between the two groups.

3.51 The *Code of Practice on the Identification and Assessment of Special Educational Needs* (1994) and the Education Act 1996 set out the arrangements by which a child's special educational needs are identified, assessed and any appropriate provision made. Key principles of the Code of Practice are that:

- all children should have the greatest possible access to abroad and balanced education.
- all special educational needs must be addressed.
- children should be educated within mainstream schools wherever possible.
- active partnership between children, their parents, schools, LEAs and health and social services is essential in order to meet children's special educational needs.

3.52 Education policy and guidance thus 'confirm and amplify the key messages of the Children Act 1989', including the right of children to be heard in the assessment of their educational needs (Russell1996, p.135).

3.53 Social services can play an important role in a Special Educational Needs assessment. They can ensure that parents have accurate information on assessment arrangements and local provision, and that the whole range of options is explained to the child and parents. They can provide an advocacy role for vulnerable children and families, including looked after children. They can facilitate integrated planning across agencies for the transition to adulthood.

Pointers for Practice

EDUCATION

- Are the child's educational needs being addressed?
- Are there barriers preventing the child accessing appropriate education?
- Is information being shared appropriately between agencies?
- Do parents and children have access to information about local provision?
- Are services from education co-ordinated and complementary to services from other agencies?

Emotional and Behavioural Development

3.54 Disabled children and young people need to complete the same tasks of emotional development as all children: early attachments are just as important for disabled babies and children, and the development of relationships, self-confidence and sexuality are just as important for young disabled people. Disabled children and young people may need additional emotional support for all the same reasons as other children and young people: for example because of disruption of family relationships; loss; academic stress; serious illness; bullying or racism. Some Child and Adolescent Mental Health Services include staff, for example clinical psychologists, who have developed specific expertise in meeting the mental health needs of disabled children. Some counsellors have also developed expertise in this area (eg. see Brearley, 1997) .

3.55 Some disabled children and young people thrive emotionally; others do not do well. The increased emphasis on listening to children should help practitioners better understand the emotional needs of disabled children at different stages in their lives.

3.56 Disabled children and young people may also need support with both the direct impact of their impairments and their experiences of prejudice and oppressive attitudes. It is important that such support is provided in ways that do not pathologise the child. Support from family, friends and professionals should not deny a child's experience of prejudice. Disabled young people and disabled adults may also be valuable sources of emotional support and understanding.

3.57 Disabled young people can face particular challenges during adolescence and the transition to adulthood (Hurst and Baldwin, 1994; Morris,1999c). Some of this is exacerbated by transitions between childhood and adult services. Sometimes different services have different ages at which this transition is deemed to take place.

> *Rebecca's gap year before university was full of exciting opportunities, but Sam's gap year is remembered as the year everything ground to a halt* (Parent of disabled young adult, personal communication) .

3.58 Recent publications clarify good practice in services involved in transition (Morris, 1999c; Department for Education & Employment, 1997). Choice, control, entitlement, consultation, involvement and inclusion are key themes.

3.59 Young disabled people from black and minority ethnic communities often face additional problems in their transition to adulthood. Services tend to be run by white people; insufficient account may be taken of the different meaning of adolescence in different cultures; young people who have spent time in residential education may have spent years with little or no contact with others from the same cultural background (Morris, 1999c).

3.60 At all ages, assessment of a child whose impairments have been caused or exacerbated by abuse raises particularly complex issues. The child's knowledge of the cause of their condition should be approached with extreme caution. Such knowledge can be truly unbearable for children, and they may genuinely not know about the abuse, even though they have apparently been told.

Pointers for Practice

EMOTIONAL AND BEHAVIOURAL DEVELOPMENT

- Are there concerns about the child's emotional development?
- Can the child access sources of emotional support available to all children?
- If not, can disabling barriers be removed?
- Are appropriate supports available for transition to adulthood?
- Is there away a disabled adult could help?

Identity

3.61 The Assessment Framework refers to the 'strength of a positive sense of individuality'. Children's life chances will be affected by their sense of their own value and worth. Developing a positive sense of identity is an important task of childhood and adolescence, no less so for disabled children and young people. It has been noted that disabled children are often defined within a one dimensional identity that is largely 'degendered, asexual, culturally unspecific and classless' (Priestley, 1998, p.220). All aspects of a child's identity should be recognised, although different aspects will assume greater or lesser significance at different developmental stages.

3.62 Recognising disability as a positive identity is not easy in contemporary society. Disabled children growing up will receive negative messages about being disabled, and need a positive internal model of disabled identity to counteract negative stereotypes. Children can internalise the messages they receive about what it means to have an impairment. It can be difficult to develop a positive sense of identity as a young disabled person especially if services are entirely focused on changing the child through treatment, therapy, or other interventions. A child's impairment is an integral part of identity, not something separate or incidental. It is, of course, not the only aspect of their identity but should be considered throughout any assessment. It has been suggested that an early acceptance of a child's condition may be important for the development of a positive identity: 'children should make their journeys as themselves' (Middleton, 1999, p.129). We are also beginning to understand the importance of a family's perception of disability on a child's identity development. As an example, a differentiation needs to be made between deaf children in deaf families and deaf children of hearing parents. If deafness is considered normal, its impact will be different in comparison to a family where it may be viewed as a major disabling condition (Loosemore-Reppen, 1999).

3.63 There are strong parallels with issues for black children growing up in a racist society. There are also key differences. In terms of family context, black children usually have black families who can provide positive role models whereas disabled children usually have non-disabled parents. Many disabled children rarely meet disabled adults and may assume that they will somehow grow out of their impairments with age. This is a sensible assumption if one meets many disabled children and no disabled adults.

3.64 The cultural identity of disabled children should be recognised. Prejudice about race and disability can compound each other. There is evidence that families from minority ethnic groups caring for a severely disabled child are even more disadvantaged than white families in similar situations (Chamba et al, 1999).

3.65 Although it is not possible for anyone professional to be fully knowledgeable about all childhood impairments and all cultural contexts, it is possible to demonstrate a willingness to learn about a child's individual needs and an openness to, and respect for, cultural differences. Of particular relevance when working with disabled children may be the cultural differences which exist within our society in relation to concepts such as dependence and independence. It is important to listen carefully to children and families' views about those differences.

3.66 In all cultures, disabled children may be perceived and treated as younger than their actual age. This is particularly so for learning disabled children and young people. Linked to this, the sexual identity of disabled children is often widely denied. Many disabled young people have very low expectations of relationships:

> *I never dreamt that I'd get married and I certainly didn't think that I'd have children. Its something out of this world to me. Being disabled they made you feel as though you had no use in the world . . . It made me feel I wasn't whole, it made me feel sort of not clean enough to have children* (Disabled woman in Humphries and Gordon, 1992, p.142).

3.67 There have been encouraging recent developments to ensure that disabled children have access to appropriate sex education (Adcock and Stanley, 1996; Scott and Kerr-Edwards,1999).

Pointers for Practice

IDENTITY

- Is the child recognised as a girl or boy, as part of a family and community, with a definite cultural identity?
- Is the child recognised and treated in ways appropriate to his or her age and stage of development?
- Is the child's identity as a sexual being recognised in line with their age and understanding?
- Does the child have access to positive role models for all the different aspects of their identity?
- What messages is the child receiving about what it means to be disabled?
- Is the child loved and valued as they are, or are they learning that they need to change to be acceptable?

Family and Social relationships

3.68 The great majority of disabled children grow up within their families and assessments should identify and support the strengths of families. All children need stable and affectionate relationships with their parents or carers, and all children need friends.

3.69 Relationships between families of disabled children and social services are often dominated by arrangements to separate children from their families through the provision of respite care (Morris, 1998b). All parents and children need breaks from each other, but natural breaks (playing out, visiting friends, joining in organised activities, staying with relatives) may be unavailable to disabled children.

3.70 Defining the purpose of any service as respite can create a confusing situation. The child's experience of the service can become incidental since its defined purpose is to give the child's parents a break. A social model perspective is helpful in identifying children's real needs, which often require seeking ways to overcome disabling barriers that prevent them accessing the social and leisure opportunities available to their non-disabled peers.

3.71 All children need friends, and disabled children can face particular barriers in establishing and maintaining friendships:

> The disabled young people we interviewed more often led limited social lives... The more severely disabled young people were least likely to have a wide circle of friends, close confidants or regular contact with their peers (Hurst and Baldwin, 1994, p.86).

3.72 Not all disabled children live at home. It is difficult to estimate how many live away from home: one figure commonly cited is that around 46,000 disabled children spend some or all of their time in residential establishments (Russell, 1994) . Many of these children maintain strong family and social relationships but it is estimated that 'well over 4,000 disabled children and young people. . . are living away from home, isolated from their families, and with little or no contact with people outside their schools, foster or residential homes and a circle of busy professionals' (Knight, 1998, p.58). An assessment should consider the requirement under the Children Act 1989 to appoint independent visitors for such isolated young people.

3.73 The continuation of relationships is important for all disabled children, particularly those who spend time away from their families, and have communication or learning impairments. If children do not read or write or use the telephone, other ways of staying in touch are necessary, for example photos, cassettes of voices, familiar sounds or music, videos, treasured belongings, objects of reference, life story books and things that smell like, taste like, or feel like home.

Pointers for Practice

FAMILY AND SOCIAL RELATIONSHIPS

- Does the child belong within a family and community?
- Does the child have secure and stable attachments?
- Does the child have friends and are their friendships valued and supported?
- Should the child have the option of an independent visitor or other advocacy arrangement?
- Are the child's relationships within their family actively supported?
- Is the child's access to education, play or family life restricted by lack of support with their communication needs?

Social Presentation

3.74 This dimension requires particular attention because disabled children and their families may experience pressure to deny or minimise or hide their impairments. 'The pressure to appear "normal"... can give rise to enormous inefficiency and stress, yet many disabled people are well into adulthood before they abandon such attempts' (French, 1993, p.46).

3.75 Denying one's situation and pretending to be 'normal' can be both exhausting and emotionally costly for children:

> *... having adults pretend that I could see more than I could and having to acquiesce in the pretence, was a theme throughout my childhood. . . as well as denying the reality of their disabilities, disabled children are frequently forced to deny painful feelings associated with their experiences because their parents and other adults simply cannot cope with them...* (French, 1993,p.69).

Pointers for Practice

SOCIAL PRESENTATION

- Is the child supported to present themselves confidently, without denying or hiding impairments? . Is the child helped to exercise choice about social presentation?

Selfcare Skills

3.76 Selfcare and independence can be a major focus of services for disabled children. Independence is often thought to be something that disabled children and young people and indeed disabled adults desire above all else, yet 'the notion of independence can be taken too far, restricting the lives of disabled people rather than enriching them' (French, 1993, p.44).

3.77 Selfcare skills should be related to children's individual ability and desire to contribute to their care rather than be dictated by age. In assessments is important to listen carefully to children's views about undertaking their own care:

Sammy was expected to spend around 90 minutes a day getting himself dressed and undressed; tasks which are very difficult because of his physical impairments. Sammy was given an opportunity to express his views about this routine and he communicated very strongly that he would rather spend that time reading or using his computer. As a result Sammy's routine was changed.

Karen wanted to learn how to transfer .from her wheelchair to a bath or bed. This proved a difficult skill that took some months for her to gain. She describes the impact of this one skill on her life as 'huge' and is very pleased she had the opportunity to learn how to do it.

3.78 Children's own priorities will vary and are likely to change over time. It is important also to be sensitive to fluctuations in children's abilities; tiredness, distress, illness or an unfamiliar environment can temporarily wipe out a skill.

Pointers for Practice

SELF-CARE SKILLS

- Are the child's priorities in terms of self-care taken into account?
- Where the child receives personal care from others, is this undertaken respectfully?
- Are procedures explained to children before they occur?

Domain: Parenting Capacity

Critically important to a child's health and development is the ability of parents or caregivers to ensure that the child's developmental needs are being appropriately and adequately responded to, and to adapt to his or her changing needs over time (Department of Health et al, 2000, paragraph 2.9).

3.79 The concept of reasonable parental care can be particularly challenging where a child is disabled. Some children need more parenting or more skilled parenting than others; some children need intensive parenting for much longer than others. Some children are parented in a far less supportive social context than others, and a consideration of the supports available to parents in responding to their child's needs is important (see next Domain). Some families have more than one disabled child which affects parenting capacity (Lawton, 1998) .

3.80 Parenting a disabled child can be very demanding, both because of the child's impairments and because of the time and energy which have to be devoted to securing services to respond to the child's needs. When children have very complex needs and the demands on parents are heavy, there can be lower expectations of what constitutes reasonable parental care. Professionals may understandably think that parents do very well considering how little help they get and thus expectations of the standard of care which a disabled child should enjoy are lowered.

3.81 A clear value base at an individual and organisational level is essential for practitioners. The explicit commitment to equality of opportunity within the Assessment Framework should prove helpful in clarifying standards and expectations for disabled children.

Pointers for Practice

PARENTING CAPACITY

- What supports are available to the help the family parent their disabled child?
- What is understood as constituting reasonable parental care given to this child?
- Are the standards for assessment of parenting capacity clear?

Basic Care

3.82 A disabled child's care needs might be more complex, take more time, or continue for more of their childhood, but basic care remains aright of all children.

3.83 A child's care needs can create barriers in their lives unless appropriate support is available; schools can be reluctant to give medication, playgroups may insist that children are out of nappies. Even services specifically for disabled children may exclude children with certain care needs, for example children who require tube feeding (see Townsley and Robinson, 1999). There may also be disagreements about whether basic care constitutes nursing or social care or is part of their education (and therefore which agency should pay). Identifying these barriers and finding ways to address them is an appropriate focus of assessment.

Pointers for Practice

BASIC CARE

- Are the child's basic care needs adequately responded to?
- If the child requires additional support, is this provided in ways that are both respectful of the child and sustainable in the long term?
- Is the child's access to education, play or family life restricted by lack of support with care needs?

Emotional Warmth

3.84 'Ensuring the child's emotional needs are met and giving the child a sense of being specially valued' (Department of Health et al, 2000, page 21) is important for all children, but may be particularly crucial for disabled children who, given the societal context, are likely to receive negative messages about their personal value.

Pointers for Practice

EMOTIONAL WARMTH

- Does the child experience warmth and affection from parents and/or caregivers?
- Does the child have secure, stable and affectionate relationships?

Ensuring Safety

3.85 Disabled children are particularly vulnerable and face an increased risk of suffering abuse in many settings (Westcott and Jones, 1999). They ought to be over-represented in our child protection systems, yet research suggests that they may be significantly under-represented (Morris, 1998b; 1999a). The mistaken assumption that disability protects from abuse contributes to the vulnerability of disabled children.

3.86 The increased vulnerability of disabled children to abuse results from social attitudes and the special treatment of disabled children; for example, disabled children tend to be more isolated, to be more dependent, to have less control over their lives and their bodies, and may be less likely to be heard or believed. Disabled children are often in the care of many more adults than other children, they are more likely to spend time in institutional settings and the usual safeguards may not be in place (Morris, 1998b; Utting,1997).

3.87 Possible indicators of abuse or significant harm may prove difficult to disentangle from the effects of a child's impairment. A multi-disciplinary approach is essential (Department of Health et al, 1999).

A seven year old boys constant masturbation was 'explained' by his autism and his attempts to touch adults sexually were initially attributed to his confusion about boundaries. Several years later his father was convicted of sexual assault of all three children in the family.

Severe self-injurious behaviour from a three year old was thought to be indicative of experience of violence at home, although there were no other indicators. As part of the assessment a second medical opinion was sought and the child was found to have a rare chromosomal disorder linked to self-injury and aggression.

Extensive bruising to the face, chest and arms of an eleven year old was said to result from falls during epileptic seizures. Medical advice was that the bruising was incompatible with falling and child protection procedures were initiated.

3.88 Possible indicators may even be perceived as safeguards against abuse:

Concerns were raised about the possible sexual abuse of a six year old girl with learning disabilities. School and residential staff felt she could not be abused because she resisted nappy changing with such violence.

3.89 Assessments should consider the safety of the different settings in a child's life. There is some evidence that institutional care should be considered a risk factor in itself (Westcott, 1994) . This information is relevant for many disabled children. For further discussion of safeguarding disabled children in institutions see Marchant and Cross (1993).

3.90 Munchausen syndrome by proxy is a very rare form of child abuse, and the possible links with childhood impairment are not yet fully understood. However, one possible consequence of repeatedly inducing illness in a child is long-term impairment. Preverbal children have been found to be at highest risk of induced illness (Schreiber and Libow, 1993) and anecdotal evidence suggests an increased incidence among disabled children (see Meadow, 1999; Precey, 1998) .

3.91 There are welcome developments both in approaches for safety skills training specifically relevant for disabled children (Briggs, 1995; Kennedy, 1993a; 1993b; Lee et al, 1998; Marchant, 1998) and in approaches to making s47 enquiries regarding the possible abuse of children whose impairments affect their communication (Marchant and Page, 1993; 1997; Aldridge and Wood, 1998; 1999).

Pointers for Practice

ENSURING SAFETY

- Are key adults in the child's life aware of the increased vulnerability of disabled children to being abused?
- Are standards for safeguards within services in place and regularly monitored?
- Can the child access the safety channels that exist for all children (e.g. helplines, complaints procedures, advocacy services)?
- If not, what alternative safeguards can be put in place?
- Have any concerns about possible significant harm been carefully considered and the subject of appropriate enquiries?

Stimulation

3.92 All children need levels of stimulation appropriate to their stage of development and sensitive to their individual needs. Ideas, resources and support may be required to help parents of disabled children (especially children with multiple impairments or dual sensory impairments) to find appropriate ways to stimulate their child. On the other hand, parents may feel exceptional pressure to provide stimulation:

> *I found that you just do everything. Everything that came: "Yes, she'll do that, oh yes, we'll go to that, yes, we'll do that". I tried to carry on doing everything and then I couldn't manage really. But then it needed someone else to come in and say 'Its alright, actually, you don't have to do all these things, and Alex will be perfectly fine if she doesn't do these things". I felt she needed so much input* (Parent of disabled girl in aMaze, 1997, p.26).

3.93 It may be an appropriate assessment task to help parents explore their child's need for stimulation and the connections with their own feelings about their child.

Pointers for Practice

STIMULATION

- Is the child offered stimulation appropriate to their needs?
- Are parents able to access resources and ideas where needed?
- Does the child have access to recreation and leisure opportunities that provide stimulation?

Guidance and Boundaries

3.94 All children need guidance and boundaries. Parenting disabled children can raise additional dilemmas when making decisions about reasonable risks. The dilemmas facing all parents may be magnified and assessments may encounter extremes of both over and under protection. Some parents of disabled children may need help to recognise that their child requires additional support or protection. Other parents need support and sometimes permission to let their disabled child take risks in their everyday lives.

3.95 Involving disabled adults in these discussions can be valuable:

> *Recently I was talking to a man with cerebral palsy and he was saying 'Let her do things, if people want to do things with hel; let her do it. OK if she breaks an arm, she breaks an arm, but other children break arms you know. Just let her be a child* (Parent of disabled girl, in Beresford, 1994) .

3.96 Disabled children are also more likely to be perceived as having challenging behaviour. The context of their lives may affect others' expectations: disabled young people can sometimes get away with less than others. It is useful to remind ourselves that most children and young people do not behave well all the time, they do not do what they are told immediately and without arguing, do not always go along with all adult suggestions, or do not always eat sensibly, get ready for school without protest or go to bed and get up again when asked.

3.97 That said, it seems that children with learning disabilities, autism, or language delay do face an increased risk of developing challenging behaviour. Physical and sensory impairments are also known to increase this likelihood. The increased likelihood of developing challenging behaviours is not necessarily a direct result of these impairments, but may be related to other factors.

3.98 Whatever the cause of a child's behaviour, and sometimes this is never absolutely clear, assessments must address the appropriateness of adult responses. Judgements about what constitutes reasonable control for disabled children can be particularly fraught. In assessments where there are issues around control of a child's behaviour, clear principles become essential (see also Mental Health Foundation (1997)) .

Pointers for Practice

GUIDANCE AND BOUNDARIES

- Is the child supported to take reasonable risks in everyday life?
- Are parents supported to enable children to take reasonable risks in everyday life?
- Are boundaries appropriate for the child's age and understanding?
- Do boundaries change over time as the child grows and develops?
- Is the child's welfare the paramount consideration?
- Are responses to a child's behaviour based on a consideration of what is in that child's best interests and what they would recognise themselves as being in their own interests, were they of the age and capacity to make such decisions themselves?
- Are restrictive measures adopted to deal with severe challenging behaviour only when there is no alternative?
- Are they used in the least detrimental manner and for the shortest possible time?
- Are measures of control part of a plan with long term strategies to meet the child's needs and encourage other behaviours?
- Have approaches been discussed by the parents, professionals and carers involved?

Points 5 -10 are adapted from Lyons (1994)

Stability

3.99 All children require stability in their lives. This does not mean absolute consistency. Most parents have breaks from their children, but these usually involve the child spending time in natural settings and with familiar people (friends, family) . Disabled children may be unable to access these natural breaks and instead might be offered segregated services. Disabled children's patterns of care should offer stability appropriate to their age and understanding. They are more likely to face discontinuity in the short term (sleeping in several different places in one week) or in the long term (multiple changes of carers or of settings).

Pointers for Practice

STABILITY

- How many adults are involved in this child's life?
- Do they change frequently? Are there long term, secure attachment figures for the child?
- How many adults take care of this child?
- How many adults take intimate care of this child?
- How many different places or settings does this child sleep in?
- Is the care provided in different settings consistent?
- Is the care well planned and is the child properly prepared for breaks?

Domain: Family And Environmental Factors

3.100 Parents' basic needs are the same whether or not their child is disabled. They need to feel supported, have breaks, feel valued and to have a family routine where they feel a sense of control. They benefit from professionals who respect them, and value and want the best for their child.

3.101 A wide range of factors can either help or hinder a family's functioning. The Assessment Framework acknowledges the inter-linking of different problems facing families. For families of disabled children this is a particularly important issue. Having a disabled child can impact on a family in many different ways. The direct effects of the child's impairment are likely to be compounded by disabling barriers facing both the child and the family.

3.102 These disabling barriers may be particularly daunting for families of disabled children who are otherwise at risk of social exclusion, for example because of their position in society, their family structure, their ethnic background, or their income.

3.103 Careful consideration of the supports available to parents in responding to their disabled child's needs is important. Many families make huge adjustments to respond to the needs of their children. Supports available to most parents are often less available to parents of disabled children. Baby-sitting and other informal supports may be much harder to find. Mainstream services (family centres, playgroups, nurseries) are often less accessible to families with disabled children. Living in a world that may relentlessly reject your child has an impact on families.

Pointers for Practice

FAMILY AND ENVIRONMENTAL FACTORS

- What factors help or hinder this family's functioning?
- What disabling barriers face this family?

- What supports are available to this family in responding to the needs of their disabled child?

Family History and Functioning

3.104 Exploration of the child's place within the family is important for disabled children as for all children. Relationships with parents and siblings require the same attention, as do parental strengths and difficulties. The birth of a child with some form of impairment, or the experience of a child acquiring an impairment is usually a significant life event, often perceived to disrupt family expectations for the future. The meaning that the impairment will hold for a family, and the family's response to such an event will depend on a range of factors. Exploring how a family has coped with other major life events may assist in placing responses in context.

3.105 Beresford (1994; 1995) emphasises the importance of defining parents as 'active agents' rather than 'passive recipients', thus acknowledging that they actively seek to manage the stresses and strains of caring for their disabled child. Services should seek to build on parents' strengths, and since parents cope in very different ways an approach sensitive to individual difference is necessary. There is good evidence that parents value highly assessments which take full account of their knowledge, understanding and aspirations for the future.

3.106 The siblings of disabled children have often been invisible to professional eyes. An assessment of a disabled child and their family should recognise the importance of siblings in each others' lives. Relationships between brothers and sisters should be valued and encouraged, including relationships where one or both children are disabled. It is essential to approach sibling relationships on an individual basis: it cannot be assumed that undertaking some caring responsibilities is harmful to siblings. The views of siblings about their relationships with each other may be an important part of the assessment.

Pointers for Practice

FAMILY HISTORY AND FUNCTIONING

- How does this family generally cope with major life events?
- What place does the disabled child have within the family?
- What supports are available to this family?
- What are the effects on the siblings of the disabled child or children?
- Does any child undertake caring responsibilities for a disabled sibling which may be detrimental to his or her own development?

Wider Family

3.107 The Assessment Framework stresses that 'Account must be taken of the diversity of family styles and structures, particularly who counts as a family and who is important to the child' (Department of Health et al, 2000, paragraph 2.15) .

3.108 Like all children, disabled children will vary in the significance they attach to their wider family. Relationships with siblings, grandparents, other relatives, friends and neighbours may be crucial at different stages in a child's life. Wider family support is also important to parents: those who receive a lot of help from their extended family tend to report fewer unmet needs (Chamba et al, 1999). The assessment should therefore consider any potential within the wider family for increased support. There is some evidence that divorce is more likely in families with disabled children and so the assessment should include sensitive enquiries into ways in which an absent parent might be able to promote the child's welfare.

3.109 An important group of people for many disabled children are those who are paid to provide support to the child or who have been in the past, for example, teachers, carers, and outreach workers. A significant proportion of adults who provide family based care for disabled children have previously worked with disabled children in general or with the particular child they later care for.

3.110 Recent research found no evidence to substantiate the stereotype of extended supportive families among minority ethnic groups. Families' experiences, needs and circumstances vary across ethnic groups: Indian and Black M rican Caribbean families reported least support from their extended family, with levels of support lower than that found among the survey of white families. The most cited reason for lack of support was that no family members lived nearby (Chamba et al, 1999). In the same study, some Asian parents expressed the belief that they should bear full responsibility for their child and this prevented them from asking for help from their extended family.

Pointers for Practice

WIDER FAMILY

- Who are the important people in this child's life?
- How are these relationships supported and preserved?
- Has the potential to offer support within the wider family (including any absent parents) been fully considered?

Housing

The provision of appropriate housing can make an important contribution to meeting the health and developmental needs of children (Department of Health et al, 2000, paragraph 5.71).

3.111 Inadequate housing is a frequent barrier affecting families with children with a wide range of impairments, not just physical or mobility impairments. Housing that is unsuitable for a disabled child affects the whole family, by making it difficult or impossible for children to enjoy normal- even essential- childhood experiences.

3.112 For the disabled child, unsuitable housing can make moving around the house, playing, contributing to family life and learning to look after themselves much harder.

3.113 Issues raised in recent research include the general quality of housing; the amount of space; safety and access problems linked to location rather than to actual buildings (Beresford, 1994; Oldman and Beresford, 1998).

3.114 Oldsman and Beresford (1999) found that three out of four families reported one or more ways in which their housing was unsuitable; four out of ten reported than their housing was poor overall; and families with disabled children were more likely to live in rented housing on low incomes than families with non-disabled children. Families with disabled children often move for reasons associated with the child's impairment.

3.115 When houses are well adapted for a particular child, the family's life can be transformed:

> *If you can get your home right you can cope. . . within 24 hours of being in this house... she was a different child!* (Parent quoted in Oldman and Beresford, 1999)

3.116 Shortcomings in housing are likely to lead to demands for other services, for example short term breaks or help with lifting a child. This can both undermine a family's wish for independence and lead to a waste of limited public funds.

Pointers for Practice

HOUSING

- Does the child's accommodation have basic amenities and facilities appropriate to the child's needs?
- Are advice and resources available to make the necessary adaptations?

Employment

3.117 This dimension includes patterns of employment and impact of work on the child. We know that parents of disabled children face additional barriers to employment: very few mothers with a disabled child work outside the home – about 2% work full time compared with 23% of the general population of mothers with children (Lawton,1998). There are particularly low levels of employment among minority ethnic families with disabled children (Chamba et al, 1999) and among parents of more than one disabled child (Tozer, 1999).

3.118 Parents believe that employment has economic, social and psychological benefits for them and for their children, and assessments may helpfully explore barriers to employment with parents who wish to work.

3.119 This dimension also includes children's experience of work and its impact on them. It is important for disabled children to be aware of the world of work and if possible to see disabled adults in employment.

Pointers for Practice

EMPLOYMENT

- Are there barriers to employment if parents wish to work?
- Is accessible, adequate child care available?
- Do disabled young people have appropriate opportunities to experience work situations?

Income

3.120 This dimension is about the sufficiency of income to meet the family's needs. Families are financially disadvantaged by having a disabled child, and it has been estimated that it costs on average three times more to bring up a severely disabled child than a non-disabled child (Dobson and Middleton, 1999). The same study found that younger disabled children are especially disadvantaged because the benefit system assumes lower costs for younger children, which is often not the case. Parents attempt to minimise the gap between their income and their spending by going into debt, spending less on themselves and other family members, and altering their lifestyles and aspirations.

3.121 Applying for financial help is a difficult process with an inherent tension: on the one hand parents are encouraged to promote their child's development but, on the other hand financial support and access to some services rests on levels of dependency. Applying for financial help can be emotionally difficult for parents:

> *I can't bear to do the DLA forms) its so painful to have to think about what she can't do and maybe will never do* (Parent of disabled girl, personal communication) .

For these reasons the assessment should ensure that families are receiving the benefits to which they are entitled and are referred, if appropriate, to the Family Fund Trust.

3.122 Additionally, parents in a number of studies report difficulty in finding out about and claiming benefits (Kagan et al, 1998; Lawton, 1998; Dobson and Middleton, 1999). Minority ethnic group families were less likely to receive benefits and less likely to be awarded benefits it the higher rates than white families. Parents who understood English well had much higher levels of benefit take-up than those with little or no understanding of English (Chamba et al, 1999).

Pointers for Practice

INCOME

- Are parents and young people clear about their financial entitlements?
- Is support available with applications for benefits?
- Is information about benefits accessible to all families?

- Have the cultural and linguistic backgrounds of the families been fully taken into account?
- Are working parents of disabled children aware of their entitlement to benefits?

Family's Social Integration

3.123 Assessments should consider the wider social context and a family's social integration or isolation. Families of disabled children can face barriers to social integration, which may be physical, financial or attitudinal.

3.124 Relationships with other families are an important part of life. Disabled children and their families may face barriers preventing them from taking part in social events or cultural or religious celebrations or holidays. Providing the appropriate form of support may enable disabled children to join with their families in such events, and on a more day to day basis may enable children to go to their local playgroup, park, school, church, swimming pool or youth club, or to visit friends of the family or relatives. Supporting the social integration of disabled children often facilitates the integration of their parents, who gain opportunities to meet local parents at the school gate, local members of their religious community, workers in local services and so on. Many families welcome introductions to support groups as a means of reducing social isolation, and gaining useful information and valued support.

Pointers for Practice

FAMILY'S SOCIAL INTEGRATION

- Does the family face barriers to their social integration?
- Can supports be provided to facilitate the child and family's integration?

Community Resources

3.125 This dimension includes the availability and accessibility of local resources to children and families. Assessments should consider barriers to the disabled child's use of community resources:

> Disabled children have the human right to take part in play and leisure activities and to freely express themselves in cultural and artistic ways. They have the right to equal access to cultural, artistic, recreational and leisure activities (Morris, 1998c, p.20).

Assessments should therefore focus on disabled children's needs for support to enable them to access leisure, recreation and play activities. The Disability Discrimination Act 1995 should result in a wide range of resources being more accessible to disabled children.

3.126 The Disability Discrimination Act 1995 has put those who provide services to the public (eg shops, banks, leisure facilities, as well as health and social services themselves) under new duties to make their services more accessible to disabled people. Since 1996, it is has generally been illegal for service providers to discriminate against disabled people by refusing to provide them with a service on the same terms as are available to the public generally. Since October 1999 service providers have been required to take "reasonable steps" to make their services accessible to disabled people who would otherwise find them impossible or unreasonably difficult to access. (Further information about the Disability Discrimination Act's requirements of service providers, including the Code of Practice on access to goods and services, is available on the Government's disability website http://www.disability.gov.uk). These duties should make it easier for disabled children to access mainstream services: they do not, however, remove the need for social services to continue to provide special support where services would otherwise be inaccessible.

3.127 Disabled adults are also a potentially valuable community resource for disabled children and their families. The disabled people's movement is paying increasing attention to children's issues (see Cross, 1998; Morris, 1998c; Shakespeare and Watson,1998).

> *I learn more from them (disabled adults) than I can learn from anybody, about what their childhoods were like...* (Parent quoted in Beresford, 1994) .

Pointers for Practice

COMMUNITY RESOURCES

- Is the child linked into their community resources?
- Can they and do they make use of community resources?
- What steps are being taken to overcome barriers to inclusion?

Involving children in the assessment process

3.128 Involving disabled children and young people in assessments has a value in its own right, quite apart from the improved quality of assessment that is likely to result in. It demonstrates to children and others a respect and valuing of the child as a person.

3.129 Workers may face a number of barriers when involving disabled children in assessments. This final section is designed to address some of these in very practical ways.

3.130 **Others may not expect this to happen.** Be clear from the start that you want to involve children in the assessment. Others may not expect it to happen: parents, children and other workers may be surprised as the child may not previously have been consulted. Children may also be unused to participation. Actively involving children in decision making may be threatening for parents – many families do not routinely involve children, disabled or not, in family decisions. Prepare parents and attend to their concerns.

3.131 **Workers may not feel confident about their own skills.** Social workers who are generally good at communicating with children are likely also to be good at communicating with disabled children, but may need encouragement and support to adapt their skills and try out new approaches. General listening and communications skills are usually more useful than attempting to become competent in a wide range of communication methods.

3.132 **Develop a broad and flexible definition of communication**. Involving children with communication impairments in meaningful ways requires us to broaden our definition of communication and to be willing to try new approaches (Marchant and Martyn, 1999) . Individualised, responsive ways of working are essential.

3.133 We often act as if speaking is the only valid way to communicate and yet we know that this is rarely the case for any child. Total communication means tuning in on all channels, attending for example: to speech; sign; symbols; body language; facial expression; gesture; behaviour; art; photographs; objects of reference; games; drawing and playing.

3.134 Recent work suggests innovative ways to engage with and consult disabled children (Beresford, 1997; Sanderson et al, 1997; Ward, 1997; Beecher, 1998; Morris, 1998d; Russell, 1998; Griffiths et al, 1999; Kirkbride, 1999; Marchant et al, 1999; Morris, 1999b; Prewett, 1999). Being alongside children – endeavouring to observe their world from their point of view – can be a potent assessment tool.

3.135 S**tandard assessment approaches may not work**. One parent arrived at her son's annual review with a blank, chewed copy of the form she had been sent to record his views. She wrote to social services:

> *I have no problem with you consulting my child. In fact I would like to know how to do so myself But sending him this questionnaire is just bizarre. I showed him the form and he tried to eat it* (Parent of 13 year old boy with severe learning disabilities and autism, personal communication).

3.136 Involve others who can support communication with the child. Find out about the child's communication from the child and from others who know the child well. If possible, ask the child whom to approach. Sometimes communication with a child will need the help of a third party. Independent interpreters are often not available for children with complex needs, whose communication methods may be very idiosyncratic. The ideal is someone who knows the child well, is trusted by the child and is as neutral as possible about the assessment.

> *Paul is 9 and communicates using eye pointing on a personalised communication board of words and symbols. He spends his time at residential school and in foster care. His social worker finds out who can communicate well with him, and offers Paul a choice of three people to help her involve him* ***in the assessment process.***
>
> This gives Paul control within safe boundaries.

3.137 **If parents or others are to be directly involved negotiate clear ground rules at the start**. Sometimes establishing direct communication with a child is far easier than anticipated:

> *Janice is 13 and communicates with gestures, signs and some words although her speech is difficult to understand. Her social worker spent time with her at home and at school. She and Janice became more confident in each others' presence and after two visits were able to communicate directly with each other without any help.*

3.138 **Be responsive and flexible.** The following are suggestions for practitioners about how to be responsive to the needs and views of each child:

- make approaches to the young people responsive and individualised;
- where appropriate, encourage or allow young people to do other things at the same time as communicating (playing, drawing, walking, eating or drinking);
- take interesting things in a bag or folder that you are willing to let the child look through;
- have lots of different ideas ready, and be prepared to abandon them all;
- be non-directive, reflect back to young people what they have said, ask open questions;
- acknowledge if things aren't going well, say if you don't understand, be willing to go back to the beginning and start again;
- listen carefully to everything being communicated, especially where there is a discrepancy between verbal and non-verbal messages;
- don't make assumptions, keep an open mind, check back;
- let it take time, go at the young person's pace, be willing to wait, be willing to take a break, to stop and try again.

Conclusion

3.139 It is an exciting time to be involved in assessment work with disabled children: knowledge and resources are developing rapidly and our understanding of what it means to be disabled are being challenged. Assessment represents a powerful force for change.

3.140 The basic needs of disabled children and their families are no different to those of any other child and family. Those involved in assessments must bear in mind the context, and be both aware of and prepared to challenge disabling barriers in a child's life. Inclusive practice has benefits beyond the effects for individual children and families. Getting assessments right for children with the most complex needs will improve practice with all children.

> *Everybody's got something different about them, and some things are just more different than others. But we're all- I don't know – different in different ways* (Disabled girl of 12, quoted in Cavet, 1999, p.91).

APPENDIX 4
Definitions of Disability and Key Legislation

Children Act 1989

In section 17 of the Children Act 1989 a child is defined as in need if:

a) *he is unlikely to achieve or maintain, or to have the opportunity of achieving or maintaining a reasonable standard of health or development without the provision for him of services by a local under this [Part] of the Act.*

b) *his health or development is likely to be significantly impaired; or further impaired; without the provision for him of such services or*

c) *he is disabled.*

'Development' means physical intellectual emotional social or behavioural development and

'health' means physical or mental health.

The Children Act mirrors the National Assistance 1948 definition of disability, which states that:

A child is disabled i/he is blind, deaf or dumb or suffers from mental disorder of any kind or is substantially and permanently handicapped by illness, injury or congenital deformity or such other disability as may be prescribed.

World Health Organisation

There have been ongoing debates in the United Kingdom and elsewhere about definitions of disability. The World Health Organisation defines disability under four key headings, namely:

a) A disorder: a medically definable condition such as spina bifida;

b) An impairment: any loss or abnormality of physiological, psychological or anatomical function or structure (eg paraplegia);

c) A disability: any restriction or loss arising from an impairment, of the ability to carry out an activity in a way or within the range of that would be considered normal for a person of a similar age (eg the ability to walk);

d) A handicap: the impact of the impairment or disability upon the individual's pursuit or achievement of the goals which he/she wishes or expects, or which may be desired or expected by him/her or by society (eg. The inability to undertake particular forms of employment or to live independently) .

The World Health Organisation definitions are currently under review.

Disability Discrimination Act 1995

The Disability Discrimination Act (1995) defines a disabled person as someone who has:

> *A physical or mental impairment which has a substantial and long-term adverse effects on his ability to carry out normal day-to-day activities.*

The Disability Rights Task Force (1999) identified a number of weaknesses within the DDA definition of disability and its interpretation. It has therefore recommended that the Disability Rights Commission, when established, should further review and consult on the question of definitions of disability.

Disabled People's International

Organisations of disabled people have become increasingly concerned at the impact of negative definitions of disability, arguing that the social model of disability should be adopted in place of a model based upon deficits. The British Council of Disabled People has adopted Disabled People's International's definitions of disability, namely that:

> Disability is the loss or limitation of the ability to take part in the normal life of the community on an equal level with others, due to physical and social barriers.

Education Act 1996

The majority of (although not all) children with disabilities will also have special educational needs. Section 316 of the Education Act 1996 defines disability in the context of special educational needs as follows:

Section 312(1)

> *A child has special educational needs' for the purposes of this Act if he has a learning difficulty which calls for special education provision to be made for him.*

A child may be defined as having a learning difficulty calling for special educational provision if:

> *He has a disability which either prevents or hinders him from making use of educational facilities of a kind generally provided for children of his age in schools within the area of the local education authority.*

Any assessment of a child with a disability should not only have regard to definitions of disability under the Children Act 1989 and the Disability Discrimination Act 1995 (with reference to access to goods and services) but also consider the implications of the child's disability for his educational development and progression.

Some Key Legislation Relevant to the Assessment of Disabled Children

The following legislation is of particular relevance to the assessment of disabled children:

The Carers (Representation and Services) Act 1995

The Carers' Act makes provision for parents and carers (including young carers) to request independent assessments of their needs, when the child or adult cared for is undergoing as assessment under Section 47 of the NHS and Community Care Act 1990, the Children Act 1989 or the Chronically Sick and Disabled Persons Act 1970.

The Children Act 1989

The Children Act 1989 brings together most public and private law relating to children in England and Wales. Section 17 clarifies the position of children with disabilities as *children in need* and therefore eligible for a range of services and support from the local authority. Schedule 2 permits a local authority to assess a child's needs at the same time as other assessments under different legislation (for example under the Education Act 1996) , *The Children Act 1989 Guidance and Regulations, Volume 6:' Children with Disabilities* gives further information.

The Chronically Sick and Disabled Persons Act 1970 (CSDPA)

Section 2 of the CSDPA requires authorities to make arrangements for the provision of a number of services (such as practical assistance in the home or access to leisure and recreational facilities) if they are satisfied that it is necessary to do so in order to meet the disabled person's needs.

The Community Care (Direct Payments) Act 1996

The Community Care (Direct Payments) Act is designed to enable local authorities to make direct payments to service users in order to purchase their own communication care.

The Carers and Disabled Children 8ill

The Carers and Disabled Children Bill proposes, subject to Royal Assent, to extend direct payments to disabled 16 and 17 year olds and to parents of disabled children.

The Disability Discrimination Act 1995 (DDA)

From December 1996 it has been unlawful for service providers to treat disabled people less favourably for a reason related to their disability. Since October 1999, service providers (including health and social services) have been required to make 'reasonable adjustments' or provide an alternative method of service when practices, policies or procedures to make it impossible or unreasonably difficult for a disabled child or adult to use the service in question. The *Code of Practice on Rights of Access: Goods, Facilities, Services and Premises* (1999) sets out the relevant duties for local authorities in the provision of services. A Disability Rights Commission was established in April 2000.

The Disabled Persons (Services, Consultation and Representation) Act 1986 (DPA)

This Act supplements the provisions of the CSDPA 1970. Section 4 requires authorities to assess need for services under Section 2 of the CSDPA. Sections 5 and 6 require authorities to identify disabled school leavers and assess their need for social services. Section 9 amends the Section 1 of the CSDPA with regard to provision of information.

The Education Act 1996

The Education Act 1996 specifies the procedures to be followed by Local Education Authorities (LEAs) with regard to the identification and assessment of children with special educational needs and any special educational provision arising from assessment. The Act is accompanied by a Code of Practice (*Code of Practice on the Identification and Assessment of Special Education Needs* (1994)) which clarifies the contributions of social services departments and child health services, as well as schools and the LEA, in assessing special educational needs.

The Local Government and Housing Act 1999

Under section 114, local housing authorities are able to give *disabled facilities grants* to disabled people (including disabled children) to help with the costs of adaptations to enable them to live as independently as possible in their own homes.

The NHS and Community Care Act 1990

The NHS and Community Care Act 1990 requires social services departments to assess the needs of persons who may require community care services and, if appropriate, to provide 'care packages' in the light of the users' circumstances. The Act relates to adults and not to children, but is relevant to assessment for transition plans.

References – Chapter 3

ABCD (1993) *Abuse and Disabled Children: Training and Resource Pack for Trainers in Child Protection and Disability*. The NSPCC, London.

Adcock K and Stanley G (1996) *Sexual Health, Education and Children and Young People with Learning Disabilities*. BILD, Kidderminster.

Alderson P (1993) *Childrens Consent to Surgery*. Open University Press, Buckingham.

Aldridge M and Wood J (1998) *Interviewing Children: A Guide for Childcare and Forensic Practitioners*. Wiley, Chichester.

Aldridge M and Wood J (1999) Interviewing child witnesses with disabilities: A survey of police officers in England and Wales. *The Police Journal*. January 1999. pp.33-42.

The aMaze Project (1997) *Through the Maze: An information handbook for parents of children with special needs*. aMaze, Brighton.

Argent Hand Kerrane A (1997) *Taking Extra Care: Respite, Shared and Permanent Care for Children with Disabilities*. BAAF, London.

Audit Commission (1994) *Seen but not Heard: Co-ordinating Community Child Health and Social Services*. HMSO, London.

Bakheit M, Chamba R, Griffiths J, Lee D and Marchant R (1999) *Recommendations for minimum standards of health care in children with cerebral palsy*. Bell-Pottinger Health Care.

Beecher W (1998) *Having a Say! Disabled Children and Effective Partnership: Section 2 – practice Initiatives and Selected Annotated References*. Council for Disabled Children, London.

Beresford B (1994) *Positively Parents: Caring for a Severely Disabled*. Child Social Policy Research Unit, York.

Beresford B (1995) *Expert Opinions: A National Survey of Parents Caring for a Severely Disabled Child*. Policy Press, Bristol.

Beresford B (1997) *Personal Accounts: Involving Disabled Children in Research*. Social Policy Research Unit, York.

Brearley G (1997) *Counselling Children with Special Needs*. Blackwell Science, Oxford.

Briggs F (1995) *Developing Personal Safety Skills in Children with Disabilities*. Jessica Kingsley, London.

Cavet J (1998) *People Don't Understand: Children, Young People and their Families living with a Hidden Disability*. National Children's Bureau, London.

Chamba R, Ahmad W; Hirst M, Lawton D and Beresford B (1999) *On the Edge: Minority Ethnic Families Caring for a Severely Disabled Child*. Policy Press, London.

Chailey Heritage (1997) *Guidelines for Good Practice in Consent to Examination or Treatment*. Chailey Heritage, Sussex.

Children Act 1989 (1989) HMSO, London.

Cross M (1998) *Proud Child; Safer Child: A Handbook for Parents and Carers of Disabled Children*. Women's Press, London.

Department for Education and Employment (1994) *The Code of Practice on the Identification and Assessment of Special Educational Needs.* HMSO, London.

Department for Education and Employment (1997) *Making Connections: A Guide for agencies helping young people with disabilities make the transition from school to adulthood.* The Stationery Office, London.

Department of Health (1991) *The Children Act 1989 Guidance and Regulations: Volume 6. Children with Disabilities.* HMSO, London.

Department of Health (1994) *Services to Disabled Children and their Families: Report of the National Inspection.* Department of Health, London.

Department of Health (1998a) *Disabled Children: Directions for their Future Care.* Department of Health, London.

Department of Health (1998b) *Removing Barriers for Disabled Children: Inspection of Services to Disabled Children and their Families.* Department of Health, London.

Department of Health (1999) *Stepping away from the edge.* Department of Health, London.

Department of Health, Department for Education and Employment and The Home Office (2000) *Framework for the Assessment of Children in Need and their Families.* The Stationery Office, London.

Department of Health, Home Office, Department for Education and Employment (1999) *Working Together to Safeguard Children: A guide to inter-agency working to safeguard and promote the welfare of children.* The Stationery Office, London.

Department of Health and the Welsh Office (1997) *People Like Us. The Report of the Review of the Safeguards for Children Living Away from Home.* The Stationery Office, London.

Disability Discrimination Act 1995 (1995) The Stationery Office, London.

Dobson Band Middleton S (1999) *Paying to Care: The Cost of Childhood Disability.* York Publishing Services, York.

Education Act 1996 (1996) The Stationery Office, London.

French S (1993) *Can you see the Rainbow? The roots of denial.* In Finkelstein V (ed) *Disabling Barriers, Enabling Environments.* Sage, London.

French S (1996) *Out of Sight, Out of Mind: The experience and effects of a 'special' residential school.* In Morris J (ed) *Encounters with Strangers: Feminism and Disability.* Women's Press, London.

Griffiths J, Cunningham G and Dick S (1999) *Onwards and Upwards: Involving Disabled Children and Young People in Decision Making.* Children in Scotland, Edinburgh.

Howlin P (1998) *Children with Autism and Asperger Syndrome: A Guide for Practioners and Carers.* Wiley, Chichester.

Humphries Sand Gordon P (1992) *Out of Sight: The experience of Disability 1900–1950.* Northcote House, London.

Hurst M and Baldwin S (1994) *Unequal Opportunities: Growing up Disabled.* HMSO, London.

Joseph Rowntree Foundation (1999) *Supporting Disabled Children and their Families: summary of research findings.* Joseph Rowntree Foundation, York.

Kagan C, Lewis Sand Heaton P (1998) *Caring to Work: Accounts of Working Parents of Disabled Children.* Family Policy Studies Centre, London.

Khan J and Russell P (1999) *Quality Protects: First analysis of management action plans with reference to disabled children and families.* Council for Disabled Children, London.

Kennedy M (1993a) *You Choose.* National Deaf Children's Society, London.

Kennedy M (1993b) *Safety and prevention programmes.* In ABCD Reader. pp.43-38. The NSPCC, London.

Kirkbride L (1999) *I'll go First: The Planning and Review Toolkit for use with Children with Disabilities.* Children's Society, London.

Knight A (1998) *Valued or Forgotten? Independent Visitors and Disabled Young People.* National Children's Bureau, London.

Lawton D (1998) *Complex Numbers: Families with more than one disabled child.* Social Policy Research Unit, York.

Lee D, McGee A and Ungar S (1998) Issues in the development of a computer based safety programme for children with severe learning difficulties. *Child Abuse Review.* **7**: 343-354.

Loosemore- Reppen G (1999) *Personal Communication.*

Lyons C (1994) *Legal Issues arising from the care and control of Children with Learning Disabilities who also present Severely Challenging Behaviour*: Mental Health Foundation, London.

McConahie H (1997) Organisation of child disability services. *Child: care, health and development.* **23**: 1, pp.3-9.

McCarthy G (1999) *Additional therapies for children with cerebral palsy.* Scope School for Parents Conference.

Marchant R (1998) *Letting it Take Time.* In Ward, L. (ed) *Innovations in Advocacy and Empowerment for People with Intellectual Disabilities.* Liseux Hall, Lancashire.

Marchant R and Cross M (1993) *Places of Safety: Institutions, disabled children and abuse.* In *ABCD Reader.* The NSPCC, London.

Marchant R and Page M (1993) *Bridging the Gap: Child Protection work with Children with Multiple Disabilities.* The NSPCC, London.

Marchant R and Page M (1997) *The Memorandum and Disabled Children.* In Westcott J and Jones J (1997) *Perspectives on the Memorandum: Policy Practice and Research.* Arena, Aldershot.

Marchant R, Jones M, Giles A and Julyan A (1999) *Listening on all Channels: Consulting with Disabled Children.* Triangle, Brighton.

Marchant R and Martyn M (1999) *Make it Happen: Communication Handbook.* Triangle, Brighton.

Meadow R (1999) Mothering to death. *Archives of Diseases in Childhood.* **80**: 359-362.

Mental Health Foundation (1997) *Don't Forget Us: children with learning disabilities and severe challenging behaviour.* Mental Health Foundation, London.

Middleton L (1996) *Making a Difference; Social Work with Disabled Children.* Venture Press, Birmingham.

Middleton L (1999) *Disabled Children; Challenging Social Exclusion.* Blackwell, Oxford.

Morris J (1995) *Gone Missing? A Research and Policy Review of Disabled Children Living away from their Families.* The Who Cares? Trust, London.

Morris J (1998a) *Still Missing? Vol 1; The Experiences of Disabled Children living away from their Families.* The Who Cares? Trust, London.

Morris J (1998b) *Still Missing? Vo12; Disabled Children and the Children Act.* The Who Cares? Trust, London.

Morris J (1998c) *Accessing Human Rights; Disabled Children and the Children Act.* Barnardo's, London.

Morris J (1998d) *Don't Leave us Out; Involving Children and Young People with Communication Impairments.* York Publishing Services, York.

Morris J (1999a) Disabled children, child protection systems and the Children Act 1989. *Child Abuse Review.* **8**:91-108.

Morris J (1999b) *Space for Us; Finding out what Disabled Children and Young People think about their Placements.* Newham Social Services Department, London.

Morris J (1999c) *Move On Up; Supporting Young Disabled People in the transition to Adulthood.* Barnardo's, London.

Mukherjee S, Beresford Band Sloper P (1999) *Unlocking key working; An analysis and evaluation of key worker services for families with disabled children.* The Policy Press/ Community Care, London.

Murphy C C, Boyle C, Schendel D, Decoufle P and Yeargin-Allsop M (1998) Epidemiology of mental retardation in children. *Mental Retardation and Developmental Disabilities Research Reviews.* **4**: 6-13.

Murray P and Penman J (1996) *Let Our Children Be; A Collection of Stories.* Parents with Attitude, Sheffield.

Oldman C and Beresford B (1998) *Homes Unfit for Children; Housing Disabled Children and their Families.* Policy Press, Bristol.

OPCS (1986) *Surveys of Disability in Great Britain. Reports 1-6*: HMSO, London.

Oliver M (1999) *Understanding Disability; From Theory to Practice.* MacMillan, London.

Oswin M (1992) *They Keep Going Away; A critical study of short term residential care services for children with learning difficulties.* Kings Fund Centre, London.

Precey G (1998) Assessment issues in working with mothers who induce illness in their children. *Child and Family Social Work, Vol 3.* Blackwell Science Ltd, London.

Prewett E (1999) *Short Term Break, Long 1erm Benefit; Family based short term care for disabled children and adults.* University of Sheffield and Joseph Rowntree Foundation, Bristol.

Priestley M (1998) Childhood disability and disabled childhoods: agendas for research. *Childhood.* **5**(2): 207-23.

Russell P (1994) *The Children Act 1989: Children and Young People with Learning Difficulties – Some Opportunities and Challenges.* Council for Disabled Children, London.

Russell P (1995) *Positive Choices: Services for Disabled Children Living Away from Home.* Council for Disabled Children, London.

Russell P (1996) *Listening to Children with special educational needs.* In Davie R and Galloway D (eds) *Listening to Children in Education.* David Fulton, London.

Russell P (1998) *Having a Say: Disabled Children and Effective Partnership in Decision Making: Section 1 The Report.* Council for Disabled Children, London.

Russell P (1999) *Personal communication.*

Rutter S and Seyman S (1999) *'He'll never join the army: A report on a survey into attitudes to people with Downs Syndrome amongst medical professionals.* Down's Syndrome Association, London.

Robinson C and Stalker K (eds) (1998) *Growing up with Disability.* Jessica Kingsley, London.

Sanderson H, Kennedy J, Richie P and Goodwin G (1997) *People, Plans and Possibilities: exploring person-centred planning.* SHS, Edinburgh.

Schreiber and Libow (1993) *Hurting for Love – Munchausen by Proxy Syndrome.* Guildford Press, London.

Scott L and Kerr-Edwards L (1999) *Talking Together... about Growing Up: A Workbook for parents of children with learning disabilities.* Family Planning Association, London.

Shakespeare T and Watson D (1998) *Theoretical Perspectives on Research with Disabled Children.* In Robinson C and Stalker K (ed) *Growing up with Disability.* Jessica Kingsley, London.

Townsley R and Robinson C (1999) What rights for disabled children? Home enteral tube feeding in the community. *Children and Society.* **13**: 48-60.

Tozer R (1999) *At the Double: Supporting families with two or more severely disabled children.* National Children's Bureau, London.

Twigg J and Atkin K (1993) *Carers Perceived: Policy and Practice in Informal Care.* OU Press, Buckingham.

Ward L (1997) *Seen and Heard: Involving Disabled Children and Young People in Research and Development Projects.* York Publishing Services, York.

Westcott H (1993) *The Abuse of Disabled Children and Adults.* The NSPCC, London.

Westcott H (1994) *Abuse of children and adults who are disabled.* In French S (ed) (1994) *On Equal Terms: working with disabled people.* Butterworth Heinemann, London.

Westcott Hand Cross M (1996) *This Far and no Further: Towards Ending the Abuse of Disabled Children.* Venture Press, Birmingham.

Westcott H and Jones D (1999) Annotation: The Abuse of Disabled Children. *Journal of Child Psychology and Psychiatry.* **40**(4): 497-506.

4

Resources to assist effective assessment of children in need

Introduction

4.1 This chapter provides information about practice materials, evidence based publications and training resources which were specifically commissioned by the Department of Health as part of the development of the Assessment Framework. It also includes other relevant training materials on which trainers, practitioners and managers may wish to draw. The practice materials are not comprehensive. They do not cover every aspect of the process of assessing children and families, nor every situation in which families may ask or are referred for help. The use of these materials will entail careful discrimination and thought being given to the individual circumstances of each child. They can provide checklists which may be useful for structuring what practitioners observe or discuss, and assist in the precise recording and systematic assembly of information for analysis. They complement but do not replace information gained through interviews and observations.

The collection and recording of information

4.2 Collecting information which will help explain what is happening to children and their families and making sense of that information are key tasks in the assessment process. These tasks require knowledge, confidence and skill, underpinned by regular training and professional supervision. Materials, which help structure practitioners' thinking about the complex worlds of the families with whom they work, which assist them to record systematically and consistently what they have seen and heard, and then aid their analysis and formulation of appropriate plans, can make a significant contribution to the development of high quality work. **Good tools cannot substitute for good practice, but good practice and good tools together can achieve excellence.**

4.3 Recently many local authority social services departments have worked on new and innovative approaches for responding to referrals of children in need. Much of that work has been on finding improved ways of collecting salient information and recording it from the point of referral onwards, and producing assessment forms which reflect a broader approach to families' needs. Some of the national voluntary child care organisations, particularly those running family centres, have found imaginative ways of involving families in identifying their children's needs and distinguishing them from their own needs as parents and adults.

4.4 The **protocols, procedures, forms and methods of record keeping and practice** resources of all authorities and agencies should be consistent with the Assessment Framework and with the principles which underpin its use.

Resources commissioned to assist the assessment process

4.5 The Department of Health commissioned a range of materials to support practice in assessment by providing ideas and increasing the repertoire of tools available to practitioners. The two main developments have been to produce a recording format to assist in the collection and analysis of information gained during an assessment of an individual child and family, and a pack of questionnaires and scales to assist assessment in particular areas, for example child wellbeing or parental mental health. These materials have been tested for their usefulness and validity with local authority and voluntary agency practitioners and managers. The assessment records will be published with the Assessment Framework and refined following further trialing and evaluation during 2000/01. The questionnaires and scales have been published in *The Family Assessment Pack of Questionnaires and Scales* (2000) which also accompanies the Assessment Framework.

Principles underpinning the use of practice materials

4.6 The principles, summarised below, which underpin good assessment work, should be applied in the use of all questionnaires, scales and other practice materials.

PRINCIPLES FOR THE USE OF MATERIALS TO ASSIST ASSESSMENT

Clarity of purpose

Clarity about aims is fundamental to all assessments. Inpractice these can be broad ranging or more focused, depending on timing and context, but in general there will be an intention to gather a range of relevant information in a manner that promotes or sustains a positive working relationship with those being assessed; in most circumstances information is of limited use if collaboration hsa broken down.

Assessment is not a static process

An assessment has many purposes but the process should be theraputic. The assessment should inform the identification of current needs as well as future work, and evaluate the progress and effectiveness of interventions. The way in which the assessment is carried out is important. It should enable those involved to gain fresh perspectives on their family situation, which are in themselves helpful and assist in taking the work forward.

Working with Children and Families is informed by professional judgement

It follows that, although working with children and families is a fundamental principle, this does not mean that every detail on information gained, or in particular the practitioner's judgement about that information, can be shared immediately and in full with those being assessed. Sustaining working relationships and positive therapeutic impact are overriding principles and timing is therefore a consideration in deciding when and how to feed back information.

Assessment does not take place in a vacuum

Assessments benefit from multiple sources of information and multiple methods. Any one source used alone is likely to give either a limited or unbalanced view. This applies to all the main approaches of interviewing, observation, and the use of standardised tests and questionnaires. Limitations should be recognised. Contrasting data from different methods and/or sources are vital to developing a deeper and more bapanced understanding of the child and family's situation.

From: The Family Assessment Pack of Questionnaires and Scales (200) (see paragraph 4.14)

Assessment records

4.7 The Department of Health has commissioned the development of age related assessment records for use by social services front line staff when collecting, collating and analysing information gathered during an assessment of a child and family. These **assessment records of children in need and parenting capacity, within the wider family and community context** (Department of Health and Cleaver, 2000) are both research and practice based, and use the developmental dimensions of the assessment framework. They are underpinned by two important premises: that most parents want to do their best for their children; and that children can be protected from the adverse consequences of parental problems, in circumstances where another significant adult responds appropriately to the child's developmental needs.

4.8 The assessment records cannot replace professional skills, but are tools to assist social workers and other colleagues in the process of assessment, recording and decision making when undertaking an assessment. As such they are designed to help social workers record:

- the child's developmental progress;
- each caregiver's parenting capacity;
- the impact of family and environmental factors.

4.9 In order to obtain the information required to complete the assessment record, practitioners should work in an age appropriate manner, with the child and openly with the child's caregivers. Where appropriate other professionals working with the child and family, such as health workers and teachers, should be involved and their knowledge of the child and family incorporated into the record and subsequent making of judgements. The information required includes identifying the child's developmental progress, who is responding to the child's needs, and areas which should be addressed to ensure optimal outcomes for the child.

4.10 Once these domains have been explored during assessment, the format in which the information is documented on the records will help professionals analyse the child's needs and the capacity of their parents/carers to respond appropriately to those needs. This understanding should inform judgements about the child's situation and decisions about how best to help the particular child, parent(s) and other family members, for example siblings or grandparents.

4.11 The assessment records were the subject of an initial feasibility study and revision process in 1999. The records will, when used well, contribute to the achievement of greater consistency and coherence in the recording of assessments, plans of action and outcomes for children. The records will continue to be consistent with the Looking After Children Assessment and Action Records which are being revised during 19992001. The assessment records will be the subject of more extensive development over a two year period that will include integrating them with the Looking After Children materials. Further work will include ensuring that information gathered for children looked after who were known to the social services department prior to being looked after builds on that already recorded, thus avoiding duplication.

4.12 Information gathered about individual children, when aggregated, will assist local authority management of and planning for children's services. Further development work will be undertaken by the Department of Health, in consultation with key players, to enable salient data on individual children to be used for management information purposes, to assist both local and national planning and management of children's services. These data will also enable judgements to be made about whether the relevant Government objectives for children's social services are being met.

4.13 **A Parenting Assessment Project** which is being undertaken by North Lincolnshire Council, Home-Start and the University of Loughborough is also relevant to the assessment framework. As part of a local parenting assessment project, a process is being developed to help front line non-social services professionals, for example health visitors and teachers visiting or in contact with families, identify those parents who might need additional support in bringing up their children. Forms have been developed, on an age related basis, to help assess the level of concern about a child, the areas of child and family vulnerability and unmet need, and to assist appropriate provision of services or referral to other agencies for help. The process and forms were piloted across agencies in two areas of North Lincolnshire beginning in June 1999. Social services departments will wish to consider taking forward similar work with other agencies to facilitate appropriate referrals of children in need and joint working with vulnerable children.

Use of questionnaires and scales in assessment

4.14 The Family Assessment Pack of Questionnaires and Scales (Department of Health, Cox and Bentovim, 2000) which accompany this practice guidance, contains questionnaires and scales for use by social work and other social services staff for specific purposes when undertaking assessments. It includes the following:

- Strengths and Difficulties Questionnaires;
- Parenting Daily Hassles Scale;
- Home Conditions Assessment;
- Adult Wellbeing Scale;
- Adolescent Wellbeing Scale;
- Recent Life Events Questionnaire;
- Family Activity Scales (in two age bands);
- Alcohol Scale.

4.15 There is a wide range of questionnaires and instruments available for use when assessing children and families. Those set out in paragraph 4.14 were selected because of their appropriateness for the task of undertaking assessments using the Assessment Framework and because they proved easy to incorporate into practice. The eight questionnaires and scales can be used following a process of familiarisation with the materials but do not require any formal training.

4.16 The chosen assessment instruments are concerned with child mental health and development, parental mental health, parenting capacity and the family environment. A description of each questionnaire or scale is given below (Figure 5). They are intended to assist staff undertaking assessments by providing a clear evidence base for judgements and recommendations. The use of these questionnaires and scales requires careful preparation and introduction to families by the practitioner, and a clear explanation of how they fit into an initial or core assessment. Each questionnaire or scale should be used for the purpose for which it was developed. They are intended to contribute to the overall assessment and should be applied with sensitivity and understanding.

Figure 5 **The Family Assessment Questionnaires and Scales**

- **The Strengths and difficulties Questionnaires** (Goodman et al, 1997; Goodman et al, 1998). These scales are a modification of the very widely used instruments to screen for emotional and behavioural problems in children and adolescents – the Rutter A+B scales for parents and teachers. Although similar to Rutter's, the strengths and Difficulties Questionnaire's wording was re-framed to focus on a child's emotional and behavioural strengths as well as difficulties. The actual questionnaire incorporates five scales: pro-social, hyperactivity, emotional problems, conduct (behavioural) problems, and peer problems. In the pack, there are versions of the scale to be completed by adult caregivers, or teachers for children from age 3 to 16, and children between the ages of 11–16. These questionnaires have been used with disabled children and their teachers and carers. They are available in 40 languages on the following website: **http://chp.iop.kcl.ac.uk/sdq/b3.html**
- **The Parenting Daily Hassles Scale** (Crnic and Greenberg, 1990; Crnic and Booth, 1991). This scale aims to assess the frequency and intensity/impact of 20 potential parenting 'daily' hassles experienced by adults caring for children. It has been used in a wide variety of research studies concerned with children and families – particularly families with young children. It has been found that parents (or caregivers) generally like filling it out, because it touches on many aspects of being a parent that are important to them.
- **The Home Conditions Assessment** (The Family Cleanliness Scale. Davie et al, 1984) addresses various aspects of the home environment (for example, smell, state of surfaces in house, floors). The total score has been found to correlate highly with indices of the development of children.
- **Adult Wellbeing Scale** (Irritability, Depression, Anxiety – IDA Scale. Snaith et al, 1978). This scale, which was based on the Irritability, Depressionand Anxiety Scale, was devised by a social worker involved in the pilot. The questions are framed in a 'personal' fashion (i.e. I feel, my appetite is…). This scale looks at how an adult is feeling in terms of their depression, anxiety and irritability. The scale allows the adult to respond from four possible answers, which enables the adult some choice, and therfore less restriction. This could enable the adult to feel more empowered.

- **The Adolescent Wellbeing Scale** (Self-rating Scale for Depression in Young People. Birleson, 1980). It was originally validated for children aged between 7–16. It involves 18 questions each relating to different aspects of a child or adolescent's life, and how they feel about these. As a result of the pilot the wording of some questions was altered in order to be more appropriate to adolescents. Although children as young as seven and eight have used it, older children's thoughts and beliefs about themselves are more stable. The scale is intended to enable practitioners to gain more insight and understanding into how an adolescent feels about their life.

- **The Recent Life Events Questionnaire** This scale was taken from Brugha et al (1985), withn nine additional items added. It focuses on recent life events (ie. those occurring in the last 12 months) but could be used over a longer time-scale. It is intended to assist in the compilation of a social history. Respondents are asked to identify which of the events still affects them. It was hoped that use of the scale will:

  - result in a fuller picture of a family's history and contribute to greater contextual understanding of the family's current situation;
  - help practitioners explore how particular recent life events have affected the carer and the family;
  - in some situations, identify life events which family members have not reported earlier.

- **The Family Activity Scale** (Derived from Th Child-Centredness Scale. Smith, 1985). These scales give practitioners an opportunity to explore with carers the environment provided for their children, through joint activities and support for in dependent activities. This includes information about the cultural and idealogical environment in which children live, as well as how their carers respond to their children's actions (for example, concerning play and independence). They aim to be independent of socio-economic resources. There are two separate scales; one for children aged 2–6, and one for children aged 7–12.

- **The Alchohol Scale** This scale was developed by Piccinelli et al (1997). Alcohol abuse is estimated to be present in about 6% of primary carers, ranking it third in frequency behind major depression and generalised anxiety. Higher rates are found in certain localities, and particularly amongst those parents known to social services departments. Drinking alcohol affects different individuals in different ways. For example, some people may be relatively unaffected by the same amount of alcohol that incapacitates others. The primary concern therefore is not the amount of alcohol consumed, but how it impacts on the individual and, more particularly, on their rolr as a parent. This questionnaire has been found to be effective in detecting individuals with alcohol disorders and those with hazardous drinking habits.

4.17 These eight questionnaires and scales have all been well evaluated. They are widely used in psychology and psychiatry but are not commonly used in social work practice. In 1998/99 they were piloted in a number of different sites within five social services departments as part of the development of the Assessment Framework and found to be helpful.

4.18 Two other instruments, the *Home Inventory* (Caldwell and Bradley, 1984) and the *Assessment of Family Competence, Strengths and Difficulties* (Bentovim and Bingley Miller (forthcoming)) based on the Family measures described by Kinston and Loader (1984) were also piloted and practitioners found them very useful. The Home

Inventory aims to obtain a picture of what the world.is like from a child's perspective and is not, therefore, exclusively focused on the care-giving activities of carers. The Assessment of Family Competence, Strengths and Difficulties provides an approach to assessing children and families which focuses on work in the following areas:

- direct assessment of the family organisation and character;
- completing a family genogram;
- undertaking family tasks;
- assessment of presenting problem/concerns and difficulties;
- exploring parents' background, childhood and developments;
- use of the family conflict tactics scale.

4.19 The pilot indicated that in order to use the above two instruments effectively, practitioners required more substantial training. The materials will be made available later in 2000 for use by practitioners and in training programmes.

4.20 Generally, these questionnaires and scales have been found to have a number of applications in practice:

- to strengthen the voice of the child or family in the assessment process;
- to clarify the nature and extent of need, either raising new issues or revealing new information during their use, or enabling practitioners to reassure families of progress;
- to provide a focus for assessment and a structure for an intervention plan;
- to provide away of structuring discussions with families about issues the families are reluctant or feel unable to discuss;
- to provide an evidence base for reports;
- to monitor progress over time, having an open and agreed understanding between staff and families of areas in which particular changes are planned.

Evidence based publications

4.21 The Department of Health commissioned child protection research studies, which are summarised in *Child Protection: Messages from Research* (Department of Health, 1995b), identified a number of areas where practitioners working with children and families indicated they would benefit from further exploration of the research findings. Four of these have been taken forward in publications on: child sexual abuse; parental mental illness, domestic violence, and problem alcohol and drug use; working with fathers; and communicating with children who may have been traumatised or maltreated. A fifth area identified was working with black and minority ethnic families. This has also been taken forward and is presented in chapter 2 in this publication.

4.22 Using an evidence based approach, the authors of the four publications above reviewed the available research, including relevant studies commissioned by the Department of Health, and their findings have informed the development of the

Assessment Framework. In addition these publications are intended to assist practitioners, managers and policy makers when assessing children and families and deciding which types of intervention are effective in a particular family situation.

4.23 Each publication is summarised below. Readers are encouraged to make extensive use of these publications to inform the evidence base of their work with children and families.

4.24 *Child Sexual Abuse. Informing Practice from Research* (Jones and Ramchandani, 1999) outlines the different ways in which professionals can help children who have experienced sexual abuse. It describes how professional intervention can improve the outcomes for sexually abused children and their families. The authors conclude:

- therapies can help children who have been sexually abused and those based on a cognitive-behavioural model should help the majority of children who are displaying symptoms of distress;
- treatment for children should not take place in isolation, but must include other forms of help, for example, support for the child's carers.

4.25 They suggest an algorithm (Figure 6) for helping a sexually abused child. This can be used by practitioners when deciding how best to help a child who has been sexually abused and by those planning appropriate resources for this group of children and their families.

4.26 *Childrens Needs – Parenting Capacity* (Cleaver et al, 1999) addresses how parental mental illness, problem alcohol and drug misuse, and domestic violence have an impact on children's development. These potential problems affect each child differently depending on their age and circumstances. The publication focuses on children of different age groups and explores both the possible negative consequences of parenting issues and the buffering or protective factors. Practitioners can draw on this knowledge when assessing and intervening in families where there are such problems. This work underpins the assessment records under development by the Department of Health and Hedy Cleaver (see paragraphs 4.7 to 4.11).

4.27 In *Working with Fathers* (Ryan, 2000) the roles of men in contemporary society are examined and the impact of fathers on their children's development is explored. Within the general context of the role of fathers in society, findings are presented from a number of child protection studies which found that fathers were not being engaged in child and family work. Even in situations where the father was a positive and valued person in his child's life, the focus of practitioners was on mothers and children. This publication provides examples from practice on how to work with different types of fathers including those who are violent and abusive, whilst ensuring children's safety.

4.28 *Communicating with children who may have been traumatised or maltreated* (Jones, forthcoming) reviews the international literature and suggests how this knowledge can be used by practitioners in their work with children, and where there are concerns to assist children to tell their story. An important consideration is ensuring that children's communications, which may be used as evidence in criminal court processes, are appropriately managed so as not to jeopardise any legal proceedings.

Figure 6[3]

An Algorithm For Helping Children Who Have Been Sexually Abused

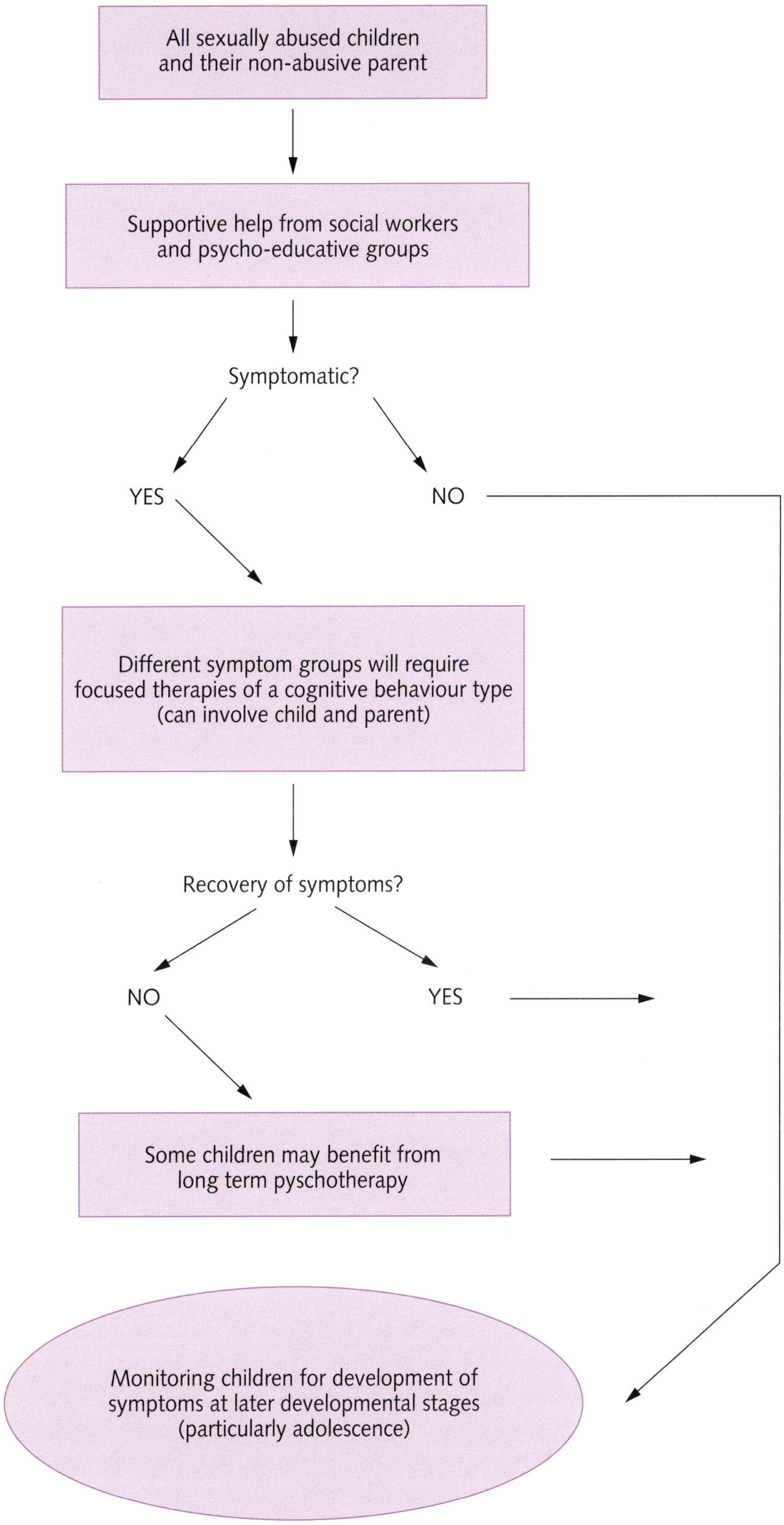

3. Reproduced with kind permission from the authors of *Child Sexual Abuse: Research into Practice* (1999) Jones D P Hand Ramchandani P. Radcliffe Medical Press, Abingdon.

4.29 Four studies (Department of Health, 2000) were undertaken to inform the development of the Assessment Framework. These were:

- *A review of the social work literature on assessment.* This work has made a significant contribution to the theoretical basis of the Assessment Framework. It also identifies that the theory of social work practice requires updating to take account of developments in practice over the past twenty years.
- *A study of different structures and types of assessments undertaken in a variety of settings* – social services departments, health service, voluntary agencies, family centres which were either single agency or multi-disciplinary contexts. It suggests the type of settings, structures and cultures that facilitate assessment work.
- *A study of the language used by social workers to describe the needs of children.* A key finding was that where the Looking After Children materials were being used by social workers, they were describing the needs of children according to the seven child developmental dimensions.
- *A summary of the findings on assessment .from child care inspections undertaken by the Social Services Inspectorate during the period 1993-1997*: The report identifies key messages for practitioners, managers and policy makers in relation to assessment.

4.30 These four studies provide a valuable source of information about contemporary practice and thinking. The intention is that they will inform the field, and assist in understanding the background and principles underpinning the Assessment Framework, as well as assist its implementation.

Training resources

4.31 Training is a critical component of any strategy to implement new policy or practice and to embed it into everyday practice. To support the development of knowledge and skills, and to provide learning opportunities for practitioners to become familiar with the Assessment Framework and associated practice materials, a training pack has been developed concurrently with the Guidance. This pack has been designed to be used also in future training on the Assessment Framework and to be adapted for a variety of training purposes. Selected training resources either commissioned by or produced with the Department of Health have also been identified to help practitioners with some of the specific issues which may arise when undertaking a child and family assessment.

4.32 *The Childs World: Assessing Children in Need. 7raining and Development Pack* was commissioned by the Department of Health and produced by the NSPCC and the University of Sheffield (2000) . It consists of:

- **A Video** of trigger material highlighting issues about assessment in a variety of different circumstances. The material is presented in six scenarios, covering different aspects of assessment practice, and by children and young people including disabled young people, describing their experiences of assessment. The scenarios focus on planning the initial stages of an initial or core assessment but can be used for all stages in the process.

- **A Training Guide** which provides trainers with activities, materials and guidance to facilitate learning for a range of different audiences, although primarily aimed at social services staff. It includes four modules:
  - Introduction to the Assessment Framework;
  - The process of assessment;
  - Assessing children's developmental needs within their family and environmental context;
  - Assessing parenting capacity to respond to their child's developmental needs within their environmental context.
- **A Reader** designed to provide practitioners, front-line managers and trainers with an overview of theory, research and practice developments relevant to assessing children in need and their families. The Reader consists of four modules:
  - The framework: background and context;
  - The assessment process: the task for practitioners and their supervisors;
  - The developmental needs of children: research, theory and practice implications;
  - Parenting capacity: factors that impact on carers ability to respond appropriately to the needs of children in their care.

4.33 The Reader can be purchased separately from the rest of the Pack (Horwath (ed), 2000). It is a valuable source of reference for those using the Assessment Framework, and provides a route to further study of contemporary theory and research by practitioners and their managers.

4.34 The objectives of the training and development pack are to provide trainers with resources to:

- support the implementation and use of the Guidance on assessing children in need and their families;
- support the implementation and continuing understanding of *Working Together to Safeguard Children* (1999) in relation to the assessment of children where there are concerns about significant harm;
- enable practitioners and managers to become familiar with the Assessment Framework and to develop the necessary knowledge, skills and attitudes to use the framework in practice;
- provide learning opportunities to improve the quality of assessments and outcomes for children in need;
- enable practitioners and managers to use the framework in the context of national and local policies and resources;
- provide a link between training based on this material and relevant qualifying and post qualifying awards.

4.35 Key texts and articles as well as training programmes are also highlighted in the directory *Undertaking Assessments of Children And Families* (Connolly and Shemmings, 1998). This publication was commissioned by the Department of Health as a resource for those involved in training and for use by individuals who may wish to pursue their own independent professional learning. The directory of training materials, key texts and programmes is divided into seven sections, covering respectively the areas of Training Packs, Videos, Open Learning Materials, Computer based Information Services, Key Texts and Articles, Post-Qualifying Courses and NVQ Based Learning Opportunities. It describes the materials briefly in order to help the reader decide which materials will be helpful for the purpose, but does not evaluate them. It is a comprehensive source of reference to inform planning the implementation and use of this Guidance through training and continuing professional development.

4.36 Two training packs were commissioned by the Department of Health to assist staff working in both adult and children's services to ensure that children's development will not be adversely affected when their parents have problems with mental illness or domestic violence respectively. They complement Cleaver et al's publication *Childrens Needs – Parenting Capacity* (1999).

Parental Mental Health

Crossing Bridges – Training resources for working with mentally ill parents and their children (1998) It contains a reader for managers, practitioners and trainers which in turn introduces and supports the associated training materials. Information is provided on:

- key topics in adult mental health
- parenting and parent – child relationships
- child development and mental health
- legislation
- implications for practice

Domestic Violence

Making an Impact. Children and Domestic Violence (1998)
This pack also contains a reader and training pack which have been designed to ensure ready availability of training for front line staff dealing with domestic violence.

4.37 A third training pack, to be published later in 2000, has been commissioned by the Department of Health to assist adult and children's services staff work together. It's focus is on working with physically disabled parents and their children, assessing their needs and providing appropriate services.

4.38 Five further training packs, which the Department of Health either commissioned or was closely involved in their development, are also relevant to practitioners. They address a number of key areas relating to the Assessment Framework. The contents of these are set out below.

Direct work with children

Turning Points: A Resource Pack for Communicating with Children (1997) NSPCC in association with Chailey Heritage, with support of the Department of Health.

This pack promotes a child-centred approach to working with children and young people, including those who are disabled. It builds on the principles of the Children Act 1989 and endorses Article 12 of the United Nations Convention on the Rights of the Child, placing emphasis on the rights of children not only to be protected, but also to have their voice heard.

Involving young people in the process of assessment

In on the Act – A Training Programme for relevant Professionals (1999) Shemmings D, School of Social Work, University of East Anglia.

The programme has four main aims:

- To raise participants' awareness of key dilemmas for practitioners when increasing the involvment of children in family support and child protection;
- To offer professionals taking part the chance to explore new ways of involving children in decision-making;
- To give participants an opportunity to improve their skills by considering practical examples from the fields of family support and child protection;
- To help professionals discuss the options and consequences of different outcomes when children are consulted about decisions which affect their lives.

Family Decision Making

Family Group Conferences: A Training Pack (1998) Morris K, Marsh P, and Wiffen J, The Family Rights Group, London

The PAck contains background information about Family Group Conferences and contains a number of exercises which address the following areas:

- The Family Group Conference Model
- The context for Family Group Conferences
- Attitudes to families and a consideration of the need for change
- Skills development
- Local knowledge

Working with separated children and young people living outside their Country of Origin

Unaccompanied Asylum-Seeking Children; A Training Pack (1995) Social Services Inspectorate, Department of Health and Surrey County Council Council. This pack contains practice guidance and information about relevant resources. It pays particular attention to sensitive issues for consideration when assessing children in these circumstances.

Assessing the progres of looked after children

- *Looking after Children: Training Resource Pack* (1995a) Department of Health. It contains a comprehensive set of materials which can be used flexibly to support up to two days of training for social workers, foster carers, residential workers, students and others who have some responsibility for looking after children. It comprises:
- **Management and Implementation Guide** This contains key information for managers and supervisors about organisational and practice issues.
- **Training Guide** Contains introductory materials, guidance on setting up a training programme, sample training programmes with workshops, reading materials, learning exercises, case examples and other resources to support staff training and development.
- **Training Video** A 50-minute VHS tape, which shows the Assessment and Action Records being used by social workers and foster carers with six children and young people and their families. Inter-agency aspects of this work are also highlighted.
- **Video Notes** A book containing notes about the video and its use in training.
- **Reader** This contains short papers which address the concepts and philosophy supporting the Looking After Children materials; the developmental dimensions; and practice issues.
- **Demonstrating Documents** Two completen sets of Looking After Children documents.

4.39 Two publications *Adoption Now: Messages from Research* (Department of Health, 1999) and the *The Children Act 1989 Now: Messages from Research* (Department of Health, forthcoming) summarise major Department of Health commissioned studies on Adoption and the Children Act 1989 respectively. These are important resources for improving practice in work with children and families.

4.40 The materials should be used extensively and imaginatively in qualifying training, continuing study and private learning by all those with responsibility for work with children and families. Of critical importance is keeping up to date to ensure a sound basis of knowledge for evidence based practice.

References – Chapter 4

Bentovim A and Bingley Miller L (forthcoming) *Assessment of Family Competence, Strengths and Difficulties.*

Birleson P (1980) The validity of depressive disorder in childhood and the development of a self-rating scale: A research report. *Journal of Child Psychology and Psychiatry.* **22**: 73-88.

Brugha T, Bebington P, Tennant C and Hurry J (1985) The list of threatening experiences: A subset of 12 life event categories with considerable long-term contextual threat. *Psychological Medicine.* **15**: 189-194.

Caldwell B M and Bradley RH(1984) *Home Observation for Measurement of the Environment – Administration Manual (revised edition).* University of Arkansas, Arkansas.

Cleaver H, Unell land Aldgate J (1999) *Childrens Needs – Parenting Capacity: The impact of parental mental illness, problem alcohol and drug use, and domestic violence on childrens development.* The Stationery Office, London.

Code of Practice for the Disability Discrimination Rights of Access – Goods, Facilities, Services and Premises. The Stationery Office, London.

Connolly J and Shemmings D (1998) *Undertaking Assessments of Children and Families: A directory of training materials, courses and key texts.* University of East Anglia, Norwich.

Crime and Disorder Act 1998 (1998) The Stationery Office, London.

Crnic K A & Greenberg M T (1990) Minor parenting stresses with young children. *Child Development.* **61**: 1628-1637.

Crnic K A & Booth CL (1991) Mothers' and fathers' perceptions of daily hassles of parenting across early childhood. *Journal of Marriage and the Family.* **53**: 1043-1050.

Davie C E, Hutt S J, Vincent E and Mason M (1984) *The young child at home.* NFER-Nelson, Windsor.

Department of Health (1995a) *Looking After Children: Training Pack.* HMSO, London.

Department of Health (1995b) *Child Protection: Messages from Research.* HMSO, London.

Department of Health (1999) *Adoption Now: Messages from Inspection.* Wiley, Chichester.

Department of Health (2000) *Studies which inform the development of the Framework for the Assessment of Children in Need and their Families.* The Stationery Office, London.

Department of Health (forthcoming) *The Children Act 1989 Now: Messages from Research.* The Stationery Office, London.

Department of Health and Cleaver H (2000) *Assessment Recording Forms.* The Stationery Office, London.

Department of Health, Cox A and Bentovim A (2000) *The Family Assessment Pack of Questionnaires and Scales*. The Stationery Office, London.

Department of Health, Home Office, Department for Education and Employment (1999) *Working Together to Safeguard Children: A guide to inter-agency working to safeguard and promote the welfare of children*. The Stationery Office, London.

Department of Health, University of Bristol, the NSPCC and Barnardos (1998) *Making an Impact: Children and Domestic Violence: Training Resource*. Barnardos, London.

Falkov A, Mayes K, Diggins M, Silverdale N, and Cox A (1998) *Crossing Bridges – Training resources for working with mentally ill parents and their children*. Pavilion Publishing, Brighton.

Goodman R (1997) The Strengths and Difficulties Questionnaire: A Research Note. *Journal of Child Psychology and Psychiatry*. **38**: 581- 586.

Goodman R, Meltzer H and Bailey V (1998) The strengths and difficulties questionnaire: A pilot study on the validity of the self-report version. *European Child and Adolescent Psychiatry*. 7: 125-130.

Horwath J. (ed) (2000) *The Childs World: Assessing Children in Need. The Reader*. The NSPCC, London.

Jones D and Ramchandani P (1999) *Child Sexual Abuse: Informing Practice from Research*. Radcliffe Medical Press. Abingdon.

Jones D P H (forthcoming) *Communicating with children who may have been traumatised or maltreated (working title).*

Kinston W and Loader P (1988) The Family Task Interview: A tool for clinical research in family interaction. *Journal of Marital and Family Therapy*. **14**: 67-87.

Marsh P and Peel M (1999) *Leaving Care in Partnership: family involvement with care leavers*. The Stationery Office, London.

Morris K, Marsh P and Wiffin J (1998) *Family Group Conferences – A Training Pack*. The Family Rights Group, London.

The NSPCC in association with Chailey Heritage and Department of Health (1997) *Turning Points: A Resource Pack for Communicating with Children*. The NSPCC, London.

The NSPCC and the University of Sheffield (2000) *The Childs World: Assessing Children in Need. Training and Development Pack*. The NSPCC, London.

Piccinelli M, Tessari E, Bortolomasi M, Piasere 0, Semenzin M, Garzotto Nand Tansella M (1997) Efficacy of the alcohol use disorders identification test as a screening tool for hazardous alcohol intake and related disorders in primary care: A validity study. *British Medical Journal*. **514**: 420-424.

Ryan M (2000) *Working with Fathers*. Radcliffe Medical Press, Abingdon.

Shemmings D (1999) *In on the Act – A Training Programme for Relevant Professionals. School of Social Work*, University of East Anglia, Norwich.

Smith M A (1985) *The Effects of Low Levels of Lead on Urban Children: The relevance of social factors*. Ph.D. Psychology, University of London.

Snaith R P, Constantopoulos A A, Jardine M Y and McGuffin P (1978) A clinical scale for the self-assessment of irritability. *British Journal of Psychiatry*. **132**: 164-171.

Social Services Inspectorate and Surrey County Council (1995) *Unaccompanied Asylum-Seeking Children: A Training Pack*. Department of Health, London.

The Family Pack of Questionnaires and Scales

A Cox and A Bentovim

Department of Health

The Family Pack of Questionnaires and Scales

A Cox and A Bentovim

London: TSO

Social Care Group

The Social Care Group is one of the four business groups in the Department of Health. It is jointly headed by the Chief Social Services Inspector and the Head of Social Care Policy. It supports Ministers in promoting high quality, cost effective services through

- national policies
- support to external social care agencies
- inspection

The Social Services Inspectorate is a part of the Social Care Group. It is headed by the Chief Social Services Inspector who is the principal professional advisor to Ministers on social services and related matters.

First published 2000

Fifth impression 2008

Family Activity Scales and Life Events Scale reproduced with the kind permission of MA Smith

Strengths and Difficulties Questionnaire reproduced with the kind permission of R Goodman

Adolscent Wellbeing Scale reproduced with the kind permission of Professor D Skuse, Editor, Journal of Child Psychology and Psychiatry and Allied Disciplines.

Alcohol Use Disuaders reproduced with the kind permission of Richard Smith, Editor, British Medical Journal.

Home Conditions reproduced with the kind permission of Routledge Publishers

Adult Wellbeing Scale reproduced with the kind permission of Dr P Snaith

Parenting Daily Hassles Scales reproduced with the kind permission of Professor R Carnic

ISBN 9780113224265

Published by The Stationery Office Ltd

Printed in the United Kingdom for The Stationery Office
ID5913501 C2 9/08

Contents

Assessing the Needs of Children and Families: Using Questionnaires and Scales

1 Introduction

This pack, which accompanies the Framework for the Assessment of Children in Need and their Families (2000), sets out how a number of questionnaires and scales can be used by social work and other social services staff when assessing children and their families. The materials were piloted in a number of child care situations within five social service departments and modified to suit children and families and the requirements of staff working in this setting. The instruments can assist staff preparing reports for the Court, by providing a clear evidence base for the judgements and recommendations made regarding a child, and inform the child care plan.

2 Summary of Questionnaires and Scales

The following eight questionnaires and scales are included in the pack:

2.1 **The Strengths and Difficulties Questionnaires** (Goodman, 1997; Goodman *et al*, 1998). These scales are a modification of the very widely used instruments to screen for emotional and behavioural problems in children and adolescents – the Rutter A + B scales for parents and teachers. Although similar to Rutter's, the Strengths and Difficulties Questionnaire's wording was re-framed to focus on a child's emotional and behavioural strengths as well as difficulties. The actual questionnaire incorporates five scales: pro-social, hyperactivity, emotional problems, conduct (behavioural) problems, and peer problems. In the pack, there are versions of the scale to be completed by adult caregivers, or teachers for children from age 3 to 16, and young people between the ages of 11–16. These questionnaires have been used with disabled children and their teachers and carers. They are available in 40 languages on the following website: *http://chp.iop.kcl.ac.uk/sdq/b3.html*

2.2 **The Parenting Daily Hassles Scale** (Crnic and Greenberg, 1990; Crnic and Booth, 1991). This scale aims to assess the frequency and intensity/impact of 20 potential parenting 'daily' hassles experienced by adults caring for children. It has been used in a wide variety of research studies concerned with children and families – particularly families with young children. It has been found that parents (or caregivers) generally like filling it out, because it touches on many aspects of being a parent that are important to them.

2.3 **Home Conditions Scale** (The Family Cleanliness Scale. Davie et al, 1984) addresses various aspects of the home environment (for example, smell, state of surfaces in house, floors). The total score has been found to correlate highly with indices of the development of children.

2.4 **Adult Wellbeing Scale** (Irritability, Depression, Anxiety – IDA Scale. Snaith *et al*, 1978). This scale, which was based on the Irritability, Depression and Anxiety Scale, was devised by a social worker involved in the pilot. The questions are framed in a 'personal' fashion (i.e. I feel, my appetite is…). This scale looks at how an adult is feeling in terms of their depression, anxiety and irritability. The scale allows the adult to respond from four possible answers, which enables the adult some choice, and therefore less restriction. This could enable the adult to feel more empowered.

2.5 **The Adolescent Wellbeing Scale** (Self-rating Scale for Depression in Young People. Birleson, 1980). It was originally validated for children aged between 7–16. It involves 18 questions each relating to different aspects of a child or adolescent's life, and how they feel about these. As a result of the pilot the wording of some questions was altered in order to be more appropriate to adolescents. Although children as young as seven and eight have used it, older children's thoughts and beliefs about themselves are more stable. The scale is intended to enable practitioners to gain more insight and understanding into how an adolescent feels about their life.

2.6 **The Recent Life Events Questionnaire** This scale was taken from Brugha *et al* (1985), with nine additional items added. It focuses on recent life events (ie. those occurring in the last 12 months) but could be used over a longer time-scale. It is intended to assist in the compilation of a social history. Respondents are asked to identify which of the events still affects them. It is intended that use of the scale will:

- result in a fuller picture of a family's history and contribute to greater contextual understanding of the family's current situation;
- help practitioners explore how particular recent life events have affected the carer and the family;
- in some situations, identify life events which family members have not reported earlier.

2.7 **The Family Activity Scale** (Derived from The Child-Centredness Scale. Smith, 1985). These scales give practitioners an opportunity to explore with carers the environment provided for their children, through joint activities and support for independent activities. This includes information about the cultural and ideological environment in which children live, as well as how their carers respond to their children's actions (for example, concerning play and independence). They aim to be independent of socio-economic resources. There are two separate scales; one for children aged 2–6, and one for children aged 7–12.

2.8 **The Alcohol Scale** This scale was developed by Piccinelli et al (1997). Alcohol abuse is estimated to be present in about 6% of primary carers, ranking it third in frequency behind major depression and generalised anxiety. Higher rates are found in certain localities, and particularly amongst those parents known to social services departments. Drinking alcohol affects different individuals in different ways. For example, some people may be relatively unaffected by the same amount of alcohol that incapacitates others. The primary concern therefore is not the amount of alcohol consumed, but how it impacts on the individual and, more particularly, on their role as a parent. This questionnaire has been found to be effective in detecting individuals with alcohol disorders and those with hazardous drinking habits.

3 Principles underpinning the use of the questionnaires and scales

3.1 **Clarity of Purpose.** Clarity about aims is fundamental to all assessment. In practice these can be broad ranging or more focused, depending on timing and context, but in general there will be an intention to gather a range of relevant information in a manner that promotes, or sustains, a working relationship with the children and families being assessed: in most circumstances information is of limited use if collaboration has broken down.

3.2 **Assessment is not a static process.** The process of assessment should be therapeutic. An assessment has many purposes. It should inform future work, and evaluate the progress of interventions. The way in which the assessment is carried out is also important. It should enable those involved to gain fresh perspectives on their family situation, which are in themselves therapeutic.

3.3 **Partnership is informed by professional judgement.** It follows that, although partnership is a fundamental principle, this does not mean that every detail of information gained, or in particular the practitioners judgement about that information, is shared immediately and in full with those being assessed. Sustaining partnership and positive therapeutic impact are overriding principles.

3.4 **Assessment does not take place in a vacuum.** Assessments benefit from multiple sources of information, and multiple methods. Any one source used alone is likely to give either a limited or unbalanced view. This applies to all the main approaches: interviewing, observation, and the use of standardised tests and questionnaires. Limitations should be recognised. Contrasting data from different methods and/or sources is vital to develop a deeper and more balanced understanding of the situation.

4 Background

4.1 Many practitioners will be unfamiliar with the use of instruments in day-to-day practice. They are often thought to be limited, judgmental, and superficial. However these are dangers with all assessment approaches. The vital issue is **how and when** an approach is used.

4.2 Standardised Questionnaires and Scales must be distinguished from Standardised and Semi-structured interviews. Questionnaires are (usually) brief, use set questions, and are frequently designed to be completed by a respondent – a person who is being assessed or contributing to the assessment, but is not themselves the professional with responsibility for pulling together the whole picture.

4.3 The respondent does not have to interact directly with the assessor while they are completing the questionnaire and can, therefore, concentrate on **voicing their needs** and concerns unimpeded. Indeed, there is evidence that responses to questionnaires can be more frank than in an interview.

4.4 Although most questionnaires have been designed to be completed by respondents, they can be used in other ways, for example as **mental check-lists** for the assessor, either with regard to what they observe or what they take up with the respondent. They can be administered verbally, or provide prompts that are the basis for further discussion.

4.5 In whatever ways they have been used or presented in day-to-day practice, questionnaires should always prompt discussion between worker and respondent. To pick up the questionnaire and leave, or ask the questions and just note the answers is not appropriate, although as a questionnaire is administered verbally it may be best to keep fuller discussions to the end.

4.6 Many questionnaires have been designed to screen for particular problems or needs. They have been standardised so that a score above a particular cut-off indicates the strong probability of a significant problem of the type for which the questionnaire is screening. This can be a useful guideline, but it must be remembered that scores above or below a particular cut-off do not guarantee the presence or absence of a significant problem in the individual case. Further discussion can help to clarify whether respondents are over-or-under-representing their needs. Furthermore, there may be highly significant needs picked up by individual questions, even when the overall score is well below the cut-off.

4.7 Questionnaires can not only be used in different ways, they can be used with different respondents, for example, foster or birth parents, residential or nursery workers, children or young people and in different contexts.

5 Testing the use of the questionnaires and scales in practice

5.1 The questionnaires and scales in this pack have been piloted by staff in a variety of settings – metropolitan, urban and rural – with adult carers of children and young people, and with some children and young people themselves. The children involved were children in need (section 17 of the Children Act, 1989): they included children who were living with their families and children who were accommodated including those who were experiencing respite care. Some of these children were being assessed as part of s47 enquiries and the names of some other children were on a child protection register. The children's needs were varied; physical, cognitive, education and behavioural. Most children had behavioural needs alone or in combination with other needs.

5.2 During piloting practitioners took time to get acclimatised to the use of the questionnaires, and indeed how to use them most effectively, but increasingly found them easy to administer and of immediate benefit. For example, they revealed needs of which staff were unaware, or modified their views of needs with which they were already familiar. Often there was increased understanding of the nature and extent of the problems facing family members. One of the instruments, the Recent Life Events Questionnaire, raised new issues on three quarters of the occasions it was used: for several other questionnaires it was more than half the times they were given.

5.3 The questionnaire proved helpful both for initial and core assessments and for reviewing progress. The context of some instruments provided a valuable focus for work with the families.

5.4 In many cases use of the questionnaires and scales helped consolidate the relationship between the staff member and family. Children and parents reported that they liked filling in the questionnaires and scales.

6 The use of the Questionnaires and Scales in practice

When should I use a questionnaire/scale?

6.1 Practitioners have to decide when and why they are going to use a particular questionnaire or scale. Piloting suggested they can be of use in almost any context, even those where the practitioner considers they already have a good grasp of the family's needs. However, questions were raised about their appropriateness in several particular circumstances.

6.2 For example, sometimes it felt inappropriate to use questionnaires where the problems potentially tapped by the instruments were not at all evident, but it is in **these** circumstances that they may be of particular value in providing a way to bring out what the respondent has thought irrelevant or been reluctant to divulge.

Where certain problems are not evident, those that **are** can be acknowledged and summarised. The questionnaire can then be introduced as a way of speedily checking out another area before discussing it in more detail if appropriate.

6.3 On occasions, it was also considered insensitive to present a questionnaire when needs in a particular area were **very** evident. In practice it often offered a way to obtain a fuller understanding or established a baseline for measuring improvement.

One approach is to summarise what the practitioner and respondent already share and explain that the questionnaire may do just that, acknowledge the extent of current understanding, or help to mark the present situation so that progress can be readily established.

6.4 Emergencies and crises were considered to be occasions when respondents would not have enough time and mental space to address a form. However, even when there is a crisis there are times when professionals are consulting with each other and carers or children are waiting. Appropriately presented a questionnaire can help carers or children feel that they are still active partners, and that the professionals are still listening.

What about when working with disabled children?

6.5 Staff working with disabled children, including those with learning disabilities, had reservations about giving carers forms concerned with children's behaviour or family activities. This was because they felt the carers would feel judged adversely for not providing an adequate range of activities for their child, or blamed for the child's behaviour. This reticence demonstrates that it is vital that the instruments are presented as ways to understand families' concerns or difficulties, not to judge them. Behavioural problems are particularly prevalent amongst disabled children, and it is especially hard to organise a full range of family activities with such children. If these facts are acknowledged to the carers, and it is explained that the questionnaire is a basis for discussion of how matters may be improved, for example how other activities might be arranged with Social Services support, then the instruments can be useful.

How do I introduce the questionnaires to families?

6.6 Whenever a questionnaire is introduced, it is not just a matter of considering its appropriateness, but explaining its purpose and potential relevance. The respondent should also be able to comprehend where it fits into the assessment as a whole and how it may be able to extend understanding of the current family situation.

What other purposes can I use a questionnaire for?

6.7 Certain questionnaires may be useful as mental checklists, either for observation or structuring discussion with the respondent. For example, this applies to the Home Conditions Scale and Alcohol Use Questionnaire. Social services staff should assess the family's physical environment. The Home Conditions Scale is a list of items that can be used in isolation from, for example, an evaluation of the quality of the parent-child relationship. However, it provides a guideline as research has found the total score to be strongly correlated with child cognitive development. In addition, the individual items can point to specific targets to work on if there is a concern that the lack of cleanliness is a danger to the child. Establishing whether the family can work to achieve these targets is another way that this and some of the other scales can be used.

6.8 In summary, a questionnaire can be introduced as a way of understanding the families' or individual members' needs or to acknowledge the extent of current shared knowledge of the family's predicament. With some it may be relevant to indicate, at the outset, that the questionnaire may provide suggestions for the support the family requires, or aspects that the carer and social worker can work on together.

7 Using information gathered to inform work with the family

7.1 Unless the questionnaire has been used simply as a mental checklist, it should be discussed with the respondent. Discussion should cover their overall thoughts and feelings about completing it, and individual items which raise possible issues or indicate improvements.

In piloting several practitioners mentioned the value of the questionnaire in making progress.

7.2 Discussion is probably best at the completion of the questionnaire, whether administered verbally or filled in by the respondent, but there will be times when it is important to pick up individual items during completion if they are of very immediate significance. For example, some carers were unhappy about the question on self-harm in the Adult Wellbeing scale. Their concerns need to be understood. If such a question is disturbing it could well mean that the respondent worries that they will be thought inadequate as a parent, or that they have indeed had thoughts of injuring themselves.

7.3 Thus practitioners should be prepared to take up issues that arise, whether indicators of needs or progress. In piloting some workers commented that observing the respondent and the way they completed the questionnaire was also valuable. It is important to remain alert while the instrument is being filled out.

7.4 When respondents are unsure of the meaning of individual items it is better to find out what they think it means before attempting to clarify, but the practitioner must be prepared to explain if necessary. In doing so, it is worth remembering that mutual understanding between family member and worker is more important than whether a form is correctly filled in.

7.5 If there has not been an opportunity to do so, the practitioner should remember to explain how using the instrument fits into broader assessment work, whenever appropriate.

7.6 Piloting suggests that it is often useful and good for the worker-family member relationship, if they score the questionnaire together, but acknowledgement of the needs expressed is the priority for further work.

7.7 Sometimes it may be appropriate to emphasis the questionnaire's screening status, and that definite conclusions should not be reached on the basis of one form. However, it is important to keep the door open to the possibility of significant needs, even if the information derived from the questionnaire does not appear to fit with other knowledge about the family.

Where needs are mutually accepted by social worker and respondent, it will not be necessary to reassure the family member.

7.8 There will be times when issues raised require the practitioner to consult with others, for example if the respondent expresses thought of self-harm, or the child has marked emotional and behavioural problems that might merit referral to another agency. As in other circumstances this will require discussion.

7.9 The questionnaire should not be administered to the same individual, or about the same individual too frequently. Responses may become less valid, or respondents irritated. At least a 3 month gap is recommended.

8 The Family Assessment Pack of Questionnaires and Scales

8.1 Each questionnaire and scale is set out in the following pages, with accompanying guidance on its use. Where appropriate, the scoring system is included separately.

8.2 The questionnaires and scales have been included in the pack also in a form for ease of photocopying. They are intended to be photocopied back-to-back and folded for use with children and families.

Department of Health

Strengths and Difficulties

QUESTIONNAIRES

Strengths and Difficulties
QUESTIONNAIRE

TO BE COMPLETED BY A MAIN CARER OF A CHILD AGED BETWEEN 3 AND 4

For each item, please mark the box for Not True, Somewhat True or Certainly True. It would help us if you answered all items as best you can even if you are not absolutely certain, or the items seem daft! Please give your answers on the basis of the child's behaviour over the last six months.

Child's Name ______________________ **Male/Female** **Date of Birth** ______________

	Not True	Somewhat True	Certainly True
Considerate of other people's feelings	☐	☐	☐
Restless, overactive, cannot stay still for long	☐	☐	☐
Often complains of headaches, stomach-aches or sickness	☐	☐	☐
Shares readily with other children (treats, toys, pencils etc.)	☐	☐	☐
Often has temper tantrums or hot tempers	☐	☐	☐
Rather solitary, tends to play alone	☐	☐	☐
Generally obedient, usually does what adults request	☐	☐	☐
Many worries, often seems worried	☐	☐	☐
Helpful if someone is hurt, upset or feeling ill	☐	☐	☐
Constantly fidgeting or squirming	☐	☐	☐
Has at least one good friend	☐	☐	☐
Often fights with other children or bullies them	☐	☐	☐
Often unhappy, downhearted or tearful	☐	☐	☐
Generally liked by other children	☐	☐	☐
Easily distracted, concentration wanders	☐	☐	☐
Nervous or clingy in new situations, easily loses confidence	☐	☐	☐
Kind to younger children	☐	☐	☐
Often argumentative with adults	☐	☐	☐
Picked on or bullied by other children	☐	☐	☐
Often volunteers to help others (parents, teachers, other children)	☐	☐	☐
Can stop and think things over before acting	☐	☐	☐
Can be spiteful to others	☐	☐	☐
Gets on better with adults than with other children	☐	☐	☐
Many fears, easily scared	☐	☐	☐
Sees tasks through to the end, good attention span	☐	☐	☐

Please complete questions on the next page...

Overall, do you think that your child has difficulties in one or more of the following areas: emotions, concentration, behaviour or being able to get on with other people?

No difficulties	Yes – minor difficulties	Yes – more serious difficulties	Yes – severe difficulties
☐	☐	☐	☐

If you have answered **'Yes'**, please answer the following questions about these difficulties:

- How long have these difficulties been present?

Less than a month	1–5 months	5–12 months	Over a year
☐	☐	☐	☐

- Do the difficulties upset or distress your child?

Not at all	Only a little	Quite a lot	A great deal
☐	☐	☐	☐

- Do the difficulties interfere with your child's everyday life in the following areas?

	Not at all	Only a little	Quite a lot	A great deal
Home life	☐	☐	☐	☐
Friendships	☐	☐	☐	☐
Learning	☐	☐	☐	☐
Leisure activities	☐	☐	☐	☐

- Do the difficulties put a burden on you or the family as a whole?

Not at all	Only a little	Quite a lot	A great deal
☐	☐	☐	☐

Signature ______________________________

Date ______________________________

Mother/Father/Other (please specify) ______________________________

Thank you very much for your help

Strengths and Difficulties

QUESTIONNAIRE

TO BE COMPLETED BY A MAIN CARER OF A CHILD AGED BETWEEN 4 AND 16

For each item, please mark the box for Not True, Somewhat True or Certainly True. It would help us if you answered all items as best you can even if you are not absolutely certain, or the items seem daft! Please give your answers on the basis of the child's behaviour over the last six months.

Child's Name ______________________ **Male/Female** **Date of Birth** ____________

	Not True	Somewhat True	Certainly True
Considerate of other people's feelings	☐	☐	☐
Restless, overactive, cannot sit still for long	☐	☐	☐
Often complains of headaches, stomach-aches or sickness	☐	☐	☐
Shares readily with other children (treats, toys, pencils etc.)	☐	☐	☐
Often has temper tantrums or hot tempers	☐	☐	☐
Rather solitary, tends to play alone	☐	☐	☐
Generally obedient, usually does what adults request	☐	☐	☐
Many worries, often seems worried	☐	☐	☐
Helpful if someone is hurt, upset or feeling ill	☐	☐	☐
Constantly fidgeting or squirming	☐	☐	☐
Has at least one good friend	☐	☐	☐
Often fights with other children or bullies them	☐	☐	☐
Often unhappy, downhearted or tearful	☐	☐	☐
Generally liked by other children	☐	☐	☐
Easily distracted, concentration wanders	☐	☐	☐
Nervous or clingy in new situations, easily loses confidence	☐	☐	☐
Kind to younger children	☐	☐	☐
Often lies or cheats	☐	☐	☐
Picked on or bullied by other children	☐	☐	☐
Often volunteers to help others (parents, teachers, other children)	☐	☐	☐
Thinks things out before acting	☐	☐	☐
Steals from home, school or elsewhere	☐	☐	☐
Gets on better with adults than with other children	☐	☐	☐
Many fears, easily scared	☐	☐	☐
Sees tasks through to the end, good attention span	☐	☐	☐

Please complete questions on the next page...

Overall, do you think that your child has difficulties in one or more of the following areas: emotions, concentration, behaviour or being able to get on with other people?

No difficulties	Yes – minor difficulties	Yes – more serious difficulties	Yes – severe difficulties
☐	☐	☐	☐

If you have answered **'Yes'**, please answer the following questions about these difficulties:

- How long have these difficulties been present?

Less than a month	1–5 months	5–12 months	Over a year
☐	☐	☐	☐

- Do the difficulties upset or distress your child?

Not at all	Only a little	Quite a lot	A great deal
☐	☐	☐	☐

- Do the difficulties interfere with your child's everyday life in the following areas?

	Not at all	Only a little	Quite a lot	A great deal
Home life	☐	☐	☐	☐
Friendships	☐	☐	☐	☐
Classroom Learning	☐	☐	☐	☐
Leisure activities	☐	☐	☐	☐

- Do the difficulties put a burden on you or the family as a whole?

Not at all	Only a little	Quite a lot	A great deal
☐	☐	☐	☐

Signature ______________________________

Date ______________________________

Mother/Father/Other (please specify) ______________________________

Thank you very much for your help

Strengths and Difficulties

QUESTIONNAIRE

TO BE COMPLETED BY A YOUNG PERSON BETWEEN 11 AND 16

Please read the questionnaire carefully. For each of the statements put a tick in the box that **you** think is most like you. It would help us if you put a tick for all the statements – even if it seems a bit daft! Please give answers on the basis of how you have been feeling over the last six months.

Your Name ______________________ **Male/Female** **Date of Birth** ____________

	Not True	Somewhat True	Certainly True
I try to be nice to people. I care about their feelings	☐	☐	☐
I get restless, I cannot sit still for long	☐	☐	☐
I get a lot of headaches, stomach-aches or sickness	☐	☐	☐
I usually share with others (food, games, pens etc.)	☐	☐	☐
I get very angry and often lose my temper	☐	☐	☐
I am usually on my own. I generally play alone or keep to myself	☐	☐	☐
I usually do as I am told	☐	☐	☐
I worry a lot	☐	☐	☐
I am helpful if someone is hurt, upset or feeling ill	☐	☐	☐
I am constantly fidgeting or squirming	☐	☐	☐
I have one good friend or more	☐	☐	☐
I fight a lot. I can make other people do what I want	☐	☐	☐
I am often unhappy, downhearted or tearful	☐	☐	☐
Other people my age generally like me	☐	☐	☐
I am easily distracted, I find it difficult to concentrate	☐	☐	☐
I am nervous in new situations. I easily lose confidence	☐	☐	☐
I am kind to younger children	☐	☐	☐
I am often accused of cheating or lying	☐	☐	☐
Other children or young people pick on or bully me	☐	☐	☐
I often volunteer to help others (parents, teachers, children)	☐	☐	☐
I think before I do things	☐	☐	☐
I take things that are not mine from home, school or elsewhere	☐	☐	☐
I get on better with adults than with people my own age	☐	☐	☐
I have many fears, I am easily scared	☐	☐	☐
I finish the things I'm doing. My attention is good	☐	☐	☐

Please complete questions on the next page...

Overall, do you think that you have difficulties in one or more of the following areas: emotions, concentration, behaviour or being able to get on with other people?

No difficulties	Yes – minor difficulties	Yes – more serious difficulties	Yes – very severe difficulties
☐	☐	☐	☐

If you have answered **'Yes'**, please answer the following questions about these difficulties:

- How long have these difficulties been present?

Less than a month	1–5 months	5–12 months	Over a year
☐	☐	☐	☐

- Do the difficulties upset or distress your child?

Not at all	Only a little	Quite a lot	A great deal
☐	☐	☐	☐

- Do the difficulties interfere with your child's everyday life in the following areas?

	Not at all	Only a little	Quite a lot	A great deal
Home life	☐	☐	☐	☐
Friendships	☐	☐	☐	☐
Classroom Learning	☐	☐	☐	☐
Leisure activities	☐	☐	☐	☐

- Do the difficulties make it harder for those around you (family, friends, teachers etc.)?

Not at all	Only a little	Quite a lot	A great deal
☐	☐	☐	☐

Signature ______________________________

Date ______________________________

Thank you very much for your help

GUIDANCE ON USING STRENGTHS AND DIFFICULTIES QUESTIONNAIRES

Background

1. Evaluation of children's emotional and behavioural development is a central component of social work assessment.

2. These questionnaires screen for child emotional and behavioural problems. These scales are similar to older scales such as Rutter A & B Scales developed for use by parents and teachers, but put a greater emphasis on strengths.

The Scales

3. The questionnaires consist of 25 items that refer to different emotions or behaviours.

4. For each item the respondent marks in one of three boxes to indicate whether the item is **not** true, **somewhat** true or **certainly** true for the child in question.

5. On the back of each questionnaire are questions that aim to address severity by scoring duration of the difficulties and their impact on the child, themselves or others.

6. Children's emotional and behavioural problems are not always evident in all situations. When they are, the problem is usually more severe. As with the Rutter scales, the Strengths and Difficulties Questionnaires have both parent and teacher versions.

7. In young children, parents' reports of their emotions and behaviour are usually more reliable than those of the children themselves, but in adolescence, parents are often unaware of their children's emotional state. There is therefore a Strengths and Difficulties questionnaire for young people aged 11–16.

8. The Rutter scales were originally devised for children aged 9–10, and have been shown to be valid for those aged 6–16. The Strengths and Difficulties Scale covers ages 4–16, and there is an additional scale for children aged 3–4.

9. The scales can be scored to produce an overall score that indicates whether the child/young person is likely to have a significant problem. Selected items can also be used to form subscales for Pro-social Behaviour, Hyperactivity, Emotional Symptoms, Conduct and Peer problems.

Use

10. The questionnaires are of value in both assessments and for evaluating progress.

11. They can give an indication of whether a child/young person is likely to have a significant emotional or behavioural problem/disorder, and what type of disorder it is.

12. During piloting, over half the children assessed scored above the cut-off scores indicating a probable disorder.

13. The most common problems were Hyperactivity, Peer and Conduct problems. These were identified in over half the children.

14. One social worker commented that the questionnaire 'gave a more in-depth look at the young person'. Another said that with the individual child/young person it could be a springboard for therapeutic action, and that it would be helpful, alongside work with the family, to monitor progress.

Administration

15. The respondent – whether parent, child or teacher – needs to understand where the use of the questionnaire fits into the overall assessment.

16. It is usually best if the respondent completes the questionnaire in the presence of the social worker. Sometimes it will be necessary for the worker to administer the scale verbally.

17. The scale takes about 10 minutes to complete.

18. It is preferable if full discussion is kept to the end, but there will be occasions when what the respondent says while completing the scale should be acknowledged immediately.

19. Fuller discussion is vital for several reasons. Firstly, it is important to establish level and nature of any difficulties more clearly. Information from other sources is also relevant for this purpose. Secondly, the overall score may be below the cut off point indicative of disorder, but there may still be issues that are important to the respondent. The response to a single item might provide the cue. Thirdly, it is crucial to understand how the child, parent and other family members are responding to how the child is, or what the child is doing/saying.

Scoring

20. This is explained on the sheet that accompanies the questionnaires.

21. Each item is scored 0, 1 or 2. Somewhat true is always scored 1, but whether Not true and Certainly true are scored 0 or 2 depends on whether the item is framed as a strength or difficulty.

22. The scoring sheet explains which item contributes to which subscales. The Pro-social scale is scored so that an absence of pro-social behaviour is a problem i.e. scores high. A child may have difficulties but if they have a low Pro-social score the outlook for intervention is better.

23. The scoring sheet has a chart, which indicates which total scores are low, average or high in the general population. High scores overall or for any subscale point to the likelihood of a significant disorder, and/or a disorder of a particular type. They do not guarantee that there will be found to be a disorder when a more thorough assessment is conducted. Neither does a low score guarantee the absence of a problem, but the instrument is useful for screening.

References

Goodman R (1997). The Strengths and Difficulties Questionnaire: A reseach note. *Journal of Child Psychology and Psychiatry*. **38**: 581–586.

Goodman R, Meltzer H and Bailey V (1998) The strengths and difficulties questionnaire: A pilot study on the validity of the self-report version. *European Child & Adolescent Psychiatry*. **7**: 125–130.

SCORING THE SELF REPORT STRENGTHS AND DIFFICULTIES QUESTIONNAIRE

The 25 items in the SDQ comprise 5 scales of 5 items each. The first stage of scoring the questionnaire is generally to score each of the 5 scales. Somewhat true is always scored as 1, but the scoring of Not True and Certainly True varies with each item. The score for each response category is given below scale by scale.

Pro-social Scale

	NOT TRUE	SOMEWHAT TRUE	CERTAINLY TRUE
I am considerate of others	2	1	0
I usually share	2	1	0
I am helpful if	2	1	0
I am kinder to younger	2	1	0
I often volunteer	2	1	0

Hyperactivity Scale

	NOT TRUE	SOMEWHAT TRUE	CERTAINLY TRUE
I am restless	0	1	2
I am constantly fidgeting	0	1	2
I am easily distracted	0	1	2
Thinks things out	2	1	0
I see tasks through	2	1	0

Emotional Symptoms Scale

	NOT TRUE	SOMEWHAT TRUE	CERTAINLY TRUE
I get a lot of headaches	2	1	0
I worry a lot	2	1	0
I am often happy	2	1	0
I am nervous in	2	1	0
I have many fears	2	1	0

Conduct Problems Scale

	NOT TRUE	SOMEWHAT TRUE	CERTAINLY TRUE
I get very angry	0	1	2
I usually do as I am told	2	1	0
I fight a lot	0	1	2
I am often accused of lying	0	1	2
I take things	0	1	2

Peer Problems Scale

	NOT TRUE	SOMEWHAT TRUE	CERTAINLY TRUE
I am rather solitary	0	1	2
I have at least one good friend	2	1	0
Other people ... like me	2	1	0
Other ... people pick on me ...	0	1	2
I get on better with adults ...	0	1	2

For each of the 5 scales the score can range from 0 to 10 provided all five items have been completed. You can prorate the scores if there are only one or two missing items.

To generate a total difficulties score, sum the four scales dealing with problems but do not include the pro-social scale. The resultant score can range from 0 to 40. Provided at least 12 of the relevant 20 items are completed, you can prorate the total if necessary.

Interpreting scores and identifying need

The provisional bandings shown below have been selected so that roughly 80% of children in the community do not have needs in these areas, 10% have some needs, and 10% have high needs.

Self completed

	LOW NEED	SOME NEED	HIGH NEED
Total difficulties score	0–15	16–19	20–40
Conduct problems score	0–3	4	5–10
Hyperactivity score	0–5	6	7–10
Emotional symptoms score	0–5	6	7–10
Peer problem score	0–3	4–5	6–10
Pro-social behaviour score	6–10	5	0–4

Department of Health

Parenting Daily Hassles

SCALES

Parenting Daily Hassles

SCALE

The statements below describe a lot of events that routinely occur in families with young children. These events sometimes make life difficult. Please read each item and circle how often it happens to you (rarely, sometimes, a lot, or constantly) and then circle how much of a 'hassle' you feel that it has been for you **FOR THE PAST 6 MONTHS**. If you have more than one child, these events can include any or all of your children.

EVENT	How often it happens				Hassle (low to high)				
1. Continually cleaning up messes of toys or food	Rarely	Sometimes	A lot	Constantly	1	2	3	4	5
2. Being nagged, whined at, complained to	Rarely	Sometimes	A lot	Constantly	1	2	3	4	5
3. Meal-time difficulties with picky eaters, complaining etc.	Rarely	Sometimes	A lot	Constantly	1	2	3	4	5
4. The kids won't listen or do what they are asked without being nagged	Rarely	Sometimes	A lot	Constantly	1	2	3	4	5
5. Baby-sitters are hard to find	Rarely	Sometimes	A lot	Constantly	1	2	3	4	5
6. The kids schedules (like pre-school or other activities) interfere with meeting your own household needs	Rarely	Sometimes	A lot	Constantly	1	2	3	4	5
7. Sibling arguments or fights require a 'referee'	Rarely	Sometimes	A lot	Constantly	1	2	3	4	5
8. The kids demand that you entertain them or play with them	Rarely	Sometimes	A lot	Constantly	1	2	3	4	5
9. The kids resist or struggle with you over bed-time	Rarely	Sometimes	A lot	Constantly	1	2	3	4	5
10. The kids are constantly underfoot, interfering with other chores	Rarely	Sometimes	A lot	Constantly	1	2	3	4	5
11. The need to keep a constant eye on where the kids are and what they are doing	Rarely	Sometimes	A lot	Constantly	1	2	3	4	5
12. The kids interrupt adult conversations or interactions	Rarely	Sometimes	A lot	Constantly	1	2	3	4	5
13. Having to change your plans because of unprecedented child needs	Rarely	Sometimes	A lot	Constantly	1	2	3	4	5
14. The kids get dirty several times a day requiring changes of clothing	Rarely	Sometimes	A lot	Constantly	1	2	3	4	5
15. Difficulties in getting privacy (eg. in the bathroom)	Rarely	Sometimes	A lot	Constantly	1	2	3	4	5
16. The kids are hard to manage in public (grocery store, shopping centre, restaurant)	Rarely	Sometimes	A lot	Constantly	1	2	3	4	5
17. Difficulties in getting kids ready for outings and leaving on time	Rarely	Sometimes	A lot	Constantly	1	2	3	4	5
18. Difficulties in leaving kids for a night out or at school or day care	Rarely	Sometimes	A lot	Constantly	1	2	3	4	5
19. The kids have difficulties with friends (eg. fighting, trouble, getting along, or no friends available)	Rarely	Sometimes	A lot	Constantly	1	2	3	4	5
20. Having to run extra errands to meet the kids needs	Rarely	Sometimes	A lot	Constantly	1	2	3	4	5

Questionnaire completed by *mother/father/adoptive parent/foster carer* (please specify)

GUIDANCE ON USING PARENTING DAILY HASSLES SCALE

Background

1. This scale aims to assess the frequency and intensity/impact of 20 experiences that can be a 'hassle' to parents.
2. It has been used in a wide variety of research concerned with children and families. The research in which it has been used includes a parenting programme with families who had major difficulties in raising young children.
3. Parents/Caregivers enjoy completing the scale, because it touches on aspects of being a parent that are very familiar. It helps them express what it feels like to be a parent.
4. During piloting, social workers reported that it depicted concisely areas of pressure felt by the carer. This helped identify areas where assistance could be provided either by the social services department or other agencies.
5. It is seen by parents as a way for them to express their needs for help with parenting.

The Scale

6. The caregiver is asked to score each of the 20 potential **Hassles** in two different ways for frequency and intensity.
7. The frequency of each type of happening provides an 'objective' marker of how often it occurs.
8. The intensity or impact score indicates the caregiver's 'subjective' appraisal of how much those events affect or 'hassle' them.
9. The time frame for this scale can be varied according to the focus of the assessment. For example, if a family is thought to have been under particular pressure in the last 2 months the parent can be asked to consider how matters have been during that period. However, if it is intended to assess progress, the same time frame should be used on each occasion. Periods of less than one month are probably too short to give a useful picture.

Use

10. The caregiver should understand the aim of filling out the questionnaire, and how it will contribute to the overall assessment.
11. The scale is probably most useful with families that are not well-known. In piloting it was found to highlight areas for future discussion, and help prioritise which parenting issues should be addressed first.
12. It can also be used to monitor change.

Administration

13. It should be given to the parent/caregiver to fill out themselves.
14. It can be read out if necessary.
15. It takes about 10 minutes to complete.
16. The scale should always be used as a basis for discussion. In general this is best kept until the parent has finished, but there will be occasions when it is vital to acknowledge, or immediately follow up comments made while it is being filled out.

Scoring

17. The scale can be used in two distinct ways: (a) the totals of the frequency and intensity scales can be obtained, or (b) scores for challenging behaviour and parenting tasks can be derived from the intensity scale.
18. To obtain frequency and intensity total scores

    (a) The frequency scale is scored: rarely = 1, sometimes = 2, a lot = 3, and constantly = 4. If the parent says that an event never occurs, never = 0.

The range for this scale is 0–80. A score of 3 or 4 for any one event indicates that it occurs with above average frequency.

(b) The intensity scale is scored by adding the parents rating of 1–5 for each item. If a 0 has been scored for frequency on an item then it should be scored 0 for intensity. The range for this scale is 0–100. A score of 4 or 5 for any one event indicates that it is at least some problem to the parent.

Scoring

19. (a) The challenging behaviour total score is obtained by adding the intensity scale scores for items: 2, 4, 8, 9, 11, 12, 16. Range: 0–35.

    (b) The parenting tasks total score is obtained by adding the intensity scale scores for items: 1, 5, 7, 10, 13, 14, 17, 20. Range: 0–40.

20. There is no cut off for any of the scales but total scores above 50 on the frequency scale or above 70 on the intensity scale indicate on the one hand a high frequency of potentially hassling happenings, and on the other that the parent is experiencing significant pressure over parenting.
21. Events occurring with frequency 3 or 4, or intensity 4 or 5, particularly those where the parent rates high intensity or impact, should be discussed to clarify the extent of need.
22. The total score on the challenging behaviour and parenting tasks scales may be useful in indicating how the parent/caregiver sees the situation, whether difficulties lie in the troublesome behaviour of the children, or the burden of meeting the 'expected' or 'legitimate' needs of the children. The subscores may also be useful in monitoring change.

References

Crnic KA & Greenberg MT (1990) Minor parenting stresses with young children. *Child Development*. **61**: 1628–1637

Crnic KA & Booth CL (1991) Mothers' and fathers' perceptions of daily hassles of parenting across early childhood. *Journal of Marriage and the Family*. **53**: 1043–1050.

Home Conditions

ASSESSMENT

GUIDANCE ON USING HOME CONDITIONS ASSESSMENT

Background

1. Social workers assess physical aspects of the home environment.
2. This scale may appear judgmental, but workers necessarily make judgements about the safety, order and cleanliness of the place in which the child lives. The use of a list helps the objectivity of observation.
3. The total score has been found to correlate highly with children's abilities, so that children from homes with low scores usually have better language and intellectual development. This does not mean that all children from high scoring homes will have poor intellectual progress.
4. Like all methods of assessment it should not be used in isolation – other sources of information, including the quality of the parent-child relationship will contribute to the overall assessment.

The Scale

5. The assessment is identical to the Family Cleanliness Scale devised by Davie and others (1984).
6. This is a list of 11 items to be observed during home visits.
7. Social presentation, namely the cleanliness of the children is included.

Use

8. The scale if best used as a mental checklist to provide a framework for observation.
9. It is particularly appropriate to use during initial assessment. Once used it is a method of keeping track of progress or deterioration.
10. In order to be able to complete the scale it is necessary to look over the home. The caregiver can be asked whether they have any problems with their housing, or whether the nature of their accommodation causes difficulties from the point of view of brining up the children. This can lead naturally to a request to look round.
11. It will usually be unhelpful to share all that has been observed with the caregiver. This could upset the establishment of partnership – a good working relationship is of overriding importance. However the worker needs to have a clear picture of the environment from the child's point of view.
12. Individual items can be a focus for a piece of work. This might be to encourage the parent to attend to something that could pose a health risk to the children, or to bring in additional support where the parent is unlikely to be able to improve matters unassisted.

Scoring

13. The scoring is binary 0 if the condition is not present, and 1 if it is.
14. Items are scored on the basis of what is observed. Why the conditions are as they are is not taken into account. Of course the worker needs to understand why matters are as they are to take appropriate action. The scale charts the child environment as it is.
15. The scale has no cut off. Depending on the age of the children different items may give more or less concern, but in general the higher the score the greater the concern.
16. Individual items may require action whatever the total score.

Reference

Davie CE, Hutt SJ, Vincent E & Mason M (1984) *The young child at home*. NFER-Nelson, Windsor

THE SCALE

1. Smell (e.g. stale cigarette smoke, rotting food)	0	1
2. Kitchen floor soiled, covered in bits, crumbs etc.	0	1
3. Floor covering in any other room soiled as above.	0	1
4. General decorative order poor – obviously in need of attention (e.g. badly stained wall paper, broken windows)	0	1

5.	Kitchen sink, draining board, work surfaces or cupboard door have not been washed for a considerable period of time	0	1
6.	Other surfaces in the house have not been dusted for a considerable period of time	0	1
7.	Cooking implements, cutlery or crockery showing ingrained dirt and or these items remain unwashed until they are needed again.	0	1
8.	Lavatory, bath or basin showing ingrained dirt.	0	1
9.	Furnishings or furniture soiled	0	1
10.	Informant's or children's, clothing clearly unwashed, or hair matted and unbrushed	0	1
11.	Garden or yard uncared for and strewn with rubbish	0	1
	Total Score		

Department of Health

Adult Wellbeing

SCALE

ADULT WELLBEING SCALE

This form has been designed so that you can show how you have been feeling in the past few days.

Read each item in turn and UNDERLINE the response which shows best how you are feeling or have been feeling in the last few days.

Please complete all of the questionnaire.

1. I feel cheerful

Yes, definitely	Yes, sometimes	No, not much	No, not at all

2. I can sit down and relax quite easily

Yes, definitely	Yes, sometimes	No, not much	No, not at all

3. My appetite is

Very poor	Fairly poor	Quite good	Very good

4. I lose my temper and shout and snap at others

Yes, definitely	Yes, sometimes	No, not much	No, not at all

5. I can laugh and feel amused

Yes, definitely	Yes, sometimes	No, not much	No, not at all

---

6. I feel I might lose control and hit or hurt someone

Sometimes	Occasionally	Rarely	Never

7. I have an uncomfortable feeling like butterflies in the stomach

Yes, definitely	Yes, sometimes	Not very often	Not at all

8. The thought of hurting myself occurs to me

Sometimes	Not very often	Hardly ever	Not at all

9. I'm awake before I need to get up

For 2 hours or more	For about 1 hour	For less than 1 hour	Not at all. I sleep until it is time to get up

10. I feel tense or 'wound up'

Yes, definitely	Yes, sometimes	No, not much	No, not at all

---

11. I feel like harming myself

Yes, definitely	Yes, sometimes	No, not much	No, not at all

12. I've kept up my old interests

Yes, most of them	Yes, some of them	No, not many of them	No, none of them

13. I am patient with other people

All the time	Most of the time	Some of the time	Hardly ever

---

14. I get scared or panicky for no very good reason

Yes, definitely	Yes, sometimes	No, not much	No, not at all

15. I get angry with myself or call myself names

Yes, definitely	Yes, sometimes	Not often	No, not at all

16. People upset me so that I feel like slamming doors or banging about

Yes, often	Yes, sometimes	Only occasionally	Not at all

---

17. I can go out on my own without feeling anxious

Yes, always	Yes, sometimes	No, not often	No, I never can

18. Lately I have been getting annoyed with myself

Very much so	Rather a lot	Not much	Not at all

GUIDANCE ON USING ADULT WELLBEING SCALE

Background

1. Parent/Caregiver mental health is a fundamental component of assessment.
2. There is evidence that some people respond more openly to a questionnaire than a face to face interview, when reporting on their mental health.
3. A questionnaire gives caregivers the opportunity to express themselves without having to face another person, however sympathetic that person may be.
4. A questionnaire is no substitute for a good relationship, but it can contribute to the development of a rapport if discussed sensitively.
5. During piloting the use of the questionnaire was found to convey the social worker's concern for the parent's wellbeing. This can be particularly valuable where the parent feels their needs are not being considered.

The Scale

6. The scale is the Irritability, Depression, Anxiety (IDA) Scale developed by Snaith *et al* (1978).
7. This scale allows respondents four possible responses to each item.
8. Four aspects of wellbeing are covered: Depression, Anxiety and Inwardly and Outwardly directed Irritability.

Use

9. In principle the questionnaire can be used with any adult, who is in contact with the child whose development and context are being assessed. In practice this will usually be the main caregiver(s).
10. In piloting social workers reported that use of the scale raised issues on more than half the occasions that it was used. Probable depression was found amongst almost half the caregivers, and significant anxiety in a third.
11. Where social workers were new to the family situation they said they learnt things they did not know. 'It helped me to be aware of the carers' needs', and 'highlighted stresses'. It helped focus on 'parents' needs and feelings'.
12. Even when parents were known to the workers it gave topics an airing and clarified areas to work on; it 'released tension'.
13. Progress can also be registered. It was 'useful to measure when things were calmer'.
14. Used flexibly it can provide openings to discuss many areas including feelings about relationships with partners and children.

Administration

15. It is vital that the respondent understands why they are being asked to complete the scale. Some will be concerned that revealing mental health needs will prejudice their chances of continuing to care for their child. For example, it can be explained that many carers of children experience considerable stress, and it is important to understand this if they are to be given appropriate support.
16. The scale is best filled out by the carer themselves in the presence of the worker, but it can be administered verbally.
17. It takes about 10 minutes to complete.
18. **Discussion is essential**. Usually this will be when the questionnaire has been completed, so the respondent has an opportunity to consider their own needs uninterrupted. However, there will be times when an important clue to how the caregiver feels may be best picked up immediately. One example occurred during piloting, when a respondent expressed distaste for questions about self-harm.

Scoring

19. The sheet accompanying the questionnaire indicates the method of scoring the 4 subscales.
20. Use of cut-off scores gives indicators of significant care needs with respect to depression, anxiety, and inwardly and outwardly directed irritability. Inward irritability can point to the possibility of self-harm. Outward irritability raises the possibility of angry actions towards the child(ren).
21. As with any screening instrument, interpretation must be in the context of other information. Some respondents will underreport distress, others exaggerate it. A high or low score on any scale does not guarantee that a significant level of need is present.
22. Most value is obtained by using the scale as a springboard for discussion.

Reference

Snaith RP, Constantopoulos AA, Jardine MY & McGuffin P (1978) A clinical scale for the self-assessment of irritability. *British Journal of Psychiatry*. **132**: 163–71.

SCORING THE ADULT WELLBEING SCALE

1. **Depression** – Questions 1,3,5,9 and 12 look at depression. The possible response scores that are shown below run from the left to the right – i.e. for question 1 'I feel cheerful', the scores would be looked at from 'yes, definitely' (0), 'yes, sometimes' (1), 'no, not at all' (3). A score of 4–6 is borderline in this scale and a score above this may indicate a problem.

QU1	QU3	QU5	QU9	QU12
0,1,2,3	3,2,1,0	0,1,2,3	3,2,1,0	0,1,2,3

2. **Anxiety** – Questions 2,7,10,14 and 17 look at anxiety. A score of 6–8 is borderline, above this level may indicate a problem in this area.

QU2	QU7	QU10	QU14	QU17
0,1,2,3	3,2,1,0	3,2,1,0	3,2,1,0	0,1,2,3

3. **Outward directed irritability** – Questions 4,6,13 and 16 look at outward directed irritability. A score of 5–7 is borderline for this scale, and a score above this may indicate a problem in this area.

QU4	QU6	QU13	QU16
3,2,1,0	3,2,1,0	0,1,2,3	3,2,1,0

4. **Inward directed irritability** – Questions 8,11,15 and 18 look at inward directed irritability. A score of 4–6 is borderline, a higher score may indicate a problem.

QU8	QU11	QU15	QU18
3,2,1,0	3,2,1,0	3,2,1,0	3,2,1,0

Use of cut-off scores gives indicators of significant care needs with respect to depression, anxiety, and inwardly and outwardly directed irritability. Inward irritability can point to the possibility of selfharm. Outward irritability raises the possibility of angry actions towards the child(ren).

As with any screening instrument, interpretation must be in the context of other information. Some respondents will underreport distress, others exaggerate. A high or low score on any scale does not guarantee that significant level of need is present.

Most value is obtained by using the scale as a springboard for discussion.

Department of Health

Adolescent Wellbeing

SCALE

Adolescent Wellbeing

SCALE FOR YOUNG PEOPLE AGED 11 TO 16

Please tick as appropriate

	Most of the time	sometimes	never
1. I look forward to things as much as I used to	☐	☐	☐
2. I sleep very well	☐	☐	☐
3. I feel like crying	☐	☐	☐
4. I like going out	☐	☐	☐
5. I feel like leaving home	☐	☐	☐
6. I get stomache-aches/cramps	☐	☐	☐
7. I have lots of energy	☐	☐	☐
8. I enjoy my food	☐	☐	☐
9. I can stick up for myself	☐	☐	☐
10. I think life isn't worth living	☐	☐	☐
11. I am good at things I do	☐	☐	☐
12. I enjoy the things I do as much as I used to	☐	☐	☐
13. I like talking to my friends and family	☐	☐	☐
14. I have horrible dreams	☐	☐	☐
15. I feel very lonely	☐	☐	☐
16. I am easily cheered up	☐	☐	☐
17. I feel so sad I can hardly bear it	☐	☐	☐
18. I feel very bored	☐	☐	☐

GUIDANCE ON USING ADOLESCENT WELLBEING SCALE

Background

1. How young people feel in themselves is a vital part of any assessment.
2. It is important to understand their worries and concerns, and whether they are depressed or even suicidal.
3. There is good evidence that the way a young person is feeling is often not recognised by their parents or caregivers. This makes it particularly important to have a way of helping them to express directly how they are feeling.
4. With very young children their reporting can fluctuate from day to day, or even hour to hour – they do not necessarily give a stable view of their situation. Evaluation of their perspective requires particular care, so questionnaires are not usually a good starting point
5. Older children and adolescents can give a more reliable report, which means that a questionnaire may be more helpful. As with some adults they often find it easier to respond to a questionnaire about feelings than face-to-face interviewing.

The Scale

6. The Adolescent Wellbeing Scale was devised by Birleson to pick up possible depression in older children and adolescents. It has been shown to be effective for this purpose.
7. The scale has 18 questions – each relating to different aspects of an adolescent's life, and how they feel about these. They are asked to indicate whether the statement applies to them most of the time, sometimes or never.
8. The scale can be used by children as young as 7 or 8, but as indicated above, responses are more reliable for those aged 11 or more.

Use

9. In piloting social workers found young people were pleased to have the opportunity to contribute to the assessment.
10. The questionnaire often helped them express their feelings. It gave 'an overall insight in a short time'. It presented a 'truer picture of the adolescent's state of mind'. 'It gave me insight into how sad and overwhelmed the young person felt'.
11. On occasions use of the scale pointed to particular issues that could be a focus for further work. It gave an opportunity for 'the young person to look at themselves'.
12. The scale has proved useful with adolescents at initial assessment, but also to monitor progress. For example, it helped 'clarify a young person's feeling about placement with their mother'.
13. During piloting over half the young people who filled out the questionnaire were above the cut-off score of 13 indicating a probable depressive disorder.

Administration

14. The young person should understand the aim of the questionnaire, and how it fits into any wider assessment.
15. Ideally it is completed by the adolescent themselves, but, if necessary, it an be administered verbally.
16. Discussion is usually best at the end, but there may be important areas that should be picked up as the result of comments made while the questionnaire is being filled out. A number of adolescents talk as they are completing the scale, and this may provide a good opportunity to promote conversation, or establish rapport.
17. During piloting the scale took about 15 minutes to complete, ensuing discussion took longer.

Scoring

18. The responses to each question are scored 0, 1 or 2. How the responses are scored depends on the nature of the statement that is being responded to as well as the response. 0 means that the response indicates no concern, 1 possible concern and 2 that the young person is indicating unhappiness or low self esteem with regard to that item.

    For example for question 8 – I enjoy my food – if no/never is ticked the score is 2. For question 17 – I feel so sad I can hardly bear it – a score of 2 would be obtained for most of the time.

19. A score of 13 or more has been found to indicate the likelihood of a depressive disorder. Discussion with the young person and information from other sources will be necessary to make a definite diagnosis. There will be some who score high, but who on careful consideration are not judged to have a depressive disorder, and others who score low who do have one.

20. In most instances the way a young person responds to the the different questions will be as important and as valuable as any score, because they can give an insight into that particular young person's needs. The reply to only one question may give the opportunity to understand their point of view.

Reference

Birleson P (1980) The validity of Depressive Disorder in Childhood and the Development of a Self-Rating Scale; a Research Report. *Journal of Child Psychology and Psychiatry*. **22**: 73–88.

Department of Health

Recent Life Events

QUESTIONNAIRE

Recent Life Events
QUESTIONNAIRE

Listed below are a number of events. Please read each item carefully and then indicate whether or not each event has happened to you in the past year.

Please tick the **YES** box if the event has occurred.
Please tick the **'still affects me'** box if **the event is still having an effect on your life**

EVENT	YES	Still affects me
Have you had a serious illness or been seriously injured?	☐	☐
Has one of your immediate family * been seriously ill or injured?	☐	☐
Have any of your close friends or other close relatives been seriously ill or injured?	☐	☐
Have any of your immediate family died?	☐	☐
Have any of your other close relatives or close friends died?	☐	☐
Have you separated from your partner (not including death)?	☐	☐
Have you had any serious problem with a close friend, neighbour or relative?	☐	☐
Have you, or an immediate family member been subject to serious racial abuse, attack or /threats	☐	☐
Have you, or an immediate family member been subject to any abuse, attack, threat – perhaps due to you or someone close to you having a disability of any kind (i.e. a mental health problem, a learning disability or a physical problem)?	☐	☐
Have you, or an immediate family member been subject to any other form of serious abuse, attack, or threat?	☐	☐
Have you or your partner been unemployed or seeking work for more than one month?	☐	☐
Have you or your partner been sacked from your job or made redundant?	☐	☐
Have you had any major financial difficulties (e.g. debts, difficulty paying bills)?	☐	☐
Have you, or an immediate family member had any Police contact or been in a court appearance?	☐	☐
Have you or an immediate member of your family been burgled or mugged?	☐	☐
Have you or another individual who lives with you given birth?	☐	☐
Have you or another individual who lives with you suffered from a miscarriage or had a stillbirth?	☐	☐
Have you moved house (through choice)?	☐	☐
Have you moved house (not through choice)?	☐	☐
Have you had any housing difficulties?	☐	☐
Have you had any other significant event (Please specify)?	☐	☐

* *immediate family includes: mother, father, sister, brother, partner, child*

GUIDANCE ON USING RECENT LIFE EVENTS QUESTIONNAIRE

Background

1. Life events are usually short-lived but may have more enduring consequences.
2. They can be distinguished from 'chronic difficulties', such as poverty or persistently discordant relationships. However life events can be both an indicator of chronic difficulties, or a precipitant of them.
3. Life events affect individuals and families in different ways, so it is important to explore how they impact on the caregivers and the family. For example, the death of a grandparent may have a practical as well as an emotional impact on the family if they have helped to support and care for the children.
4. Negative life events such as divorce, death of someone close, physical illness and unemployment have the capacity to affect any family member, not just those directly involved. Losing a parent at a young age, particularly before 11, has been reported to independently influence wellbeing in both childhood and adult life.
5. Most negative life events can be seen as involving the experience of loss, or threat of loss, including the loss of self esteem. Some apparently positive events such as job promotion may act in this way.
6. An important issue is whether an event is felt to continue to exert a negative affect. This aspect has not always been included in questionnaires.

The Questionnaire

7. This Life Events questionnaire has been developed from one devised by Brugha *et al* (1985), with 9 additional items.
8. The scale aims to look at recent life events, those occurring in the last 12 months and whether the respondent thinks they have a continuing influence. However, it can be used to evaluate events and impact over a longer period if desired.
9. It can contribute to a social history, or provide an opportunity to re-evaluate whether known events are continuing to exert an influence.

Use

10. It is expected that it will be used mostly with main caregivers, but it could be of value with potential caregivers and separated parents.
11. In piloting it was found to be 'extremely' useful in both initial assessment and continuing work. It raised new issues on three out of every four occasions on which it was used.
12. With new families the questionnaire 'gave further insight into the carer's background'. It 'put into perspective the reasons why the mother was down'.
13. With respondents with whom workers were already familiar it revealed information not previously known. It identified issues that 'the family had not considered stressful or told me'. 'It highlighted issues that were and were not still having an effect'. One social worker reported that they were able to find out the 'carer's view of issues'.
14. It is clear that social workers should be prepared for what may emerge if this instrument is used.

Administration

15. The scale should be given to the respondent, usually a main caregiver, after appropriate preparation. This will depend on whether the context is an assessment or a review.
16. It may be helpful to acknowledge that the worker appreciates that thinking about important family events may stir up painful memories.
17. The questionnaires take about 15 minutes to complete, but discussion can take considerably longer.
18. Although not used in this way in the piloting, it could form a valuable basis for a family discussion. This would require further preparation and negotiation.

Scoring

19. The initial scoring is binary. 1 if the life event has happened, and 0 if it has not.
20. The number of events that the respondent considers are still affecting them is then counted.
21. In piloting respondents reported up to 17 events in the last year, of which up to 10 were still having an affect. The average number of events was between 7 & 8, of which about half were still considered by the caregiver to be affecting them.
22. The questionnaire does not have a cut off point. It is scored on the basis that the more life events the adult has been through, the higher the score, and therefore the **greater** the **likelihood** of some form of longer term impact on the adult, child and or family. This will be particularly so if the person considers the events still affect them.

Reference

Brugha T, Bebington P, Tennant C and Hurry J (1985) The list of threatening experiences: A subset of 12 life events categories with considerable long-term contextual threat. *Psychological Medicine*. **15**: 189–194.

Department of Health

Family Activity

SCALES

Family Activity

SCALE FOR CHILDREN AGED 2 TO 6

Could you let me know the sort of things you do as a family, or with your child/children both regularly and in the last year. Below are some examples of activities you may have done.

If you have done any of these activities **within the timescale written in bold**, please tick in the box provided. You may also like to mention other activities you have done. You ca do this by filling in the lines at the end of this sheet.

	Activity if YES , please tick
Have you read a story to your child **in the last week**?	☐
Has your child eaten with you and other family members at least **once in the last week**?	☐
Did you do anything special for your child on their **last birthday**, such as a cake, party, trip to the park etc.?	☐
Have you gone with your child/family to the park, playground, farm or similar **in the last month**?	☐
Have you gone with your child/family to a local event, such as county show, fete, **in the last 6 months**?	☐
Have you ever belonged to a mother/toddler baby group of any kind for **at least 3 months**?	☐
Have you and your child/family visited friends who have young children **in the last month**?	☐
Has the family been away for the day out to somewhere different **in the last 6 months** (town/into town/ to the seaside/day trip)?	☐
Has your child had a friend to visit **in the last 6 months**?	☐
Has your child been to visit relatives or friends as a treat for her/him **in the last 6 months**?	☐

Are there any other things you have done as a family/with your child in the last:

Week

Month

Last 6 months

Family Activity

SCALE FOR CHILDREN AGED 7 TO 12

Could you let me know the sort of things you do as a family, or with your child/children both regularly and in the last year. Some examples of the kind of activities you may have done are listed below.

If you have done any of these activities **within the time-scale written in bold**, please tick in the box provided.

You may also like to mention other activities you have done in the space provided at the bottom of the page.

	Activity if YES, please tick
Had a friend of your child to visit – **in the last month**?	☐
Had a birthday celebration (i.e. party/cake)?	☐
Been to the cinema/museum/zoo/panto/local event – **in the last 3 months**?	☐
Been swimming/skating/other (participant) sport – **in the last 3 months**?	☐
Been away on holiday with the family/to the seaside – **in the past year**?	☐
Been to the park/for a picnic/local farm – **in the last 3 months**?	☐
Has – or had – any pets **in the past year**?	☐
Attended any special classes/clubs i.e. football, dance – **in the last 3 months**?	☐
Been to stay with relatives or friends (without parents) – **in the last year**?	☐
Visited own friends (i.e. for a meal/for the day) – **in the last 3 months**	
Belongs to a children's library?	☐

Are there any other things you have done as a family/with your child in the last:

Week

Month

Last 6 months

GUIDANCE ON USING FAMILY ACTIVITY SCALES

Background

1. The study of parenting styles has explored several different dimensions, including warmth/coldness and authoritarian/permissive approaches. Related dimensions are control and child-centredness.
2. Newson and Newson (1968) in their study of families in the general population, found that mothers felt strongly about their child's compliance because having children who behave well, and do not 'show them up' in public was important for their self esteem. At the same time, many mothers also recognised that they needed to concede some autonomy to their children.
3. Referring to 'child-centredness' Newson & Newson (1976) said:
   'The keynote to this is the parents' recognition of the child's status as an individual with rights and feelings that are worthy of respect'.
   One example cited by the Newsons was the extent to which mothers were prepared to accept their 4-year-old's claim that they were busy.
4. The concept of child-centredness underlies many schemes for observing parent-child interaction, and there is evidence that it is an important determinant of good child development.
5. What people do together and how they conduct joint activity is an important indicator of the quality of their relationship.

The Scale

6. The Family Activity Scale is derived from a Child-Centredness Scale devised by Marjorie Smith (1985).
7. Child-centredness is seen to be reflected in appropriate opportunities for the child to be involved in autonomous activities of their own choice, or family activities that the parents judge to be potentially enjoyable or fulfilling for the child.
8. There are two versions – one for children aged 2–6, and one for children aged 7–12.
9. The scale aims to identify the extent of joint, child-centred family activity and independent/autonomous child activity, such as pursuit of hobbies and relationships outside the home, and selfcare.
10. The activities in the scale are intended to be relatively independent of family income.
11. It is not expected that families will provide all the activities or opportunities. To some extent this will depend on the characteristics of the child and the context of the family.
12. There are circumstances, for example low income families living in isolated rural areas and those with a disabled child, where access to some of the activities is not possible without additional support.
13. The scale is not intended to judge parents in a critical way, but provide an opportunity to encourage relevant activity, and assess the need for support to enable it to take place.

Use

14. The scale has been used successfully with children as well as caregivers.
15. In piloting it was reportedly 'extremely useful' in initial assessment.
16. Used with both parents separately it highlighted differences in parent perceptions.
17. Used both with caregivers alone and with the children it helped with work on family relationships.
18. On one occasion the children's enthusiastic account of joint family activity gave weight to the view that there had been considerable improvements in the function of the family concerned.
19. When children took part it helped them to feel included, and was thought to have been confidence-building.
20. Specific items were useful as a focus for work to extend joint family activity. Where there is a lack of resource available to the family or a disabled child relevant support can be discussed, and if appropriate, provided.

Administration

21. It is as always important to introduce the scale in a fashion that is appropriate to the family in question. With families that are new to the worker, the need to understand the family can be put forward. For those that are well known there is the need to get a fuller picture of how the family is at the present time – the questionnaire can be a way to broaden the focus of discussion. Where there a disabled child there is a need to understand

how this restricts family activity, and whether there are ways to ensure that the needs of all family members are met.

22. The scale will usually be used with main caregivers, but, as indicated, it can be used with parent(s) and children together.

23. The scale takes about 10 minutes to complete if used with a single adult, but discussion or any relevant work that develops will naturally take longer.

Scoring

24. Each item is scored 1 if it has occurred, or 0 if it did not, and the item scores are summed to give a total score from 0–11 for the list of specific activities, and 0–3 for the items at the bottom of the scale, which allow for activities that have not been specified.

25. To be scored the interviewer must satisfy themselves that the motivation for the action was from the parents and that it was for the child(ren)'s enjoyment or stimulation. For example, staying with the grandmother as a treat during the holidays would count, but staying with a relative because the parents were going on holiday would not. Family pets only count if the child has a special responsibility for looking after them, otherwise only pets 'belonging to the child count'.

26. There is not cut-off score. The questionnaire is scored on a continuum: the higher the score, the more child-centred are the family activities.

27. Formal scoring – adding up the number of activities that have occurred in the specified time periods – can give a general indication of family child-centredness, but parental attitude to the various possibilities on the list, and their motivation to provide suitable opportunities, will contribute to the overall assessment.

28. In evaluating the meaning of the scoring and family circumstances, the development of the child and presence/absence of disability will all need to be considered.

Reference

Smith M (1985) *The Effects of Low Levels of Lead on Urban Children: The relevance of social factors*. Ph.D. Psychology, University of London.

Department of Health

Alcohol Use

QUESTIONNAIRE

Alcohol Use – QUESTIONNAIRE

Please circle the answer most relevant to you

1. **How often do you have a drink containing alcohol?**

NEVER	MONTHLY OR LESS	TWO TO FOUR TIMES A WEEK	TWO OR THREE TIMES A WEEK	FOUR TIMES A ~~MONTH~~ week

2. **How many drinks containing alcohol do you have on a typical day when you are drinking?**

1 or 2	3 or 4	5 or 6	7 to 9	10 or more

3. **How often during the past year have you found that you were not able to stop drinking once you had started?**

NEVER	LESS THAN MONTHLY	MONTHLY	WEEKLY	DAILY, OR ALMOST DAILY

4. **How often during the past year have you failed to do what was normally expected of you because of drinking?**

NEVER	LESS THAN MONTHLY	MONTHLY	WEEKLY	DAILY, OR ALMOST DAILY

5. **Has a relative or friend, doctor or other health worker been concerned about your drinking or suggested you cut down?**

NO	YES, BUT NOT IN THE PAST YEAR	YES DURING THE PAST YEAR

ALCOHOL USE QUESTIONNAIRE

Background

1. Alcohol misuse is estimated to be present in about 6% of primary carers, ranking it third in frequency behind major depression and generalised anxiety. Higher rates are found in certain localities, particularly amongst parents known to Social Services Departments.
2. Drinking alcohol affects different individuals in different ways. For example, some people may be relatively unaffected by the same amount of alcohol that incapacitates others.
3. The primary concern therefore is not the amount of alcohol consumed but how it impacts on the individual, and more particularly on their role as a parent.
4. Drinking alcohol can affect a carer's behaviour towards their partner or children, even if their alcohol consumption is within the Department of Health's guidelines for safe drinking. This may be particularly true if the parent has a vulnerable personality.
5. Drinking alcohol may contribute to incidents where there is loss of temper or parental rows. Deep sleep due to alcohol may reduce the parents' awareness of distress in young children at night.
6. Children of parents who misuse alcohol are more likely to have: developmental delays, social problems, emotional detachment, and delinquency.
7. Research has found that individuals who misuse alcohol are more likely to have a parent or relative who misused alcohol.
8. Children of alcoholics are reported to abuse alcohol or drugs more than children who have grown up with non-alcoholics, and are 2–4 times more likely to have a psychiatric disorder.

The Questionnaire

9. This questionnaire has been found to be effective in detecting adults with alcohol disorders and those with hazardous drinking.
10. The questionnaire is designed to be self administered. Research has found that adults may be more honest in completing this type of questionnaire than in a face-to-face interview.
11. The questionnaire can be scored (see overleaf), but **should be viewed primarily as a tool** to help to raise the subject of alcohol, and to provide the opportunity to address any issues that may arise, particularly in the responses to questions 3, 4 and 5.
12. The questionnaire covers:
    - Frequency of alcohol consumption (question 1)
    - Number of drinks consumed in a typical day (question 2)
    - Ability to control drinking (question 3)
    - Failure to carry out expected tasks as consequence of the effects of alcohol (question 4)
    - Whether others are concerned about the individuals drinking (question 5)

Use

13. The questionnaire can be useful to provide a baseline, either at initial or core assessment or during ongoing work.
14. The questionnaire can help to detect drinking issues in circumstances where alcohol problems are not suspected. Drinking habits are often hidden, even from other family members.
15. It is important that the questionnaire is used as a basis for discussion of drinking patterns. For example, it may be useful to explore with carers how they manage their children when they are drinking. If they go the pub – what happens to the children?
16. Where the worker is uncertain how to interpret the response to the questionnaire they should consult a professional who is experienced in this field.

Administration

17. The introduction of the questionnaire will have to be carefully planned, particularly with carers from communities where the use of alcohol is frowned upon. One approach is to explain that it is important to understand families' approach to drinking alcohol, and that asking parents to fill out a questionnaire can be a useful starting point for discussion. It can be emphasised that the worker is not for or against drinking, but from the children's point of view it is helpful to know what part it plays in day to day family life.
18. Although designed to be self-administered, the questionnaire can also be used as a series of initial probes for use by the worker.

Scoring

Question 1: Never = **0**, Monthly or less =**1**, Two to four times a week = **2**,
Two or three times a week = **3**, Four or more times a week = **4**

Question 2: 1 or 2 = **0**, 3 or 4 = **1**, 5 or 6 = **2**, 7 to 9 = **3**, 10 or more = **4**

Question 3: Never = **0**, Less than monthly = **1**, Monthly = **2**, Weekly = **3**,
Daily or almost daily = **4**.

Question 4: Never = **0**, Less than monthly = **1**, Monthly = **2**, Weekly = **3**,
Daily or almost daily = **4**.

Question 5: No = **0**, Yes, but not in the past year = **2**, Yes during the past year = **4**.

Interpretation of Scoring

1. A score of 5 or more indicates that there may be an alcohol problem, and that there should be fuller evaluation. It needs to be remembered that although people may be more honest filling in a questionnaire than face to face, they are still likely to underestimate consumption and effects.
2. If questions 3, 4 or 5 are checked as other than *No* or *Never* there is likely to be concern that the pattern of drinking may be having an impact on the children.
3. Interpretation may be helped by looking at the Department of Health guidelines.

   The Department of Health guidelines for safe drinking state that:

   For men, drinking between 3 and 4 units a day or less indicates no significant risk to health (1 unit = approximately ½ a pint of beer, 1 measure of spirit, or 1 glass of wine). Regularly drinking 4 our more units of alcohol a day indicates an increased risk to health.

   For women, drinking between 2 and 3 units a day or less, indicates no significant risk to health. Regularly drinking over 3 units a day signifies an increased risk to health.

Reference:

Piccinelli M, Tessari E, Bortolomasi M, Piasere O, Semenzin M, Garzotto N & Tansella M (1997) Efficacy of the alcohol use disorders identification test as a screening tool for hazardous alcohol intake and related disorders in primary care: A validity study. *British Medical Journal*. **514**: 420–424.

References

Birleson P (1980) The validity of depressive disorder in childhood and the development of a self-rating scale: A research report. *Journal of Child Psychology & Psychiatry.* **22**: 73–88.

Brugha T, Bebington P, Tennant C and Hurry J (1985) The list of threatening experiences: A subset of 12 life event categories with considerable long-term contextual threat. *Psychological Medicine.* **15**: 189–194.

Crnic K A & Greenberg M T (1990) Minor parenting stresses with young children. *Child Development.* **61**: 1628–1637.

Crnic K A & Booth C L (1991) Mothers' and fathers' perceptions of daily hassles of parenting across early childhood. *Journal of Marriage and the Family.* **53**: 1043–1050.

Davie C E, Hutt S J, Vincent E and Mason M (1984) *The young child at home.* NFER-Nelson, Windsor.

Department of Health, Department for Education and Employment, Home Office (2000) *The Framework for the Assessment of Children in Need and their Families.* The Stationery Office, London.

Goodman R (1997) The Strengths and Difficulties Questionnaire: A Research Note. *Journal of Child Psychology and Psychiatry.* **38**: 581–586.

Goodman R, Meltzer H and Bailey V (1998) The strengths and difficulties questionnaire: A pilot study on the validity of the self-report version. *European Child and Adolescent Psychiatry.* **7**: 125–130.

Piccinelli M, Tessari E, Bortolomasi M, Piasere O, Semenzin M, Garzotto N and Tansella M (1997) Efficacy of the alcohol use disorders identification test as a screening tool for hazardous alcohol intake and related disorders in primary care: A validity study. *BritishMedical Journal.* **514**: 420–424.

Smith M A (1985) *The Effects of Low Levels of Lead on Urban Children: The relevance of social factors.* Ph.D. Psychology, University of London.

Snaith R P, Constantopoulos A A, Jardine M Y and McGuffin P (1978) A clinical scale for the self-assessment of irritability. *British Journal of Psychiatry.* **132**: 164–171.

Acknowledgements

The Department of Health is grateful to the professionals whose names are listed in the references for their permission to use their respective questionnaires and scales in this pack, and for agreeing to some amendments which enabled the instruments to be customised.

We acknowledge with thanks the social services staff who managed and participated in this study, and advised us on how best to present and use the materials. In particular, we thank the children and families whose feedback was invaluable in refining the scales and questionnaires and suggesting how they might be best used. We are grateful also to Steve Walker and Carol Wickes for their creative assistance with design and presentation.

In the Chair of the Development Group

Jenny Gray	Social Services Inspector, Department of Health

Consultants to the Project

Dr Arnon Bentovim	Consultant, Child and Family Psychiatrist, The London Child and Family Consultation Service and Honorary Consultant, Institute of Child Health, Great Ormond Street Hospital.
Liza Bingley Miller	Social Work Consultant (from November 1998)
Professor Antony Cox	Emeritus Professor of Child and Adolescent Psychiatry, Guy's, King's College and St Thomas' Hospitals Medical School
Natalie Silverdale	Research Assistant, Lambeth Healthcare NHS Trust (until December 1998)
Dr Marjorie Smith	Deputy Director, The Thomas Coram Research Unit

Members of the Development Group

Rohan Barnet	Essex Social Services Department (from July 1998)
Rita Crowne	Service Manager, Bournemouth Borough Council
Ann Goldsmith	Children's Assessment and Family Support County Manager, Essex Social Services Department (until July 1998)
John Griffen	Children with Disabilities Team, London Borough of Westminster

Ann Gross	Section Head – Child Protection, Department of Health (until September 1998)
Maurice Lindsay	Bath and North East Somerset Social Services Department
Steve Walker	Training and Development Manager, Kingston upon Thames Social Services Department

 ISBN 0 11 322426 5

Department of Health

Parenting Daily Hassles

SCALE

Name of Child: ______________________

Completed by: ______________________

Relationship to child: ______________________

Date: ______________________

Parenting Daily Hassles
SCALE

The statements below describe a lot of events that routinely occur in families with young children. These events sometimes make life difficult. Please read each item and circle how often it happens to you (rarely, sometimes, a lot, or constantly) and then circle how much of a 'hassle' you feel that it has been for you **FOR THE PAST 6 MONTHS**. If you have more than one child, these events can include any or all of your children.

EVENT	How often it happens				Hassle (low to high)				
1. Continually cleaning up messes of toys or food	Rarely	Sometimes	A lot	Constantly	1	2	3	4	5
2. Being nagged, whined at, complained to	Rarely	Sometimes	A lot	Constantly	1	2	3	4	5
3. Meal-time difficulties with picky eaters, complaining etc.	Rarely	Sometimes	A lot	Constantly	1	2	3	4	5
4. The kids won't listen or do what they are asked without being nagged	Rarely	Sometimes	A lot	Constantly	1	2	3	4	5
5. Baby-sitters are hard to find	Rarely	Sometimes	A lot	Constantly	1	2	3	4	5
6. The kids schedules (like pre-school or other activities) interfere with meeting your own household needs	Rarely	Sometimes	A lot	Constantly	1	2	3	4	5
7. Sibling arguments or fights require a 'referee'	Rarely	Sometimes	A lot	Constantly	1	2	3	4	5
8. The kids demand that you entertain them or play with them	Rarely	Sometimes	A lot	Constantly	1	2	3	4	5
9. The kids resist or struggle with you over bed-time	Rarely	Sometimes	A lot	Constantly	1	2	3	4	5
10. The kids are constantly underfoot, interfering with other chores	Rarely	Sometimes	A lot	Constantly	1	2	3	4	5
11. The need to keep a constant eye on where the kids are and what they are doing	Rarely	Sometimes	A lot	Constantly	1	2	3	4	5
12. The kids interrupt adult conversations or interactions	Rarely	Sometimes	A lot	Constantly	1	2	3	4	5
13. Having to change your plans because of unprecedented child needs	Rarely	Sometimes	A lot	Constantly	1	2	3	4	5
14. The kids get dirty several times a day requiring changes of clothing	Rarely	Sometimes	A lot	Constantly	1	2	3	4	5
15. Difficulties in getting privacy (eg. in the bathroom)	Rarely	Sometimes	A lot	Constantly	1	2	3	4	5
16. The kids are hard to manage in public (grocery store, shopping centre, restaurant)	Rarely	Sometimes	A lot	Constantly	1	2	3	4	5
17. Difficulties in getting kids ready for outings and leaving on time	Rarely	Sometimes	A lot	Constantly	1	2	3	4	5
18. Difficulties in leaving kids for a night out or at school or day care	Rarely	Sometimes	A lot	Constantly	1	2	3	4	5
19. The kids have difficulties with friends (eg. fighting, trouble, getting along, or no friends available)	Rarely	Sometimes	A lot	Constantly	1	2	3	4	5
20. Having to run extra errands to meet the kids needs	Rarely	Sometimes	A lot	Constantly	1	2	3	4	5

Questionnaire completed by *mother/father/adoptive parent/foster carer* (please specify)

Scoring

19. (a) The challenging behaviour total score is obtained by adding the intensity scale scores for items: 2, 4, 8, 9, 11, 12, 16. Range: 0–35.

    (b) The parenting tasks total score is obtained by adding the intensity scale scores for items: 1, 5, 7, 10, 13, 14, 17, 20. Range: 0–40

20. There is no cut off for any of the scales but total scores above 50 on the frequency scale or above 70 on the intensity scale indicate on the one hand a high frequency of potentially hassling happenings, and on the other that the parent is experiencing significant pressure over parenting.

21. Events occurring with frequency 3 or 4, or intensity 4 or 5, particularly those where the parent rates high intensity or impact, should be discussed to clarify the extent of need.

22. The total score on the challenging behaviour and parenting tasks scales may be useful in indicating how the parent/caregiver sees the situation, whether difficulties lie in the troublesome behaviour of the children, or the burden of meeting the 'expected' or 'legitimate' needs of the children. The subscores may also be useful in monitoring change.

Reference

Crnic KA & Greenberg MT (1990) Minor parenting stresses with young children. *Child Development*. **61**: 1628-1637

Crnic KA & Booth CL (1991) Mothers' and fathers' perceptions of daily hassles of parenting across early childhood. *Journal of Marriage and the Family*. **53**: 1043–1050.

 ISBN 0 11 322426 5

Department of Health

Parenting Daily Hassles

GUIDANCE ON USING SCALE

PARENTING DAILY HASSLES SCALE

Background

1. This scale aims to assess the frequency and intensity/impact of 20 experiences that can be a 'hassle' to parents.
2. It has been used in a wide variety of research concerned with children and families. The research in which it has been used includes a parenting programme with families who had major difficulties in raising young children.
3. Parents/Caregivers enjoy completing the scale, because it touches on aspects of being a parent that are very familiar. It helps them express what it feels like to be a parent.
4. During piloting, social workers reported that it depicted concisely areas of pressure felt by the carer. This helped identify areas where assistance could be provided either by the social services department or other agencies.
5. It is seen by parents as a way for them to express their needs for help with parenting.

The Scale

6. The caregiver is asked to score each of the 20 potential **Hassles** in two different ways for **frequency** and **intensity**.
7. The frequency of each type of happening provides an 'objective' marker of how often it occurs.
8. The intensity or impact score indicates the caregiver's 'subjective' appraisal of how much those events affect or 'hassle' them.
9. The time frame for this scale can be varied according to the focus of the assessment. For example, if a family is thought to have been under particular pressure in the last 2 months the parent can be asked to consider how matters have been during that period. However, if it is intended to assess progress, the same time frame should be used on each occasion. Periods of less than one month are probably too short to give a useful picture.

Use

10. The caregiver should understand the aim of filling out the questionnaire, and how it will contribute to the overall assessment.
11. The scale is probably most useful with families that are not well-known. In piloting it was found to highlight areas for future discussion, and help prioritise which parenting issues needed to be addressed first.
12. It can also be used to monitor change.

Administration

13. It should be given to the parent/caregiver to fill out themselves.
14. It can be read out if necessary.
15. It takes about 10 minutes to complete.
16. The scale should always be used as a basis for discussion. In general this is best kept until the parent has finished, but there will be occasions when it is vital to acknowledge, or immediately follow up comments made while it is being filled out.

Scoring

17. The scale can be used in two distinct ways: (a) the totals of the frequency and intensity scales can be obtained, or (b) scores for challenging behaviour and parenting tasks can be derived from the intensity scale.
18. To obtain frequency and intensity total scores

    a) The frequency scale is scored: rarely = 1, sometimes = 2, a lot = 3, and constantly = 4. If the parent says that an event never occurs, never = 0. The range for this scale is 0–80. A score of 3 or 4 for any one event indicates that it occurs with above average frequency.

    b) The intensity scale is scored by adding the parents rating of 1–5 for each item. If a 0 has been scored for frequency on an item then it should be scored 0 for intensity. The range for this scale is 0–100. A score of 4 or 5 for any one event indicates that it is at least some problem to the parent.

 ISBN 0 11 322426 5

Department of Health

Strengths and Difficulties

QUESTIONNAIRE

Name of Child: ______________________

Completed by: ______________________

Relationship to child: ______________________

Date: ______________________

19. Fuller discussion is vital for several reasons. Firstly, it is important to establish level and nature of any difficulties more clearly. Information from other sources is also relevant for this purpose. Secondly, the overall score may be below the cut off point indicative of disorder, but there may still be issues that are important to the respondent. The response to a single item might provide the cue. Thirdly, it is crucial to understand how the child, parent and other family members are responding to how the child is, or what the child is doing/saying.

Scoring

20. This is explained on the sheet that accompanies the questionnaires.

21. Each item is scored 0, 1 or 2. Somewhat true is always scored 1, but whether Not true and Certainly true are scored 0 or 2 depends on whether the item is framed as a strength or difficulty.

22. The scoring sheet explains which item contributes to which subscales. The Pro-social scale is scored so that an absence of pro-social behaviour is a problem i.e. scores high. A child may have difficulties but if they have a low Pro-social score the outlook for intervention is better.

23. The scoring sheet has a chart, which indicates which total scores are low, average or high in the general population. High scores overall or for any subscale point to the likelihood of a significant disorder, and/or a disorder of a particular type. They do not guarantee that there will be found to be a disorder when a more thorough assessment is conducted. Neither does a low score guarantee the absence of a problem, but the instrument is useful for screening.

References

Goodman R (1997). The Strengths and Difficulties Questionnaire: A reseach note. *Journal of Child Psychology and Psychiatry*. **38**: 581–586.

Goodman R, Meltzer H and Bailey V (1998) The strengths and difficulties questionnaire: A pilot study on the validity of the self-report version. *European Child & Adolescent Psychiatry*. **7**: 125–130.

 ISBN 0 11 322426 5

DH Department of Health

Strengths and Difficulties

GUIDANCE ON USING QUESTIONNAIRES

STRENGTHS AND DIFFICULTIES QUESTIONNAIRES

Background

1. Evaluation of children's emotional and behavioural development is a central component of social work assessment.
2. These questionnaires screen for child emotional and behavioural problems. These scales are similar to older scales such as Rutter A & B Scales developed for use by parents and teachers, but put a greater emphasis on strengths.

The Scales

3. The questionnaires consist of 25 items that refer to different emotions or behaviours.
4. For each item the respondent marks in one of three boxes to indicate whether the item is **not** true, **somewhat** true or **certainly** true for the child in question.
5. On the back of each questionnaire are questions that aim to address severity by scoring duration of the difficulties and their impact on the child, themselves or others.
6. Children's emotional and behavioural problems are not always evident in all situations. When they are, the problem is usually more severe. As with the Rutter scales, the Strengths and Difficulties Questionnaires have both parent and teacher versions.
7. In young children, parents' reports of their emotions and behaviour are usually more reliable than those of the children themselves, but in adolescence, parents are often unaware of their children's emotional state. There is therefore a Strengths and Difficulties questionnaire for young people aged 11–16.
8. The Rutter scales were originally devised for children aged 9–10, and have been shown to be valid for those aged 6–16. The Strengths and Difficulties Scale covers ages 4–16, and there is an additional scale for children aged 3–4.
9. The scales can be scored to produce an overall score that indicates whether the child/young person is likely to have a significant problem. Selected items can also be used to form subscales for Pro-social Behaviour, Hyperactivity, Emotional Symptoms, Conduct and Peer problems.

Use

10. The questionnaires are of value in both assessments and for evaluating progress.
11. They can give an indication of whether a child/young person is likely to have a significant emotional or behavioural problem/disorder, and what type of disorder it is.
12. During piloting over half the children assessed scored above the cut-off scores indicating a probable disorder.
13. The most common problems were Hyperactivity, Peer and Conduct problems. These were identified in over half the children.
14. One social worker commented that the questionnaire 'gave a more in-depth look at the young person'. Another said that with the individual child/young person it could be a springboard for therapeutic action, and that it would be helpful, alongside work with the family, to monitor progress.

Administration

15. The respondent whether parent, child or teacher needs to understand where the use of the questionnaire fits into the overall assessment.
16. It is usually best if the respondent completes the questionnaire in the presence of the social worker. Sometimes it will be necessary for the worker to administer the scale verbally.
17. The scale takes about 10 minutes to complete.
18. It is preferable if full discussion is kept to the end, but there will be occasions when what the respondent says while completing the scale should be acknowledged immediately.

Interpreting scores and identifying need

The provisional bandings shown below have been selected so that roughly 80% of children in the community do not have needs in these areas, 10% have some needs, and 10% have high needs.

Self completed	LOW NEED	SOME NEED	HIGH NEED
Total difficulties score	0–15	16–19	20–40
Conduct problems score	0–3	4	5–10
Hyperactivity score	0–5	6	7–10
Emotional symptoms score	0–5	6	7–10
Peer problem score	0–3	4–5	6–10
Pro-social behaviour score	6–10	5	0–4

 ISBN 0 11 322426 5

Department of Health

Strengths and Difficulties

SCORING

SCORING THE SELF REPORT STRENGTHS AND DIFFICULTIES QUESTIONNAIRE

The 25 items in the SDQ comprise 5 scales of 5 items each. The first stage of scoring the questionnaire is generally to score each of the 5 scales. Somewhat true is always scored as 1, but the scoring of Not True and Certainly True varies with each item. The score for each response category is given below scale by scale.

Pro-social Scale

	NOT TRUE	SOMEWHAT TRUE	CERTAINLY TRUE
I am considerate of others	2	1	0
I usually share	2	1	0
I am helpful if	2	1	0
I am kinder to younger	2	1	0
I often volunteer	2	1	0

Hyperactivity Scale

	NOT TRUE	SOMEWHAT TRUE	CERTAINLY TRUE
I am restless	0	1	2
I am constantly fidgeting	0	1	2
I am easily distracted	0	1	2
Thinks things out	2	1	0
I see tasks through	2	1	0

Emotional Symptoms Scale

	NOT TRUE	SOMEWHAT TRUE	CERTAINLY TRUE
I get a lot of headaches	2	1	0
I worry a lot	2	1	0
I am often happy	2	1	0
I am nervous in	2	1	0
I have many fears	2	1	0

Conduct Problems Scale

	NOT TRUE	SOMEWHAT TRUE	CERTAINLY TRUE
I get very angry	0	1	2
I usually do as I am told	2	1	0
I fight a lot	0	1	2
I am often accused of lying	0	1	2
I take things	0	1	2

Peer Problems Scale

	NOT TRUE	SOMEWHAT TRUE	CERTAINLY TRUE
I am rather solitary	0	1	2
I have at least one good friend	2	1	0
Other people … like me	2	1	0
Other … people pick on me …	0	1	2
I get on better with adults …	0	1	2

For each of the 5 scales the score can range from 0 to 10 provided all five items have been completed. You can prorate the scores if there are only one or two missing items.

To generate a total difficulties score, sum the four scales dealing with problems but do not include the pro-social scale. The resultant score can range from 0 to 40. Provided at least 12 of the relevant 20 items are completed, you can prorate the total if necessary.

Strengths and Difficulties

QUESTIONNAIRE

TO BE COMPLETED BY A MAIN CARER OF A CHILD AGED BETWEEN 3 AND 4

For each item, please mark the box for Not True, Somewhat True or Certainly True. It would help us if you answered all items as best you can even if you are not absolutely certain, or the items seem daft! Please give your answers on the basis of the child's behaviour over the last six months.

Child's Name ______________________ **Male/Female** **Date of Birth** ______________

	Not True	Somewhat True	Certainly True
Considerate of other people's feelings			
Restless, overactive, cannot stay still for long			
Often complains of headaches, stomach-aches or sickness			
Shares readily with other children (treats, toys, pencils etc.)			
Often has temper tantrums or hot tempers			
Rather solitary, tends to play alone			
Generally obedient, usually does what adults request			
Many worries, often seems worried			
Helpful if someone is hurt, upset or feeling ill			
Constantly fidgeting or squirming			
Has at least one good friend			
Often fights with other children or bullies them			
Often unhappy, downhearted or tearful			
Generally liked by other children			
Easily distracted, concentration wanders			
Nervous or clingy in new situations, easily loses confidence			
Kind to younger children			
Often argumentative with adults			
Picked on or bullied by other children			
Often volunteers to help others (parents, teachers, other children)			
Can stop and think things over before acting			
Can be spiteful to others			
Gets on better with adults than with other children			
Many fears, easily scared			
Sees tasks through to the end, good attention span			

Please turn over – there are a few more questions on the other side...

Overall, do you think that your child has difficulties in one or more of the following areas: emotions, concentration, behaviour or being able to get on with other people?

No difficulties	Yes – minor difficulties	Yes – more serious difficulties	Yes – severe difficulties
☐	☐	☐	☐

If you have answered **'Yes'**, please answer the following questions about these difficulties:

- How long have these difficulties been present?

Less than a month	1–5 months	5–12 months	Over a year
☐	☐	☐	☐

- Do the difficulties upset or distress your child?

Not at all	Only a little	Quite a lot	A great deal
☐	☐	☐	☐

- Do the difficulties interfere with your child's everyday life in the following areas?

	Not at all	Only a little	Quite a lot	A great deal
Home life	☐	☐	☐	☐
Friendships	☐	☐	☐	☐
Learning	☐	☐	☐	☐
Leisure activities	☐	☐	☐	☐

- Do the difficulties put a burden on you or the family as a whole?

Not at all	Only a little	Quite a lot	A great deal
☐	☐	☐	☐

Signature ______________________________

Date ______________________________

Mother/Father/Other (please specify) ______________________________

Thank you very much for your help

Strengths and Difficulties

QUESTIONNAIRE

TO BE COMPLETED BY A MAIN CARER OF A CHILD AGED BETWEEN 4 AND 16

For each item, please mark the box for Not True, Somewhat True or Certainly True. It would help us if you answered all items as best you can even if you are not absolutely certain, or the items seem daft! Please give your answers on the basis of the child's behaviour over the last six months.

Child's Name ______________________ **Male/Female** **Date of Birth** ______________

	Not True	Somewhat True	Certainly True
Considerate of other people's feelings	☐	☐	☐
Restless, overactive, cannot sit still for long	☐	☐	☐
Often complains of headaches, stomach-aches or sickness	☐	☐	☐
Shares readily with other children (treats, toys, pencils etc.)	☐	☐	☐
Often has temper tantrums or hot tempers	☐	☐	☐
Rather solitary, tends to play alone	☐	☐	☐
Generally obedient, usually does what adults request	☐	☐	☐
Many worries, often seems worried	☐	☐	☐
Helpful if someone is hurt, upset or feeling ill	☐	☐	☐
Constantly fidgeting or squirming	☐	☐	☐
Has at least one good friend	☐	☐	☐
Often fights with other children or bullies them	☐	☐	☐
Often unhappy, downhearted or tearful	☐	☐	☐
Generally liked by other children	☐	☐	☐
Easily distracted, concentration wanders	☐	☐	☐
Nervous or clingy in new situations, easily loses confidence	☐	☐	☐
Kind to younger children	☐	☐	☐
Often lies or cheats	☐	☐	☐
Picked on or bullied by other children	☐	☐	☐
Often volunteers to help others (parents, teachers, other children)	☐	☐	☐
Thinks things out before acting	☐	☐	☐
Steals from home, school or elsewhere	☐	☐	☐
Gets on better with adults than with other children	☐	☐	☐
Many fears, easily scared	☐	☐	☐
Sees tasks through to the end, good attention span	☐	☐	☐

Please turn over – there are a few more questions on the other side ...

Overall, do you think that your child has difficulties in one or more of the following areas: emotions, concentration, behaviour or being able to get on with other people?

No difficulties	Yes – minor difficulties	Yes – more serious difficulties	Yes – severe difficulties
☐	☐	☐	☐

If you have answered **'Yes'**, please answer the following questions about these difficulties:

- How long have these difficulties been present?

Less than a month	1–5 months	5–12 months	Over a year
☐	☐	☐	☐

- Do the difficulties upset or distress your child?

Not at all	Only a little	Quite a lot	A great deal
☐	☐	☐	☐

- Do the difficulties interfere with your child's everyday life in the following areas?

	Not at all	Only a little	Quite a lot	A great deal
Home life	☐	☐	☐	☐
Friendships	☐	☐	☐	☐
Classroom Learning	☐	☐	☐	☐
Leisure activities	☐	☐	☐	☐

- Do the difficulties put a burden on you or the family as a whole?

Not at all	Only a little	Quite a lot	A great deal
☐	☐	☐	☐

Signature ______________________________

Date ______________________________

Mother/Father/Other (please specify) ______________________________

Thank you very much for your help

Strengths and Difficulties

QUESTIONNAIRE

TO BE COMPLETED BY A YOUNG PERSON BETWEEN 11 AND 16

Please read the questionnaire carefully. For each of the statements put a tick in the box that **you** think is most like you. It would help us if you put a tick for all the statements – even if it seems a bit daft! Please give answers on the basis of how you have been feeling over the last six months.

Your Name ______________________ **Your age** ______________________

	Not True	Somewhat True	Certainly True
I try to be nice to people. I care about their feelings			
I get restless, I cannot sit still for long			
I get a lot of headaches, stomach-aches or sickness			
I usually share with others (food, games, pens etc.)			
I get very angry and often lose my temper			
I am usually on my own. I generally play alone or keep to myself			
I usually do as I am told			
I worry a lot			
I am helpful if someone is hurt, upset or feeling ill			
I am constantly fidgeting or squirming			
I have one good friend or more			
I fight a lot. I can make other people do what I want			
I am often unhappy, downhearted or tearful			
Other people my age generally like me			
I am easily distracted, I find it difficult to concentrate			
I am nervous in new situations. I easily lose confidence			
I am kind to younger children			
I am often accused of cheating or lying			
Other children or young people pick on or bully me			
I often volunteer to help others (parents, teachers, children)			
I think before I do things			
I take things that are not mine from home, school or elsewhere			
I get on better with adults than with people my own age			
I have many fears, I am easily scared			
I finish the things I'm doing. My attention is good			

Please turn over – there are a few more questions on the other side ...

Overall, do you think that you have difficulties in one or more of the following areas: emotions, concentration, behaviour or being able to get on with other people?

No difficulties	Yes – minor difficulties	Yes – more serious difficulties	Yes – very severe difficulties
☐	☐	☐	☐

If you have answered **'Yes'**, please answer the following questions about these difficulties:

- How long have these difficulties been present?

Less than a month	1–5 months	5–12 months	Over a year
☐	☐	☐	☐

- Do the difficulties upset or distress your child?

Not at all	Only a little	Quite a lot	A great deal
☐	☐	☐	☐

- Do the difficulties interfere with your child's everyday life in the following areas?

	Not at all	Only a little	Quite a lot	A great deal
Home life	☐	☐	☐	☐
Friendships	☐	☐	☐	☐
Classroom Learning	☐	☐	☐	☐
Leisure activities	☐	☐	☐	☐

- Do the difficulties make it harder for those around you (family, friends, teachers etc.)?

Not at all	Only a little	Quite a lot	A great deal
☐	☐	☐	☐

Signature ______________________________

Date ______________________________

Thank you very much for your help

Strengths and Difficulties QUESTIONNAIRE

RECORD SHEET

Name ______________________________

Age ____________ Male/Female

Strengths and Difficulties Questionaire completed by:

MAIN CARER ON ______________________

Teacher on ______________________

Self on ______________________

SCALE	LOW NEEDS	SOME NEEDS	HIGH NEEDS
CONDUCT PROBLEMS			
MAIN CARER	0–2	3	4–10
Teacher	0–2	3	4–10
Self	**0–3**	**4**	**5–10**
HYPERACTIVITY			
MAIN CARER	0–5	6	7–10
Teacher	0–5	6	7–10
Self	**0–5**	**6**	**7–10**
EMOTIONAL SYMPTOMS			
MAIN CARER	0–3	4	5–10
Teacher	0–4	5	6–10
Self	**0–5**	**6**	**7–10**
PEER PROBLEMS			
MAIN CARER	0–2	3	4–10
Teacher	0–3	4	5–10
Self	**0–3**	**4–5**	**6–10**
PRO-SOCIAL BEHAVIOUR			
MAIN CARER	6–10	5	0–4
Teacher	6–10	5	0–4
Self	**6–10**	**5**	**0–4**
TOTAL DIFFICULTIES			
MAIN CARER	0–13	14–16	17–40
Teacher	0–11	12–15	16–40
Self	**0–15**	**16–19**	**20–40**

 ISBN 0 11 322426 5

Strengths and Difficulties QUESTIONNAIRE

SCORE SHEET

Conduct	Hyperactivity	Emotional	Peer	Pro-social
Total				

 ISBN 0 11 322426 5

Department of Health

Adolescent Wellbeing

SCALE

Name of Young Person

____

Date: ______________________

Adolescent Wellbeing

SCALE FOR YOUNG PEOPLE AGED 11 TO 16

Please tick as appropriate

	Most of the time	sometimes	never
1. I look forward to things as much as I used to	☐	☐	☐
2. I sleep very well	☐	☐	☐
3. I feel like crying	☐	☐	☐
4. I like going out	☐	☐	☐
5. I feel like leaving home	☐	☐	☐
6. I get stomache-aches/cramps	☐	☐	☐
7. I have lots of energy	☐	☐	☐
8. I enjoy my food	☐	☐	☐
9. I can stick up for myself	☐	☐	☐
10. I think life isn't worth living	☐	☐	☐
11. I am good at things I do	☐	☐	☐
12. I enjoy the things I do as much as I used to	☐	☐	☐
13. I like talking to my friends and family	☐	☐	☐
14. I have horrible dreams	☐	☐	☐
15. I feel very lonely	☐	☐	☐
16. I am easily cheered up	☐	☐	☐
17. I feel so sad I can hardly bear it	☐	☐	☐
18. I feel very bored	☐	☐	☐

Scoring

18. The responses to each question are scored 0, 1 or 2. How the responses are scored depends on the nature of the statement that is being responded to as well as the response. 0 means that the response indicates no concern, 1 possible concern and 2 that the young person is indicating unhappiness or low self esteem with regard to that item.

    For example for question 8 – I enjoy my food – if no/never is ticked the score is 2. For question 17 – I feel so sad I can hardly bear it – a score of 2 would be obtained for most of the time.

19. A score of 13 or more has been found to indicate the likelihood of a depressive disorder. Discussion with the young person and information from other sources will be necessary to make a definite diagnosis. There will be some who score high, but who on careful consideration are not judged to have a depressive disorder, and others who score low who do have one.

20. In most instances the way a young person responds to the the different questions will be as important and as valuable as any score, because they can give an insight into that particular young person's needs. The reply to only one question may give the opportunity to understand their point of view.

Reference

Birleson P (1980) The validity of Depressive Disorder in Childhood and the Development of a Self-Rating Scale; a Research Report. *Journal of Child Psychology and Psychiatry*. **22**: 73–88.

 ISBN 0 11 3224265

Department of Health

Adolescent Wellbeing

GUIDANCE ON USING SCALE

ADOLESCENT WELLBEING SCALE

Background

1. How young people feel in themselves is a vital part of any assessment.
2. It is important to understand their worries and concerns, and whether they are depressed or even suicidal.
3. There is good evidence that the way a young person is feeling is often not recognised by their parents or caregivers. This makes it particularly important to have a way of helping them to express directly how they are feeling.
4. With very young children their reporting can fluctuate from day to day, or even hour to hour – they do not necessarily give a stable view of their situation. Evaluation of their perspective requires particular care, so questionnaires are not usually a good starting point
5. Older children and adolescents can give a more reliable report, which means that a questionnaire may be more helpful. As with some adults they often find it easier to respond to a questionnaire about feelings than face-to-face interviewing.

The Scale

6. The Adolescent Wellbeing Scale was devised by Birleson to pick up possible depression in older children and adolescents. It has been shown to be effective for this purpose.
7. The scale has 18 questions – each relating to different aspects of an adolescent's life, and how they feel about them. They are asked to indicate whether the statement applies to them most of the time, sometimes or never.
8. The scale can be used by children as young a 7 or 8, but as indicated above, responses are more reliable for those aged 11 or more.

Reference

Birleson P (1980) The validity of Depressive Disorder in Childhood and the Development of a Self-Rating Scale; a Research Report. *Journal of Child Psychology and Psychiatry*. **22**: 73–88.

Use

9. In piloting social workers found young people were pleased to have the opportunity to contribute to the assessment.
10. The questionnaire often helped them express their feelings. It gave 'an overall insight in a short time'. It presented a 'truer picture of the adolescent's state of mind'. 'It gave me insight into how sad and overwhelmed the young person felt'.
11. On occasions use of the scale pointed to particular issues that could be a focus for further work. It gave an opportunity for 'the young person to look at themselves'.
12. The scale has proved useful with adolescents at initial assessment, but also to monitor progress. For example it helped 'clarify a young person's feeling about placement with their mother'.
13. During piloting over half the young people who filled out the questionnaire were above the cut-off score of 13 indicating a probable depressive disorder.

Administration

14. The young person needs to understand the aim of the questionnaire, and how it fits into any wider assessment.
15. Ideally it is completed by the adolescent themselves, but, if necessary, it an be administered verbally.
16. Discussion is usually best at the end, but there may be important areas that need to be picked up as the result of comments made while the questionnaire is being filled out. A number of adolescents talk as they are completing the scale, and this may provide a good opportunity to promote conversation, or establish rapport.
17. During piloting the scale took about 15 minutes to complete, ensuing discussion took longer.

 ISBN 0 11 322426 5

Department of Health

Adult Wellbeing

THE SCALE

Name of Child: ______________________________

Completed by: ______________________________

Relationship to child: ______________________________

Date: ______________________________

ADULT WELLBEING SCALE

This form has been designed so that you can show how you have been feeling in the past few days.

Read each item in turn and UNDERLINE the response which shows best how you are feeling or have been feeling in the last few days.

Please complete all of the questionnaire.

1. I feel cheerful

Yes, definitely | Yes, sometimes | No, not much | No, not at all

2. I can sit down and relax quite easily

Yes, definitely | Yes, sometimes | No, not much | No, not at all

3. My appetite is

Very poor | Fairly poor | Quite good | Very good

4. I lose my temper and shout and snap at others

Yes, definitely | Yes, sometimes | No, not much | No, not at all

5. I can laugh and feel amused

Yes, definitely | Yes, sometimes | No, not much | No, not at all

---

6. I feel I might lose control and hit or hurt someone

Sometimes | Occasionally | Rarely | Never

7. I have an uncomfortable feeling like butterflies in the stomach

Yes, definitely | Yes, sometimes | Not very often | Not at all

8. The though of hurting myself occurs to me

Sometimes | Not very often | Hardly ever | Not at all

9. I'm awake before I need to get up

For 2 hours or more | For about 1 hour | For less than 1 hour | Not at all. I sleep until it is time to get up

10. I feel tense or 'wound up'

Yes, definitely | Yes, sometimes | No, not much | No, not at all

---

11. I feel like harming myself

Yes, definitely | Yes, sometimes | No, not much | No, not at all

12. I've kept up my old interests

Yes, most of them | Yes, some of them | No, not many of them | No, none of them

13. I am patient with other people

All the time | Most of the time | Some of the time | Hardly ever

14. I get scared or panicky for no very good reason

Yes, definitely | Yes, sometimes | No, not much | No, not at all

15. I get angry with myself or call myself names

Yes, definitely | Yes, sometimes | Not often | No, not at all

---

16. People upset me so that I feel like slamming doors or banging about

Yes, often | Yes, sometimes | Only occasionally | Not at all

17. I can go out on my own without feeling anxious

Yes, always | Yes, sometimes | No, not often | No, I never can

18. Lately I have been getting annoyed with myself

Very much so | Rather a lot | Not much | Not at all

Scoring

19. The sheet accompanying the questionnaire indicates the method of scoring the 4 subscales.
20. Use of cut-off scores gives indicators of significant care needs with respect to depression, anxiety, and inwardly and outwardly directed irritability.
21. Inward irritability can point to the possibility of self-harm. Outward irritability raises the possibility of angry actions towards the child(ren).
22. As with any screening instrument, interpretation must be in the context of other information. Some respondents will underreport distress, others exaggerate it. A high or low score on any scale does not guarantee that a significant level of need is present.
23. Most value is obtained by using the scale as a springboard for discussion.

Reference

Snaith RP, Constantopoulos AA, Jardine MY & McGuffin P (1978) A clinical scale for the self-assessment of irritability. *British Journal of Psychiatry*. **132**: 163–71.

 ISBN 0 11 322426 5

Department of Health

Adult Wellbeing

GUIDANCE ON USING THE SCALE

ADULT WELLBEING SCALE

Background

1. Parent/Caregiver mental health is a fundamental component of assessment.
2. There is evidence that some people respond more openly to a questionnaire than a face to face interview, when reporting on their mental health.
3. A questionnaire gives caregivers the opportunity to express themselves without having to face another person, however sympathetic that person may be.
4. A questionnaire is no substitute for a good relationship, but it can contribute to the development of a rapport if discussed sensitively.
5. During piloting the use of the questionnaire was found to convey the social worker's concern for the parent's wellbeing. This can be particularly valuable where the parent feels their needs are not being considered.

The Scale

6. The scale is the Irritability, Depression, Anxiety (IDA) Scale developed by Snaith *et al* (1978).
7. This scale allows respondents four possible responses to each item.
8. Four aspects of wellbeing are covered: Depression, Anxiety and Inwardly and Outwardly directed Irritability.

Use

9. In principle the questionnaire can be used with any adult, who is in contact with the child whose development and context are being assessed. In practice this will usually be the main caregiver(s).
10. In piloting, social workers reported that use of the scale raised issues on more than half the occasions that it was used. Probable depression was found amongst almost half the caregivers, and significant anxiety in a third.
11. Where social workers were new to the family situation they said they learnt things they did not know. 'It helped me to be aware of the carers' needs', and 'highlighted stresses'. It helped focus on 'parents' needs and feelings'.
12. Even when parents were known to the workers it gave topics an airing and clarified areas to work on; it 'released tension'.
13. Progress can also be registered. It was 'useful to measure when things were calmer'.
14. Used flexibly it can provide openings to discuss many areas including feelings about relationships with partners and children.

Administration

15. It is vital that the respondent understands why they are being asked to complete the scale. Some will be concerned that revealing mental health needs will prejudice their chances of continuing to care for their child. For example, it can be explained that many carers of children experience considerable stress, and it is important to understand this if they are to be given appropriate support.
16. The scale is best filled out by the carer themselves in the presence of the worker, but it can be administered verbally.
17. It takes about 10 minutes to complete.
18. **Discussion is essential**. Usually this will be when the questionnaire has been completed, so the respondent has an opportunity to consider their own needs uninterrupted. However, there will be times when an important clue to how the caregiver feels may be best picked up immediately. One example occurred during piloting, when a respondent expressed distaste for questions about self-harm.

SCORING THE ADULT WELLBEING SCALE

1. **Depression** – Questions 1,3,5,9 and 12 look at depression. The possible response scores that are shown below run from the left to the right – i.e. for question 1 'I feel cheerful', the scores would be looked at from 'yes, definitely' (0), 'yes, sometimes' (1), 'no, not at all' (3), A score of 4–6 is borderline in this scale and a score above this may indicate a problem

QU1	QU3	QU5	QU9	QU12
0,1,2,3	3,2,1,0	0,1,2,3	3,2,1,0,	0,1,2,3,

2. **Anxiety** – Questions 2,7,10,14 and 17 look at anxiety. A score of 6–8 is borderline, above this level may indicate a problem in this area.

QU2	QU7	QU10	QU14	QU17
0,1,2,3	3,2,1,0	3,2,1,0	3,2,1,0,	0,1,2,3,

3. **Outward directed irritability** – Questions 4,6,13 and 16 look at outward directed irritability. A score of 5–7 is borderline for this scale, and a score above this may indicate a problem in this area.

QU4	QU6	QU13	QU16
3,2,1,0	3,2,1,0	0,1,2,3	3,2,1,0,

4. **Inward directed irritability** – Questions 8,11,15 and 18 look at inward directed irritability. A score of 4–6 is borderline, a higher score may indicate a problem.

QU8	QU11	QU15	QU18
3,2,1,0	3,2,1,0	3,2,1,0	3,2,1,0,

Use of cut-off scores gives indicators of significant care needs with respect to depression, anxiety, and inwardly and outwardly directed irritability. Inward irritability can point to the possibility of self-harm. Outward irritability raises the possibility of angry actions towards the child(ren).

As with any screening instrument, interpretation must be in the context of other information. Some respondents will underreport distress, others exaggerate. A high or low score on any scale does not guarantee that significant level of need is present.

Most value is obtained by using the scale as a springboard for discussion.

 ISBN 0 11 322426 5

DH Department of Health

Adult Wellbeing

SCORING THE SCALE

Alcohol Use:

The Department of Health guidelines for safe drinking state that:

For men, drinking between 3 and 4 units a day or less indicates no significant risk to health (1 unit = approximately ½ a pint of beer, 1 measure of spirit, or 1 glass of wine). Regularly drinking 4 our more units of alcohol a day indicates an increased risk to health.

For women, drinking between 2 and 3 units a day *or less*, indicates no significant risk to health. Regularly drinking over 3 units a day signifies an increased risk to health.

 ISBN 0 11 322426 5

DH Department of Health

Alcohol Use

QUESTIONNAIRE

Name of Child: ______________________

Completed by: ______________________

Relationship to child: ______________________

Date: ______________________

Alcohol Use – QUESTIONNAIRE

Please circle the answer most relevant to you

1. How often do you have a drink containing alcohol?

NEVER	MONTHLY OR LESS	TWO TO FOUR TIMES A WEEK	TWO OR THREE TIMES A WEEK	FOUR TIMES A MONTH

2. How many drinks containing alcohol do you have on a typical day when you are drinking?

1 or 2	3 or 4	5 or 6	7 to 9	10 or more

3. How often during the past year have you found that you were not able to stop drinking once you had started?

NEVER	LESS THAN MONTHLY	MONTHLY	WEEKLY	DAILY, OR ALMOST DAILY

4. How often during the past year have you failed to do what was normally expected of you because of drinking?

NEVER	LESS THAN MONTHLY	MONTHLY	WEEKLY	DAILY, OR ALMOST DAILY

5. Has a relative or friend, doctor or other health worker been concerned about your drinking or suggested you cut down?

NO	YES, BUT NOT IN THE PAST YEAR	YES DURING THE PAST YEAR

Scoring

Question 1: Never = **0**, Monthly or less =**1**, Two to four times a week = **2**, Two or three times a week = **3**, Four or more times a week = **4**

Question 2: 1 or 2 = **0**, 3 or 4 = **1**, 5 or 6 = **2**, 7 to 9 = **3**, 10 or more = **4**

Question 3: Never = **0**, Less than monthly = **1**, Monthly = **2**, Weekly = **3**, Daily or almost daily = **4**.

Question 4: Never = **0**, Less than monthly = **1**, Monthly = **2**, Weekly = **3**, Daily or almost daily = **4**.

Question 5: No = **0**, Yes, but not in the past year = **2**, Yes during the past year = **4**.

Interpretation of Scoring

1. A score of 5 or more indicates that there may be an alcohol problem, and that there should be fuller evaluation. It should be remembered that although people may be more honest filling in a questionnaire than face-to-face, they are still likely to underestimate consumption and effects.
2. If questions 3, 4 or 5 are checked as other than *No* or *Never* there is likely to be concern that the pattern of drinking may be impacting on the children.
3. Interpretation may be helped by looking at the Department of Health guidelines:

The Department of Health guidelines for safe drinking state that:

For men, drinking between 3 and 4 units a day or less indicates no significant risk to health (1 unit = approximately ½ a pint of beer, 1 measure of spirit, or 1 glass of wine). Regularly drinking 4 our more units of alcohol a day indicates an increased risk to health.

For women, drinking between 2 and 3 units a day or less, indicates no significant risk to health. Regularly drinking over 3 units a day signifies an increased risk to health.

Reference:

Piccinelli M, Tessari E, Bortolomasi M, Piasere O, Semenzin M, Garzotto N & Tansella M (1997) Efficacy of the alcohol use disorders identification test as a screening tool for hazardous alcohol intake and related disorders in primary care: A validity study. *British Medical Journal*. **514**: 420-424.

 ISBN 0 11 322426 5

Department of Health

Alcohol Use

GUIDANCE ON QUESTIONNAIRE

ALCOHOL USE QUESTIONNAIRE

Background

1. Alcohol misuse is estimated to be present in about 6% of primary carers, ranking it third in frequency behind major depression and generalised anxiety. Higher rates are found in certain localities, particularly amongst parents known to Social Services Departments.
2. Drinking alcohol affects different individuals in different ways. For example, some people may be relatively unaffected by the same amount of alcohol that incapacitates others.
3. The primary concern therefore is not the amount of alcohol consumed but how it impacts on the individual, and more particularly on their role as a parent.
4. Drinking alcohol can affect a carer's behaviour towards their partner or children, even if their alcohol consumption is within the Department of Health guidelines for safe drinking. This may be particularly true if the parent has a vulnerable personality.
5. Drinking alcohol may contribute to incidents where there is loss of temper or parental rows. Deep sleep due to alcohol may reduce the parents' awareness of distress in young children at night.
6. Children of parents who misuse alcohol are more likely to have: developmental delays, social problems, emotional detachment, and delinquency.
7. Research has found that individuals who misuse alcohol are more likely to have a parent or relative who misused alcohol.
8. Children of alcoholics are reported to abuse alcohol or drugs more than children who have grown up with non-alcoholics, and are 2–4 times more likely to have a psychiatric disorder.

The Questionnaire

9. This questionnaire has been found to be effective in detecting adults with alcohol disorders and those with hazardous drinking.
10. The questionnaire is designed to be self administered. Research has found that adults may be more honest in completing this type of questionnaire than in a face-to-face interview.
11. The questionnaire can be scored (see overleaf), but should be viewed primarily as a tool to help to raise the subject of alcohol, and to provide the opportunity to address any issues that may arise, particularly in the responses to questions 3, 4 and 5.
12. The questionnaire covers:
    - Frequency of alcohol consumption (question 1)
    - Number of drinks consumed in a typical day (question 2)
    - Ability to control drinking (question 3)
    - Failure to carry out expected tasks as consequence of the effects of alcohol (question 4)
    - Whether others are concerned about the individuals drinking (question 5)

Use

13. The questionnaire can be useful to provide a baseline, either at initial or core assessment or during ongoing work.
14. The questionnaire can help to detect drinking issues in circumstances where alcohol problems are not suspected. Drinking habits are often hidden, even from other family members.
15. It is important that the questionnaire is used as a basis for discussion of drinking patterns. For example, it may be useful to explore with carers how they manage their children when they are drinking. If they go the pub – what happens to the children?
16. Where the worker is uncertain how to interpret the response to the questionnaire they should consult a professional who is experienced in this field.

Administration

17. The introduction of the questionnaire will have to be carefully planned, particularly with carers from communities where the use of alcohol is frowned upon. One approach is to explain that it is important to understand families' approach to drinking alcohol, and that asking parents to fill out a questionnaire can be a useful starting point for discussion. It can be emphasised that the worker is not for or against drinking, but from the children's point of view it is helpful to know what part it plays in day to day family life.
18. Although designed to be self-administered, the questionnaire can also be used as a series of initial probes for use by the worker.

 ISBN 0 11 322426 5

Department of Health

Family Activity
SCALE

Name of Child/ren: ______________________

Completed by: ______________________

Relationship to child/ren: ______________________

Date: ______________________

Family Activity

SCALE FOR CHILDREN AGED 2 TO 6

Could you let me know the sort of things you do as a family, or with your child/children both regularly and in the last year. Below are some examples of activities you may have done.

If you have done any of these activities **within the time-scale written in bold**, please tick in the box provided. You may also like to mention other activities you have done. You can do this by filling in the lines at the end of this sheet.

	Activity if YES , please tick
Have you read a story to your child **in the last week**?	☐
Has your child eaten with you and other family members at least **once in the last wee**k?	☐
Did you do anything special for your child on their **last birthday**, such as a cake, party, trip to the park etc.?	☐
Have you gone with your child/family to the park, playground, farm or similar **in the last month**?	☐
Have you gone with your child/family to a local event, such as county show, fete, **in the last 6 months**?	☐
Have you ever belonged to a mother/toddler or baby group of any kind for **at least 3 months**?	☐
Have you and your child/family visited friends who have young children **in the last month**?	☐
Has the family been away for the day out to somewhere different **in the last 6 months** (town/into town/ to the seaside/day trip)?	☐
Has your child had a friend to visit **in the last 6 months**?	☐
Has your child been to visit relatives or friends as a treat for her/him **in the last 6 months**?	☐

Are there any other things you have done as a family/with your child in the last:

Week

____

____

Month

____

____

6 months

____

____

____

____

____

____

 ISBN 0 11 322426 5

Department of Health

Family Activity

SCALE

Name of Child/ren: ______________________

Completed by: ______________________

Relationship to child/ren: ______________________

Date: ______________________

Family Activity

SCALE FOR CHILDREN AGED 7 TO 12

Could you let me know the sort of things you do as a family, or with your child/children both regularly and in the last year. Some examples of the kind of activities you may have done are listed below.

If you have done any of these activities **within the time-scale written in bold**, please tick in the box provided.

You may also like to mention other activities you have done in the space provided at the bottom of the page.

	Activity if YES , please tick
Had a friend of your child to visit **in the last month**?	☐
Had a birthday celebration (i.e. party/cake)?	☐
Been to the cinema/museum/zoo/panto/local event – **in the last 3 months**?	☐
Been swimming/skating/other (participant) sport – **in the last 3 months**?	☐
Been away on holiday with the family/to the seaside – **in the past year**?	☐
Been to the park/for a picnic/local farm – **in the last 3 months**?	☐
Has – or had – any pets **in the past year**?	☐
Attended any special classes/clubs i.e. football, dance – **in the last 3 months**?	☐
Been to stay with relatives or friends (without parents) – **in the last year**?	☐
Visited own friends (i.e. for a meal/for the day) – **in the last 3 months**	
Belongs to a children's library?	☐

Are there any other things you have done as a family/with your child in the last:

Week

Month

6 months

continued from 3b

family is at the present time – the questionnaire can be a way to broaden the focus of discussion. Where there a disabled child there is a need to understand how this restricts family activity, and whether there are ways to ensure that the needs of all family members are met.

22. The scale will usually be used with main caregivers, but, as indicated, it can be used with parent(s) and children together.
23. The scale takes about 10 minutes to complete if used with a single adult, but discussion or any relevant work that develops will naturally take longer.

Scoring

24. Each item is scored 1 if it has occurred, or 0 if it did not, and the item scores are summed to give a total score from 0–11 for the list of specific activities, and 0–3 for the items at the bottom of the scale, which allow for activities that have not been specified.
25. To be scored the interviewer must satisfy themselves that the motivation for the action was from the parents and that it was for the child(ren)'s enjoyment or stimulation. For example staying with the grandmother as a treat during the holidays would count, but staying with a relative because the parents were going on holiday would not. Family pets only count if the child has a special responsibility for looking after them, otherwise only pets 'belonging to the child count'.
26. There is not cut-off score. The questionnaire is scored on a continuum: the higher the score, the more child-centred are the family activities.
27. Formal scoring – adding up the number of activities that have occurred in the specified time periods – can give a general indication of family child-centredness, but parental attitude to the various possibilities on the list, and their motivation to provide suitable opportunities, will contribute to the overall assessment.
28. In evaluating the meaning of the scoring, family circumstances, the development of the child, presence/absence of disability all should be considered.

Reference

Smith M (1985) *The Effects of Low Levels of Lead on Urban Children: The relevance of social factors*. Ph.D. Psychology, University of London.

 ISBN 0 11 322426 5

Department of Health

Family Activity

GUIDANCE ON USING SCALES

FAMILY ACTIVITY SCALE

Background

1. The study of parenting styles has explored several different dimensions, including warmth/coldness and authoritarian/permissive approaches. Related dimensions are control and child-centredness.
2. Newson and Newson (1968) in their study of families in the general population, found that mothers felt strongly about their child's compliance because having children who behave well, and do not 'show them up' in public was important for their self esteem. At the same time, many mothers also recognised that they needed to concede some autonomy to their children.
3. Referring to 'child-centredness' Newson & Newson (1976) said:
   'The keynote to this is the parents' recognition of the child's status as an individual with rights and feelings that are worthy of respect'.
   One example cited by the Newsons was the extent to which mothers were prepared to accept their 4-year-old's claim that they were busy.
4. The concept of child-centredness underlies many schemes for observing parent-child interaction, and there is evidence that it is an important determinant of good child development.
5. What people do together and how they conduct joint activity is an important indicator of the quality of their relationship.

The Scale

6. The Family Activity Scale is derived from a Child-Centredness Scale devised by Marjorie Smith (1985).
7. Child-centredness is seen to be reflected in appropriate opportunities for the child to be involved in autonomous activities of their own choice, or family activities that the parents judge to be potentially enjoyable or fulfilling for the child.
8. There are two versions – one for children aged 2–6, and one for children aged 7–12.
9. The scale aims to identify the extent of joint, child-centred family activity and independent/autonomous child activity, such as pursuit of hobbies and relationships outside the home, and self-care.
10. The activities in the scale are intended to be relatively independent of family income.
11. It is not expected that families will provide all the activities or opportunities. To some extent this will depend on the characteristics of the child and the context of the family.
12. There are circumstances, for example low income families living in isolated rural areas and those with a disabled child, where access to some of the activities is not possible without additional support.
13. The scale is not intended to judge parents in a critical way, but provide an opportunity to encourage relevant activity, and assess the need for support to enable it to take place.

Use

14. The scale has been used successfully with children as well as caregivers
15. In piloting it was reportedly 'extremely useful' in initial assessment.
16. Used with both parents separately it highlighted differences in parent perceptions.
17. Used both with caregivers alone and with the children it helped with work on family relationships.
18. On one occasion the children's enthusiastic account of joint ,family activity gave weight to the view that there had been considerable improvements in the function of the family concerned.
19. When children took part it helped them to feel included, and was thought to have been confidence-building.
20. Specific items were useful as the focus for work to extend joint family activity. Where there is a lack of resource available to the family, or a disabled child relevant support can be discussed, and if appropriate, provided.

Administration

21. It is as always important to introduce the scale in a fashion that is appropriate to the family in question. With families that are new to the worker, the need to understand the family can be put forward. For those that are well known there is the need to get a fuller picture of how the

continued on 3a

ISBN 0 11 322426 5

Department of Health

Home Conditions

ASSESSMENT

Name of Child: ______________________

Completed by: ______________________

Relationship to child: ______________________

Date: ______________________

HOME CONDITIONS ASSESSMENT

Background

1. Social workers assess physical aspects of the home environment.
2. This scale may appear judgmental, but workers necessarily make judgements about the safety, order and cleanliness of the place in which the child lives. The use of a list helps the objectivity of observation.
3. The total score has been found to correlate highly with children's abilities, so that children from homes with low scores usually have better language and intellectual development. This does not mean that all children from high scoring homes will have poor intellectual progress.
4. Like all methods of assessment it should not be used in isolation – other sources of information, including the quality of the parent-child relationship will contribute to the overall assessment.

The Scale

5. The assessment is identical to the Family Cleanliness Scale devised by Davie and others (1984).
6. This is a list of 11 items to be observed during home visits.
7. Social presentation, namely the cleanliness of the children is included.

Use

8. The scale if best used as a mental checklist to provide a framework for observation.
9. It is particularly appropriate to use during initial assessment. Once used it is a method of keeping track of progress or deterioration.
10. In order to be able to complete the scale it is necessary to look over the home. The caregiver can be asked whether they have any problems with their housing, or whether the nature of their accommodation causes difficulties from the point of view of brining up the children. This can lead naturally to a request to look round.
11. It will usually be unhelpful to share all that has been observed with the caregiver. This could upset the establishment of partnership – a good working relationship is of overriding importance. However the worker needs to have a clear picture of the environment from the child's point of view.
12. Individual items can be a focus for a piece of work. This might be to encourage the parent to attend to something that could pose a health risk to the children, or to bring in additional support where the parent is unlikely to be able to improve matters unassisted.

References

Davie CE, Hutt SJ, Vincent E & Mason M (1984) *The young child at home*. NFER-Nelson, Windsor

The Scale

1.	Smell (e.g. stale cigarette smoke, rotting food)	0	1
2.	Kitchen floor soiled, covered in bits, crumbs etc.	0	1
3.	Floor covering in any other room soiled as above.	0	1
4.	General decorative order poor – obviously in need of attention (e.g. badly stained wall paper, broken windows)	0	1
5.	Kitchen sink, draining board, work surfaces or cupboard door have not been washed for a considerable period of time	0	1
6.	Other surfaces in the house have not been dusted for a considerable period of time	0	1
7.	Cooking implements, cutlery or crockery showing ingrained dirt and/or these items remain unwashed until they are needed again.	0	1
8.	Lavatory, bath or basin showing ingrained dirt.	0	1
9.	Furnishings or furniture soiled	0	1
10.	Informant's or children's, clothing clearly unwashed, or hair matted and unbrushed	0	1
11.	Garden or yard uncared for and strewn with rubbish	0	1
	Total Score		

 ISBN 0 11 322426 5

Department of Health

Recent Life Events

QUESTIONNAIRE

Name of Child: ______________________

Completed by: ______________________

Relationship to child: ______________________

Date: ______________________

Recent Life Events

QUESTIONNAIRE

Listed below are a number of events. Please read each item carefully and then indicate whether or not each event has happened to you in the past year.

Please tick the **YES** box if the event has occurred.
Please tick the **'still affects me'** box if **the event is still having an effect on your life**

EVENT	YES	Still affects me
Have you had a serious illness or been seriously injured?	☐	☐
Has one of your immediate family * been seriously ill or injured?	☐	☐
Have any of your close friends or other close relatives been seriously ill or injured?	☐	☐
Have any of your immediate family died?	☐	☐
Have any of your other close relatives or close friends died?	☐	☐
Have you separated from your partner (not including death)?	☐	☐
Have you had any serious problem with a close friend, neighbour or relative?	☐	☐
Have you, or an immediate family member been subject to serious racial abuse, attack or /threats	☐	☐
Have you, or an immediate family member been subject to any abuse, attack, threat - perhaps due to you or someone close to you having a disability of any kind (i.e. a mental health problem, a learning disability or a physical problem)?	☐	☐
Have you, or an immediate family member been subject to any other form of serious abuse, attack, or threat?	☐	☐
Have you or your partner been unemployed or seeking work for more than one month?	☐	☐
Have you or your partner been sacked from your job or made redundant?	☐	☐
Have you had any major financial difficulties (e.g. debts, difficulty paying bills)?	☐	☐
Have you, or an immediate family member had any Police contact or been in a court appearance?	☐	☐
Have you or an immediate member of your family been burgled or mugged?	☐	☐
Have you or another individual who lives with you given birth?	☐	☐
Have you or another individual who lives with you suffered from a miscarriage or had a stillbirth?	☐	☐
Have you moved house (through choice)?	☐	☐
Have you moved house (not through choice)?	☐	☐
Have you had any housing difficulties?	☐	☐
Have you had any other significant event (Please specify)?	☐	☐

* *immediate family includes: mother, father, sister, brother, partner, child*

Scoring

19. The initial scoring is binary. 1 if the life event has happened, and 0 if it has not.

20. The number of events that the respondent considers are still affecting them is then counted.

21. In piloting respondents reported up to 17 events in the last year, of which up to 10 were still having an affect. The average number of events was between 7 & 8, of which about half were still considered by the caregiver to be affecting them.

22. The questionnaire does not have a cut off point. It is scored on the basis that the more life events the adult has been through, the higher the score, and therefore the *greater* the *likelihood* of some form of longer term impact on the adult, child and or family. This will be particularly so if the person considers the events still affect them.

Reference

Brugha T, Bebington P, Tennant C and Hurry J (1985) The list of threatening experiences: A subset of 12 life events categories with considerable long-term contextual threat. *Psychological medicine*. **15**: 189–194.

 ISBN 0 11 322426 5

DH Department of Health

Recent Life Events

GUIDANCE ON USING QUESTIONNAIRE

RECENT LIFE EVENTS QUESTIONNAIRES

Background

1. Life events are usually short-lived but may have more enduring consequences.
2. They can be distinguished from 'chronic difficulties', such as poverty or persistently discordant relationships. However life events can be both an indicator of chronic difficulties, or a precipitant of them.
3. Life events affect individuals and families in different ways, so it is important to explore how they impact on the caregivers and the family. For example, the death of a grandparent may have a practical as well as an emotional impact on the family if they have helped to support and care for the children.
4. Negative life events such as divorce, death of someone close, physical illness and unemployment have the capacity to affect any family member, not just those directly involved. Losing a parent at a young age, particularly before 11, has been reported to independently influence wellbeing in both childhood and adult life.
5. Most negative life events can be seen as involving the experience of loss, or threat of loss, including the loss of self esteem. Some apparently positive events such as job promotion may act in this way.
6. An important issue is whether an event is felt to continue to exert a negative affect. This aspect has not always been included in questionnaires.

The Questionnaire

7. This Life Events questionnaire has been developed from one devised by Brugha et al (1985), with 9 additional items.
8. The scale aims to look at recent life events, those occurring in the last 12 months and whether the respondent thinks they have a continuing influence. However it can be used to evaluate events and impact over a longer period if desired.
9. It can contribute to a social history, or provide an opportunity to re-evaluate whether known events are continuing to exert an influence.

Use

10. It is expected that it will be used mostly with main caregivers, but it could be of value with potential caregivers and separated parents.
11. In piloting it was found to be 'extremely' useful in both initial assessment and continuing work. It raised new issues on three out of every four occasions on which it was used.
12. With new families the questionnaire 'gave further insight into the carer's background'. It 'put into perspective the reasons why the mother was down'.
13. With respondents with whom workers were already familiar it revealed information not previously known. It identified issues that 'the family had not considered stressful or told me'. 'It highlighted issues that were and were not still having an effect'. One social worker reported that they were able to find out the 'carer's view of issues'.
14. It is clear that social workers should be prepared for what may emerge if this instrument is used.

Administration

15. The scale should be given to the respondent, usually a main caregiver, after appropriate preparation. This will depend on whether the context is an assessment or a review.
16. It may be helpful to acknowledge that the worker appreciates that thinking about important family events may stir up painful memories.
17. The questionnaires take about 15 minutes to complete, but discussion can take considerably longer.
18. Although not used in this way in the piloting, it could form a valuable basis for a family discussion. This would require further preparation and negotiation.

INITIAL ASSESSMENT RECORD

In completing this initial assessment, if it is known a core assessment will be required, social work staff should make a professional judgement about whether it is necessary to complete all sections before beginning a Core Assessment.

Name ______________________________

Gender ______________ *Date of birth* ______________

Address ______________________________

____

____

____

Telephone number ______________________________

Date Initial Assessment commenced	*Date completed*

The Government's Objectives for Children's Social Services (1999) requires an initial assessment to be completed within 7 working days.

Agencies contacted/involved during Initial Assessment (please tick)

G.P.	☐	H.V.	☐	Nursery	☐	E.W.O.	☐	School	☐
Community Mental Health	☐	Community Paediatrician	☐	Dentist	☐	Y.O.T.	☐	Police	☐
School Nurse	☐	Other ______	☐			Other ______	☐		

Reason for Initial Assessment, including views of child/ young person and parents/carers

Summary

Summary of developmental needs of child or young person, parents'/carers' capacities to respond to the child's needs appropriately, and any family or environmental factors impacting on the child/family

____

____

____

____

____

____

____

Further action

Allocation of specific services	**Date service provided:**	**Referral to other agencies**	**Date of referral:**
Service: ______	|__|__|__|	Agency: ______	|__|__|__|
Service: ______	|__|__|__|	Agency: ______	|__|__|__|
Service: ______	|__|__|__|	Agency: ______	|__|__|__|
Service: ______	|__|__|__|	Agency: ______	|__|__|__|

Hold strategy discussion ☐ Initiate s47 enquiries ☐

Date |__|__|__| Date |__|__|__|

Practice note: Core assessment should be commenced at the point s47 enquiries are initiated.

Immediate legal action to protect child ☐

Type of legal action ______ Date |__|__|__|

Core assessment ☐ Date Core assessment commenced |__|__|__|

Specialist assessment(s) commissioned Yes ☐ No ☐

Reason(s) for Further Action:

Signature of worker completing assessment ______ Date |__|__|__|

Signature of Team Manager ______ Date |__|__|__|

Copy of Assessment given to family members as appropriate ☐ Date sent/given |__|__|__|

Allocated to ______ Team ______ Date |__|__|__|

Signed ______ Team Manager ______

 ISBN 0 11 322437 0

REFERRAL AND INITIAL INFORMATION RECORD

SSD Case Numbers ______________ Date referral received |__|__|__|

Is the parent/carer aware of the referral? Yes ☐ No ☐ Re-Referral ☐

Child/Young Person's name, address and responsible LA

Family name ______________ Forenames ______________ Dob ______________ Gender ______________

Address ______________

Postcode ______________ Tel. ______________

Current address if different from above ______________

Postcode ______________ Tel. ______________

SSD Team ______________ Responsible local authority ______________

Child/Young Person's Principal carers

Name	Relationship to child/young person	Parental Responsibility
______________	______________	Yes ☐ No ☐
______________	______________	Yes ☐ No ☐

Referred by ______________ Agency/rel. to child/young person ______________

Address ______________

Postcode ______________ Tel. ______________

Does referrer wish to remain anonymous Yes ☐ No ☐

Child/young person's religion ______________ Child/young person's ethnicity: ______________

Caribbean	☐	Indian	☐	White British	☐	White and Black Caribbean	☐	Chinese	☐
African	☐	Pakistani	☐	White Irish	☐	White and Black African	☐	Any other ethnic group	☐
Any other Black background	☐	Bangladeshi	☐	Any other White background	☐	White and Asian	☐	Not given	☐

Any other Asian background ☐ Any other mixed background ☐

If other, please specify ______________ Child's first language ______________ Parent(s) first language ______________

Is an interpreter or signer required? Yes ☐ No ☐ Has this been arranged? Yes ☐ No ☐

Other household members (including non-family members)

Surname	Forename	DoB	SSD case number if appropriate	Relationship to child	Tick if also referred to SSD

Significant family members who are not members of child's household

Name ______________ Name ______________

Relationship ______________ Relationship ______________

Address ______________ Address ______________

Tel. ______________ Tel. ______________

Information on statutory status

	Yes	No	*Please give details:*		
Child/young person or other child(ren)/young person(s) in family is/has on a disability register	☐	☐	Name	Date(s)	
Child/young person or other child(ren)/young person(s) in family is/has on a child protection register	☐	☐	Name	Date(s)	Category
Child/young person or other family member(s) has/have been looked after a local authority	☐	☐	Name	Date(s)	

Other SSD cases associated with the child/young person

Name ______ Case No. ______ Name ______ Case No. ______

Name ______ Case No. ______ Name ______ Case No. ______

Key agencies *(please tick if currently working with the family)*

G.P.	☐	Tel. ______	H.V.	☐	Tel. ______
Nursery	☐	Tel. ______	E.W.O.	☐	Tel. ______
School	☐	Tel. ______	Police	☐	Tel. ______
Y.O.T.	☐	Tel. ______	Dentist	☐	Tel. ______
Community Mental Health	☐	Tel. ______	Community Paediatrician	☐	Tel. ______
School Nurse	☐	Tel. ______	Other	☐	Tel. ______

Reason for referral/request for services:

Name of staff member completing this referral ______ Signature ______ Date ______

Further action: **Practice note: ensure this referral is collated with previous referrals or files**

Provision of information and advice ☐ Referral to other agencies (please state which) ☐

Initial assessment (to be completed within 7 working days) ☐ ______

No further action ☐

Reason for Further Action

Name of Team Manager ______ Signature ______ Date ______

 ISBN 0 11 322436 2

CORE ASSESSMENT RECORD

Child aged 0–2 years

Name ______________________________

Gender ______________ *Date of birth* ______________

Address ______________________________

____

____

____

Telephone number ______________________________

Name of social worker completing assessment:

____

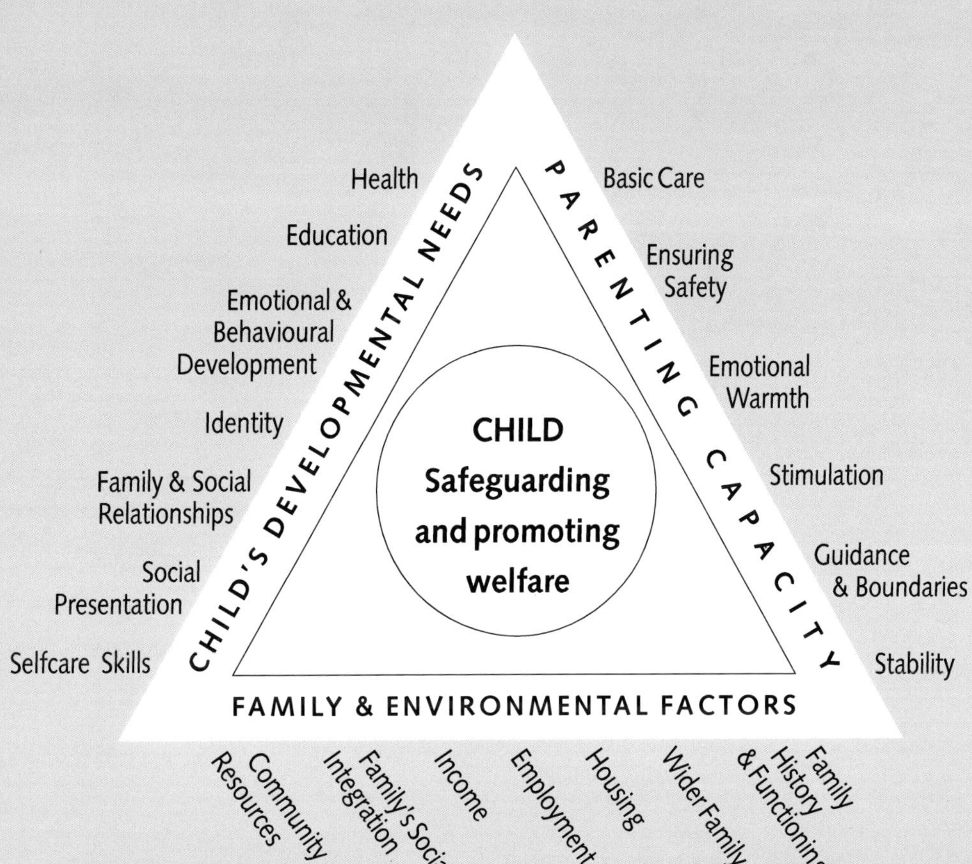

Contents

Undertaking the core assessment

- The Core Assessment Record provides a framework for systematically recording the findings from the core assessment. Whilst the Assessment Record provides some guidance on the areas that should be covered in a core assessment, it is a tool and should not be used as a substitute for a professionally informed assessment process, analysis and judgement.
- The questionnaires and scales published in the accompanying materials to the **Framework for the Assessment of Child in Need and their Families** may be useful in obtaining the information in specific areas (Department of Health, Cox and Bentovim, 2000). The Assessment Record indicates where particular questionnaires and scales may be useful. Practitioners may also choose to use other assessment tools to assist them.
- The Core Assessment Record may be completed in a number of different ways. For example, the social worker may wish to discuss each area with the family before completing the record and then share this with the family. Alternatively, having undertaken some or all of the core assessment the social worker may wish to complete the form with the child's parents or carers.
- Parents and carers invariably want to do the best for their children. Completing the record will help social workers to recognise the strengths that families have as well as identifying areas where they may need further help.
- Completing the core assessment should always be done in a way that helps parents or carers, children and other relevant family members to have their say and encourages them to take part. Space has been provided within the forms for parents/carers and older children to be involved in the assessment.
- It is expected that other agencies should be involved, as appropriate, during the core assessment process. Parental permission to contact other agencies should be obtained except in cases where the safety of the child would be jeopardised (paragraphs 7.27 to 7.38 of **Working Together to Safeguard Children** provides guidance on this issue). Permissions should be obtained from other agencies to share their information with the family.
- It is important that all sections of the Core Assessment Record are considered carefully. The analysis of the information gathered should be recorded in the plan. In some cases it will not be appropriate to complete particular sections, and in such situations the reason why should be recorded in the summary section. The information gathered is then used to develop case objectives and plans.
- In competing the record, it should be possible to see what help and support the child and family need, and which agencies might be best placed to give that help. This might include more detailed assessments of specific issues.
- Families should be provided with the following information:

Complaints procedures	date provided ______________
Information on access to records	date provided ______________
Other relevant/available information *(please specify)*	date provided ______________

Sources of information

Dates child and family members seen

Name	Date(s) seen

Agencies consulted/involved as part of the assessment

Agency	Person	Contact number

Questionnaires, Scales or other Instruments used in assessment

Questionnaire/Scale/Instrument	Date(s) used

Specialist Assessments

Agency/person who undertook the assessment	Purpose of the assessment	Date(s) assessment commissioned and completed

Details concerning a core assessment

D1 What is the reason for undertaking the core assessment?

Date core assessment started

Date core assessment ended

The Government's Objectives for Childen's Social Services (1999) require the core assessment to be completed within 35 working days.

D2 Are there specific communication needs for child/parent (eg. impairment affecting communication or English is not the first language)?
If so, what action has been taken to address this ie. use of an interpreter or a signer?

Background details concerning the child

(This information supplements the information recorded on the Referral and Initial Assessment Record)

B/K1 Significant relatives who are not part of the child's household

Birth father Parental responsibility Yes ☐ No ☐ Name ______________________

Address ______________________

Brothers and sisters

Name(s)	Age	Address

Others (please specify)

Name(s)	Relationship to child	Address

B/K2 If the child has any health conditions, impairment(s) or a genetically inherited condition – please give details
(include for example: physical disability, sensory impairment, Down's syndrome, encephalitis, autism, sickle cell anaemia, cystic fibrosis)

B/K3 Key events which may have had an impact on the child
(for example: death of brother or sister, circumstances surrounding conception)

B/K4 Other key events experienced by siblings or other family members which may affect the child

Key research sources

The Assessment Record is based on research information drawn from a number of sources

Assessment

Cleaver H, Wattam C and Cawson P (1998) *Assessing Risk in Child Protection*. NSPCC, London.

Department of Health, Department for Education and Employment and Home Office (2000) *Framework for the Assessment of Child in Need and their Families*. The Stationery Office, London.

Department of Health, Cox A and Bentovim A (2000) *The Family Assessment Pack of Questionnaires and Scales*. The Stationery Office, London.

The NSPCC and University of Sheffield (2000) *The Child's World: Assessing Children in Need. Training and Development Pack*. NSPCC, London.

Sinclair R, Garnett L and Berridge D (1995) *Social Work and Assessment with Adolescents*. National Children's Bureau, London.

Ward H (ed) (1995) *Looking After Children: Research into Practice*. HMSO, London.

Child development

Department of Health (1996) *Focus on Teenagers: Research into Practice*. HMSO, London.

Department of Health (1997) *Young Carers: Making a Start*. Department of Health, London.

Fahlberg VI (1994) *A Child's Journey Through Placement*. BAAF, London.

Jones DPH (forthcoming) *Communicating with children who may have been traumatised or maltreated*.

Rutter R and Rutter M (1992) *Developing Minds: Challenge and Continuity across the Life Span*. Penguin, Harmondsworth.

Smith PK and Cowie H (1993) *Understanding Children's Development* (2nd Edition). Blackwell, Oxford.

Varma VP (1991) *The Secret Life of Vulnerable Children*. Routledge, London.

Parenting capacity

Cleaver H, Unell I and Aldgate J (1999) *Children's Needs — Parenting Capacity: The impact of parental mental illness, problem alcohol and drug use, and domestic violence on children's development*. The Stationery Office, London.

Falkov A, Mayes K, Diggins M, Silverdale N and Cox A(1998) *Crossing Bridges — Training resources for working with mentally ill parents and their children*. Pavilion Publishing, Brighton.

Reder, P and Lucey, C (1995) *Assessment of Parenting: Psychiatric and psychological contributions*. Routledge, London.

Family and environmental factors

Cochran M (ed) (1993) *Parenting: an ecological perspective*. Lawrence Erlbaum Associates, New Jersey.

Cochran M, Larner M, Riley D, Gunnarsson L and Henderson C (eds) (1990) *Extending families: the social networks of parents and their children*. Cambridge University Press, Cambridge.

Jack G and Jordan B (1999) Social capital and child welfare. *Children and Society*. 13 (5): 242-256.

Wallace SA, Crown JM, Berger M and Cox AD (1997) *Child and Adolescent Mental Health*. In Stevens A and Rafferty J (1997) *Health Care Needs Assessment: 2nd Series*. Radcliffe Medical Press, Oxford.

Iwanec D (1995) *The emotionally abused and neglected child*. Wiley, Chichester.

Stevenson O (1998) *Neglected Children: Issues and Dilemmas*. Blackwell Science, Oxford.

Child's developmental needs

Health

Normally well is defined *as unwell for 1 week or less in the last 6 months.*

Details of immunisations in health record held by parents.

Immunisations 2-4 months: Diphtheria/Tetanus/ Whooping cough; Polio;Hib; meningococcal C vaccine

12-15 months: Measles/Mumps/ Rubella.

Babies of substance using mothers may suffer: tremors screaming,

Child's needs | **Summary/clarification of child's needs**

		Yes	No
H1	The child is normally well	☐	☐
H2	Weight/height at expected level	☐	☐
H3	Hearing/vision is satisfactory	☐	☐
H4	Child eats well	☐	☐
H5	Child has a regular sleep pattern	☐	☐
H6	Has been appropriately immunised	☐	☐
H7	Symptoms/signs of exposure to drugs/alcohol in utero	☐	☐
H8	Has an ongoing health problem (ie diabetes, asthma, epilepsy)	☐	☐
H9	Has had many accidental injuries	☐	☐
H10	Usually happy with parent/carer	☐	☐
H11	Other	☐	☐

Disabled children can face barriers in accessing routine medical care.

All children should be taken regularly to the dentist from 2 years of age.

To gather further information consider using the Home Conditions Assessment.

Black families may have less access to preventative and support services than white families.

Parental capacity | **Summary/clarification of family strengths or issues identified**
Note when issue is not relevant

	Basic care	Yes	No
H12	Child is given an adequate and nutritious diet including fluids	☐	☐
H13	Child is bathed regularly	☐	☐
H14	Child's teeth regularly cleaned	☐	☐
H15	Child is dressed to suit the weather	☐	☐
H16	Home, including child's bed is clean	☐	☐
H17	Child's routine medical appointments are generally kept	☐	☐
H18	Appropriate contact with the health visitor and G.P.	☐	☐
H19	Parent has adequate explanation as to why immunisations not up to date	☐	☐
H20	Other	☐	☐

	Ensuring safety		
H21	Injuries have always been appropriately attended to	☐	☐
H22	Parent takes action to prevent common accidents	☐	☐
H23	Child is protected from abuse	☐	☐
H24	Marks on the child's body have an acceptable explanation	☐	☐
H25	Other	☐	☐

Parental capacity

Summary/clarification of family strengths or issues identified
Note when issue is not relevant

Poverty and poor social conditions are related to poor child health and development and increased risk of accidents.

Disabled children may need special help or equipment for exercise.

Parents with severe problems may not always be able to concentrate long enough to complete the baby's feeding or nappy change.

Eating and sleeping patterns need to be set within the context of the family's culture.

		Yes	*No*	
	Emotional warmth			
H26	Child is usually with a parent/carer when awake	☐	☐	
H27	Parents/carers give comfort when child is ill/distressed/injured	☐	☐	
H28	Other	☐	☐	
	Stimulation			
H29	Child is encouraged to be active within a safe environment	☐	☐	
H30	Child is taken out regularly	☐	☐	
H31	Other			
	Guidance and Boundaries			
H32	Child's nappy is changed regularly	☐	☐	
H33	Parent/carer tries to ensure that the child gets adequate and undisturbed sleep	☐	☐	
H34	Parent/carer provides the child with an adequate and nutritious diet	☐	☐	
H35	Other	☐	☐	
	Stability			
H36	Parent/carer provides regular and consistent routines for the child (mealtimes, bedtimes, bath times)	☐	☐	
H37	Other	☐	☐	

Social worker's summary of the child's needs in this area and the extent to which parents are responding appropriately

Education

Soon after birth children respond to sound and voices. By 2 there is an increase in vocabulary.

After 6 months children start to engage in social play. Pretend play starts at approx. 12–15 months.

Consider referring children with communication difficulties for a specialist assessment (i.e. speech therapist).

	Child's needs			**Summary/clarification of child's needs**
E1	Child is making expected progress with speech and language	☐	☐	
E2	Child responds appropriately to sounds and voices	☐	☐	
E3	Child shows curiosity about his/her environment, people, toys etc	☐	☐	
E4	Child plays at an age-appropriate level	☐	☐	
E5	Child responds to instructions during second year of life	☐	☐	
E6	Other	☐	☐	

When a child has not reached an expected developmental milestone consider referring for a specialist assessment.

When a parent has a learning disability only 15% of children are similarly affected.

Safe outside play areas are important because accidents are the major cause of death amongst children.

	Parental capacity			**Summary/clarification of family strengths or issues identified** **Note when issue is not relevant**
	Basic care	*Yes*	*No*	
E7	Child has a range of safe toys/objects to play with	☐	☐	
E8	Child has frequent opportunities to communicate/play with others	☐	☐	
E9	Other	☐	☐	
	Ensuring safety			
E10	Child has somewhere safe to play at home	☐	☐	
E11	Parent ensures that out of home play areas are safe	☐	☐	
E12	Child is closely supervised by an adult in and out of the home	☐	☐	
E13	Other			

Parental capacity

Summary/clarification of family strengths or issues identified
Note when issue is not relevant

Parents own problems may mean they respond less frequently to their child's cues.

To gather further information consider using the Family Activity Scale.

All children need adequate and appropriate stimulation.

When a child has profound or complex impairments it may be necessary to check with a specialist before completing this section.

The key to children's educational progress is a parent or significant adult who takes an interest in their learning and offers praise and encouragement.

	Emotional warmth	*Yes*	*No*	
E14	Parent responds to the child's efforts to communicate/talk	☐	☐	
E15	Parent enjoys communicating with the child	☐	☐	
E16	Parent shows approval of the child's achievement	☐	☐	
E17	Other	☐	☐	
	Stimulation			
E18	Parent talks, sings and plays with the child	☐	☐	
E19	Parent reads to/looks at books with/watches TV with the child	☐	☐	
E20	Child has some freedom to explore his/her environment	☐	☐	
E21	Other	☐	☐	
	Guidance and Boundaries			
E22	Toys/play are suitable to child's stage of development	☐	☐	
E23	Child is 'overstimulated' e.g. given too many toys at once	☐	☐	
E24	Distractions are minimised	☐	☐	
E25	Other	☐	☐	
	Stability			
E26	Parent/carer consistently encourages the child to learn	☐	☐	
E27	Child's toys/books are looked after	☐	☐	
E28	Other	☐	☐	

Social worker's summary of the child's needs in this area and the extent to which parents are responding appropriately

Children who show poor attachment may be suffering from substance withdrawal symptoms.

Short lived temper tantrums are to be expected.

To gather further information consider using The Parenting Daily Hassles Scale.

Children who are abused or witness domestic violence may wake up screaming or crying.

Child's needs

		Yes	No
B&S1	Child is usually happy	☐	☐
B&S2	When the child is crying he/she can usually be readily comforted	☐	☐
B&S3	Child is often wary/anxious	☐	☐
B&S4	Temper tantrums lasting 15 mins occur daily	☐	☐
B&S5	Child readily engages in joint play with familiar adults	☐	☐
B&S6	Child can play quietly for at least brief periods	☐	☐
B&S7	Mealtimes and bedtimes are generally hassle free	☐	☐
B&S8	Child is beginning to feed/dress him/herself	☐	☐
B&S9	Other		

Summary/clarification of child's needs

Children as young as 18 months can become distressed during angry exchanges between adults.

Most at risk are children who are victims of aggression, or are neglected.

Children who are abused or witness domestic violence are particularly traumatised.

Younger or disabled children may be at greater risk than older, more articulate children because they are less able to tell anyone about their experiences and distress.

A disabled child may not protest when left with strangers because they have been handled by many unknown people. Nonetheless it remains a matter for concern.

Parental capacity

	Basic care	Yes	No
B&S10	Parents are responsive to the child's emotional needs	☐	☐
B&S11	Disagreements between parents/carers are resolved in non-violent ways	☐	☐
B&S12	Other	☐	☐
	Ensuring safety		
B&S13	Child is left with strangers	☐	☐
B&S14	Child is smacked or physically chastised	☐	☐
B&S15	Parent/carers have sought help or advice if they are experiencing difficulties in managing the child's behaviour	☐	☐
B&S16	Other	☐	☐

Summary/clarification of family strengths or issues identified
Note when issue is not relevant

Parental capacity

Summary/clarification of family strengths or issues identified
Note when issue is not relevant

	Yes	No
Emotional warmth		
B&S17 Child is comforted when distressed	☐	☐
B&S18 Child is exposed to frequent criticism/hostility	☐	☐
B&S19 Parent takes pleasure in appropriate physical contact with their child	☐	☐
B&S20 Other	☐	☐
Stimulation		
B&S21 Child is often exposed to parental emotional distress	☐	☐
B&S22 Child is encouraged to play with others	☐	☐
B&S23 Other	☐	☐
Guidance and Boundaries		
B&S24 Parent uses a variety of positive methods to get the child to behave	☐	☐
B&S25 There are clear family rules and limits about behaviour	☐	☐
B&S26 Child is helped to control his/her feelings	☐	☐
B&S27 Child is taught how to behave with other children and adults	☐	☐
B&S28 Other	☐	☐
Stability		
B&S29 Child's behaviour is responded to in a relatively consistent manner	☐	☐
B&S30 Parents/carers generally support each other in applying family rules	☐	☐
B&S31 Parent responses to the child are reasonably predictable	☐	☐
B&S32 Other	☐	☐

Depression can affect parents' capacity to care about their child.

Positive methods for encouraging good behaviour include: praise, negotiation, modelling, rewards, distraction, play, persuasion and explanation.

Social worker's summary of the child's needs in this area and the extent to which parents are responding appropriately

Identity and Social Presentation

9-12 months is the beginning of self identity.

At end of second year children can recognise self in mirror and are aware of physical differences.

At 6–9 months children reach for familiar persons.

By 12–18 months children develop a sense of me and mine.

Child's needs

		Yes	*No*
ID&P1	Child is self confident	☐	☐
ID&P2	Child has a positive view of self	☐	☐
ID&P3	Child takes pride in his/her achievements	☐	☐
ID&P4	Child responds to own name by 1 year and knows own name by 2 years	☐	☐
ID&P5	Child approaches familiar persons		
ID&P6	Child asserts 'rights' with sibs/ peers by 2 years	☐	☐
ID&P7	After 2 years, the child knows his or her own gender	☐	☐
ID&P8	Other	☐	☐

Summary/clarification of child's needs

Children who grow up in families which experience many stresses and problems will need positive messages to avoid developing a negative self image and poor self esteem. Disabled children need even more help.

Disabled children have a right to be dressed appropriately but their dress should not impede movement, endanger stability or aggravate their skin.

Parental capacity

	Basic care	*Yes*	*No*
ID&P9	Child's clothes are clean: not soiled with urine, excrement, or food	☐	☐
ID&P10	Child's clothes are routinely washed	☐	☐
ID&P11	The name by which the child is known is consistent within the family	☐	☐
ID&P12	Other	☐	☐
	Ensuring safety		
ID&P13	Child's dress is appropriate for age, gender, culture and religion and where necessary impairment	☐	☐
ID&P14	Parents help the child to distinguish familiar and trusted people from strangers	☐	☐
ID&P15	Other	☐	☐

Summary/clarification of family strengths or issues identified
Note when issue is not relevant

Parental capacity

Summary/clarification of family strengths or issues identified
Note when issue is not relevant

For children to develop a positive self image they need to feel loved and valued for themselves.

In all cultures disabled children may be treated as younger than their actual age. This is a particular risk for a learning disabled child.

Children who are routinely rejected come to see themselves as unloved and unlovable.

	Emotional warmth	*Yes*	*No*
ID&P16	Parent often shows spontaneous affection to the child	☐	☐
ID&P17	Child is valued for his/her self	☐	☐
ID&P18	Parent shows pride in the child	☐	☐
ID&P19	Other	☐	☐
	Stimulation		
ID&P20	Child is encouraged to do appropriate things for him/herself	☐	☐
ID&P21	Child is offered simple choices	☐	☐
ID&P22	Child's efforts to be independent are respected	☐	☐
ID&P23	Other	☐	☐
	Guidance and Boundaries		
ID&P24	Child is taught to respect others and other's possessions	☐	☐
ID&P25	Other	☐	☐
	Stability		
ID&P26	Child is accepted as a member of the family	☐	☐
ID&P26	Child is included in family celebrations, e.g. birthdays	☐	☐
ID&P27	Child is reassured when separated from the parent	☐	☐
ID&P28	Other	☐	☐

Social worker's summary of the child's needs in this area and the extent to which parents are responding appropriately

Family and Social Relationships

By 1 year children are able to distinguish strangers from familiar people.

Strong attachment relationships can be formed with a number of carers.

At 2 children develop an awareness of the emotions of others.

Child's needs | **Summary/clarification of child's needs**

		Yes	*No*
F1	Child shows attachment behaviour to main carers by 1 year	☐	☐
F2	Child is relaxed in the presence of main carers	☐	☐
F3	Child plays happily with siblings	☐	☐
F4	By 2 child is gentle and kind to other children and animals	☐	☐
F5	By 2 child is beginning to share with familiar peers and siblings	☐	☐
F6	By 2 child is playing comfortably along-side peers	☐	☐
F7	Other	☐	☐

Parental problems may result in children being looked after by a large number of different people.

A good attachment relationship is associated with parents being emotionally available and consistent in their parenting.

Love and affection are shown in different ways depending on culture and individual characteristics.

Parental capacity | **Summary/clarification of family strengths or issues identified**
Note when issue is not relevant

	Basic care	*Yes*	*No*
F8	A small number of familiar and appropriate adults look after the child	☐	☐
F9	Parents behave towards child in a way that encourages a strong, positive relationship to develop	☐	☐
F10	Parents/carers spend sufficient time with the child to sustain a strong relationship	☐	☐
F11	Other	☐	☐

	Ensuring safety		
F12	Siblings are generally gentle with the child	☐	☐
F13	Parents/carers monitor interactions between child and siblings	☐	☐
F14	Other	☐	☐

Parental capacity

Summary/clarification of family strengths or issues identified
Note when issue is not relevant

The presence of a supportive adult can help stressed parents to cope.

For a disabled child, practical and social barriers can make taking the child out difficult, but it remains essential to the child's wellbeing.

Of central importance to a child in all families is a loving and protective relationship.

Continuity and stability are key aspects of the attachment process.

	Emotional warmth	*Yes*	*No*	
F15	Parent/carer responds sensitively to the child	☐	☐	
F16	Parent/carer encourages affectionate family relationships	☐	☐	
F17	Other	☐	☐	
	Stimulation			
F18	Child is taken to meet other parents and children	☐	☐	
F19	Child visits family friends and relatives	☐	☐	
F20	Other	☐	☐	
	Guidance and Boundaries			
F21	Parent's relationships with others provides a good example to child	☐	☐	
F22	Child is taught to take turns	☐	☐	
F23	Child is encouraged to negotiate	☐	☐	
F24	Child is discouraged from violent or cruel behaviour	☐	☐	
F25	Other	☐	☐	
	Stability			
F26	There is a stable pattern of care in the child's day to day life	☐	☐	
F27	Child has a long-term, stable relationship with at least 1 adult	☐	☐	
F28	There is continuity of carers	☐	☐	
F29	A limited number of known, safe adults deliver intimate care	☐	☐	
F30	Other	☐	☐	

Social worker's summary of the child's needs in this area and the extent to which parents are responding appropriately

Issues affecting parents'/carers' capacities to respond appropriately to the child's needs

	Parental issues	*Yes*	*No*	*Professional/agency involved*	*Note identity of parent/carer for whom the issue is relevant. Record strengths and difficulties*
C1	Illness:				
	Physical	☐	☐		
	Mental	☐	☐		
C2	Disability:				
	Physical	☐	☐		
	Learning	☐	☐		
	Sensory impairment	☐	☐		
C3	Period in care during childhood	☐	☐		
C4	Childhood abuse	☐	☐		
C5	Known history of child abuse	☐	☐		
C6	Known history of violence	☐	☐		
C7	Problem drinking/ drug use	☐	☐		
C8	Other	☐	☐		

Social worker's summary of how the above issues have an impact on the parents'/carers' capacities to respond appropriately to the child's needs

Family and Environmental Factors which may impact on the child and parenting capacity

Include all household and relevant family members, living in or out of the home, when exploring family history and functioning.

To gather further information consider using: The Recent Life Events Questionnaire; A genogram; An eco-map.

How parents bring up their children is rooted in their own childhood experiences.

Consider whether a separate carers' assessment is required.

Both positive and negative parenting styles can be passed from one generation to another.

To gather further information consider using: The Adult Well-being Scale; The Alcohol Scale.

Wider family may extend beyond blood relatives to include people who feel like family to parent or child.

	Family History	*Yes*	*No*	**Additional details as appropriate Note identity of person for whom the issue is relevant**
FE1	Has a member of the household experienced a stressful childhood?	☐	☐	
	Note childhood abuse; in care	☐	☐	
FE2	Have the family suffered a traumatic loss or crisis which is unresolved? (e.g. bereavement)	☐	☐	
FE3	Other	☐	☐	
	Family Functioning			
FE4	Does child's impairment/behaviour have a negative impact on siblings?	☐	☐	
FE5	Child's impairment/behaviour affects parent(s) capacity to continue care	☐	☐	
FE6	Does a member of the household experience:			
	poor mental health	☐	☐	
	poor physical health	☐	☐	
	behaviour problem	☐	☐	
	physical disability	☐	☐	
	learning disability	☐	☐	
	sensory impairment	☐	☐	
	problem alcohol/drug use	☐	☐	
FE7	Has an adult member of the house-hold got a history of violence?	☐	☐	
FE8	Are there frequent family rows?	☐	☐	
FE9	Other.	☐	☐	
	Wider Family			
FE10	Do wider family provide:			
	Practical help	☐	☐	
	Emotional support	☐	☐	
	Financial help	☐	☐	
	Information and advice	☐	☐	
FE11	Is there an adult in the home who helps the parent care for the child?	☐	☐	
FE12	Other.	☐	☐	

Additional details as appropriate
Note identify of person for whom the issue is relevant

Basic amenities include safe water, heating, cooking facilities, food storage, sleeping arrangements and cleanliness.

The Home Conditions Assessment may help gather this information.

Housing

	Yes	No
FE13 Is the family homeless?	☐	☐
FE14 Is the family vulnerable to eviction or in temporary accommodation?	☐	☐
FE15 Is the house and its immediate surroundings safe for the child?	☐	☐
FE16 Does home have basic amenities?	☐	☐
FE17 Does home require any adaptations to meet the child's needs?	☐	☐
FE18 Is the home overcrowded?		
FE19 Other	☐	☐

Jobs may be lost because parents' circumstances result in them behaving in a bizarre or unpredictable way.

Parents' circumstances may mean too much family income is used to satisfy parental needs.

Adult services may help a disabled parent respond to their child's needs.

Employment

	Yes	No
FE20 Is a parent in paid employment?	☐	☐
FE21 Does parent's pattern of work adversely impact on child care?	☐	☐
FE22 Is employment reasonably secure?	☐	☐
FE23 Are family members who seek employment adequately supported?	☐	☐
FE24 Other	☐	☐

The family may be vulnerable to future financial problems (i.e. extraordinary medical, funeral expenses, need to help out a relative).

Income

	Yes	No
FE25 Are all entitled benefits claimed?	☐	☐
FE26 Are household bills paid regularly?	☐	☐
FE27 Is the family managing on the income they receive?	☐	☐
FE28 If in debt, is this increasing?	☐	☐
FE29 Is the family worried about future financial commitments?	☐	☐
FE30 Other	☐	☐

Social isolation and rejection by the community may have affected the family for generations.

Family's Social Integration

	Yes	No
FE31 Does the family feel accepted within their community?	☐	☐
FE32 Do family members experience discrimination/harassment?	☐	☐
FE33 Does the family have local friends?	☐	☐
FE34 Is the family involved in local organisations/activities?	☐	☐
FE35 Other		

Additional details as appropriate

Community resources include: shops, play areas, mother and toddler groups, health clinics etc.

In assessing community resources note: availability, accessibility and standard, and if appropriate to child and family needs.

Community Resources	*Yes*	*No*
FE36 Are there accessible community resources?	☐	☐
FE37 Does the family take advantage of community resources?	☐	☐
FE38 Other	☐	☐

Social worker's summary of how the family and environmental factors have an impact on the child and parents'/carers' capacities to respond appropriately to child's needs.

Plan for the child in need

- Having completed the information gathering, the following pages should be used to analyse the strengths and needs of the child and family members and to identify goals and specific objectives. This information is then used to formulate a plan of action. The decision about which methods are used and services are provided to achieve specific objectives should be evidence based. The expectations of a plan for a child in need are outlined in paragraphs 4.32 to 4.37 of the **Framework for the Assessment of Children in Need and Their Families** (2000).
- The plan for a child in need has been designed to enable it to be used for all children in need, including these about whom there are concerns they are suffering or likely to suffer significant harm.
- The plan should identify how the following will be addressed:
  - The identified developmental needs of the child;
  - Issues which impact negatively on parents/carers' capacity to respond to the child and needs of their child, drawing on their strengths;
  - Wider family and environmental factors which have a negative impact on the child and family, drawing on strengths in the wider family and community.
- The plan should be specific about the actions to be taken, identify who is responsible for each action, and any services or resources that will be required to ensure that the objectives set can be achieved within the agreed time scales. Statutory reviews should take place within statutory time limits and it is good practice for Child In Need plans to be reviewed at least every 6 months. Reviews should be formally recorded.
- The outcome section of the table should be completed following a review of the plan. When completing the outcome section record the outcome for each objective and whether the circumstances have; improved, remained the same, or deteriorated.
- The last page records which family members and agencies are party to the plan and the date when the plan will be reviewed. This should be signed by the child (where appropriate), family members/carers and the social worker.

Summary of child's developmental needs and strengths

Information gathered in the core assessment

Summarise the child's developmental needs and strengths

Parents should be involved in the assessment

This space is for parents/carers to write their views of the child's strengths and needs

Summary of parenting capacity: Needs and strengths

Information gathered in the core assessment

Summarise how the parental issues, needs and strengths, which have been identified in the core assessment have an impact on the capacity of each parent/carer to respond appropriately to the child's needs

Parents should be involved in the assessment

This space is for parents/carers to write their views of their own strengths and difficulties and what impact they think these have on the child's development

Summary of wider family and environmental factors: Needs and strengths

Information gathered in the core assessment

Summarise how family and environment issues, which have been identified in the core assessment, have an impact either directly on the child or on the capacity of the parents/carers to respond appropriately to the child's needs

Parents should be involved in the assessment

This space is for parents/carers to write their views of the strengths and difficulties in their wider family and environment and what impact they think these have on the child's development

Analysis of the information gathered during the core assessment

The analysis should list the factors which have an impact on different aspects of the child's development and parenting capacity, and explore the relationship between them. This process of analysing the information available about the child's needs, parenting capacity and wider family and environmental factors should result in a clear understanding of the child's needs, and what types of service provision would best address these needs to ensure the child has the opportunity to achieve their potential

The child: Objectives and plans

Child's developmental needs	*Objectives and plan of action*	*Person/Agency responsible*	*Objective to be achieved by (date)*	*Outcome (to be completed at the review)*
Health				
Education				
Identity: Social presentation				
Family and social relationships				
Emotional and behavioural development: Selfcare skills				

The Parents/Carers: Objectives and plans

Parenting capacity	*Objective and plan of action*	*Person/Agency responsible*	*Objective to be achieved by (date)*	*Outcome (to be completed at the review)*
Basic care				
Ensuring safety				
Emotional warmth				
Stimulation				
Guidance and Boundaries				
Stability				

Wider Family and Environmental Factors: Objectives and plans

Family and environmental factors	*Objective and plan of action*	*Person/Agency responsible*	*Objective to be achieved by (date)*	*Outcome (to be completed at the review)*
Family history and functioning				
Wider family				
Housing				
Employment and/or income				
Family social integration				
Community resources				

Views of all parties

These objectives and plans should have been discussed with all interested parties/agencies
Family members/agencies who are party to the plan

Name (please print)	Signature	Contact Number

Agreed date for the review: __________

Lead professional/agency for the review: __________

If the objectives and plans have not been discussed with any of the parties/agencies concerned, please give reasons

What steps will be taken and who is responsible if any party/agency wants to alter these objectives and plans?

Date plan reviewed in supervision	Signature of Line Manger/Supervisor

Parents'/carers' comments

I have seen the contents of this assessment form

Parent/carer's signature ______________________ **Date** ___/___/___

Parent/carer signature ______________________ **Date** ___/___/___

Parents/carers comments on the assessment

Have all relevant family members been given a copy of the assessment record? **Yes** ☐ **No** ☐

If not, what arrangements have been made to ensure this happens?

Social Worker's Signature ______________________ **Date** ___/___/___

Management information

Ethnicity of the child:

Caribbean	☐	Indian	☐	White British	☐	White and Black Caribbean	☐	Chinese	☐
African	☐	Pakistani	☐	White Irish	☐	White and Black African	☐	Any other ethnic group	☐
Any other Black background	☐	Bangladeshi	☐	Any other White background	☐	White and Asian	☐	Not given	☐

Any other Asian background ☐ Any other mixed background ☐

If other, please specify ______________________

Immigration status if applicable:

Asylum seeking ☐ Refugee status ☐ Exceptional leave to remain ☐

Home Office registration number: ______________________

(H6) Details of immunisations:

Has the child been appropriately immunised? Yes ☐ No ☐

2–4 months: Diphtheria, Tetanus, Whooping cough, Polio, Hib, Men C 12–18 months: Measles/Mumps/Rubella

Child protection register:

Is the child's name on the Child Protection Register? Yes ☐ No ☐

Category ____________ Date of registration ____________

Has the child previously been on the Child Protection Register? Yes ☐ No ☐

Category	Date of registration	Date of deregistration

Court Order(s)

Is the child the subject of a court order? Yes ☐ No ☐

Was the child previously subject of a court order? Yes ☐ No ☐

Type of Order(s)	Date Order(s) made:	Type of Order(s)	Date Order(s) made	Date Order(s) revoked/changed

 ISBN 0 11 322419 2

CORE ASSESSMENT RECORD

Child aged 3–4 years

Name ______________________________

Gender ______________ *Date of birth* ______________

Address ______________________________

____

____

____

Telephone number ______________________________

Name of social worker completing assessment:

____

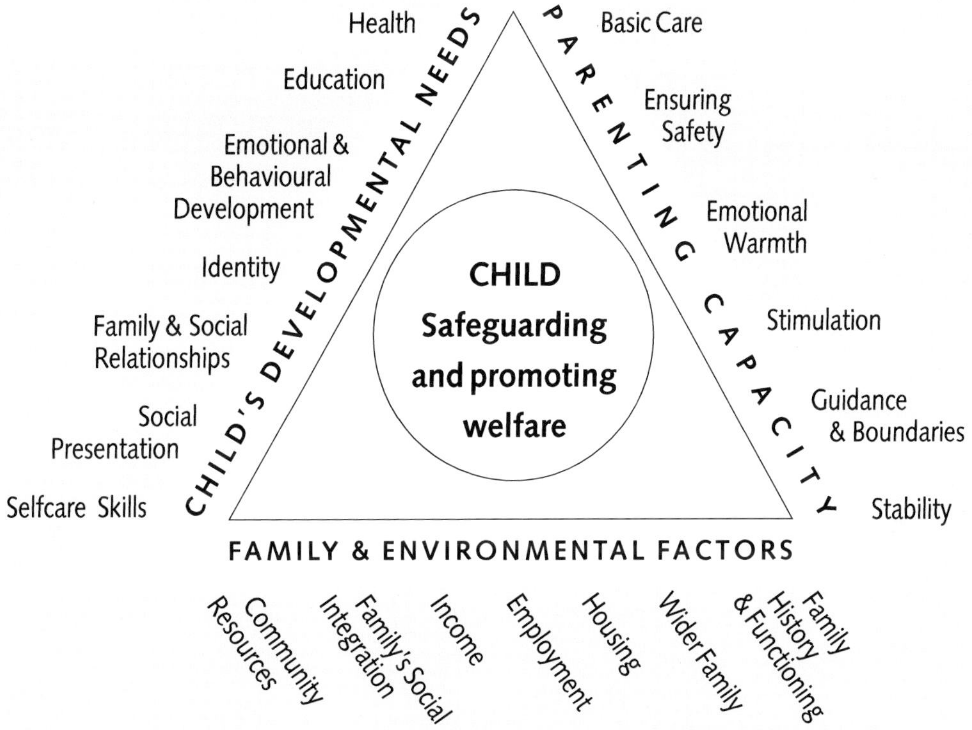

Contents

Undertaking the core assessment

- The Core Assessment Record provides a framework for systematically recording the findings from the core assessment. Whilst the Assessment Record provides some guidance on the areas that should be covered in a core assessment, it is a tool and should not be used as a substitute for a professionally informed assessment process, analysis and judgement.
- The questionnaires and scales published in the accompanying materials to the **Framework for the Assessment of Child in Need and their Families** may be useful in obtaining the information in specific areas (Department of Health, Cox and Bentovim, 2000). The Assessment Record indicates where particular questionnaires and scales may be useful. Practitioners may also choose to use other assessment tools to assist them.
- The Core Assessment Record may be completed in a number of different ways. For example, the social worker may wish to discuss each area with the family before completing the record and then share this with the family. Alternatively, having undertaken some or all of the core assessment the social worker may wish to complete the form with the child's parents or carers.
- Parents and carers invariably want to do the best for their children. Completing the record will help social workers to recognise the strengths that families have as well as identifying areas where they may need further help.
- Completing the core assessment should always be done in a way that helps parents or carers, children and other relevant family members to have their say and encourages them to take part. Space has been provided within the forms for parents/carers and older children to be involved in the assessment.
- It is expected that other agencies should be involved as appropriate during the core assessment process. Parental permission to contact other agencies should be obtained except in cases where the safety of the child would be jeopardised (paragraphs 7.27 to 7.38 of **Working Together to Safeguard Children** provides guidance on this issue). Permissions should be obtained from other agencies to share their information with the family.
- It is important that all sections of the Core Assessment Record are considered carefully. The analysis of the information gathered should be recorded in the plan. In some cases it will not be appropriate to complete particular sections, and in such situations the reason why should be recorded in the summary section. The information gathered is then used to develop case objectives and plans.
- In competing the record, it should be possible to see what help and support the child and family need, and which agencies might be best placed to give that help. This might include more detailed assessments of specific issues.
- Families should be provided with the following information:

Complaints procedures	date provided ____________
Information on access to records	date provided ____________
Other relevant/available information *(please specify)*	date provided ____________

Sources of information

Dates child and family members seen

Name	Date(s) seen

Agencies consulted/involved as part of the assessment

Agency	Person	Contact number

Questionnaires, Scales or other Instruments used in assessment

Questionnaire/Scale/Instrument	Date(s) used

Specialist Assessments

Agency/person who undertook the assessment	Purpose of the assessment	Date(s) assessment commissioned and completed

Details concerning a core assessment

D1 What is the reason for undertaking the core assessment?

Date core assessment started

Date core assessment ended

The Government's Objectives for Childen's Social Services (1999) require the core assessment to be completed within 35 working days.

D2 Are there specific communication needs for child/parent (eg. impairment affecting communication or English is not the first language)?
If so, what action has been taken to address this ie. use of an interpreter or a signer?

Background details concerning the child

(This information supplements the information recorded on the Referral and Initial Assessment Record)

B/K1 Significant relatives who are not part of the child's household

Birth father Parental responsibility Yes ☐ No ☐ Name ____________________

Address ____

Brothers and sisters

Name(s)	Age	Address

Others (please specify)

Name(s)	Relationship to child	Address

B/K2 If the child has any health conditions, impairment(s) or a genetically inherited condition – please give details
(include for example: physical disability, sensory impairment, Down's syndrome, encephalitis, autism, sickle cell anaemia, cystic fibrosis)

B/K3 Key events which may have had an impact on the child
(for example: death of brother or sister, circumstances surrounding conception)

B/K4 Other key events experienced by siblings or other family members which may affect the child

Key research sources

The Assessment Record is based on research information drawn from a number of sources

Assessment

Cleaver H, Wattam C and Cawson P (1998) *Assessing Risk in Child Protection*. NSPCC, London.

Department of Health, Department for Education and Employment and Home Office (2000) *Framework for the Assessment of Child in Need and their Families*. The Stationery Office, London.

Department of Health, Cox A and Bentovim A (2000) *The Family Assessment Pack of Questionnaires and Scales.* The Stationery Office, London.

The NSPCC and University of Sheffield (2000) *The Child's World: Assessing Children in Need. Training and Development Pack*. NSPCC, London.

Sinclair R, Garnett L and Berridge D (1995) *Social Work and Assessment with Adolescents*. National Children's Bureau, London.

Ward H (ed) (1995) *Looking After Children: Research into Practice*. HMSO, London.

Child development

Department of Health (1996) *Focus on Teenagers: Research into Practice*. HMSO, London.

Department of Health (1997) *Young Carers: Making a Start*. Department of Health, London.

Fahlberg VI (1994) *A Child's Journey Through Placement.* BAAF, London.

Jones DPH (forthcoming) *Communicating with children who may have been traumatised or maltreated*.

Rutter R and Rutter M (1992) *Developing Minds: Challenge and Continuity across the Life Span*. Penguin, Harmondsworth.

Smith PK and Cowie H (1993) *Understanding Children's Development* (2nd Edition). Blackwell, Oxford.

Varma VP (1991) *The Secret Life of Vulnerable Children.* Routledge, London.

Parenting capacity

Cleaver H, Unell I and Aldgate J (1999) *Children's Needs — Parenting Capacity: The impact of parental mental illness, problem alcohol and drug use, and domestic violence on children's development.* The Stationery Office, London.

Falkov A, Mayes K, Diggins M, Silverdale N and Cox A(1998) *Crossing Bridges — Training resources for working with mentally ill parents and their children.* Pavilion Publishing, Brighton.

Reder, P and Lucey, C (1995) *Assessment of Parenting: Psychiatric and psychological contributions.* Routledge, London.

Family and environmental factors

Cochran M (ed) (1993) *Parenting: an ecological perspective.* Lawrence Erlbaum Associates, New Jersey.

Cochran M, Larner M, Riley D, Gunnarsson L and Henderson C (eds) (1990) *Extending families: the social networks of parents and their children*. Cambridge University Press, Cambridge.

Jack G and Jordan B (1999) Social capital and child welfare. *Children and Society*. 13 (5): 242-256.

Wallace SA, Crown JM, Berger M and Cox AD (1997) *Child and Adolescent Mental Health*. In Stevens A and Rafferty J (1997) *Health Care Needs Assessment: 2nd Series.* Radcliffe Medical Press, Oxford.

Iwanec D (1995) *The emotionally abused and neglected child*. Wiley, Chichester.

Stevenson O (1998) *Neglected Children: Issues and Dilemmas*. Blackwell Science, Oxford.

Child's developmental needs

Health

Normally well is defined as *unwell for 1 week or less in the last 6 months.*

Details of immunisations in health record held by parents.

Children of 3 years should have had the following immunisations Diphtheria/Tetanus/ Whooping cough; Polio; Hib; Meningococcal C vaccine and Measles/ Mumps/Rubella.

By 4 most can use the toilet by themselves.

Child's needs | **Summary/clarification of child's needs**

		Yes	No
H1	Child is normally well	☐	☐
H2	Weight/height at expected level	☐	☐
H3	Hearing/vision is satisfactory	☐	☐
H4	Child eats well	☐	☐
H5	Child frequently soils the bed	☐	☐
H6	Child is clean and dry in the day	☐	☐
H7	Child has a regular sleep pattern	☐	☐
H8	Has been appropriately immunised	☐	☐
H9	Has a persistent health problem	☐	☐
H10	Has had many accidental injuries	☐	☐
H11	Other	☐	☐

To gather further information consider using the Home Conditions Assessment.

Disabled children can face barriers in accessing routine dental and medical care.

All children should be taken regularly to the dentist.

Black families may have less access to preventative and support services than white families.

The significance of the physical symptoms of the child's illness may not always be easily identified or understood. This may influence the way parents respond.

Parental capacity | **Summary/clarification of family strengths or issues identified**
Note when issue is not relevant

	Basic care	Yes	No
H12	Child is given an adequate and nutritious diet including fluids	☐	☐
H13	Child is bathed regularly	☐	☐
H14	Child's teeth are cleaned regularly	☐	☐
H15	Dress is appropriate to weather	☐	☐
H16	Home, including child's bed, is clean	☐	☐
H17	Child's routine medical/dental appointments are generally kept	☐	☐
H18	Appropriate contact with H.V./ G.P.	☐	☐
H19	Parent has adequate explanation as to why immunisations not up to date	☐	☐
H20	Other	☐	☐
	Ensuring safety		
H21	Periodic bouts of illness have a recognised medical explanation	☐	☐
H22	Injuries have always been appropriately attended to	☐	☐
H23	Parent takes action to prevent common accidents	☐	☐
H24	Child is protected from abuse	☐	☐
H25	Marks on the child's body have an acceptable explanation	☐	☐
H26	Other	☐	☐

Parental capacity

Summary/clarification of family strengths or issues identified
Note when issue is not relevant

Poverty and poor social conditions are related to poor child health and development and increased risk of accidents.

Disabled children may need special help or equipment for exercise.

Parents with severe problems may not be able to always concentrate long enough to ensure that the child's physical needs are adequately met.

Eating and sleeping patterns need to be set within the context of the family's culture.

		Yes	*No*
	Emotional warmth		
H27	Child is usually with a parent/carer when awake	☐	☐
H28	Parents/carers give comfort when child is ill/distressed/injured	☐	☐
H29	Other	☐	☐
	Stimulation		
H30	Child is encouraged to be active within a safe environment	☐	☐
H31	Child is taken out regularly	☐	☐
H32	Other	☐	☐
	Guidance and Boundaries		
H33	Parent/carer tries to ensure that the child gets adequate and undisturbed sleep	☐	☐
H34	Parent/carer provides the child with an adequate and nutritious diet	☐	☐
H35	Other	☐	☐
	Stability		
H36	Parent/carer provides regular and consistent routines for the child (mealtimes, bedtimes, bath times)	☐	☐
H37	Other	☐	☐

Social worker's summary of the child's needs in this area and the extent to which parents are responding appropriately

Most children of 3–4 understand colour names, count to 3, enjoy matching shapes etc, looking at books, understand pretend play.

Consider referring children with communication difficulties for a specialist assessment (i.e. speech therapist).

Child's needs

		Yes	No
E1	Child is making expected progress with speech and language	☐	☐
E2	Child plays at age-appropriate level	☐	☐
E3	Child shows an interest in stories and play materials	☐	☐
E4	Child is able to settle to task and can concentrate for approximately 10 minutes	☐	☐
E5	Child responds to instructions	☐	☐
E6	Other	☐	☐

Summary/clarification of child's needs

When a child has not reached anexpected developmental milestone consider referring for a specialist assessment.

When a parent has a learning disability only 15% of children are similarly affected.

Safe outside play areas are important because accidents are the major cause of death amongst children.

At 3 many children benefit from regular attendance at pre-school.

Parents' circumstances may mean they are unable to take the child to pre-school or they may delegate the task to others. These adults should present no risk to the child.

Pre-school may be less accessible to a disabled child.

Parental capacity

	Basic care	Yes	No
E7	Child has a range of safe toys/ objects to play with	☐	☐
E8	Child has frequent opportunities to communicate/play with others	☐	☐
E9	Other	☐	☐
	Ensuring safety		
E10	Parent shows approval of child's achievements	☐	☐
E11	Child has somewhere safe to play at home	☐	☐
E12	Parent ensures that out of home play areas are safe	☐	☐
E13	The child is closely supervised by an adult in and out of the home	☐	☐
E14	If the child attends pre-school he/she is always collected	☐	☐
E15	A small number of safe adults, known to the child, take and collect the child from pre-school	☐	☐
E16	Other	☐	☐

Summary/clarification of family strengths or issues identified
Note when issue is not relevant

Parental capacity

Summary/clarification of family strengths or issues identified
Note when issue is not relevant

Parents own problems may mean they are less able to offer the stimulation a child of this age needs.

All children need adequate and appropriate stimulation.

To gather further information consider using the Family Activity Scale.

When a child has profound or complex impairments it may be necessary to check with a specialist before completing this section.

The key to children's educational progress is a parent or significant adult who takes an interest in their learning and offers praise and encouragement.

	Emotional warmth	*Yes*	*No*	
E17	Parent generally responds positively to child's conversation	☐	☐	
E18	Parent offers praise when child attempts new activities	☐	☐	
E19	Parent supports child when attempts at new activities fail	☐	☐	
E20	Other	☐	☐	
	Stimulation			
E21	Child is encouraged to talk and join in conversation	☐	☐	
E22	Parent regularly reads, tells stories, plays counting games, watches TV with child	☐	☐	
E23	Child explores new places outside the home under supervision	☐	☐	
E24	Other	☐	☐	
	Guidance and Boundaries			
E25	The child has a range of toys/play materials suitable to his/her stage of development	☐	☐	
E26	Distractions are minimised	☐	☐	
E27	Child usually arrives at pre-school on time	☐	☐	
E28	Other	☐	☐	
	Stability			
E29	Parent/carer consistently encourages the child to learn	☐	☐	
E30	If child goes to pre-school, attendance is regular	☐	☐	
E31	Child's toys/books are looked after	☐	☐	
E32	Other	☐	☐	

Social worker's summary of the child's needs in this area and the extent to which parents are responding appropriately

When distressed most children will turn to adults for comfort.

Short lived temper tantrums are to be expected.

To gather further information consider using The Parenting Daily Hassles Scale.

Consider using the Strengths and Difficulties Questionnaire.

Any self harm must be treated seriously and appropriate help sought.

When a child is disabled or sensory impaired behaviours such as rocking or constant screaming are significant and must not be dismissed.

By 4 years about half of all children can dress without supervision.

Child's needs | **Summary/clarification of child's needs**

		Yes	*No*	Summary/clarification of child's needs
B&S1	Child is usually happy	☐	☐	
B&S2	When crying the child can usually be readily comforted	☐	☐	
B&S3	Child is often wary/anxious	☐	☐	
B&S4	Temper tantrums lasting 15 mins occur daily	☐	☐	
B&S5	Child readily engages in joint play with familiar adults	☐	☐	
B&S6	Child generally sleeps through the night	☐	☐	
B&S7	Mealtimes and bedtimes are generally hassle free	☐	☐	
B&S8	Child relates well to others (does not bite, pinch or attack)	☐	☐	
B&S9	Child's challenging/disruptive behaviour affects his/her safety	☐	☐	
B&S10	Child inflicts injuries on him/her self (i.e. scratching, head banging)	☐	☐	
B&S11	Child trusts known adults	☐	☐	
B&S12	Child attempts to dress him/herself	☐	☐	
B&S13	Child feeds him/herself	☐	☐	
B&S14	Other	☐	☐	

Most at risk are children who are victims of aggression, or are neglected.

Children who are abused or witness domestic violence are particularly traumatised.

Younger or disabled children may be at greater risk than older, more articulate children because they are less able to tell anyone about their experiences and distress.

A disabled child may not protest when left with strangers because they have been handled by many unknown people. Nonetheless it remains a matter for concern.

Parental capacity | **Summary/clarification of family strengths or issues identified**
Note when issue is not relevant

	Basic care	*Yes*	*No*	Summary/clarification
B&S15	Disagreements between parents/carers are resolved in non-violent ways	☐	☐	
B&S16	Parents teach the child basic self care skills	☐	☐	
B&S17	Other	☐	☐	
	Ensuring safety			
B&S18	Child is left with strangers	☐	☐	
B&S19	Child is hit or physically chastised	☐	☐	
B&S20	Parents/carers have sought help or advice if they are experiencing difficulties in managing the child's behaviour	☐	☐	
B&S21	Other	☐	☐	

	Parental capacity			**Summary/clarification of family strengths or issues identified** **Note when issue is not relevant**
	Emotional warmth	*Yes*	*No*	
B&S22	Child is comforted when distressed	☐	☐	
B&S23	Child is exposed to frequent criticism/hostility	☐	☐	
B&S24	Child is encouraged to talk about fears and worries	☐	☐	
B&S25	Parent takes pleasure in appropriate physical contact with the child	☐	☐	
B&S26	Other	☐	☐	
	Stimulation			
B&S27	Child is often exposed to parents' emotional distress	☐	☐	
B&S28	Child is encouraged to share and play with others	☐	☐	
B&S29	Other	☐	☐	
	Guidance and Boundaries			
B&S30	Parent uses a variety of positive methods to get the child to behave	☐	☐	
B&S31	Child is encouraged to play alongside adults doing household tasks/ to put toys away	☐	☐	
B&S32	There are clear family rules and limits about behaviour	☐	☐	
B&S33	Child is helped to control feelings	☐	☐	
B&S34	Parents do not burden the child with their own problems	☐	☐	
B&S35	Child is protected from witnessing odd or frightening adult behaviour	☐	☐	
B&S36	Other	☐	☐	
	Stability			
B&S37	Child is responded to in a relatively consistent and predictable manner	☐	☐	
B&S38	Parents/carers generally support each other in applying family rules	☐	☐	
B&S39	Other	☐	☐	

Depression can affect parent's capacity to care about their child.

Positive methods for encouraging good behaviour include: praise, negotiation, modelling, rewards, distraction, play, persuasion and explanation.

Social worker's summary of the child's needs in this area and the extent to which parents are responding appropriately

Identity and Social Presentation

At this age most children know their first and last name, age and gender.

Child's needs

		Yes	No
ID&P1	Child is self confident	☐	☐
ID&P2	Child has a positive view of self	☐	☐
ID&P3	Child takes pride in achievements	☐	☐
ID&P4	Child knows own name/age/ gender	☐	☐
ID&P5	Child asserts rights with sibs/ peers	☐	☐
ID&P6	Has a developing sense of own culture	☐	☐
ID&P7	Child's language and behaviour are usually socially appropriate	☐	☐
ID&P8	Other	☐	☐

Summary/clarification of child's needs

Children who grow up in families which experience many stresses and problems will need positive messages to avoid developing a negative self image and poor self esteem. Disabled children need even more help.

Disabled children have a right to be dressed appropriately but their dress should not impede movement, endanger stability or aggravate their skin.

Parental capacity

	Basic care	Yes	No
ID&P9	Child's clothes are clean: not soiled with urine, excrement, or food	☐	☐
ID&P10	Child's clothes are routinely washed	☐	☐
ID&P11	The name by which the child is known is consistent within the family	☐	☐
ID&P12	Other	☐	☐
	Ensuring safety		
ID&P13	Child's dress is appropriate for age, gender, culture and religion and where necessary, impairment	☐	☐
ID&P14	Parents help the child to distinguish familiar and trusted people from strangers	☐	☐
ID&P15	Other	☐	☐

Summary/clarification of family strengths or issues identified
Note when issue is not relevant

Parental capacity

Summary/clarification of family strengths or issues identified
Note when issue is not relevant

For children to develop a positive self image they need to feel loved and valued for themselves.

In all cultures disabled children may be treated as younger than their actual age. This is a particular risk for learning disabled children.

When parents are overwhelmed by their own problems children may be left to meet their own basic needs (i.e. for food, drinks, bedtimes).

Children who are routinely rejected come to see themselves as unloved and unlovable.

	Emotional warmth	*Yes*	*No*
ID&P16	Parent often shows spontaneous affection to the child	☐	☐
ID&P17	Child is valued for his/her self	☐	☐
ID&P18	Parent shows pride in child	☐	☐
ID&P19	Other	☐	☐

	Stimulation		
ID&P20	Child is encouraged to do appropriate things for his/her self	☐	☐
ID&P21	Child is offered simple choices	☐	☐
ID&P22	Child's efforts to be independent are respected	☐	☐
ID&P23	Other	☐	☐

	Guidance and Boundaries		
ID&P24	Parent teaches respect for others and other's possessions	☐	☐
ID&P25	Parents teach/encourage appropriate behaviour in public settings, including modesty	☐	☐
ID&P26	Child is frequently left to look after him/herself	☐	☐
ID&P27	Other	☐	☐

	Stability		
ID&P28	Child is accepted as a member of the family	☐	☐
ID&P29	Child is included in family celebrations, e.g. birthdays	☐	☐
ID&P30	Child is reassured when separated from the parent	☐	☐
ID&P31	The home provides the child with a stable base	☐	☐
ID&P32	Other	☐	☐

Social worker's summary of the child's needs in this area and the extent to which parents are responding appropriately

Family and Social Relationships

Strong attachment relationships can be formed with a number of carers.

Children of this age show pro- social behaviour such as sharing, helping or comforting.

Children of this age are less distressed by short separations from key carers than are infants.

Child's needs — **Summary/clarification of child's needs**

		Yes	*No*
F1	Child shows attachment behaviour/ is relaxed with main carers	☐	☐
F2	Child plays happily with siblings	☐	☐
F3	Child is gentle and kind to children and animals	☐	☐
F4	Child shares with familiar peers/siblings	☐	☐
F5	Child plays comfortably with peers		
F6	Child relates differently towards known people as opposed to strangers	☐	☐
F7	Other	☐	☐

Parental problems may result in the child being looked after by a large number of different people.

A good attachment relationship is associated with parents being emotionally available and consistent in their parenting.

Love and affection are shown in different ways depending on culture and individual characteristics.

Parental capacity — **Summary/clarification of family strengths or issues identified**
Note when issue is not relevant

	Basic care	*Yes*	*No*
F8	A small number of familiar and appropriate adults look after the child	☐	☐
F9	Parent/carers behave towards the child in a way that will encourage a strong, positive relationship to develop	☐	☐
F10	Parent/carer spends enough time with the child to sustain a strong relationship	☐	☐
F11	Other	☐	☐
	Ensuring safety		
F12	Siblings are generally gentle with the child	☐	☐
F13	Parent monitors interactions between child and siblings	☐	☐
F14	Child is protected from witnessing adult sexual behaviour	☐	☐
F15	Other	☐	☐

Parental capacity

Summary/clarification of family strengths or issues identified
Note when issue is not relevant

The presence of a supportive adult can help stressed parents to cope.

For a disabled child, practical and social barriers can make taking the child out difficult, but it remains essential to the child's wellbeing.

Of central importance to a child in all families is a loving and protective relationship.

	Emotional warmth	*Yes*	*No*
F16	Parents'/carers' relationships with others provides a good example to the child	☐	☐
F17	Parent/carer encourages affectionate family relationships	☐	☐
F18	Other	☐	☐

	Stimulation		
F19	Child is taken to meet other parents and children	☐	☐
F20	Child visits family friends and relatives	☐	☐
F21	Other	☐	☐

	Guidance and Boundaries		
F22	Child is taught to take turns	☐	☐
F23	Child is encouraged to negotiate	☐	☐
F24	Child is discouraged from violent or cruel behaviour	☐	☐
F25	Other	☐	☐

Continuity and stability are key aspects of the attachment process

	Stability		
F26	There is a stable pattern of care in the child's day to day life	☐	☐
F27	Child has a long-term, stable relationship with at least 1 adult	☐	☐
F28	There is continuity of carers	☐	☐
F29	A limited number of known, safe adults deliver intimate care	☐	☐
F30	Other.	☐	☐

Social worker's summary of the child's needs in this area and the extent to which parents are responding appropriately

Issues affecting parents'/carers' capacities to respond appropriately to the child's needs

	Parental issues	*Yes*	*No*	*Professional/agency involved*	*Note identity of parent/carer for whom the issue is relevant. Record strengths and difficulties*
C1	Illness:				
	Physical	☐	☐		
	Mental	☐	☐		
C2	Disability:				
	Physical	☐	☐		
	Learning	☐	☐		
	Sensory impairment	☐	☐		
C3	Period in care during childhood	☐	☐		
C4	Childhood abuse	☐	☐		
C5	Known history of child abuse	☐	☐		
C6	Known history of violence	☐	☐		
C7	Problem drinking/ drug use	☐	☐		
C8	Other	☐	☐		

Social worker's summary of how the above issues have an impact on the parents'/carers' capacities to respond appropriately to the child's needs

Family and Environmental Factors which may impact on the child and parenting capacity

Additional details as appropriate
Note identity of person for whom the issue is relevant

Include all household and relevant family members, living in or out of the home, when exploring family history and functioning.

To gather further information consider using: The Recent Life Events Questionnaire; A genogram; An eco map.

How parents bring up their children is rooted in their own childhood experiences.

Consider whether a separate carers' assessment is required.

Both positive and negative parenting styles can be passed from one generation to another.

To gather further information consider using: The Adult Well-being Scale; The Alcohol Scale.

Wider family may extend beyond blood relatives to include people who feel like family to parent or child.

	Family History	*Yes*	*No*	Additional details
FE1	Has a member of the household experienced a stressful childhood?	☐	☐	
	Note childhood abuse; in care			
FE2	Have the family suffered a traumatic loss or crisis which is unresolved? (e.g. bereavement)	☐	☐	
FE3	Other	☐	☐	
	Family Functioning			
FE4	Does child's impairment/behaviour have a negative impact on siblings?	☐	☐	
FE5	Child's impairment/behaviour affects parent(s) capacity to continue care	☐	☐	
FE6	Does a member of the household experience:			
	poor mental health	☐	☐	
	poor physical health	☐	☐	
	behaviour problem	☐	☐	
	physical disability	☐	☐	
	learning disability	☐	☐	
	sensory impairment	☐	☐	
	problem alcohol/drug use	☐	☐	
FE7	Has an adult member of the household got a history of violence?	☐	☐	
FE8	Are there frequent family rows?	☐	☐	
FE9	Other	☐	☐	
	Wider Family			
FE10	Do wider family provide:			
	practical help	☐	☐	
	emotional support	☐	☐	
	financial help	☐	☐	
	information and advice	☐	☐	
FE11	Is there an adult in the home who helps the parent care for the child?	☐	☐	
FE12	Other	☐	☐	

Additional details as appropriate
Note identity of person for whom the issue is relevant

Basic amenities include safe water, heating, cooking facilities, food storage, sleeping arrangements and cleanliness.

The Home Conditions Assessment may help gather this information.

Housing	*Yes*	*No*
FE13 Is the family homeless?	☐	☐
FE14 Is the family vulnerable to eviction or in temporary accommodation?	☐	☐
FE15 Is the house and its immediate surroundings safe for the child?	☐	☐
FE16 Does home have basic amenities?	☐	☐
FE17 Does home require any adaptations to meet the child's needs?	☐	☐
FE18 Is the home overcrowded?		
FE19 Other	☐	☐

Jobs may be lost because parents' circumstances result in them behaving in a bizarre or unpredictable way.

Parents' circumstances may mean too much family income is used to satisfy parental needs.

Adult services may help a disabled parent respond to their child's needs.

The family may be vulnerable to future financial problems (i.e. extraordinary medical, funeral expenses, need to help out a relative).

Employment	*Yes*	*No*
FE20 Is a parent in paid employment?	☐	☐
FE21 Does parent's pattern of work adversely impact on child care?	☐	☐
FE22 Is employment reasonably secure?	☐	☐
FE23 Are family members who seek employment adequately supported?	☐	☐
FE24 Other	☐	☐

Income		
FE25 Are all entitled benefits claimed?	☐	☐
FE26 Are household bills paid regularly?	☐	☐
FE27 Is the family managing on the income they receive?	☐	☐
FE28 If in debt, is this increasing?	☐	☐
FE29 Is the family worried about future financial commitments?	☐	☐
FE30 Other	☐	☐

Social isolation and rejection by the community may have affected the family for generations.

Family's Social Integration		
FE31 Does the family feel accepted within their community?	☐	☐
FE32 Do family members experience discrimination/harassment?	☐	☐
FE33 Does the family have local friends?	☐	☐
FE34 Is the family involved in local organisations/activities?	☐	☐
FE35 Other		

Additional details as appropriate

Community resources include: shops, play areas, play groups and nurseries, health clinics etc.

In assessing community resources note: availability, accessibility and standard and if appropriate to child and family needs.

Community Resources	*Yes*	*No*
FE36 Are there accessible community resources?	☐	☐
FE37 Does the family take advantage of community resources?	☐	☐
FE38 Other	☐	☐

Social worker's summary of how the family and environmental factors have an impact on the child and parents'/carers' capacities to respond appropriately to their children's needs.

Plan for the child in need

- Having completed the information gathering, the following pages should be used to analyse the strengths and needs of the child and family members and to identify goals and specific objectives. This information is then used to formulate a plan of action. The decision about which methods are used and services are provided to achieve specific objectives should be evidence based. The expectations of a plan for a child in need are outlined in paragraphs 4.32 to 4.37 of the **Framework for the Assessment of Children in Need and Their Families** (2000).
- The plan for a child in need has been designed to enable it to be used for all children in need, including these about whom there are concerns they are suffering or likely to suffer significant harm.
- The plan should identify how the following will be addressed:
  - The identified developmental needs of the child;
  - Issues which impact negatively on parents/carers' capacity to respond to the child and needs of their child, drawing on their strengths;
  - Wider family and environmental factors which have a negative impact on the child and family, drawing on strengths in the wider family and community.
- The plan should be specific about the actions to be taken, identify who is responsible for each action, and any services or resources that will be required to ensure that the objectives set can be achieved within the agreed time scales. Statutory reviews should take place within statutory time limits and it is good practice for Child In Need plans to be reviewed at least every 6 months. Reviews should be formally recorded.
- The outcome section of the table should be completed following a review of the plan. When completing the outcome section record the outcome for each objective and whether the circumstances have; improved, remained the same, or deteriorated.
- The last page records which family members and agencies are party to the plan and the date when the plan will be reviewed. This should be signed by the child (where appropriate), family members/carers and the social worker.

Summary of child's developmental needs and strengths

Information gathered in the core assessment

Summarise the child's developmental needs and strengths

Parents should be involved in the assessment

This space is for parents/carers to write their views of the child's strengths and needs

Summary of parental capacity: Needs and strengths

Information gathered in the core assessment

Summarise how the parental issues, needs and strengths, which have been identified in the core assessment have an impact on the capacity of each parent/carer to respond appropriately to the child's needs

Parents should be involved in the assessment

This space is for parents/carers to write their views of their own strengths and difficulties and what impact they think these have on the child's development

Summary of wider family and environmental factors: Needs and strengths

Information gathered in the core assessment

Summarise how family and environment issues, which have been identified in the core assessment, have an impact either directly on the child or on the capacity of the parents/carers to respond appropriately to the child's needs

Parents should be involved in the assessment

This space is for parents/carers to write their views of the strengths and difficulties in their wider family and environment and what impact they think these have on the child's development

Analysis of the information gathered during the core assessment

The analysis should list the factors which have an impact on different aspects of the child's development and parenting capacity, and explore the relationship between them. This process of analysing the information available about the child's needs, parenting capacity and wider family and environmental factors should result in a clear understanding of the child's needs, and what types of service provision would best address these needs to ensure the child has the opportunity to achieve their potential

The child: objectives and plans

Child's developmental needs	*Objectives and plan of action*	*Person/Agency responsible*	*Objective to be achieved by (date)*	*Outcome (to be completed at the review)*
Health				
Education				
Identity: Social presentation				
Family and social relationships				
Emotional and behavioural development: Self care skills				

The parents/carers: Objectives and plans

Parenting capacity	*Objective and plan of action*	*Person/Agency responsible*	*Objective to be achieved by (date)*	*Outcome (to be completed at the review)*
Basic care				
Ensuring safety				
Emotional warmth				
Stimulation				
Guidance and boundaries				
Stability				

Wider Family and Environmental Factors: Objectives and plans

Family and environmental factors	*Objective and plan of action*	*Person/Agency responsible*	*Objective to be achieved by (date)*	*Outcome (to be completed at the review)*
Family history and functioning				
Wider family				
Housing				
Employment and/or income				
Family social integration				
Community resources				

Views of all parties

These objectives and plans should have been discussed with all interested parties/agencies
Family members/agencies who are party to the plan

Name (please print)	Signature	Contact Number

Agreed date for the review: ____________________

Lead professional/agency for the review: ____________________

If the objectives and plans have not been discussed with any of the parties/agencies concerned, please give reasons

What steps will be taken and who is responsible if any party/agency wants to alter these objectives and plans?

Date plan reviewed in supervision	Signature of Line Manger/Supervisor

Parents/carer's comments

I have seen the contents of this assessment form

Parent/carer's signature .... **Date** |__|__|__|

Parent/carer signature .... **Date** |__|__|__|

Parents/carers comments on the assessment

Have all relevant family members been given a copy of the assessment record? **Yes** ☐ **No** ☐

If not, what arrangements have been made to ensure this happens?

Social Worker's Signature .... **Date** |__|__|__|

Management information

Ethnicity of the child:

Caribbean	☐	Indian	☐	White British	☐	White and Black Caribbean	☐	Chinese	☐
African	☐	Pakistani	☐	White Irish	☐	White and Black African	☐	Any other ethnic group	☐
Any other Black background	☐	Bangladeshi	☐	Any other White background	☐	White and Asian	☐	Not given	☐

Any other Asian background ☐ Any other mixed background ☐

If other, please specify ____________________

Immigration status if applicable:

Asylum seeking ☐ Refugee status ☐ Exceptional leave to remain ☐

Home Office registration number: ____________________

(H8) Details of immunisations:

Has the child been appropriately immunised? Yes ☐ No ☐

2–4 months: Diphtheria/Tetanus, Whooping cough, Polio, Hib, Men C. 12–15 months: Measles/Mumps/Rubella

3–5 years: Diphtheria, Tetanus, Polio, Measles/Mumps/Rubella.

Child protection register:

Is the child's name on the Child Protection Register? Yes ☐ No ☐

Category __________ Date of registration __________

Has the child previously been on the Child Protection Register? Yes ☐ No ☐

Category	Date of registration	Date of deregistration

Court Order(s)

Is the child the subject of a court order? Yes ☐ No ☐

Was the child previously subject of a court order? Yes ☐ No ☐

Type of Order(s)	Date Order(s) made:	Type of Order(s)	Date Order(s) made	Date Order(s) revoked/changed

 ISBN 0 11 322420 6

CORE ASSESSMENT RECORD

Child aged 5–9 years

Name ______________________________

Gender ______________ *Date of birth* ______________

Address ______________________________

____

____

____

Telephone number ______________________________

Name of social worker completing assessment:

____

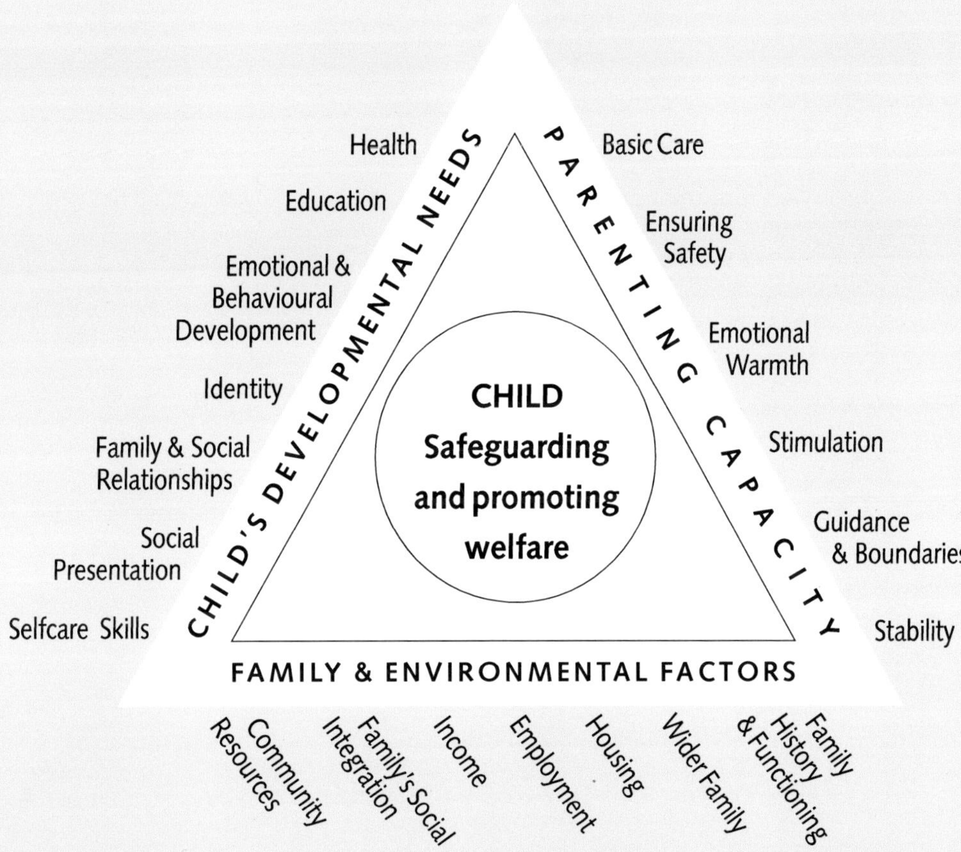

Contents

Undertaking the core assessment

- The Core Assessment Record provides a framework for systematically recording the findings from the core assessment. Whilst the Assessment Record provides some guidance on the areas that should be covered in a core assessment, it is a tool and should not be used as a substitute for a professionally informed assessment process, analysis and judgement.
- The questionnaires and scales published in the accompanying materials to the **Framework for the Assessment of Child in Need and their Families** may be useful in obtaining the information in specific areas (Department of Health, Cox and Bentovim, 2000). The Assessment Record indicates where particular questionnaires and scales may be useful. Practitioners may also choose to use other assessment tools to assist them.
- The Core Assessment Record may be completed in a number of different ways. For example, the social worker may wish to discuss each area with the family before completing the record and then share this with the family. Alternatively, having undertaken some or all of the core assessment the social worker may wish to complete the form with the child's parents or carers.
- Parents and carers invariably want to do the best for their children. Completing the record will help social workers to recognise the strengths that families have as well as identifying areas where they may need further help.
- Completing the core assessment should always be done in a way that helps parents or carers, children and other relevant family members to have their say and encourages them to take part. Space has been provided within the forms for parents/carers and older children to be involved in the assessment.
- It is expected that other agencies will be involved, as appropriate, during the core assessment process. Parental permission to contact other agencies should be obtained except in cases where the safety of the child would be jeopardised (paragraphs 7.27 to 7.38 of **Working Together to Safeguard Children** provides guidance on this issue). Permissions should be obtained from other agencies to share their information with the family.
- It is important that all sections of the Core Assessment Record are considered carefully. The analysis of the information gathered should be recorded in the plan. In some cases it will not be appropriate to complete particular sections, and in such situations the reason why should be recorded in the summary section. The information gathered is then used to develop case objectives and plans.
- In competing the record, it should be possible to see what help and support the child and family need, and which agencies might be best placed to give that help. This might include more detailed assessments of specific issues.
- Families should be provided with the following information:

Complaints procedures	date provided ______________________
Information on access to records	date provided ______________________
Other relevant/available information *(please specify)*	date provided ______________________

Sources of information

Dates child and family members seen

Name	Date(s) seen

Agencies consulted/involved as part of the assessment

Agency	Person	Contact number

Questionnaires, Scales or other Instruments used in assessment

Questionnaire/Scale/Instrument	Date(s) used

Specialist Assessments

Agency/person who undertook the assessment	Purpose of the assessment	Date(s) assessment commissioned and completed

Details concerning a core assessment

D1 What is the reason for undertaking the core assessment?

Date core assessment started

Date core assessment ended

The Government's Objectives for Childen's Social Services (1999) require the core assessment to be completed within 35 working days.

D2 Are there specific communication needs for child/parent (eg. impairment affecting communication or English is not the first language)?
If so, what action has been taken to address this ie. use of an interpreter or a signer?

Background details concerning the child

(This information supplements the information recorded on the Referral and Initial Assessment Record)

B/K1 Significant relatives who are not part of the child's household

Birth father Parental responsibility Yes ☐ No ☐ Name ______

Address ______

Brothers and sisters

Name(s)	Age	Address

Others (please specify)

Name(s)	Relationship to child	Address

B/K2 If the child has any health conditions, impairment(s) or a genetically inherited condition – please give details
(include for example: physical disability, sensory impairment, Down's syndrome, encephalitis, autism, sickle cell anaemia, cystic fibrosis)

B/K3 Key events which may have had an impact on the child
(for example: death of brother or sister, circumstances surrounding conception)

B/K4 Other key events experienced by siblings or other family members which may affect the child

Key research sources

The Assessment Record is based on research information drawn from a number of sources

Assessment

Cleaver H, Wattam C and Cawson P (1998) *Assessing Risk in Child Protection*. NSPCC, London.

Department of Health, Department for Education and Employment and Home Office (2000) *Framework for the Assessment of Child in Need and their Families*. The Stationery Office, London.

Department of Health, Cox A and Bentovim A (2000) *The Family Assessment Pack of Questionnaires and Scales.* The Stationery Office, London.

The NSPCC and University of Sheffield (2000) *The Child's World: Assessing Children in Need. Training and Development Pack*. NSPCC, London.

Sinclair R, Garnett L and Berridge D (1995) *Social Work and Assessment with Adolescents*. National Children's Bureau, London.

Ward H (ed) (1995) *Looking After Children: Research into Practice*. HMSO, London.

Child development

Department of Health (1996) *Focus on Teenagers: Research into Practice*. HMSO, London.

Department of Health (1997) *Young Carers: Making a Start*. Department of Health, London.

Fahlberg VI (1994) *A Child's Journey Through Placement*. BAAF, London.

Jones DPH (forthcoming) *Communicating with children who may have been traumatised or maltreated*.

Rutter R and Rutter M (1992) *Developing Minds: Challenge and Continuity across the Life Span*. Penguin, Harmondsworth.

Smith PK and Cowie H (1993) *Understanding Children's Development* (2nd Edition). Blackwell, Oxford.

Varma VP (1991) *The Secret Life of Vulnerable Children.* Routledge, London.

Parenting capacity

Cleaver H, Unell I and Aldgate J (1999) *Children's Needs — Parenting Capacity: The impact of parental mental illness, problem alcohol and drug use, and domestic violence on children's development.* The Stationery Office, London.

Falkov A, Mayes K, Diggins M, Silverdale N and Cox A(1998) *Crossing Bridges — Training resources for working with mentally ill parents and their children.* Pavilion Publishing, Brighton.

Reder, P and Lucey, C (1995) *Assessment of Parenting: Psychiatric and psychological contributions.* Routledge, London.

Family and environmental factors

Cochran M (ed) (1993) *Parenting: an ecological perspective.* Lawrence Erlbaum Associates, New Jersey.

Cochran M, Larner M, Riley D, Gunnarsson L and Henderson C (eds) (1990) *Extending families: the social networks of parents and their children*. Cambridge University Press, Cambridge.

Jack G and Jordan B (1999) Social capital and child welfare. *Children and Society*. 13 (5): 242-256.

Wallace SA, Crown JM, Berger M and Cox AD (1997) *Child and Adolescent Mental Health*. In Stevens A and Rafferty J (1997) *Health Care Needs Assessment: 2nd Series.* Radcliffe Medical Press, Oxford.

Iwanec D (1995) *The emotionally abused and neglected child*. Wiley, Chichester.

Stevenson O (1998) *Neglected Children: Issues and Dilemmas*. Blackwell Science, Oxford.

Child's developmental needs

Health

Normally well is defined as *unwell for 1 week or less in the last 6 months.*

Details of immunisations in health record held by parents.

Child at 5 has had the full course of the following immunisations Polio, Hib, Diphtheria, Tetanus, Whooping cough, Men C, Measles/Mumps/Rubella.

When children start school they may have had a medical examination.

Child's needs		*Yes*	*No*	**Summary/clarification of child's needs**
H1	Weight/height at expected level	☐	☐	
H2	Hearing/vision is satisfactory	☐	☐	
H3	Child is normally well	☐	☐	
H4	Child has a regular sleep pattern	☐	☐	
H5	Child eats well	☐	☐	
H6	Child frequently wets the bed	☐	☐	
H7	Soils without physical explanation	☐	☐	
H8	Has been appropriately immunised	☐	☐	
H9	Has an ongoing health problem (i.e. diabetes, asthma, epilepsy)	☐	☐	
H10	Has had many accidental injuries	☐	☐	
H11	Other	☐	☐	

To gather further information consider using the Home Conditions Assessment.

Disabled children can face barriers in accessing routine dental and medical care.

Black families may have less access to preventative and support services than white families.

The significance of the physical symptoms of children's illnesses may not always be easily identified or understood. This may influence the way parents respond.

Parental capacity				**Summary/clarification of family strengths or issues identified** **Note when issue is not relevant**
	Basic care	*Yes*	*No*	
H12	Child is given an adequate and nutritious diet including fluids	☐	☐	
H13	Parent ensures child bathes regularly	☐	☐	
H14	Parent ensures that the child's teeth are regularly cleaned	☐	☐	
H15	Dress is appropriate to weather	☐	☐	
H16	The home, including the child's bed, is clean	☐	☐	
H17	Child's medical/dental appointments are generally kept	☐	☐	
H18	Parent has adequate explanation as to why immunisations are not up to date	☐	☐	
H19	Other	☐	☐	
	Ensuring safety			
H20	Injuries have always been appropriately attended to	☐	☐	
H21	Injuries have an understandable accidental cause	☐	☐	
H22	Child is protected from abuse	☐	☐	
H23	Marks on the child's body have an acceptable explanation	☐	☐	
H24	Other	☐	☐	

Parental capacity

Summary/clarification of family strengths or issues identified
Note when issue is not relevant

Poverty and poor social conditions are related to poor child health and development and increased risk of accidents.

Increasing numbers of children are suffering obesity. Regular physical exercise is an important preventative measure.

Disabled children may need special help or equipment for exercise.

Disabled or children with a health problem need information and opportunities to help them understand and learn about themselves.

Eating and sleeping patterns need to be set within the context of the family's culture.

		Yes	*No*
	Emotional warmth		
H25	Parents/carers give comfort when child is ill/distressed/injured	☐	☐
H26	Other	☐	☐
	Stimulation		
H27	Child is encouraged to be active	☐	☐
H28	Child plays regularly out of doors	☐	☐
H29	Other	☐	☐
	Guidance and Boundaries		
H30	Parent/carer tries to ensure the child gets adequate and undisturbed sleep	☐	☐
H31	Parent/carer provides the child with an adequate and nutritious diet	☐	☐
H32	Child is supervised by responsible adults, or plays in an environment parents have checked is safe	☐	☐
H33	Other	☐	☐
	Stability		
H34	Parent/carer provides regular and consistent routines for the child (mealtimes, bedtimes, bath times)	☐	☐
H35	Other	☐	☐

Social worker's summary of the child's needs in this area and the extent to which parents are responding appropriately

SATs are given to pupils in the summer term of Years 2, 6, & 9 (ages 7, 11 & 14).

At 7 years most children are performing at level 2 of Key Stage 1.

School refusal at this age is rare. Black pupils often underachieve at school.

Black pupils are 4 times more likely to be excluded than white pupils. Excluded black children are usually of higher ability with fewer chronic disruptive behaviours than white pupils who are excluded.

Child's needs

		Yes	*No*
E1	Child's educational progress is satisfactory in reading, writing and maths. **Note SATS results**	☐	☐
E2	Child is happy to go to school	☐	☐
E3	Child attends school regularly (note number of unauthorised days absent in past year)	☐	☐
E4	Child arrives at school on time	☐	☐
E5	Child has a friend at school	☐	☐
E6	Child has a good relationship with a member of staff	☐	☐
E7	Child responds appropriately to adult instruction	☐	☐
E8	Child shows challenging/disruptive behaviour at school	☐	☐
E9	Child's lack of concentration impedes learning	☐	☐
E10	Child is excluded from school	☐	☐
E11	Other	☐	☐

Summary/clarification of child's needs

date	*Subject*	*level*
	English	
	Maths	
	Science	

When a parent has a learning disability only 15% of children are similarly affected.

Not all children with impairments will need a statement of Special Educational Needs.

Disabled children may need financial help, equipment or adaptations to allow them to get to school.

Parents' circumstances may mean they are unable to take the child to school, or may delegate the task to others.

These adults must not present a risk to the child.

Parental capacity

	Basic care	*Yes*	*No*
E12	Child has a range of safe appropriate toys/learning materials	☐	☐
E13	Parent/carer regularly attends school events	☐	☐
E14	Parent/carer supports and encourages homework	☐	☐
E15	If child is not achieving at school: Is there an Individual Education Plan?	☐	☐
	Is there a statement of Special Educational Needs?	☐	☐
E16	Other	☐	☐
	Ensuring safety		
E17	Home has safe play areas	☐	☐
E18	Where appropriate, the child is always accompanied to school	☐	☐
E19	Responsible, known adults take and fetch the child from school	☐	☐
E20	Where necessary, parents have taken action over bullying	☐	☐
E21	Other	☐	☐

Summary/clarification of family strengths or issues identified
Note when issue is not relevant

Parental capacity

Summary/clarification of family strengths or issues identified
Note when issue is not relevant

Parents own problems may mean they are not always able to offer the intellectual stimulation a child of this age needs.

To gather further information consider using the Family Activity Scale.

	Emotional warmth	*Yes*	*No*
E22	Parent shows an interest in the child's school work	☐	☐
E23	Parent shows approval of educational achievements	☐	☐
E24	Parent places great pressure on the child to achieve	☐	☐
E25	Other	☐	☐

All children need adequate and appropriate stimulation. When a child has profound or complex impairments it may be helpful to check with a specialist before completing this section.

	Stimulation		
E26	Parent regularly reads, tells stories, plays counting games, watches TV with child	☐	☐
E27	Other	☐	☐

	Guidance and Boundaries		
E28	Parent supports regular school attendance	☐	☐
E29	Ensures prompt attendance	☐	☐
E30	Supports school rules	☐	☐
E31	Ensures child is ready on time for school	☐	☐
E32	Other	☐	☐

The key to children's educational progress is a parent or significant adult who takes an interest in their learning and offers praise and encouragement.

	Stability		
E33	Parent/carer consistently encourages learning	☐	☐
E34	Child's toys/books/school work are looked after	☐	☐
E35	Other	☐	☐

Social worker's summary of the child's needs in this area and the extent to which parents are responding appropriately

Emotional and Behavioural Development

Consider using the Strengths and Difficulties Questionnaire.

When a child is disabled or sensory impaired behaviours such as rocking or constant screaming are significant and should not be dismissed.

At this age concepts of ownership may not be fully established.

Self harm must be treated seriously and appropriate help sought.

Children may cope with upsetting parental behaviours by withdrawing or running away.

	Child's needs	Yes	No	**Summary/clarification of child's needs**
B1	Child is usually happy	☐	☐	
B2	Temper tantrums lasting 15 mins occur weekly	☐	☐	
B3	Child is gaining control over the expression of strong emotions	☐	☐	
B4	Child's challenging/disruptive behaviour affects his/her safety	☐	☐	
B5	Child enjoys appropriate physical closeness with familiar adults	☐	☐	
B6	Child talks about feelings with a trusted adult	☐	☐	
B7	Shares/takes turns with others	☐	☐	
B8	Has some understanding of the concept of ownership	☐	☐	
B9	Child inflicts injuries on him/her self (i.e. scratching, head banging)	☐	☐	
B10	Child is preoccupied with violence	☐	☐	
B11	Child bullies other children	☐	☐	
B12	Child wanders from home	☐	☐	
B13	Child spends long periods alone	☐	☐	
B14	Other	☐	☐	

Depression can affect parent's capacity to care about their child.

Most at risk are children who are victims of aggression, or are neglected.

Consider whether the feelings and behaviour that troubles the child and parent would benefit from specialist assessment and help.

	Parental capacity	Yes	No	**Summary/clarification of family strengths or issues identified** **Note when issue is not relevant**
	Basic care			
B15	Parent/carer loves the child unconditionally (i.e. without strings attached)	☐	☐	
B16	Family disagreements are resolved in non-violent ways	☐	☐	
B17	Other	☐	☐	
	Ensuring safety			
B18	Child's whereabouts are always known	☐	☐	
B19	Child is frequently left alone	☐	☐	
B20	Child is hit or physically chastised	☐	☐	
B21	Parents/carers have sought help or advice if they are experiencing difficulties in managing the child's behaviour	☐	☐	
B22	Other	☐	☐	

Parental capacity

Summary/clarification of family strengths or issues identified
Note when issue is not relevant

Children who are abused or witness domestic violence are particularly traumatised.

Children may have difficulty talking about their feelings and find it easier to discuss them in retrospect.

Discussing feelings becomes more difficult when children depend on non verbal methods of communication.

To gather further information consider using The Parenting Daily Hassles Scale.

Positive methods for encouraging good behaviour include: praise, negotiation, modelling, rewards distraction, play, persuasion and explanation.

When children witness violence they have difficulty in controlling their own emotions and behaviour.

		Yes	*No*
	Emotional warmth		
B23	Child is comforted when frightened or distressed	☐	☐
B24	Child is exposed to frequent criticism/hostility	☐	☐
B25	Child is encouraged to talk about fears and worries	☐	☐
B26	Other	☐	☐
	Stimulation		
B27	Child is often exposed to parents' emotional distress	☐	☐
B28	Child is encouraged to share and play with others	☐	☐
B29	Other	☐	☐
	Guidance and Boundaries		
B30	Parent uses a variety of positive methods to get the child to behave	☐	☐
B31	Child is encouraged to help adults doing household tasks/to put toys away	☐	☐
B32	There are clear family rules and limits about behaviour	☐	☐
B33	Child is helped to control feelings	☐	☐
B34	Parents do not burden the child with their own problems	☐	☐
B35	Child is protected from witnessing odd or frightening adult behaviour	☐	☐
B36	Other	☐	☐
	Stability		
B37	Child is responded to in a relatively consistent and predictable manner	☐	☐
B38	Parents/carers generally support each other in applying family rules	☐	☐
B39	Other	☐	☐

Social worker's summary of the child's needs in this area and the extent to which parents are responding appropriately

Identity

Cultural identity develops from all aspects of the child's experience.

The way in which black disabled children define themselves is affected by their personal experience of both racism and disability.

Dual heritage does not always result in identity problems/conflicts.

Racism and bullying are common-place in the lives of black children

Child's needs | **Summary/clarification of child's needs**

	Child's needs	*Yes*	*No*
ID1	Child is self confident	☐	☐
ID2	Child takes pride in his/her appearance	☐	☐
ID3	Child takes pride in achievements	☐	☐
ID4	Child is able to stand up for him/herself appropriately	☐	☐
ID5	Child has a developing sense of his/her own culture	☐	☐
ID6	Knows full name/birthdate/address	☐	☐
ID7	Can identify important relatives	☐	☐
ID8	Child is comfortable with his/her own racial identity	☐	☐
ID9	Other	☐	☐

Parental capacity

Summary/clarification of family strengths or issues identified
Note when issue is not relevant

Children who grow up in families which experience many stresses and problems will need positive messages to avoid developing a negative self image and poor self esteem. Disabled children need even more help.

	Basic care	*Yes*	*No*
ID10	Child's clothes are clean: not soiled with urine, excrement, or food	☐	☐
ID11	Child's clothes are routinely washed	☐	☐
ID12	Parents see the child as having unique strengths and encourages them	☐	☐
ID13	Other	☐	☐

Disabled children have a right to be dressed appropriately but their dress should not impede movement, endanger stability or aggravate their skin.

	Ensuring safety		
ID14	Child's dress is appropriate for age, gender, culture and religion and where necessary, impairment	☐	☐
ID15	Child is supervised appropriately taking into account the child's personality and developmental level	☐	☐
ID16	Parents support the child who is exposed to racism or bullying	☐	☐
ID17	Other	☐	☐

Parental capacity

Summary/clarification of family strengths or issues identified
Note when issue is not relevant

For children to develop a positive self image they need to feel loved and valued for themselves.

In all cultures disabled children may be treated as younger than their actual age. This is a particular risk for learning disabled children.

	Emotional warmth	*Yes*	*No*
ID18	Parent often shows spontaneous affection to child	☐	☐
ID19	Child is valued for his/her self	☐	☐
ID20	Parent/carer shows pride in child	☐	☐
ID21	Child's efforts/achievements are praised	☐	☐
ID22	Parent supports the child when exposed to harassment or racism	☐	☐
ID23	Other	☐	☐

Children need positive role models of the same racial/ethnic origins as him/ herself.

Children frequently believe they can control their parent's disturbing behaviour through magical thinking and actions.

	Stimulation		
ID24	Child has the opportunity to learn own cultural traditions/ language	☐	☐
ID25	Child's efforts to be independent are respected	☐	☐
ID26	Other	☐	☐

Children often suffer if they are included in the imaginary world of a mentally ill parent.

	Guidance and Boundaries		
ID27	Child is taught respect/toleration of others and of different family/ cultural traditions	☐	☐
ID28	Family is tolerant of different cultures, ethnic groups etc	☐	☐
ID29	Child is protected from parental mental illness/symptoms	☐	☐
ID30	Child is comforted/reassured when parent's behaviour is disturbing	☐	☐
ID31	Other		

Children who are routinely rejected come to see themselves as unloved and unlovable.

	Stability		
ID32	Child accepted as a family member	☐	☐
ID33	Child is included in family celebrations, e.g. birthdays	☐	☐
ID34	Parent ensures that day to day living has order and stability		
ID35	Other	☐	☐

Social worker's summary of the child's needs in this area and the extent to which parents are responding appropriately

Family and Social Relationships

Strong attachment relationships can be formed with a number of carers.

Children who are unaccompanied asylum seekers experience acute loss.

Family values are increasingly internalised.

Children can help look after younger siblings and parents but should not have overall responsibility.

	Child's needs	Yes	No	**Summary/clarification of child's needs**
F1	Child shows strong attachment to a parent	☐	☐	
F2	Child is relaxed with parents/carers	☐	☐	
F3	Child plays happily/shares with siblings and familiar peers	☐	☐	
F4	Child is gentle and kind to children and animals	☐	☐	
F5	Child has a friend	☐	☐	
F6	Child bullies other children	☐	☐	
F7	Child's sexual knowledge and behaviour is age-appropriate	☐	☐	
F8	Child frequently looks after younger brothers and sisters	☐	☐	
F9	Child frequently looks after his/her parent/carer	☐	☐	
F10	Other	☐	☐	

Family or child centred issues may result in the child being looked after by a large number of different people (i.e. family, friends, hospital care, or social services respite care).

A disabled child may not protest when left with strangers because they have been handled by many unknown people. Nonetheless it remains a matter for concern.

	Parental capacity	Yes	No	**Summary/clarification of family strengths or issues identified** **Note when issue is not relevant**
	Basic care			
F11	A small number of familiar and appropriate adults look after the child	☐	☐	
F12	Parent/carer spends enough time with the child to sustain a strong relationship	☐	☐	
F13	Other	☐	☐	
	Ensuring safety			
F14	Siblings are generally gentle with the child	☐	☐	
F15	Parent monitors interactions between child and siblings	☐	☐	
F16	Child does not witness adult sexual behaviour	☐	☐	
F17	Child does not witness adult violence	☐	☐	
F18	Child is left alone at night	☐	☐	
F19	Other	☐	☐	

Parental capacity

Summary/clarification of family strengths or issues identified
Note when issue is not relevant

A good attachment relationship is associated with parents being emotionally available and consistent in their parenting.

Love and affection are shown in different ways depending on culture and individual characteristics.

The presence of a supportive adult can help stressed parents to cope.

For a disabled child, practical and social barriers can make taking the child out difficult, but it remains essential to the child's well being.

Of central importance to a child in all families is a loving and protective relationship.

Continuity and stability are key aspects of the attachment process.

Untrained agency staff are not appropriate people to care for a disabled child.

	Emotional warmth	*Yes*	*No*	Summary/clarification
F20	Parents/carers' relationships with others provides a good example to the child	☐	☐	
F21	Parent/carer encourages affectionate family relationships	☐	☐	
F22	Other	☐	☐	
	Stimulation			
F23	Child is taken to meet other parents and children	☐	☐	
F24	Child sees friends outside school	☐	☐	
F25	Child has friends to visit at home	☐	☐	
F26	Other	☐	☐	
	Guidance and Boundaries			
F27	Child is encouraged to negotiate	☐	☐	
F28	Child is discouraged from violent or cruel behaviour	☐	☐	
F29	Child is frequently left to look after siblings	☐	☐	
F30	Child has major responsibility for parental care	☐	☐	
F31	Other	☐	☐	
	Stability			
F32	There is a stable pattern of care in the child's day to day life	☐	☐	
F33	Child has a long-term, stable relationship with at least 1 adult	☐	☐	
F34	There is continuity of carers	☐	☐	
F35	A limited number of known, appropriate adults deliver intimate care	☐	☐	
F36	Other	☐	☐	

Social worker's summary of the child's needs in this area and the extent to which parents are responding appropriately

Social presentation

	Child's needs	Yes	No	Summary/clarification of child's needs
Children can make themselves understood by people outside the family.	P1 Child's language and behaviour do not cause offence or embarrassment outside the family	☐	☐	
	P2 Child values adult attention	☐	☐	
	P3 Child is happy to talk/communicate about family and home	☐	☐	
	P4 Child is self-confident and appropriately open with adults	☐	☐	
	P5 Child is overly friendly with strangers	☐	☐	
	P6 Child is self-confident and open with peers	☐	☐	
	P7 Child plays with friends outside school hours	☐	☐	
Most children have learnt to adjust their conversation and behaviour to suit a variety of different situations.	P8 Child relates differently and appropriately towards known people and strangers	☐	☐	
	P9 Other	☐	☐	

	Parental capacity	Yes	No	Summary/clarification of family strengths or issues identified Note when issue is not relevant
	Basic care			
A child who is well cared for will look as if someone is paying adequate attention to his/her personal needs. For example, it should be clear from the child's appearance that he or she frequently bathes and his/her clothes as regularly washed and mended.	P10 Parents/carers ensure that child's personal hygiene is adequate	☐	☐	
	P11 Other	☐	☐	
	Ensuring safety			
	P12 Parents/carers teach the child how to behave appropriately with strangers	☐	☐	
	P13 Parents/carers teach appropriate behaviour in public settings, including modesty	☐	☐	
	P14 Parents/carers ensure the child is supervised/supported in potentially dangerous settings	☐	☐	
	P15 Other	☐	☐	

The experience of racism, harassment or bullying may result in children having low self esteem.

When families are experiencing difficulties children keep silent because they fear telling some one will result in them 'getting into trouble', or being 'taken away'.

Children often shun social events or keep friends at bay in an attempt to keep the family's circumstances secret.

Parental capacity

Summary/clarification of family strengths or issues identified
Note when issue is not relevant

	Emotional warmth	*Yes*	*No*
P16	Parents/carers encourage the child to be self-confident	☐	☐
P17	Parents/carers praise the child for good social behaviour	☐	☐
P18	Family members support each other over decisions about child's clothes and appearance	☐	☐
P19	Other	☐	☐
	Stimulation		
P20	Parents/carers encourage the child to bring his/her friends home	☐	☐
P21	Child is encouraged to join in organised social activities	☐	☐
P22	Child is encouraged to join in mixed age family activities	☐	☐
P22	Other	☐	☐
	Guidance and Boundaries		
P23	Parents/carers teach the child appropriate 'good manners' and respect for others	☐	☐
P24	Parent's relationships with neighbours and those in authority are generally harmonious	☐	☐
P25	Family members are engaged in criminal/antisocial activities	☐	☐
P26	Other	☐	☐
	Stability		
P27	Parents/carers engage in regular social activities with other adults	☐	☐
P28	The family feels accepted by the local community	☐	☐
P2	Other	☐	☐

Social worker's summary of the child's needs in this area and the extent to which parents are responding appropriately

Selfcare skills

Younger children will need help with personal hygiene.

Although older children can generally manage their own personal hygiene, nonetheless they may need some monitoring.

Child's needs	Yes	No	Summary/clarification of child's needs
S1 Child has age appropriate self care skills – can attend to own personal hygiene (i.e. bathe, clean teeth, brush hair)	☐	☐	
S2 Child has a realistic sense of personal danger	☐	☐	
S3 Child can get drinks and some food for him/her self	☐	☐	
S4 Child can answer telephone	☐	☐	
S5 Older child can make calls	☐	☐	
S6 Older child can do simply cooking under supervision	☐	☐	
S7 Child accepts adult help with day to day tasks	☐	☐	
S8 Child behaves like a little adult	☐	☐	
S9 Other	☐	☐	

Children will be able to help, but should not have overall responsibility for household chores.

When parents' own concerns overwhelm them children may be left responsible for organising their day to day living (i.e. bedtimes, meals, getting to school, cooking, shopping, cleaning).

Parental capacity

Summary/clarification of family strengths or issues identified
Note when issue is not relevant

Basic care	Yes	No	Summary
S10 Parent/carer takes main responsibility for the day to day care of the child	☐	☐	
S11 Parents/carers encourage the child to take responsibility for aspects of self care appropriate to age/stage of development	☐	☐	
S12 Other	☐	☐	
Ensuring safety			
S13 A parent/carer supervises/monitors the child's self care to ensure safety	☐	☐	
S14 An adult has overall responsibility for looking after the home	☐	☐	
S15 Other	☐	☐	

Parental capacity	Yes	No	Summary/clarification of family strengths or issues identified Note when issue is not relevant
Emotional warmth			
S16 Child is praised for appropriate self care	☐	☐	
S17 Other	☐	☐	
Stimulation			
S18 Child is encouraged to gain appropriate self care skills	☐	☐	
S19 Other	☐	☐	
Guidance and Boundaries			
S20 Parents place appropriate boundaries on self care activities according to the child's personality and stage of development	☐	☐	
S21 The child is taught self care and safety in and out of the home (i.e. road safety, 'stranger danger', how to avoid/ cope with every day dangers)	☐	☐	
S22 Child knows how and who to contact when help is needed to cope with parental problems	☐	☐	
S23 Other	☐	☐	
Stability			
S24 There are stable arrangements for living and child care	☐	☐	
S25 Parents/carers maintain the main responsibility for the care of the family	☐	☐	
S26 Other	☐	☐	

Safe outside play areas are important because accidents are the major cause of death amongst children.

Parents' own difficulties may result in young children assuming a major role in looking after the family.

Although children of this age can help look after a sick or disabled parent, an adult should retain overall responsibility.

Social worker's summary of the child's needs in this area and the extent to which parents are responding appropriately

Issues affecting parents'/carers' capacities to respond appropriately to the child's needs

	Parental issues	*Yes*	*No*	*Professional/agency involved*	*Note identity of parent/carer for whom the issue is relevant. Record strengths and difficulties*
C1	Illness:				
	Physical	☐	☐		
	Mental	☐	☐		
C2	Disability:				
	Physical	☐	☐		
	Learning	☐	☐		
	Sensory impairment	☐	☐		
C3	Period in care during childhood	☐	☐		
C4	Childhood abuse	☐	☐		
C5	Known history of child abuse	☐	☐		
C6	Known history of violence	☐	☐		
C7	Problem drinking/ drug use	☐	☐		
C8	Other	☐	☐		

Social worker's summary of how the above issues have an impact on the parents'/carers' capacities to respond appropriately to the child's needs

Family and environmental factors which may impact on the child and parenting capacity

Additional details as appropriate
Note identity of person for whom the issue is relevant

Include all house hold and relevant family members, living in or out of the home, when exploring family history and functioning.

To gather further information consider using: The Recent Life Events Questionnaire; A genogram; An eco map.

How parents bring up their children is rooted in their own childhood experiences.

Consider whether a separate carers' assessment is required.

Both positive and negative parenting styles can be passed from one generation to another.

To gather further information consider using: The Adult Well-being Scale; The Alcohol Scale.

	Family History	*Yes*	*No*
FE1	Has a member of the household experienced a stressful childhood?	☐	☐
	Note childhood abuse; in care		
FE2	Have the family suffered a traumatic loss or crisis which is unresolved? (e.g. bereavement)	☐	☐
FE3	Other	☐	☐

	Family Functioning		
FE4	Does child's impairment/behaviour have a negative impact on siblings?	☐	☐
FE5	Child's impairment/behaviour affects parent(s) capacity to continue care	☐	☐
FE6	Does a member of the household experience:		
	poor mental health	☐	☐
	poor physical health	☐	☐
	behaviour problem	☐	☐
	physical disability	☐	☐
	learning disability	☐	☐
	sensory impairment	☐	☐
	problem alcohol/drug use	☐	☐
FE7	Has an adult member of the house-hold got a history of violence?	☐	☐
FE8	Are there frequent family rows?	☐	☐
FE9	Other	☐	☐

Wider family may extend beyond blood relatives to include people who feel like family to parent or child.

	Wider Family		
FE10	Do wider family provide:		
	Practical help	☐	☐
	Emotional support	☐	☐
	Financial help	☐	☐
	Information and advice	☐	☐
FE11	Is there an adult in the home who helps the parent care for the child?	☐	☐
FE12	Other	☐	☐

Additional details as appropriate
Note identity of person for whom the issue is relevant

Basic amenities include safe water, heating, cooking facilities, food storage, sleeping arrangements and cleanliness.

The Home Conditions Assessment may help gather this information.

Housing

	Yes	No
FE13 Is the family homeless?	☐	☐
FE14 Is the family vulnerable to eviction or in temporary accommodation?	☐	☐
FE15 Is the house and its immediate surroundings safe for the child?	☐	☐
FE16 Does home have basic amenities?	☐	☐
FE17 Does home require any adaptations to meet the child's needs?	☐	☐
FE18 Is the home overcrowded?		
FE19 Other	☐	☐

Jobs may be lost because parents' circumstances result in them behaving in a bizarre or unpredictable way.

Parents' circumstances may mean too much family income is used to satisfy parental needs.

Adult services may help a disabled parent respond to their child's needs.

Employment

	Yes	No
FE20 Is a parent in paid employment?	☐	☐
FE21 Does parent's pattern of work adversely impact on child care?	☐	☐
FE22 Is employment reasonably secure?	☐	☐
FE23 Are family members who seek employment adequately supported?	☐	☐
FE24 Other	☐	☐

The family may be vulnerable to future financial problems (i.e. extraordinary medical, funeral expenses, need to help out a relative).

Income

FE25 Are all entitled benefits claimed?	☐	☐
FE26 Are household bills paid regularly?	☐	☐
FE27 Is the family managing on the income they receive?	☐	☐
FE28 If in debt, is this increasing?	☐	☐
FE29 Is the family worried about future financial commitments?	☐	☐
FE30 Other	☐	☐

Social isolation and rejection by the community may have affected the family for generations.

Family's Social Integration

FE31 Does the family feel accepted within their community?	☐	☐
FE32 Do family members experience discrimination/harassment?	☐	☐
FE33 Does the family have local friends?	☐	☐
FE34 Is the family involved in local organisations/activities?	☐	☐
FE35 Other		

Additional details as appropriate

Community resources include: shops, recreation areas, after school clubs, health clinics etc.

In assessing community resources note: availability, accessibility and standard and if appropriate to child and family needs.

	Community Resources	*Yes*	*No*
FE36	Are there accessible community resources?	☐	☐
FE37	Does the family take advantage of community resources?	☐	☐
FE38	Other	☐	☐

Social worker's summary of how the family and environmental factors have an impact on the child and parents'/carers' capacities to respond appropriately to their child's needs.

Plan for the child in need

- Having completed the information gathering, the following pages should be used to analyse the strengths and needs of the child and family members and to identify goals and specific objectives. This information is then used to formulate a plan of action. The decision about which methods are used and services are provided to achieve specific objectives should be evidence based. The expectations of a plan for a child in need are outlined in paragraphs 4.32 to 4.37 of the **Framework for the Assessment of Children in Need and Their Families** (2000).
- The plan for a child in need has been designed to enable it to be used for all children in need, including these about whom there are concerns they are suffering or likely to suffer significant harm.
- The plan should identify how the following will be addressed:
  - The identified developmental needs of the child;
  - Issues which impact negatively on parents/carers' capacity to respond to the child and needs of their child, drawing on their strengths;
  - Wider family and environmental factors which have a negative impact on the child and family, drawing on strengths in the wider family and community.
- The plan should be specific about the actions to be taken, identify who is responsible for each action, and any services or resources that will be required to ensure that the objectives set can be achieved within the agreed time scales. Statutory reviews should take place within statutory time limits and it is good practice for Child In Need plans to be reviewed at least every 6 months. Reviews should be formally recorded.
- The outcome section of the table should be completed following a review of the plan. When completing the outcome section record the outcome for each objective and whether the circumstances have; improved, remained the same, or deteriorated.
- The last page records which family members and agencies are party to the plan and the date when the plan will be reviewed. This should be signed by the child (where appropriate), family members/carers and the social worker.

Summary of child's developmental needs and strengths

Information gathered in the core assessment

Summarise the child's developmental needs and strengths

The child (where appropriate) and parents should be involved in the assessment

This space is for parents/carers to write their views of the child's strengths and needs

Summary of parenting capacity: Needs and strengths

Information gathered in the core assessment

Summarise how the parental issues, needs and strengths, which have been identified in the core assessment have an impact on the capacity of each parent/carer to respond appropriately to the child's needs

Parents should be involved in the assessment

This space is for parents/carers to write their views of their own strengths and difficulties and what impact they think these have on the child's development

Summary of wider family and environmental factors: Needs and strengths

Information gathered in the core assessment

Summarise how family and environment issues, which have been identified in the core assessment, have an impact either directly on the child or on the capacity of the parents/carers to respond appropriately to the child's needs

Parents should be involved in the assessment

This space is for parents/carers to write their views of the strengths and difficulties in their wider family and environment and what impact they think these have on the child's development

Analysis of the information gathered during the core assessment

The analysis should list the factors which have an impact on different aspects of the child's development and parenting capacity, and explore the relationship between them. This process of analysing the information available about the child's needs, parenting capacity and wider family and environmental factors should result in a clear understanding of the child's needs, and what types of service provision would best address these needs to ensure the child has the opportunity to achieve their potential

The child: Objectives and plans

Child's developmental needs	*Objectives and plan of action*	*Person/Agency responsible*	*Objective to be achieved by (date)*	*Outcome (to be completed at the review)*
Health				
Education				
Emotional and behavioural development				
Identity				
Family and social relationships				
Social presentation				
Selfcare skills				

The parents/carers: Objectives and plans

Parenting capacity	*Objective and plan of action*	*Person/Agency responsible*	*Objective to be achieved by (date)*	*Outcome (to be completed at the review)*
Basic care				
Ensuring safety				
Emotional warmth				
Stimulation				
Guidance and Boundaries				
Stability				

Wider Family and Environmental Factors: Objectives and plans

Family and environmental factors	*Objective and plan of action*	*Person/Agency responsible*	*Objective to be achieved by (date)*	*Outcome (to be completed at the review)*
Family history and functioning				
Wider family				
Housing				
Employment and/or income				
Family social integration				
Community resources				

Views of all parties

These objectives and plans should have been discussed with all interested parties/agencies
Family members/agencies who are party to the plan

Name (please print)	Signature	Contact Number

Agreed date for the review: ______________________

Lead professional/agency for the review: ______________________

If the objectives and plans have not been discussed with any of the parties/agencies concerned, please give reasons

What steps will be taken and who is responsible if any party/agency wants to alter these objectives and plans?

Date plan reviewed in supervision	Signature of Line Manger/Supervisor

Parents'/carers' comments

I have seen the contents of this assessment form

Parent/carer's signature ______________________ Date |__|__|__|

Parent/carer signature ______________________ Date |__|__|__|

Parents'/carers' comments on the assessment

Have all relevant family members been given a copy of the assessment record? Yes ☐ No ☐

If not, what arrangements have been made to ensure this happens?

Social Worker's Signature ______________________ Date |__|__|__|

Management information

Ethnicity of the child:

Caribbean	☐	Indian	☐	White British	☐	White and Black Caribbean	☐	Chinese	☐
African	☐	Pakistani	☐	White Irish	☐	White and Black African	☐	Any other ethnic group	☐
Any other Black background	☐	Bangladeshi	☐	Any other White background	☐	White and Asian	☐	Not given	☐

Any other Asian background ☐ Any other mixed background ☐

If other, please specify ______________________

Immigration status if applicable:

Asylum seeking ☐ Refugee status ☐ Exceptional leave to remain ☐

Home Office registration number: ______________________

(H8) Details of immunisations:

Has the child been appropriately immunised? Yes ☐ No ☐

2–4 months: Diphtheria, Tetanus, Whooping cough, Polio, Hib, Men C. 12–15 months: Measles/Mumps/Rubella

3–5 years: Diphtheria, Tetanus, Polio, Measles/Mumps/Rubella.

Child protection register:

Is the child's name on the Child Protection Register? Yes ☐ No ☐

Category ____________ Date of registration ____________

Has the child previously been on the Child Protection Register? Yes ☐ No ☐

Category	Date of registration	Date of deregistration

Court Order(s)

Is the child the subject of a court order? Yes ☐ No ☐

Was the child previously subject of a court order? Yes ☐ No ☐

Type of Order(s)	Date Order(s) made:	Type of Order(s)	Date Order(s) made	Date Order(s) revoked/changed

 ISBN 0 11 322421 4

CORE ASSESSMENT RECORD

Young person aged 10–14 years

Name ______________________________

Gender ______________ *Date of birth* ______________

Address ______________________________

____

____

____

Telephone number ______________________________

Name of social worker completing assessment:

____

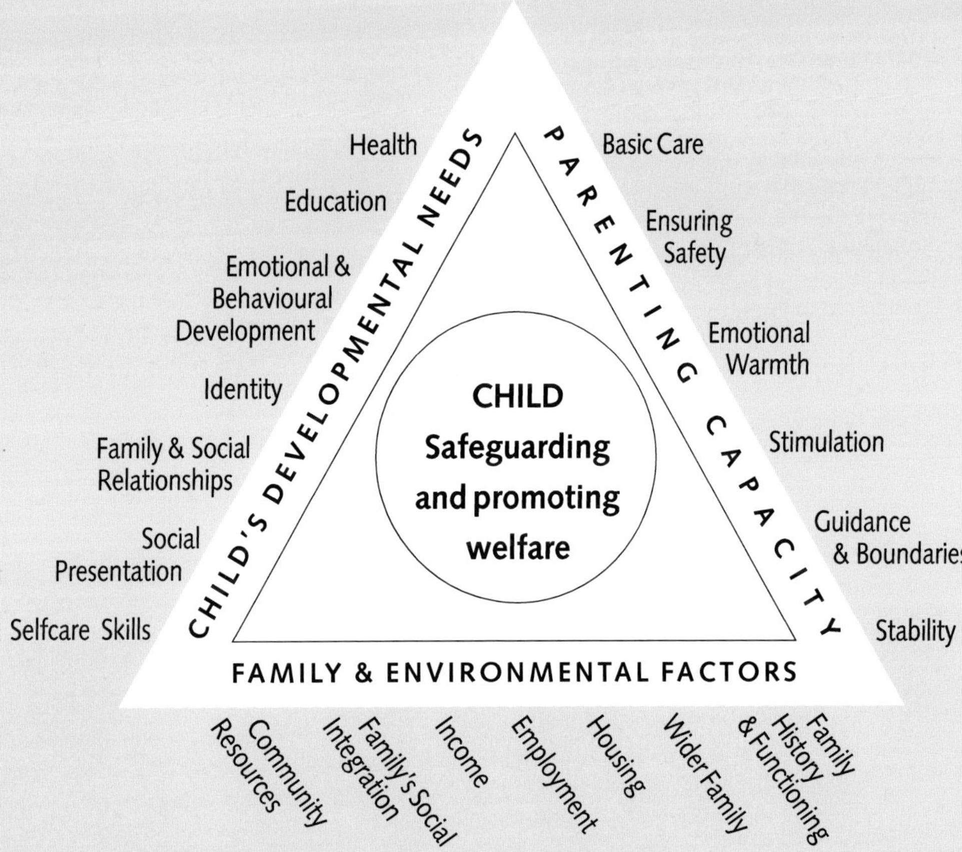

Contents

Undertaking the core assessment

- The Core Assessment Record provides a framework for systematically recording the findings from the core assessment. Whilst the Assessment Record provides some guidance on the areas that should be covered in a core assessment, it is a tool and should not be used as a substitute for a professionally informed assessment process, analysis and judgement.
- The questionnaires and scales published in the accompanying materials to the **Framework for the Assessment of Child in Need and their Families** may be useful in obtaining the information in specific areas (Department of Health, Cox and Bentovim, 2000). The Assessment Record indicates where particular questionnaires and scales may be useful. Practitioners may also choose to use other assessment tools to assist them.
- The Core Assessment Record may be completed in a number of different ways. For example, the social worker may wish to discuss each area with the family before completing the record and then share this with the family. Alternatively, having undertaken some or all of the core assessment the social worker may wish to complete the form with the child's parents or carers.
- Parents and carers invariably want to do the best for their children. Completing the record will help social workers to recognise the strengths that families have as well as identifying areas where they may need further help.
- Completing the core assessment should always be done in a way that helps parents or carers, children and other relevant family members to have their say and encourages them to take part. Space has been provided within the forms for parents/carers and older children to be involved in the assessment.
- It is expected that other agencies should be involved as appropriate during the core assessment process. Parental permission to contact other agencies should be obtained except in cases where the safety of the child would be jeopardised (paragraphs 7.27 to 7.38 of **Working Together to Safeguard Children** provides guidance on this issue). Permissions should be obtained from other agencies to share their information with the family.
- It is important that all sections of the Core Assessment Record are considered carefully. The analysis of the information gathered should be recorded in the plan. In some cases it will not be appropriate to complete particular sections, and in such situations the reason why should be recorded in the summary section. The information gathered is then used to develop case objectives and plans.
- In competing the record, it should be possible to see what help and support the child and family need, and which agencies might be best placed to give that help. This might include more detailed assessments of specific issues.
- Families should be provided with the following information:

Complaints procedures	date provided ________________
Information on access to records	date provided ________________
Other relevant/available information *(please specify)*	date provided ________________

Sources of information

Dates young person and family members seen

Name	Date(s) seen

Agencies consulted/involved as part of the assessment

Agency	Person	Contact number

Questionnaires, Scales or other Instruments used in assessment

Questionnaire/Scale/Instrument	Date(s) used

Specialist Assessments

Agency/person who undertook the assessment	Purpose of the assessment	Date(s) assessment commissioned and completed

Details concerning a core assessment

D1 What is the reason for undertaking the core assessment?

Date core assessment started |___|___|___|

Date core assessment ended |___|___|___|

The Government's Objectives for Childen's Social Services (1999) require the core assessment to be completed within 35 working days.

D2 Are there specific communication needs for young person/parent (eg. impairment affecting communication or English is not the first language)?
If so, what action has been taken to address this ie. use of an interpreter or a signer?

Background details concerning the young person

(This information supplements the information recorded on the Referral and Initial Assessment Record)

B/K1 Significant relatives who are not part of the young person's household

Birth father Parental responsibility Yes ☐ No ☐ Name ____________________

Address ____________________

Brothers and sisters

Name(s) Age Address

____

____

____

Others (please specify)

Name(s) Relationship to child Address

____

____

B/K2 If the young person has any health conditions, impairment(s) or a genetically inherited condition – please give details (include for example: physical disability, sensory impairment, Down's syndrome, encephalitis, autism, sickle cell anaemia, cystic fibrosis)

B/K3 Key events which may have had an impact on the young person
(for example: death of brother or sister, circumstances surrounding conception)

B/K4 Other key events experienced by siblings or other family members which may affect the young person

Key research sources

The Assessment Record is based on research information drawn from a number of sources

Assessment

Cleaver H, Wattam C and Cawson P (1998) *Assessing Risk in Child Protection*. NSPCC, London.

Department of Health, Department for Education and Employment and Home Office (2000) *Framework for the Assessment of Child in Need and their Families*. The Stationery Office, London.

Department of Health, Cox A and Bentovim A (2000) *The Family Assessment Pack of Questionnaires and Scales.* The Stationery Office, London.

The NSPCC and University of Sheffield (2000) *The Child's World: Assessing Children in Need. Training and Development Pack*. NSPCC, London.

Sinclair R, Garnett L and Berridge D (1995) *Social Work and Assessment with Adolescents*. National Children's Bureau, London.

Ward H (ed) (1995) *Looking After Children: Research into Practice*. HMSO, London.

Child development

Department of Health (1996) *Focus on Teenagers: Research into Practice*. HMSO, London.

Department of Health (1997) *Young Carers: Making a Start*. Department of Health, London.

Fahlberg VI (1994) *A Child's Journey Through Placement.* BAAF, London.

Jones DPH (forthcoming) *Communicating with children who may have been traumatised or maltreated*.

Rutter R and Rutter M (1992) *Developing Minds: Challenge and Continuity across the Life Span*. Penguin, Harmondsworth.

Smith PK and Cowie H (1993) *Understanding Children's Development* (2nd Edition). Blackwell, Oxford.

Varma VP (1991) *The Secret Life of Vulnerable Children.* Routledge, London.

Parenting capacity

Cleaver H, Unell I and Aldgate J (1999) *Children's Needs — Parenting Capacity: The impact of parental mental illness, problem alcohol and drug use, and domestic violence on children's development.* The Stationery Office, London.

Falkov A, Mayes K, Diggins M, Silverdale N and Cox A(1998) *Crossing Bridges — Training resources for working with mentally ill parents and their children.* Pavilion Publishing, Brighton.

Reder, P and Lucey, C (1995) *Assessment of Parenting: Psychiatric and psychological contributions.* Routledge, London.

Family and environmental factors

Cochran M (ed) (1993) *Parenting: an ecological perspective.* Lawrence Erlbaum Associates, New Jersey.

Cochran M, Larner M, Riley D, Gunnarsson L and Henderson C (eds) (1990) *Extending families: the social networks of parents and their children*. Cambridge University Press, Cambridge.

Jack G and Jordan B (1999) Social capital and child welfare. *Children and Society*. 13 (5): 242-256.

Wallace SA, Crown JM, Berger M and Cox AD (1997) *Child and Adolescent Mental Health*. In Stevens A and Rafferty J (1997) *Health Care Needs Assessment: 2nd Series.* Radcliffe Medical Press, Oxford.

Iwanec D (1995) *The emotionally abused and neglected child*. Wiley, Chichester.

Stevenson O (1998) *Neglected Children: Issues and Dilemmas*. Blackwell Science, Oxford.

Young person's developmental needs

Health

Normally well is defined as *unwell for1 week or less in the last 6 months.*

Young people with difficulties in verbal communication should use a form of signing.

Between 10–14 young people should have had the following immunisations: BCG (tuberculosis).

Young people need factual information about puberty, sex and contraception.

Half of conceptions to under-age girls result in live births.

Parenthood at this age has long term consequences for a young person's life chances.

Young person's needs | **Summary/clarification of young person's needs**

		Yes	*No*	Summary/clarification
H1	Young person is normally well	☐	☐	
H2	Experiences frequent accidents	☐	☐	
H3	Physical development is satisfactory	☐	☐	
H4	Has a chronic physical illness/ disability	☐	☐	
H5	Experiences frequent infections	☐	☐	
H6	Wets the bed at least monthly	☐	☐	
H7	Soils without physical explanation	☐	☐	
H8	Has a regular sleep pattern	☐	☐	
H9	Has been appropriately immunised	☐	☐	
H10	Is an occasional/non smoker	☐	☐	
H11	Is not addicted to illicit drugs	☐	☐	
H12	Regularly drinks alcohol with other young people	☐	☐	
H13	Eats an adequate, nutritious diet	☐	☐	
H14	Has an accurate knowledge about puberty, sex and contraception	☐	☐	
H15	Has been/is pregnant or has fathered a child	☐	☐	
H16	Other	☐	☐	

To gather further information consider using the Home Conditions Assessment.

Black families may have less access to preventative and support services than white families.

Poverty and poor social conditions are related to poor health and development and increased risk of accidents.

Parental capacity | **Summary/clarification of family strengths or issues identified**
Note when issue is not relevant

	Basic care	*Yes*	*No*	Summary/clarification
H17	A healthy diet is provided at home	☐	☐	
H18	Illnesses receive appropriate medical attention	☐	☐	
H19	Injuries are attended to	☐	☐	
H20	Parent ensures home is hygienic	☐	☐	
H21	Other	☐	☐	
	Ensuring safety			
H22	Periodic bouts of illness have a recognised medical explanation	☐	☐	
H23	Injuries have an understandable accidental cause	☐	☐	
H24	Marks on young person's body have an acceptable explanation	☐	☐	
H25	Other	☐	☐	

Parental capacity

Summary/clarification of family strengths or issues identified
Note when issue is not relevant

		Yes	*No*
	Emotional warmth		
H26	Parent encourages the young person to take care of his/her own health	☐	☐
H27	Parent shows approval of the young person taking care of own health	☐	☐
H28	Parent is sympathetic to the young person's symptoms or injuries	☐	☐
H29	Other	☐	☐
	Stimulation		
H30	Parent promotes involvement in physical activity	☐	☐
H31	Parent advises about health issues	☐	☐
H32	Other	☐	☐
	Guidance and Boundaries		
H33	Parent supports sex education	☐	☐
H34	Parent supports health education	☐	☐
H35	Parent's use of alcohol sets the young person a good example	☐	☐
H36	Parent uses illicit drugs	☐	☐
H37	Other	☐	☐
	Stability		
H38	Parent ensures medical and dental appointments are kept	☐	☐
H39	Parents support each other in promoting/caring for the young person's health	☐	☐
H40	Other	☐	☐

Increasing numbers of children are suffering obesity.

Regular physical exercise is an important preventative measure.

Disabled young people may need special help or equipment for exercise.

Disabled or young people with a health problem need information and opportunities to help them understand and learn about themselves

When one parent is a problem drinker, the non drinking parent may not always be able to protect the young person.

Parental problem drug use is associated with young people using illicit drugs.

Social worker's summary of the young person's needs in this area and the extent to which parents are responding appropriately

Education

SATs are given to pupils in the summer term of Years 2, 6, & 9 (ages 7, 11 & 14).

At 11 years most young people are performing at level 4: at 14 years most perform at levels 5–6.

Black pupils often underachieve at school

Black pupils are 4 times more likely to be excluded than white pupils. Excluded black children are usually of higher ability with fewer chronic disruptive behaviours than white children who are excluded.

Non school attendance may be related to bullying.

Young person's needs | **Summary/clarification of young person's needs**

		Yes	*No*	*date*	*Subject*	*level*
E1	Young person's educational progress is at expected level **Note SATs results**	☐	☐		English	
					Maths	
					Science	
E2	Usually happy to go to school	☐	☐			
E3	Attends school regularly (note number of unauthorised days absent in past year)	☐	☐			
E4	Usually arrives at school on time	☐	☐			
E5	Young person has a friend at school	☐	☐			
E6	Young person is bullied at school	☐	☐			
E7	Shows challenging/disruptive behviour at school	☐	☐			
E8	Has a good relationship with a member of staff	☐	☐			
E9	Young person responds positively to teaching	☐	☐			
E10	Young person's lack of concentration impedes learning	☐	☐			
E11	Young person has been permanently excluded from school	☐	☐			
E12	Other	☐	☐			

When a parent has a learning disability only 15% of children are similarly affected.

Not all young people with impairments will need a statement of Special Educational Needs.

Disabled young people may need financial help, equipment or adaptations to enable them to get to school.

Persistent non school attendance can place great strain on families.

Parental capacity | **Summary/clarification of family strengths or issues identified**
Note when issue is not relevant

	Basic care	*Yes*	*No*	
E13	Parent tries to ensure regular school attendance	☐	☐	
E14	Parent/carer supports and encourages homework	☐	☐	
E15	If the young person is not achieving at school:			
	Is there an Individual Education Plan?	☐	☐	
	Is there a statement of Special Educational Needs?	☐	☐	
E16	Other	☐	☐	
	Ensuring safety			
E17	Parent tries to ensure the journey to and from school is safe	☐	☐	
E18	Where necessary, parents have taken action over bullying	☐	☐	
E19	Other	☐	☐	

Parental capacity			**Summary/clarification of family strengths or issues identified** **Note when issue is not relevant**
Emotional warmth	*Yes*	*No*	
E20 Parent shows an interest in the young person's school work	☐	☐	
E21 Parent shows approval of educational efforts and achievements	☐	☐	
E22 Parent supports the young person over educational difficulties	☐	☐	
E23 Parent places great pressure on young person to achieve	☐	☐	
E24 Other	☐	☐	
Stimulation			
E25 Parent encourages academic and sporting activities	☐	☐	
E26 Parent encourages the young person to learn new skills	☐	☐	
E27 Other	☐	☐	
Guidance and Boundaries			
E28 Parent tries to ensure prompt school attendance	☐	☐	
E29 Supports school rules/discipline	☐	☐	
E30 Attempts to shield and support the young person from family problems that may interfere with schooling	☐	☐	
E31 Other	☐	☐	
Stability			
E32 Parent regularly attends school events/parents' meetings	☐	☐	
E33 Young person's books/school work are looked after	☐	☐	
E34 Parents agree with each other in supporting education	☐	☐	
E35 Other	☐	☐	

Parents own problems may mean they are not always able to offer the intellectual stimulation a young person of this age needs.

To gather further information consider using the Family Activity Scale.

All children need adequate and appropriate stimulation. When a young person has profound or complex impairments it may be helpful to check with a specialist before completing this section.

Many young carers believe that looking after a parent or younger sisters and brothers interferes with their schooling.

The key to children's educational progress is a parent or significant adult who takes an interest in their learning and offers praise and encouragement.

Social worker's summary of the young person's needs in this area and the extent to which parents to responding appropriately

Emotional and Behavioural Development

To gather further information consider using the Strengths and Difficulties Questionnaire and The Adolescent Well being Scale.

When a young person is disabled or sensory impaired behaviours such as rocking or constant screaming are significant and should not be dismissed.

Young people may cope with upsetting parental behaviours by withdrawing or running away.

Self harm must be treated seriously and appropriate help sought.

At this age concepts of ownership are fully established.

Young person's needs

		Yes	*No*
B1	Young person is usually happy	☐	☐
B2	Temper tantrums lasting 15 mins occur monthly	☐	☐
B3	Frequently withdraws emotionally	☐	☐
B4	Often stays away from home/out late without parental permission	☐	☐
B5	Has run away from home	☐	☐
B6	Young person copes with anger and frustration	☐	☐
B7	Challenging/disruptive behaviours affect young person's safety	☐	☐
B8	Enjoys appropriate physical closeness with familiar adults	☐	☐
B9	Talks about feelings with a trusted adult	☐	☐
B10	Shares/takes turns with others	☐	☐
B11	Inflicts injuries on him/herself (i.e. scratching, cutting, head banging)	☐	☐
B12	Is preoccupied with violence	☐	☐
B13	Bullies other children	☐	☐
B14	Respects the concept of ownership	☐	☐
B15	Has been cautioned or convicted within past year (note number)	☐	☐
B16	Other	☐	☐

Summary/clarification of young person's needs

Depression can affect parent's capacity to care about their child.

Most at risk are victims of parental aggression or neglect.

Consider whether the feelings and behaviour that troubles the young person and parent would benefit from specialist assessment and help.

Parental capacity

	Basic care	*Yes*	*No*
B17	Parent/carer assures the young person they will always be there for them	☐	☐
B18	Family disagreements are resolved in non-violent ways	☐	☐
B19	Other	☐	☐

	Ensuring safety		
B20	Parent tries to ensure whereabouts of young person are known	☐	☐
B21	Young person is hit or physically chastised	☐	☐
B22	Help is sought over unresolvable relationship problems	☐	☐
B23	Other	☐	☐

Summary/clarification of family strengths or issues identified
Note when issue is not relevant

Parental capacity

Summary/clarification of family strengths or issues identified
Note when issue is not relevant

Young people who are abused or witness family violence are particularly traumatised.

Discussing feelings becomes more difficult when a young person depends on non-verbal methods of communication.

To gather further information consider using The Parenting Daily Hassles Scale.

	Emotional warmth	*Yes*	*No*
B24	Young person is comforted when frightened or distressed	☐	☐
B25	Young person is exposed to frequent criticism/hostility	☐	☐
B26	Young person is encouraged to talk about fears and worries	☐	☐
B27	Other	☐	☐
	Stimulation		
B28	Young person is often exposed to parents' emotional distress	☐	☐
B29	Young person is encouraged to share with others	☐	☐
B30	Other	☐	☐
	Guidance and Boundaries		
B31	Parent uses a variety of positive methods to gain the young person's co-operation/good behaviour	☐	☐
B32	There are clear family rules and limits about behaviour	☐	☐
B33	Parent teaches respect for the law	☐	☐
B34	Young person is encouraged to help with household tasks	☐	☐
B35	Parents do not burden the young person with their own problems	☐	☐
B36	Young person is protected from seeing frightening adult behaviour	☐	☐
B37	Other	☐	☐
	Stability		
B38	Young person responded to in a consistent and predictable manner	☐	☐
B39	Parents/carers generally support each other in applying family rules	☐	☐
B40	Other	☐	☐

Positive methods for encouraging co-operation include: praise, negotiation, modelling, rewards, distraction, play, persuasion, explanation.

When young people witness violence they have difficulty in controlling their own emotions and behaviour.

Social worker's summary of the young person's needs in this area and the extent to which parents are responding appropriately

Identity

Cultural identity develops from all aspects of a person's experience.

The way in which black disabled children define themselves is affected by their personal experience of both racism and disability.

Dual heritage does not always result in identity problems/conflicts.

Racism and bullying are common-place in the lives of black young people.

Young person's needs | **Summary/clarification of young person's needs**

	Young person's needs	Yes	No	Summary/clarification of young person's needs
ID1	Young person is self confident	☐	☐	
ID2	Takes pride in his/her appearance	☐	☐	
ID3	Takes pride in achievements	☐	☐	
ID4	Has a developing sense of his/her own culture	☐	☐	
ID5	Is comfortable with his/her own racial identity	☐	☐	
ID6	Is at ease with his/her sexual orientation	☐	☐	
ID7	Is confident when relating to friends of either sex	☐	☐	
ID8	Is able to make decisions on appropriate matters	☐	☐	
ID9	Blames him/herself for parent's troubles	☐	☐	
ID10	Feels everything is out of control	☐	☐	
ID11	Other	☐	☐	

Parental capacity

Summary/clarification of family strengths or issues identified
Note when issue is not relevant

Young people who grow up in families which experience many stresses and problems will need positive messages to avoid developing a negative self image and poor self esteem. Disabled young people need even more help.

	Basic care	Yes	No	Summary/clarification
ID12	Clothes and appearance is in line with the young person's wishes	☐	☐	
ID13	Young person's clothes are routinely washed	☐	☐	
ID14	Parents see the young person as having unique strengths and encourages them	☐	☐	
ID15	Other	☐	☐	

Disabled young people have a right to be dressed appropriately but their dress should not impede movement, endanger stability or aggravate their skin.

	Ensuring safety	Yes	No	Summary/clarification
ID16	Young person's dress is appropriate for age, gender, culture and religion and where necessary, impairment	☐	☐	
ID17	Young person is supervised appropriately taking into account the child's personality and developmental level	☐	☐	
ID18	Young person is encouraged to talk about worries and concerns	☐	☐	
ID19	Parents support the young person who is exposed to racism, bullying or harassment	☐	☐	
ID20	Other	☐	☐	

Parental capacity

Summary/clarification of family strengths or issues identified
Note when issue is not relevant

For young people to develop a positive self image they need to feel loved and valued for themselves.

In all cultures disabled young people may be treated as younger than their actual age. This is a particular risk for learning disabled children.

Emotional warmth	*Yes*	*No*	
ID21 Parent often shows spontaneous affection to the young person	☐	☐	
ID22 Shows pride in the young person	☐	☐	
ID23 Young person's efforts/ achievements are praised	☐	☐	
ID24 Friendships are supported where appropriate	☐	☐	
ID25 Other	☐	☐	

Young people need positive role models of the same racial/ethnic origins as him/ herself.

Young people often suffer if they are included in the imaginary world of a mentally ill parent.

Stimulation			
ID26 Has the opportunity to learn own cultural traditions/language	☐	☐	
ID27 Independence is encouraged	☐	☐	
ID28 Is given control over appropriate aspects of his/her life	☐	☐	
ID29 Other	☐	☐	

Guidance and Boundaries			
ID30 Is taught respect and toleration	☐	☐	
ID31 Family is tolerant of different cultures, ethnic groups etc	☐	☐	
ID32 Young person is protected from parental mental illness/symptoms	☐	☐	
ID33 Young person is reassured when parent's behaviour is disturbing	☐	☐	
ID34 Other	☐	☐	

Although at times rebellious and moody, most young people remain integrated within the family culture and participate in important family celebrations.

Young people who are routinely rejected come to see themselves as unloved and unlovable.

Stability			
ID35 Is included in family celebrations	☐	☐	
ID36 Is accepted as a family member	☐	☐	
ID37 Parent ensures that day to day living has order and stability	☐	☐	
ID38 Other	☐	☐	

Social worker's summary of the young person's needs in this area and the extent to which parents are responding appropriately

Family and Social Relationships

Young unaccompanied asylum seekers experience acute loss.

A close, supportive friend can help young people cope with family problems.

Family values have been internalised.

Young people can look after younger siblings and sick parents but should not have overall responsibility.

Young person's needs

		Yes	No
F1	Young person has a strong, positive relationship with a parent	☐	☐
F2	Young person has a close friend	☐	☐
F3	Bullies other children	☐	☐
F4	Is generally kind to younger children and animals	☐	☐
F5	Regularly visits/spends time with friends	☐	☐
F6	Has an adult in whom he/she confides	☐	☐
F7	Sexual knowledge and behaviour is age-appropriate	☐	☐
F8	Young person frequently looks after brothers and sisters for long periods	☐	☐
F9	Frequently looks after parent/carer	☐	☐
F10	Other	☐	☐

Summary/clarification of young person's needs

Family issues or difficulties experienced by the young person may result in him/ her being looked after by a large number of different people (i.e. family, friends, hospital care, or social services respite care).

A disabled child may not protest when left with strangers because they have been handled by many unknown people. Nonetheless it remains a matter for concern.

Parental capacity

Summary/clarification of family strengths or issues identified
Note when issue is not relevant

	Basic care	Yes	No
F11	A small number of familiar and appropriate adults look after the young person	☐	☐
F12	Parent/carer spends enough time with the young person to sustain a strong relationship	☐	☐
F13	Other	☐	☐

	Ensuring safety	Yes	No
F14	The relationship between the young person and other children in the family is generally good	☐	☐
F15	Parent monitors interactions between young person and siblings	☐	☐
F16	Young person does not witness/ become involved in adult sexual behaviour	☐	☐
F17	Does not witness/become involved in adult violence	☐	☐
F18	Young person is frequently left alone at night	☐	☐
F19	Other	☐	☐

Parental capacity

Summary/clarification of family strengths or issues identified
Note when issue is not relevant

Love and affection are shown in different ways depending on culture and individual characteristics.

A supportive adult can help stressed parents to cope.

Other young people may be valuable sources of support and can greatly influence ideas and actions.

When a young person is disabled, practical and social barriers can make getting out difficult, but it remains essential to their wellbeing.

Young carers can feel stigmatised and get little recognition or respect for their contribution.

Of central importance to a young person in all families is a loving and protective relationship.

Untrained agency staff are not appropriate people to care for a disabled young person.

	Emotional warmth	*Yes*	*No*
F20	Parents/carers' relationships with others provides a good example to the young person	☐	☐
F21	Parent/carer encourages affectionate family relationships	☐	☐
F22	Other	☐	☐
	Stimulation		
F23	Young person has sufficient time to pursue his/her own interests	☐	☐
F24	Sees friends outside school	☐	☐
F25	Has friends to visit at home	☐	☐
F26	Other	☐	☐
	Guidance and Boundaries		
F27	Is encouraged to negotiate	☐	☐
F28	Is discouraged from violent or cruel behaviour	☐	☐
F29	Is given clear guidance on appropriate sexual behaviour	☐	☐
F30	Task of caring for the family is kept to a manageable level	☐	☐
F31	Parent tries to ensure young person does not associate with unsuitable adults/peers	☐	☐
F32	Other	☐	☐
	Stability		
F33	There is a stable pattern of care to day to day life	☐	☐
F34	There is continuity of carers	☐	☐
F35	A limited number of known, appropriate adults deliver intimate care	☐	☐
F36	Other	☐	☐

Social worker's summary of the young person's needs in this area and the extent to which parents are responding appropriately

Social presentation

Young people have well developed social skills. They can readily adjust their conversation and behaviour to suit a variety of different situations.

Trusted and respected adults can influence young people's behaviour.

Young people are very conscious of their appearance and sensitive to criticism, particularly from their peers.

Young person's needs | **Summary/clarification of young person's needs**

	Young person's needs	*Yes*	*No*
P1	Young person's language and behaviour do not cause offence or embarrassment outside the family	☐	☐
P2	Personal hygiene is adequate	☐	☐
P3	Young person values adult attention	☐	☐
P4	Talks/communicates about family without great difficulty	☐	☐
P5	Young person is self-confident and appropriately open with adults	☐	☐
P6	Is willing to listen to the advice of trusted and respected adults	☐	☐
P7	Young person is overly friendly with strangers	☐	☐
P8	Young person is self-confident and open with peers	☐	☐
P9	Young person spends time with friends outside school hours	☐	☐
P10	Other	☐	☐

Young people may be bullied or rejected at school because their clothes are soiled and inappropriate, or their personal hygiene is poor.

The experience of bullying, racism, harassment or being left out can lead to low self esteem and may affect the young person's behaviour.

Parental capacity

Summary/clarification of family strengths or issues identified
Note when issue is not relevant

	Basic care	*Yes*	*No*
P11	Parents/carers ensure that personal hygiene is satisfactory	☐	☐
P12	Clothes and appearance are in line with the young person's wishes	☐	☐
P13	Parents/carers' behaviour sets a good example to the young person	☐	☐
P14	Other	☐	☐
	Ensuring safety		
P15	Parents/carers encourage the young person to behave appropriately with strangers	☐	☐
P16	Parents/carers teach appropriate behaviour in public settings	☐	☐
P17	Parents/carers ensure the young person is supervised/supported in potentially dangerous settings	☐	☐
P18	Other	☐	☐

Parental capacity

Summary/clarification of family strengths or issues identified
Note when issue is not relevant

When families are experiencing difficulties young people keep silent because they fear telling someone will result in them 'getting into trouble', or being 'taken away'.

	Emotional warmth	*Yes*	*No*
P19	Parents/carers encourage the young person to be self-confident	☐	☐
P20	Praise the young person for good social behaviour	☐	☐
P21	Family members support each other over decisions on the young person's clothes and appearance	☐	☐
P22	Other	☐	☐

Young people often shun social events or keep friends at bay in an attempt to keep the family's circumstances secret.

	Stimulation		
P23	Parents/carers encourage the young person to bring his/her friends home	☐	☐
P24	Give the young person the opportunity to meet friends outside school	☐	☐
P25	Allow some control over clothes and appearance	☐	☐
P26	Other	☐	☐

Difficulties in relating well with adults outside the family, for example teachers, may lead to poor relationships, feelings of detachment and poor school results.

	Guidance and Boundaries		
P27	Give guidance on appropriate 'good manners' and respect for others	☐	☐
P28	Parents' relationships with neighbours and those in authority are generally harmonious	☐	☐
P29	Family members are engaged in criminal/antisocial activities	☐	☐
P30	Other	☐	☐

	Stability		
P31	Parents/carers engage in regular social activities with other adults	☐	☐
P32	The family feels accepted by the local community	☐	☐
P33	Other	☐	☐

Social worker's summary of the young person's needs in this area and the extent to which parents are responding appropriately

Selfcare skills

Older young people without impairments are generally able to look after their personal hygiene.

The personal hygiene of younger teenagers may need some monitoring.

Young people are able to prepare simple meals, use the telephone with confidence and react appropriately to an emergency.

Young people often wish to do things with friends rather than family.

Young person's needs | **Summary/clarification of young person's needs**

		Yes	No
S1	Young person has age appropriate self care skills – can attend to own personal hygiene (i.e. bathe, clean teeth, brush hair)	☐	☐
S2	Has a realistic sense of personal danger	☐	☐
S3	Can get drinks and do simple cooking	☐	☐
S4	Can answer and use the telephone	☐	☐
S5	Young person accepts adult help with day to day tasks with reasonable grace	☐	☐
S6	Can travel alone on journeys the parent/carer considers safe	☐	☐
S7	Can handle money and buy food and clothes	☐	☐
S8	Can make own social arrangements	☐	☐
S9	Other	☐	☐

At this age it is expected that young people will help, but should not have overall responsibility for household chores.

When parents' own concerns overwhelm them young people may be left responsible for organising their day to day living (i.e. bed-times, meals, getting to school, cooking, shopping, cleaning).

Parental capacity | **Summary/clarification of family strengths or issues identified**
Note when issue is not relevant

Basic care

		Yes	No
S10	Parent/carer takes main responsibility for the day to day care of the young person	☐	☐
S11	Parents/carers encourage the young person to take responsibility for aspects of self care appropriate to age/stage of development	☐	☐
S12	Other	☐	☐

Ensuring safety

		Yes	No
S13	A parent/carer monitors the young person's self care to ensure safety	☐	☐
S14	An adult has overall responsibility for looking after the home	☐	☐
S15	Other	☐	☐

Parental capacity

Summary/clarification of family strengths or issues identified
Note when issue is not relevant

Parents' own difficulties may result in young people assuming a major role in looking after the family.

Although young people can help look after a sick or disabled parent or younger sisters and brothers, an adult should retain overall responsibility.

Young carers may become extremely skilled in carrying out everyday household chores and in looking after themselves.

Feeling responsible for the family can lead young carers to feel tied to the home and unable to join in outside leisure and social activities.

		Yes	*No*	
	Emotional warmth			
S16	Young person is praised for appropriate self care including cooking, shopping etc	☐	☐	
S17	Other	☐	☐	
	Stimulation			
S18	Young person is encouraged to gain appropriate self care skills (i.e. money management)	☐	☐	
S19	Other	☐	☐	
	Guidance and Boundaries			
S20	Parents place appropriate boundaries on selfcare activities according to the young person's personality and stage of development	☐	☐	
S21	The young person is taught self care and safety in and out of the home (i.e. 'stranger danger', how to avoid/cope with every day dangers)	☐	☐	
S22	Young person knows how and who to contact when help is needed to cope with parental issues	☐	☐	
S23	Other	☐	☐	
	Stability			
S24	There are stable arrangements for living	☐	☐	
S25	Parents/carers maintain the major responsibility for the care of the family	☐	☐	
S26	Other	☐	☐	

Social worker's summary of the young person's needs in this area and the extent to which parents are responding appropriately

Issues affecting parents'/carers' capacity to respond appropriately to the young person's needs

	Parental issues	*Yes*	*No*	*Professional/agency involved*	*Note identity of parent/carer for whom the issue is relevant. Record strengths and difficulties*
C1	Illness:				
	Physical	☐	☐		
	Mental	☐	☐		
C2	Disability:				
	Physical	☐	☐		
	Learning	☐	☐		
	Sensory impairment	☐	☐		
C3	Period in care during childhood	☐	☐		
C4	Childhood abuse	☐	☐		
C5	Known history of child abuse	☐	☐		
C6	Known history of violence	☐	☐		
C7	Problem drinking/ drug use	☐	☐		
C8	Other	☐	☐		

Social worker's summary of how the above issues have an impact on the parents'/carers' capacities to respond appropriately to the young person's needs

Family and environmental factors which may impact on the young person and parenting capacity

Additional details as appropriate
Note identity of person for whom the issue is relevant

Include all household and relevant family members, living in or out of the home, when exploring family history and functioning.

To gather further information consider using: The Recent Life Events Questionnaire; A genogram; An eco map.

How parents bring up their children is rooted in their own childhood experiences.

Consider whether a separate carers' assessment is required.

Both positive and negative parenting styles can be passed from one generation to another.

To gather further information consider using: The Adult Well-being Scale; The Alcohol Scale.

Wider family may extend beyond blood relatives to include people who feel like family to parent or child.

	Family History	*Yes*	*No*	
FE1	Has a member of the household experienced a stressful childhood?	☐	☐	
	Note childhood abuse; in care			
FE2	Have the family suffered a traumatic loss or crisis which is unresolved? (e.g. bereavement)	☐	☐	
FE3	Other	☐	☐	
	Family Functioning			
FE4	Does young person's impairment/ behaviour have a negative impact on siblings?	☐	☐	
FE5	Young person's impairment/ behaviour affects parent(s) capacity to continue care	☐	☐	
FE6	Does a member of the household experience:			
	poor mental health	☐	☐	
	poor physical health	☐	☐	
	behaviour problem	☐	☐	
	physical disability	☐	☐	
	learning disability	☐	☐	
	sensory impairment	☐	☐	
	problem alcohol/drug use	☐	☐	
FE7	Has an adult member of the house-hold got a history of violence?	☐	☐	
FE8	Are there frequent family rows?	☐	☐	
FE9	Other	☐	☐	
	Wider Family			
FE10	Do wider family provide:			
	practical help	☐	☐	
	emotional support	☐	☐	
	financial help	☐	☐	
	information and advice	☐	☐	
FE11	Is there an adult in the home who helps the parent care for the young person?	☐	☐	
FE12	Other	☐	☐	

Additional details as appropriate
Note identity of person for whom the issue is relevant

Basic amenities include safe water, heating, cooking facilities, food storage, sleeping arrangements and cleanliness.

The Home Conditions Assessment may help gather this information.

Housing	*Yes*	*No*
FE13 Is the family homeless?	☐	☐
FE14 Is the family vulnerable to eviction or in temporary accommodation?	☐	☐
FE15 Is the house and its immediate surroundings safe for the young person?	☐	☐
FE16 Does home have basic amenities?	☐	☐
FE17 Does home require any adaptations to meet the young person's needs?	☐	☐
FE18 Is the home overcrowded?		
FE19 Other	☐	☐

Jobs may be lost because parents' circumstances result in them behaving in a bizarre or unpredictable way.

Parents' circumstances may mean too much family income is used to satisfy parental needs.

Adult services may help a disabled parent respond to their child's needs.

The family may be vulnerable to future financial problems (i.e. extraordinary medical, funeral expenses, need to help out a relative).

Employment	*Yes*	*No*
FE20 Is a parent in paid employment?	☐	☐
FE21 Does parent's pattern of work adversely impact on child care?	☐	☐
FE22 Is employment reasonably secure?	☐	☐
FE23 Are family members who seek employment adequately supported?	☐	☐
FE24 Other	☐	☐

Income		
FE25 Are all entitled benefits claimed?	☐	☐
FE26 Are household bills paid regularly?	☐	☐
FE27 Is the family managing on the income they receive?	☐	☐
FE28 Does the young person receive an appropriate allowance	☐	☐
FE29 If in debt, is this increasing?	☐	☐
FE30 Is the family worried about future financial commitments?	☐	☐
FE31 Other	☐	☐

Social isolation and rejection by the community may have affected the family for generations.

Family's Social Integration		
FE32 Does the family feel accepted within their community?	☐	☐
FE33 Do family members experience discrimination/harassment?	☐	☐
FE34 Does the family have local friends?	☐	☐
FE35 Is the family involved in local organisations/activities?	☐	☐
FE36 Other	☐	☐

Additional details as appropriate

Community resources include: shops, recreation areas, after-school clubs, health clinics etc.

In assessing community resources note: availability, accessibility and standard and if appropriate to child and family needs.

Community Resources	*Yes*	*No*
FE37 Are there accessible community resources?	☐	☐
FE38 Does the family take advantage of community resources?	☐	☐
FE39 Other	☐	☐

Social worker's summary of how the family and environmental factors have an impact on the young person and parents/carers

Plan for the child in need

- Having completed the information gathering, the following pages should be used to analyse the strengths and needs of the child and family members and to identify goals and specific objectives. This information is then used to formulate a plan of action. The decision about which methods are used and services are provided to achieve specific objectives should be evidence based. The expectations of a plan for a child in need are outlined in paragraphs 4.32 to 4.37 of the **Framework for the Assessment of Children in Need and Their Families** (2000).
- The plan for a child in need has been designed to enable it to be used for all children in need, including these about whom there are concerns they are suffering or likely to suffer significant harm.
- The plan should identify how the following will be addressed:
  - The identified developmental needs of the child;
  - Issues which impact negatively on parents/carers' capacity to respond to the child and needs of their child, drawing on their strengths;
  - Wider family and environmental factors which have a negative impact on the child and family, drawing on strengths in the wider family and community.
- The plan should be specific about the actions to be taken, identify who is responsible for each action, and any services or resources that will be required to ensure that the objectives set can be achieved within the agreed time scales. Statutory reviews should take place within statutory time limits and it is good practice for Child In Need plans to be reviewed at least every 6 months. Reviews should be formally recorded.
- The outcome section of the table should be completed following a review of the plan. When completing the outcome section record the outcome for each objective and whether the circumstances have; improved, remained the same, or deteriorated.
- The last page records which family members and agencies are party to the plan and the date when the plan will be reviewed. This should be signed by the child (where appropriate), family members/carers and the social worker.

Summary of young person's developmental needs and strengths

Information gathered in the core assessment

Summarise the young person's developmental needs and strengths

The young person (where appropriate) and parents should be involved in the assessment

This space is for young people and parents/carers to write their views of the young person's strengths and needs

Summary of parenting capacity: Needs and strengths

Information gathered in the core assessment

Summarise how the parental issues, needs and strengths, which have been identified in the core assessment have an impact on the capacity of each parent/carer to respond appropriately to the young person's needs

The young person (where appropriate) and parents should be involved in the assessment

This space is for the young person and parents/carers to write their views of their own strengths and difficulties and what impact they think these have on the young person's development

Summary of wider family and environmental factors: Needs and strengths

Information gathered in the core assessment

Summarise how family and environment issues, which have been identified in the core assessment, have an impact either directly on the young person or on the capacity of the parents/carers to respond appropriately to the young person's needs

The young person (where appropriate) and parents should be involved in the assessment

This space is for the young person and parents/carers to write their views of the strengths and difficulties in their wider family and environment and what impact they think these have on the young person's development

Analysis of the information gathered during the core assessment

The analysis should list the factors which have an impact on different aspects of the young person's development and parenting capacity, and explore the relationship between them. This process of analysing the information available about the young person's needs, parenting capacity and wider family and environmental factors should result in a clear understanding of the young person's needs, and what types of service provision would best address these needs to ensure the young person has the opportunity to achieve their potential

The young person: Objectives and plans

Young person's developmental needs	*Objectives and plan of action*	*Person/Agency responsible*	*Objective to be achieved by (date)*	*Outcome (to be completed at the review)*
Health				
Education				
Emotional and behavioural development				
Identity				
Family and social relationships				
Social presentation				
Selfcare skills				

The parents/carers: Objectives and plans

Parenting capacity	*Objective and plan of action*	*Person/Agency responsible*	*Objective to be achieved by (date)*	*Outcome (to be completed at the review)*
Basic care				
Ensuring safety				
Emotional warmth				
Stimulation				
Guidance and Boundaries				
Stability				

Wider Family and Environmental Factors: Objectives and plans

Family and environmental factors	*Objective and plan of action*	*Person/Agency responsible*	*Objective to be achieved by (date)*	*Outcome (to be completed at the review)*
Family history and functioning				
Wider family				
Housing				
Employment and/or income				
Family social integration				
Community resources				

Views of all parties

These objectives and plans should have been discussed with all interested parties/agencies
Family members/agencies who are party to the plan

Name (please print)	Signature	Contact Number

Agreed date for the review: ______________________

Lead professional/agency for the review: ______________________

If the objectives and plans have not been discussed with any of the parties/agencies concerned, please give reasons

What steps will be taken and who is responsible if any party/agency wants to alter these objectives and plans?

Date plan reviewed in supervision	Signature of Line Manger/Supervisor

Parents/carer's comments

I have seen the contents of this assessment form

Parent/carer's signature ______________________ Date |___|___|___|

Parent/carer signature ______________________ Date |___|___|___|

Parents/carers comments on the assessment

Have all relevant family members been given a copy of the assessment record? Yes ☐ No ☐

If not, what arrangements have been made to ensure this happens?

Social Worker's Signature ______________________ Date |___|___|___|

Management information

Ethnicity of the young person:

Caribbean	☐	Indian	☐	White British	☐	White and Black Caribbean	☐	Chinese	☐
African	☐	Pakistani	☐	White Irish	☐	White and Black African	☐	Any other ethnic group	☐
Any other Black background	☐	Bangladeshi	☐	Any other White background	☐	White and Asian	☐	Not given	☐

Any other Asian background ☐ Any other mixed background ☐

If other, please specify ______

Immigration status if applicable:

Asylum seeking ☐ Refugee status ☐ Exceptional leave to remain ☐

Home Office registration number: ______

(H9) Details of immunisations:

Has the young person been appropriately immunised? Yes ☐ No ☐

Between 10–14 young people should have and the following immunisations: BCG (tuberculosis) and if school leavers aged 13: Diphtheria, Tetanus and Polio.

(H15) Childbirth

The girl has been/is pregnant Yes ☐ No ☐

The boy has fathered a child Yes ☐ No ☐

Child protection register:

Is the young person's name on the Child Protection Register? Yes ☐ No ☐

Category ______ Date of registration ______

Has the young person previously been on the Child Protection Register? Yes ☐ No ☐

Category	Date of registration	Date of deregistration

Education details of the young person

(E1) SATs results show young person at the end of Key Stage 3 (child of 14) performs at level 5–6 for:

English	Yes	☐	No	☐
Maths	Yes	☐	No	☐
Science	Yes	☐	No	☐

(E3) Number school days missed within past year through unauthorised absence ____________

(E11) Young person is excluded from school Yes ☐ No ☐

Court Order(s)

Is the young person the subject of a court order? Yes ☐ No ☐

Was the young person previously subject of a court order? Yes ☐ No ☐

Type of Order(s)	Date Order(s) made:	Type of Order(s)	Date Order(s) made	Date Order(s) revoked/changed

(B15) Offending within the past year

Number of cautions within the past year ____________

Number of convictions within the past year ____________

Additional Management Information

Additional Notes

Additional Notes

 ISBN 0 11 322422 2

CORE ASSESSMENT RECORD

Young person aged 15 years and over

Name ______________________________

Gender ______________ *Date of birth* ______________

Address ______________________________

____

____

____

Telephone number ______________________________

Name of social worker completing assessment:

____

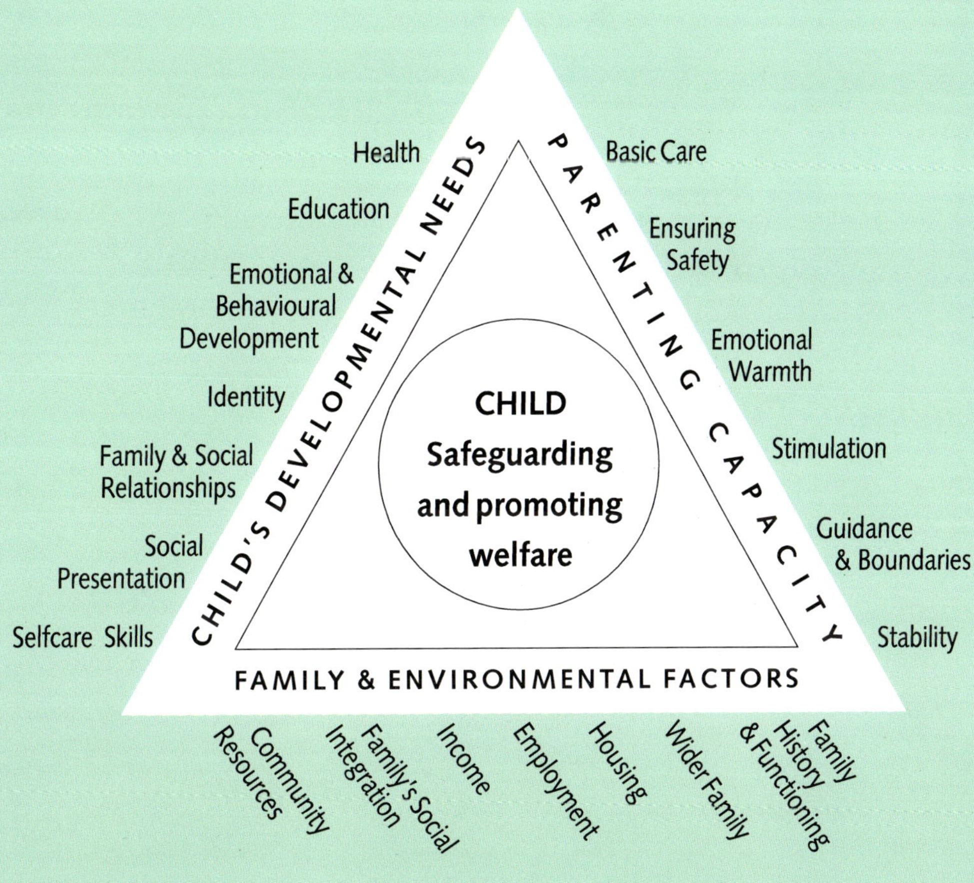

Contents

Undertaking the core assessment

- The Core Assessment Record provides a framework for systematically recording the findings from the core assessment. Whilst the Assessment Record provides some guidance on the areas that should be covered in a core assessment, it is a tool and should not be used as a substitute for a professionally informed assessment process, analysis and judgement.
- The questionnaires and scales published in the accompanying materials to the **Framework for the Assessment of Child in Need and their Families** may be useful in obtaining the information in specific areas (Department of Health, Cox and Bentovim, 2000). The Assessment Record indicates where particular questionnaires and scales may be useful. Practitioners may also choose to use other assessment tools to assist them.
- The Core Assessment Record may be completed in a number of different ways. For example, the social worker may wish to discuss each area with the family before completing the record and then share this with the family. Alternatively, having undertaken some or all of the core assessment the social worker may wish to complete the form with the child's parents or carers.
- Parents and carers invariably want to do the best for their children. Completing the record will help social workers to recognise the strengths that families have as well as identifying areas where they may need further help.
- Completing the core assessment should always be done in a way that helps parents or carers, children and other relevant family members to have their say and encourages them to take part. Space has been provided within the forms for parents/carers and older children to be involved in the assessment.
- It is expected that other agencies should be involved as appropriate during the core assessment process. Parental permission to contact other agencies should be obtained except in cases where the safety of the child would be jeopardised (paragraphs 7.27 to 7.38 of **Working Together to Safeguard Children** provides guidance on this issue). Permissions should be obtained from other agencies to share their information with the family.
- It is important that all sections of the Core Assessment Record are considered carefully. The analysis of the information gathered should be recorded in the plan. In some cases it will not be appropriate to complete particular sections, and in such situations the reason why should be recorded in the summary section. The information gathered is then used to develop case objectives and plans.
- In competing the record, it should be possible to see what help and support the child and family need, and which agencies might be best placed to give that help. This might include more detailed assessments of specific issues.
- Families should be provided with the following information:

Complaints procedures	date provided ______
Information on access to records	date provided ______
Other relevant/available information *(please specify)*	date provided ______

Sources of information

Dates young person and family members seen

Name	Date(s) seen

Agencies consulted/involved as part of the assessment

Agency	Person	Contact number

Questionnaires, Scales or other Instruments used in assessment

Questionnaire/Scale/Instrument	Date(s) used

Specialist Assessments

Agency/person who undertook the assessment	Purpose of the assessment	Date(s) assessment commissioned and completed

Details concerning a core assessment

D1 What is the reason for undertaking the core assessment?

Date core assessment started

Date core assessment ended

The Government's Objectives for Childen's Social Services (1999) require the core assessment to be completed within 35 working days.

D2 Are there specific communication needs for young person/parent (eg. impairment affecting communication or English is not the first language)?
If so, what action has been taken to address this ie. use of an interpreter or a signer?

Background details concerning the young person

(This information supplements the information recorded on the Referral and Initial Assessment Record)

B/K1 Significant relatives who are not part of the young person's household

Birth father Parental responsibility Yes ☐ No ☐ Name ____________________

Address ____________________

Brothers and sisters

Name(s) Age Address

____

____

____

Others (please specify)

Name(s) Relationship to child Address

____

____

B/K2 If the young person has any health conditions, impairment(s) or a genetically inherited condition – please give details (include for example: physical disability, sensory impairment, Down's syndrome, encephalitis, autism, sickle cell anaemia, cystic fibrosis)

B/K3 Key events which may have had an impact on the young person
(for example: death of a close relative, pregnancy, parenthood)

B/K4 Other key events experienced by siblings or other family members which may affect the young person

Key research sources

The Assessment Record is based on research information drawn from a number of sources

Assessment

Cleaver H, Wattam C and Cawson P (1998) *Assessing Risk in Child Protection*. NSPCC, London.

Department of Health, Department for Education and Employment and Home Office (2000) *Framework for the Assessment of Child in Need and their Families*. The Stationery Office, London.

Department of Health, Cox A and Bentovim A (2000) *The Family Assessment Pack of Questionnaires and Scales.* The Stationery Office, London.

The NSPCC and University of Sheffield (2000) *The Child's World: Assessing Children in Need. Training and Development Pack*. NSPCC, London.

Sinclair R, Garnett L and Berridge D (1995) *Social Work and Assessment with Adolescents*. National Children's Bureau, London.

Ward H (ed) (1995) *Looking After Children: Research into Practice*. HMSO, London.

Child development

Department of Health (1996) *Focus on Teenagers: Research into Practice*. HMSO, London.

Department of Health (1997) *Young Carers: Making a Start*. Department of Health, London.

Fahlberg VI (1994) *A Child's Journey Through Placement.* BAAF, London.

Jones DPH (forthcoming) *Communicating with children who may have been traumatised or maltreated*.

Rutter R and Rutter M (1992) *Developing Minds: Challenge and Continuity across the Life Span*. Penguin, Harmondsworth.

Smith PK and Cowie H (1993) *Understanding Children's Development* (2nd Edition). Blackwell, Oxford.

Varma VP (1991) *The Secret Life of Vulnerable Children.* Routledge, London.

Parenting capacity

Cleaver H, Unell I and Aldgate J (1999) *Children's Needs — Parenting Capacity: The impact of parental mental illness, problem alcohol and drug use, and domestic violence on children's development.* The Stationery Office, London.

Falkov A, Mayes K, Diggins M, Silverdale N and Cox A(1998) *Crossing Bridges — Training resources for working with mentally ill parents and their children.* Pavilion Publishing, Brighton.

Reder, P and Lucey, C (1995) *Assessment of Parenting: Psychiatric and psychological contributions.* Routledge, London.

Family and environmental factors

Cochran M (ed) (1993) *Parenting: an ecological perspective.* Lawrence Erlbaum Associates, New Jersey.

Cochran M, Larner M, Riley D, Gunnarsson L and Henderson C (eds) (1990) *Extending families: the social networks of parents and their children*. Cambridge University Press, Cambridge.

Jack G and Jordan B (1999) Social capital and child welfare. *Children and Society*. 13 (5): 242-256.

Wallace SA, Crown JM, Berger M and Cox AD (1997) *Child and Adolescent Mental Health*. In Stevens A and Rafferty J (1997) *Health Care Needs Assessment: 2nd Series.* Radcliffe Medical Press, Oxford.

Iwanec D (1995) *The emotionally abused and neglected child*. Wiley, Chichester.

Stevenson O (1998) *Neglected Children: Issues and Dilemmas*. Blackwell Science, Oxford.

Young person's developmental needs

Health

Normally well is defined as unwell for 1 week or *less in the last 6 months.*

Young people should have had the following immunisations: BCG (tuberculosis) and for school leavers: Diphtheria, Tetanus and Polio.

To gather further information consider using the Alcohol Scale.

Young people need factual information about sex and contraception.

Half of conceptions to under-age girls result in live births.

Parenthood at this age has long term consequences for a young person's life chances.

Young person's needs | **Summary/clarification of young person's needs**

		Yes	*No*
H1	Young person is normally well	☐	☐
H2	Experiences frequent accidents	☐	☐
H3	Has a chronic physical illness/ disability	☐	☐
H4	Wets or soils without physical explanation	☐	☐
H5	Has a regular sleep pattern	☐	☐
H6	Has been appropriately immunised	☐	☐
H7	Is responsible for own health	☐	☐
H8	Is an occassional/non smoker	☐	☐
H9	Is not addicted to illicit drugs	☐	☐
H10	Alcohol consumption is within the young person's control	☐	☐
H11	Eats an adequate, nutritious diet	☐	☐
H12	Has an accurate knowledge about sex and contraception	☐	☐
H13	Has a responsible, trusted adult to whom he/she can talk about sex and contraception	☐	☐
H14	Has been/is pregnant or has fathered a child	☐	☐
H15	Other	☐	☐

To gather further information consider using the Home Conditions Assessment.

Black families may have less access to preventative and support services than white families.

Poverty and poor social conditions are related to poor health and development and increased risk of accidents.

Parental capacity | **Summary/clarification of family strengths or issues identified**
Note when issue is not relevant

	Basic care	*Yes*	*No*
H16	A healthy diet is provided at home	☐	☐
H17	Parents ensure illnesses and injuries receive appropriate medical attention	☐	☐
H18	Parent ensures home is hygienic	☐	☐
H19	Other	☐	☐
	Ensuring safety		
H20	Periodic bouts of illness have a recognised medical explanation	☐	☐
H21	Injuries have an understandable accidental cause	☐	☐
H22	Marks on young person's body have an acceptable explanation	☐	☐
H23	Other	☐	☐

Parental capacity			Summary/clarification of family strengths or issues identified Note when issue is not relevant
Emotional warmth	*Yes*	*No*	
H24 Parent encourages the young person to take care of his/her own health	☐	☐	
H25 Parent shows approval of the young person taking care of own health	☐	☐	
H26 Parent is sympathetic to the young person's symptoms or injuries	☐	☐	
H27 Accepts young person's sexual orientation	☐	☐	
H28 Other	☐	☐	
Stimulation			
H29 Parent promotes involvement in physical activity	☐	☐	
H30 Parent advises about health issues	☐	☐	
H31 Ensures information on the risks to health of having unprotected sex (i.e. without a condom)	☐	☐	
H32 Ensures information is available about sexuality and sexual orientation	☐	☐	
H32 Other	☐	☐	
Guidance and Boundaries			
H34 Parent supports sex education	☐	☐	
H35 Parent supports health education	☐	☐	
H36 Parents' use of alcohol sets the young person a good example	☐	☐	
H37 Parent uses illicit drugs	☐	☐	
H38 Other	☐	☐	
Stability			
H39 Parent ensures medical and dental appointments are kept	☐	☐	
H40 Parents support each other in promoting/caring for the young person's health	☐	☐	
H41 Other	☐	☐	

Increasing numbers of young people are suffering obesity.

Regular physical exercise is an important preventative measure.

Disabled young people may need special help or equipment for exercise.

Disabled or young people with a health problem need information and opportunities to help them understand and learn about themselves.

When one parent is a problem drinker, the non drinking parent may not always be able to protect the young person.

Parental problem drug use is associated with young people using illicit drugs.

Social worker's summary of the young person's needs in this area and the extent to which parents are responding appropriately

Education

SATs are given to pupils in the summer term of Years 2, 6, & 9 (ages 7, 11 & 14).

At 15–16 years most young people are performing at level 6-7 at key stage 4.

Black pupils often underachieve at school

Black pupils are 4 times more likely to be excluded than white pupils. Excluded black children are usually of higher ability with fewer chronic disruptive behaviours than white pupils who are excluded.

Non school/work attendance may be related to bullying.

Young person's needs

Summary/clarification of young person's needs

		Yes	*No*
E1	Young person's educational progress is at expected level **Note SATs results**	☐	☐
E2	At 16 or over has at least 1 GCSE at grade A-G or a GNVQ	☐	☐
E3	Young person attends:		
	School/further education	☐	☐
	Full-time/part-time work	☐	☐
E4	Is excluded from school	☐	☐
	Unemployed less than 6 months	☐	☐
	Unemployed more than 6 months	☐	☐
E5	Attends school regularly (note number of unauthorised days absent in past year)	☐	☐
E6	Punctuality is good	☐	☐
E7	Challenging/disruptive behaviour at school/work/training	☐	☐
E8	Young person has a friend(s) at school/training/work place	☐	☐
E9	Has a good relationship with a member of staff	☐	☐
E10	Responds positively to instruction	☐	☐
E11	Young person's lack of concentration impedes learning	☐	☐
E12	Other	☐	☐

date	*Subject*	*level*
....	English	....
....	Maths	....
....	Science	....

When a parent has a learning disability only 15% of children are similarly affected.

Not all young people with impairments will need a statement of Special Educational Needs.

Disabled young people may need financial help, equipment or adaptations to enable them to get to school/work.

Persistent non school attendance or unemployment can place great strain on families.

Parental capacity

Summary/clarification of family strengths or issues identified
Note when issue is not relevant

	Basic care	*Yes*	*No*
E13	Parent tries to ensure regular school/work attendance	☐	☐
E14	Parent/carer supports and encourages homework	☐	☐
E15	If the young person is not achieving at school:		
	Is there an Individual Education Plan?	☐	☐
	Is there a statement of Special Educational Needs?	☐	☐
E16	Other	☐	☐

	Ensuring safety		
E17	Parent tries to ensure the journey to and from school/work is safe	☐	☐
E18	Where necessary, parents have taken action over bullying	☐	☐
E19	Other	☐	☐

Parental capacity

Summary/clarification of family strengths or issues identified
Note when issue is not relevant

Parents own problems may mean they are not always able to offer the intellectual stimulation a young person needs.

To gather further information consider using the Family Activity Scale.

Examinations can cause great stress.

Emotional warmth	*Yes*	*No*
E20 Parent shows an interest in the young person's work	☐	☐
E21 Parent shows approval of educational efforts and achievements	☐	☐
E22 Parent supports the young person over school/work difficulties	☐	☐
E23 Parent places great pressure on young person to achieve	☐	☐
E24 Other	☐	☐

All children need adequate and appropriate stimulation. When a young person has profound or complex impairments it may be helpful to check with a specialist before completing this section.

Stimulation		
E25 School leavers/unemployed are encouraged to find work	☐	☐
E26 Parent encourages the young person to learn new skills	☐	☐
E27 Other	☐	☐

Looking after a parent or sibling may interfere with a young person's work.

Guidance and Boundaries		
E28 Parent tries to ensure prompt school/work attendance	☐	☐
E29 Supports school rules/discipline	☐	☐
E30 Attempts to shield and support the young person from family problems that may interfere with schooling/work	☐	☐
E31 Other	☐	☐

The key to educational progress is a parent or significant adult who takes an interest in their learning and offers praise and encouragement.

Stability		
E31 Parent regularly attends school events/parents' meetings	☐	☐
E32 Young person's books/school work are looked after	☐	☐
E33 Parents agree with each other in supporting education/work ethic	☐	☐
E34 Other	☐	☐

Social worker's summary of the young person's needs in this area and the extent to which parents are responding appropriately

Emotional and Behavioural Development

To gather further information consider using the Strengths and Difficulties Questionnaire and The Adolescent Wellbeing Scale.

Depressive feelings and disorders increase in young adult hood. Girls are more prone than boys.

Young people may cope with upsetting parental behaviours by withdrawing or running away.

A quarter of homeless 16–25s left home because of domestic violence.

Self harm must be treated seriously and appropriate help sought.

Young person's needs | **Summary/clarification of young person's needs**

		Yes	No
B1	Young person is usually happy	☐	☐
B2	Frequently withdraws emotionally	☐	☐
B3	Young person generally feels life is not worth living	☐	☐
B4	Often stays away from home/out late without parental permission	☐	☐
B5	Has run away from home	☐	☐
B6	Young person copes with anger and frustration	☐	☐
B7	Talks about feelings with a trusted adult(s)	☐	☐
B8	Inflicts injuries on him/herself (i.e. scratching, cutting, head banging)	☐	☐
B9	Has/is seeing a mental health professional	☐	☐
B10	Is preoccupied with violence	☐	☐
B11	Challenging/disruptive behaviour affects safety of young person	☐	☐
B12	Bullies others	☐	☐
B13	Respects the concept of ownership	☐	☐
B14	Has been cautioned or convicted within past year	☐	☐
B15	Other	☐	☐

Depression can affect parent's capacity to care about their child.

Most at risk are victims of parental aggression or neglect.

When a young person is disabled or sensory impaired, behaviours such as rocking or constant screaming must not be dismissed.

Consider whether the feelings and behaviour that troubles the young person and parent would benefit from specialist assessment and help.

Parental capacity | **Summary/clarification of family strengths or issues identified**
Note when issue is not relevant

	Basic care	Yes	No
B16	Parent/carer assures the young person they will always be there for them	☐	☐
B17	Family disagreements are resolved in non-violent ways	☐	☐
B18	Other	☐	☐

	Ensuring safety		
B19	Tries to ensure young person's general whereabouts are known	☐	☐
B20	Young person is hit or physically chastised	☐	☐
B21	Help is sought over unresolvable relationship problems	☐	☐
B22	Other	☐	☐

Parental capacity

Summary/clarification of family strengths or issues identified
Note when issue is not relevant

Young people who are abused or witness family violence are particularly traumatised.

Discussing feelings becomes more difficult when a young person depends on non verbal methods of communication.

To gather further information consider using The Parenting Daily Hassles Scale.

	Emotional warmth	*Yes*	*No*
B23	Young person is comforted when frightened or distressed	☐	☐
B24	Young person is exposed to frequent criticism/hostility	☐	☐
B25	Young person is encouraged to talk about fears and worries	☐	☐
B26	Other	☐	☐
	Stimulation		
B27	Young person is often exposed to parents' emotional distress	☐	☐
B28	Young person is encouraged to share with others	☐	☐
B29	Other	☐	☐

Positive methods for encouraging co-operation include: praise, negotiation, modelling, rewards, distraction, persuasion and explanation.

When young people witness violence they have difficulty in controlling their own emotions and behaviour.

	Guidance and Boundaries	*Yes*	*No*
B30	Parent uses a variety of positive methods to gain the young person's co-operation/good behaviour	☐	☐
B31	There are clear family rules and limits about behaviour	☐	☐
B32	Parent teaches respect for the law	☐	☐
B33	Young person is encouraged to help with household tasks	☐	☐
B34	Parents do not burden the young person with their own problems	☐	☐
B35	Young person is protected from seeing frightening adult behaviour	☐	☐
B36	Other	☐	☐
	Stability		
B37	Young person is responded to in a consistent and predictable manner	☐	☐
B38	Parents/carers generally support each other in applying family rules	☐	☐
B39	Other	☐	☐

Social worker's summary of the young person's needs in this area and the extent to which parents are responding appropriately

Identity

Cultural identity develops from all aspects of a person's experience.

The way in which black disabled young people define themselves is affected by their personal experience of both racism and disability.

Dual heritage does not always result in identity problems/conflicts.

Racism and bullying are common place in the lives of black young people.

Young person's needs	Yes	No	Summary/clarification of young person's needs
ID1 Young person is self confident	☐	☐	
ID2 Takes pride in his/her appearance	☐	☐	
ID3 Takes pride in achievements	☐	☐	
ID4 Has a sense of his/her own culture	☐	☐	
ID5 Is comfortable with his/her own racial identity	☐	☐	
ID6 Is at ease with his/her sexual orientation	☐	☐	
ID7 Is confident when relating to friends of either sex	☐	☐	
ID8 Chooses own friends	☐	☐	
ID9 Is able to make decisions on appropriate matters	☐	☐	
ID10 Blames him/herself for parent's troubles	☐	☐	
ID11 Feels everything is out of control	☐	☐	
ID12 Other	☐	☐	

Young people who grow up in families which experience many stresses and problems will need positive messages to avoid developing a negative self image and poor self esteem. Disabled young people need even more help.

Disabled young people have a right to be dressed appropriately but their dress should not impede movement, endanger stability or aggravate their skin.

Parental capacity	Yes	No	Summary/clarification of family strengths or issues identified Note when issue is not relevant
Basic care			
ID13 Clothes and appearance are acceptable to the young person	☐	☐	
ID14 Parents see the young person as having unique strengths and encourages them	☐	☐	
ID15 Other	☐	☐	
Ensuring safety			
ID16 Young person's dress is appropriate for age, gender, culture and religion and where necessary, impairment	☐	☐	
ID17 Young person is supervised appropriately taking into account personality and developmental level	☐	☐	
ID18 Young person is encouraged to talk about worries and concerns			
ID19 Young person is supported if exposed to harassment or racism	☐	☐	
ID20 Other	☐	☐	

Parental capacity

Summary/clarification of family strengths or issues identified
Note when issue is not relevant

For young people to develop a positive self image they need to feel loved and valued for themselves.

Emotional warmth	*Yes*	*No*
ID21 Parent often shows spontaneous affection to the young person	☐	☐
ID22 Shows pride in the young person	☐	☐
ID23 Young person's efforts/ achievements are praised	☐	☐
ID24 Friendships are supported where appropriate	☐	☐
ID25 Other	☐	☐

Young people need positive role models of the same racial/ethnic origins as him/ herself.

In all cultures disabled young people may be treated as younger than their actual age; a particular risk for the learning disabled children.

Stimulation		
ID26 Has the opportunity to learn own cultural traditions/language	☐	☐
ID27 Independence is encouraged	☐	☐
ID28 Is given control over appropriate aspects of his/her life	☐	☐
ID29 Other	☐	☐

Young people often suffer if they are included in the imaginary world of a mentally ill parent.

Guidance and Boundaries		
ID30 Is taught respect and toleration	☐	☐
ID31 Family is tolerant of different cultures, ethnic groups etc	☐	☐
ID32 Young person is protected from parental mental illness/symptoms	☐	☐
ID33 Young person is reassured when parent's behaviour is disturbing	☐	☐
ID34 Other	☐	☐

Although at times rebellious and moody, most young people remain integrated within the family culture and participate in important family celebrations.

Young people who are routinely rejected come to see themselves as unloved and unlovable.

Stability		
ID35 Is included in family celebrations	☐	☐
ID36 Is accepted as a family member	☐	☐
ID37 Parent ensures that day to day living has order and stability	☐	☐
ID38 Other	☐	☐

Social worker's summary of the young person's needs in this area and the extent to which parents are responding appropriately

Family and social relationships

Young unaccompanied asylum seekers experience acute loss.

Young people can look after younger siblings and sick parents but should not have overall responsibility.

A first love affair has great emotional impact. Breaking up can be very stressful.

Close friends can help a young person cope with family problems.

Young person's needs | **Summary/clarification of young person's needs**

		Yes	No
F1	Young person has a strong, positive relationship with a parent	☐	☐
F2	Looks after the family	☐	☐
F3	Young person has a close friend(s)	☐	☐
F4	Is not cruel to other people or to animals	☐	☐
F5	Regularly visits/spends time with friends	☐	☐
F6	Has an adult in whom he/she confides	☐	☐
F7	Sexual knowledge and behaviour is age-appropriate	☐	☐
F8	Has a steady sexual partner	☐	☐
F9	Young person has own child(ren)	☐	☐
F10	Is looking after own child(ren)	☐	☐
F11	Other	☐	☐

Family issues or difficulties experienced by the young person may result in him/ her living with a large number of different people (i.e. family, friends, hospital care, or social services respite care).

A disabled child may not protest when left with strangers because they have been handled by many unknown people. Nonetheless it remains a matter for concern.

Long lasting rifts with the family are rare.

Parental capacity | **Summary/clarification of family strengths or issues identified**
Note when issue is not relevant

	Basic care	Yes	No
F12	When away from home the young person stays with appropriate adults	☐	☐
F13	Parent/carer spends enough time with the young person to sustain a strong relationship	☐	☐
F14	Other	☐	☐

	Ensuring safety		
F15	The relationship between the young person and other children in the family is generally good	☐	☐
F16	Parent monitors interactions between young person and siblings	☐	☐
F17	Young person does not witness/ become involved in adult sexual behaviour	☐	☐
F18	Does not witness/become involved in adult violence	☐	☐
F19	Other	☐	☐

Parental capacity

Summary/clarification of family strengths or issues identified
Note when issue is not relevant

Love and affection are shown in different ways depending on culture and individual characteristics.

A supportive adult can help stressed parents to cope.

Other young people may be valuable sources of support and can greatly influence ideas and actions.

When a young person is disabled, practical and social barriers can make getting out difficult, but it remains essential to their wellbeing.

	Emotional warmth	*Yes*	*No*
F20	Parents/carers' relationships with others provides a good example to the young person	☐	☐
F21	Parent/carer encourages affectionate family relationships	☐	☐
F22	Other	☐	☐

	Stimulation		
F23	Young person has sufficient time to pursue his/her own interests	☐	☐
F24	Is enabled to spend time with friends	☐	☐
F25	Other	☐	☐

Young carers can feel stigmatised and get little recognition or respect for their contribution.

	Guidance and Boundaries		
F26	Is encouraged to negotiate	☐	☐
F27	Is discouraged from violent or cruel behaviour	☐	☐
F28	Is given clear guidance on appropriate sexual behaviour	☐	☐
F29	Task of caring for the family is kept to a manageable level	☐	☐
F30	Parent tries to ensure young person does not associate with unsuitable adults/peers	☐	☐
F31	Other	☐	☐

Of central importance to a young person in all families is a loving and protective relationship.

Untrained agency staff are not appropriate people to care for a disabled young person.

	Stability		
F32	There is a stable pattern of care to day to day life	☐	☐
F33	There is continuity of carers	☐	☐
F34	A limited number of known, appropriate adults deliver intimate care	☐	☐
F35	Other	☐	☐

Social worker's summary of the young person's needs in this area and the extent to which parents are responding appropriately

Social presentation

Young people have well developed social skills. They can readily adjust their conversation and behaviour to suit a variety of different situations.

A considerable proportion of money is spent on clothing and toiletries.

Young people are very conscious of their appearance and sensitive to criticism, particularly from their peers.

Trusted and respected adults can influence young people's behaviour.

Young person's needs | **Summary/clarification of young person's needs**

		Yes	*No*
P1	Young person's language and behaviour do not cause offence or embarrassment outside the family	☐	☐
P2	Personal hygiene is adequate	☐	☐
P3	Has control over own clothes and appearance	☐	☐
P4	Talks/communicates about family without great difficulty	☐	☐
P5	Young person is self-confident and appropriately open with adults	☐	☐
P6	Is willing to listen to the advice of trusted and respected adults	☐	☐
P7	Young person is overly friendly with strangers	☐	☐
P8	Young person is self-confident and open with peers	☐	☐
P9	Young person spends time with friends outside the home	☐	☐
P10	Other	☐	☐

Young people may be bullied or rejected at school or work because their clothes are soiled and inappropriate, or their personal hygiene is poor.

The experience of bullying, racism, harassment or being left out can lead to low self esteem and may affect the young person's behaviour.

Parental capacity | **Summary/clarification of family strengths or issues identified**
Note when issue is not relevant

	Basic care	*Yes*	*No*
P11	Parents/carers try to ensure that personal hygiene is satisfactory	☐	☐
P12	Clothes and appearance is in line with the young person's wishes	☐	☐
P13	Parents try to ensure any body piecing is carried out responsibly	☐	☐
P14	Parents/carers' behaviour sets a good example to the young person	☐	☐
P15	Other	☐	☐
	Ensuring safety		
P16	Parents/carers encourage the young person to behave appropriately with strangers	☐	☐
P17	Parents/carers teach appropriate behaviour in public settings	☐	☐
P18	Parents/carers ensure the young person is supported in potentially dangerous settings	☐	☐
P19	Other	☐	☐

Parental capacity

Summary/clarification of family strengths or issues identified
Note when issue is not relevant

When families are experiencing difficulties young people keep silent because they fear telling someone will result in them 'getting into trouble', or being 'taken away'.

	Emotional warmth	*Yes*	*No*
P20	Parents/carers encourage the young person to be self-confident	☐	☐
P21	Praise the young person for good social behaviour	☐	☐
P22	Family members support each other over decisions on the young person's clothes and appearance	☐	☐
P23	Other	☐	☐
	Stimulation		
P24	Parents/carers encourage the young person to bring his/her friends home	☐	☐
P25	Encourage young person to join in social activities outside the home	☐	☐
P26	Allow control over clothes and appearance	☐	☐
P27	Other	☐	☐
	Guidance and Boundaries		
P28	Give guidance on appropriate 'good manners' and respect for others	☐	☐
P29	Parents relationships with neighbours and those in authority are generally harmonious	☐	☐
P30	Family members are engaged in criminal/antisocial activities	☐	☐
P31	Other.	☐	☐
	Stability		
P32	Parents/carers engage in regular social activities with other adults.	☐	☐
P33	The family feels accepted by the local community.	☐	☐
P34	Other.	☐	☐

Young people often shun social events or keep friends at bay in an attempt to keep the family's circumstances secret.

Difficulties in relating well with adults outside the family, for example teachers, workmates or supervisors may lead to poor relationships, feelings of detachment and poor school results, or progress at work.

Social worker's summary of the young person's needs in this area and the extent to which parents are responding appropriately

Selfcare skills

Young people without impairments are able to look after their own personal hygiene.

Young people are able to prepare simple meals, use the telephone.

Can cope appropriately with an emergency.

Young people often wish to do things with friends rather than family.

Young people who leave home at an early age often do so because of family conflict, abuse, or because parents are no longer prepared to let them stay.

Young person's needs | **Summary/clarification of young person's needs**

		Yes	*No*
S1	Young person has age appropriate self care skills — looks after his/her own personal hygiene	☐	☐
S2	Understands the consequences of his/her own actions	☐	☐
S3	Can prepare simple meals	☐	☐
S4	Is solely responsible for looking after the home	☐	☐
S5	Can answer and use the telephone	☐	☐
S6	Young person accepts adult help with day to day tasks with reasonable grace	☐	☐
S7	Can plan journeys and travel alone	☐	☐
S8	Can appropriately control own finances	☐	☐
S9	Makes own social arrangements	☐	☐
S10	Has slept/lived on the streets	☐	☐
S11	Lives in own accommodation	☐	☐
S12	Other	☐	☐

When parents' own concerns overwhelm them young people may be left responsible for organising their own day to day living and that of younger brothers and sisters (i.e. bed-times, meals, getting to school or work, shopping).

Parental capacity | **Summary/clarification of family strengths or issues identified**
Note when issue is not relevant

	Basic care	*Yes*	*No*
S13	Parent/carer takes main responsibility for the day to day care of the young person	☐	☐
S14	Parents/carers encourage the young person to take responsibility for aspects of self care appropriate to age/stage of development	☐	☐
S15	Other	☐	☐

	Ensuring safety		
S16	A parent/carer monitors the young person's self care to ensure safety	☐	☐
S17	Young person has overall responsibility for looking after the home	☐	☐
S18	Other	☐	☐

Parental capacity

Summary/clarification of family strengths or issues identified
Note when issue is not relevant

	Emotional warmth	Yes	No
S19	Young person is praised for appropriate self care including cooking, shopping etc	☐	☐
S20	Other	☐	☐

	Stimulation		
S21	Young person is encouraged to gain appropriate self care skills (i.e. money management)	☐	☐
S22	Parent and young person with special educational needs are planning for greater independence	☐	☐
S23	Other	☐	☐

Parents' own difficulties may result in young people assuming a major role in looking after the family.

Although young people can help look after a sick or disabled parent or younger sisters and brothers, an adult should retain overall responsibility.

Young carers may become extremely skilled in carrying out everyday household chores and in looking after themselves.

	Guidance and Boundaries		
S24	Parents place appropriate boundaries on self care activities according to the young person's personality and stage of development	☐	☐
S25	The young person is taught self care and safety in and out of the home (i.e. how to avoid/cope with every day dangers)	☐	☐
S26	Young person knows how and who to contact when help is needed to cope with parental issues	☐	☐
S27	Other	☐	☐

Feeling responsible for the family can lead young carers to feel tied to the home and unable to join in outside leisure and social activities.

	Stability		
S28	There are stable arrangements for living	☐	☐
S29	Parents/carers maintain the main responsibility for the care of the family	☐	☐
S30	Other	☐	☐

Social worker's summary of the young person's needs in this area and the extent to which parents are responding appropriately

Issues affecting parents'/carers' capacities to respond appropriately to the young person's needs

	Parental issues	*Yes*	*No*	*Professional/agency involved*	*Note identity of parent/carer for whom the issue is relevant. Record strengths and difficulties*
C1	Illness:				
	Physical	☐	☐		
	Mental	☐	☐		
C2	Disability:				
	Physical	☐	☐		
	Learning	☐	☐		
	Sensory impairment	☐	☐		
C3	Period in care during childhood	☐	☐		
C4	Childhood abuse	☐	☐		
C5	Known history of child abuse	☐	☐		
C6	Known history of violence	☐	☐		
C7	Problem drinking/ drug use	☐	☐		
C8	Other	☐	☐		

Social worker's summary of how the above issues have an impact on the parents'/carers' capacities to respond appropriately to the young person's needs

Family and environmental factors which may impact on the young person and parenting capacity

Include all household and relevant family members, living in or out of the home, when exploring family history and functioning.

To gather further information consider using: The Recent Life Events Questionnaire; A genogram; An eco-map.

How parents bring up their children is rooted in their own childhood experiences.

Consider whether a separate carers' assessment is required.

Both positive and negative parenting styles can be passed from one generation to another.

To gather further information consider using: The Adult Well-being Scale; The Alcohol Scale.

Wider family may extend beyond blood relatives to include people who feel like family to parent or child.

		Yes	*No*	**Additional details as appropriate** **Note identity of person for whom the issue is relevant**
	Family History			
FE1	Has a member of the household experienced a stressful childhood?	☐	☐	
	Note childhood abuse; in care			
FE2	Have the family suffered a traumatic loss or crisis which is unresolved? (e.g. bereavement)	☐	☐	
FE3	Other	☐	☐	
	Family Functioning			
FE4	Does young person's impairment/ behaviour have a negative impact on siblings?	☐	☐	
FE5	Young person's impairment/ behaviour affects parent(s) capacity to continue care	☐	☐	
FE6	Does a member of the household experience:			
	poor mental health	☐	☐	
	poor physical health	☐	☐	
	behaviour problem	☐	☐	
	physical disability	☐	☐	
	learning disability	☐	☐	
	sensory impairment	☐	☐	
	problem alcohol/drug use	☐	☐	
FE7	Has an adult member of the house-hold got a history of violence?	☐	☐	
FE8	Are there frequent family rows?	☐	☐	
FE9	Other	☐	☐	
	Wider Family			
FE10	Do wider family provide:			
	practical help	☐	☐	
	emotional support	☐	☐	
	financial help	☐	☐	
	information and advice	☐	☐	
FE11	Is there an adult in the home who helps the parent care for the young person?	☐	☐	
FE12	Other	☐	☐	

Additional details as appropriate
Note identity of person for whom the issue is relevant

Basic amenities include safe water, heating, cooking facilities, food storage, sleeping arrangements and cleanliness.

The Home Conditions Assessment may help gather this information.

Housing	*Yes*	*No*
FE13 Is the family homeless?	☐	☐
FE14 Is the family vulnerable to eviction or in temporary accommodation?	☐	☐
FE15 Is the house and its immediate surroundings safe for the young person?	☐	☐
FE16 Does home have basic amenities?	☐	☐
FE17 Does home require any adaptations to meet the young person's needs?	☐	☐
FE18 Is the home overcrowded?		
FE19 Other	☐	☐

Jobs may be lost because parents' circumstances result in them behaving in a bizarre or unpredictable way.

Parents' circumstances may mean too much family income is used to satisfy parental needs.

Adult services may help a disabled parent respond to their child's needs.

Employment	*Yes*	*No*
FE20 Is a parent in paid employment?	☐	☐
FE21 Does parent's pattern of work adversely impact on child care?	☐	☐
FE22 Is employment reasonably secure?	☐	☐
FE23 Are family members who seek employment adequately supported?	☐	☐
FE24 Other	☐	☐

The family may be vulnerable to future financial problems (i.e. extraordinary medical, funeral expenses, need to help out a relative).

Income		
FE25 Are all entitled benefits claimed?	☐	☐
FE26 Are household bills paid regularly?	☐	☐
FE27 Is the family managing on the income they receive?	☐	☐
FE28 Does the young person receive an appropriate allowance	☐	☐
FE29 If in debt, is this increasing?	☐	☐
FE30 Is the family worried about future financial commitments?	☐	☐
FE31 Other	☐	☐

Social isolation and rejection by the community may have affected the family for generations.

Family's Social Integration		
FE32 Does the family feel accepted within their community?	☐	☐
FE33 Do family members experience discrimination/harassment?	☐	☐
FE34 Does the family have local friends?	☐	☐
FE35 Is the family involved in local organisations/activities?	☐	☐
FE36 Other	☐	☐

Additional details as appropriate

Community resources include: shops, recreation areas, health clinics etc.

In assessing community resources note: availability, accessibility and standard, and if appropriate to child and family needs.

Community Resources	*Yes*	*No*
FE37 Are there accessible community resources?	☐	☐
FE38 Does the family take advantage of community resources?	☐	☐
FE39 Other	☐	☐

Social worker's summary of how the family and environmental factors have an impact on the young person and parents/carers

Plan for the child in need

- Having completed the information gathering, the following pages should be used to analyse the strengths and needs of the child and family members and to identify goals and specific objectives. This information is then used to formulate a plan of action. The decision about which methods are used and services are provided to achieve specific objectives should be evidence based. The expectations of a plan for a child in need are outlined in paragraphs 4.32 to 4.37 of the **Framework for the Assessment of Children in Need and Their Families** (2000).
- The plan for a child in need has been designed to enable it to be used for all children in need, including these about whom there are concerns they are suffering or likely to suffer significant harm.
- The plan should identify how the following will be addressed:
    - The identified developmental needs of the child;
    - Issues which impact negatively on parents/carers' capacity to respond to the child and needs of their child, drawing on their strengths;
    - Wider family and environmental factors which have a negative impact on the family, drawing on strengths in the wider family and community.
- The plan should be specific about the actions to be taken, identify who is responsible for each action, and any services or resources that will be required to ensure that the objectives set can be achieved within the agreed time scales. Statutory reviews should take place within statutory time limits and it is good practice for Child In Need plans to be reviewed at least every 6 months. Reviews should be formally recorded.
- The outcome section of the table should be completed following a review of the plan. When completing the outcome section record the outcome for each objective and whether the circumstances have; improved, remained the same, or deteriorated.
- The last page records which family members and agencies are party to the plan and the date when the plan will be reviewed. This should be signed by the child (where appropriate), family members/carers and the social worker.

Summary of young person's developmental needs and strengths

Information gathered in the core assessment

Summarise the young person's developmental needs and strengths

The young person (where appropriate) and parents should be involved in the assessment

This space is for young people and parents/carers to write their views of the young person's strengths and needs

Summary of parenting capacity: Needs and strengths

Information gathered in the core assessment

Summarise how the parental issues, needs and strengths, which have been identified in the core assessment have an impact on the capacity of each parent/carer to respond appropriately to the young person's needs

The young person (where appropriate) and parents should be involved in the assessment

This space is for the young person and parents/carers to write their views of their own strengths and difficulties and what impact they think these have on the young person's development

Summary of wider family and environmental factors: Needs and strengths

Information gathered in the core assessment

Summarise how family and environment issues, which have been identified in the core assessment, have an impact either directly on the young person or on the capacity of the parents/carers to respond appropriately to the young person's needs

The young person (where appropriate) and parents should be involved in the assessment

This space is for the young person and parents/carers to write their views of the strengths and difficulties in their wider family and environment and what impact they think these have on the young person's development

Analysis of the information gathered during the core assessment

The analysis should list the factors which have an impact on different aspects of the young person's development and parenting capacity, and explore the relationship between them. This process of analysing the information available about the young person's needs, parenting capacity and wider family and environmental factors should result in a clear understanding of the young person's needs, and what types of service provision would best address these needs to ensure the young person has the opportunity to achieve their potential

The young person: Objectives and plans

Young person's developmental needs	*Objectives and plan of action*	*Person/Agency responsible*	*Objective to be achieved by (date)*	*Outcome (to be completed at the review)*
Health				
Education				
Emotional and behavioural development				
Identity				
Family and social relationships				
Social presentation				
Selfcare skills				

The parents/carers: Objectives and plans

Parenting capacity	*Objective and plan of action*	*Person/Agency responsible*	*Objective to be achieved by (date)*	*Outcome (to be completed at the review)*
Basic care				
Ensuring safety				
Emotional warmth				
Stimulation				
Guidance and Boundaries				
Stability				

Wider Family and Environmental Factors: Objectives and plans

Family and environmental factors	*Objective and plan of action*	*Person/Agency responsible*	*Objective to be achieved by (date)*	*Outcome (to be completed at the review)*
Family history and functioning				
Wider family				
Housing				
Employment and/or income				
Family social integration				
Community resources				

Views of all parties

These objectives and plans should have been discussed with all interested parties/agencies
Family members/agencies who are party to the plan

Name (please print)	Signature	Contact Number

Agreed date for the review: ______

Lead professional/agency for the review: ______

If the objectives and plans have not been discussed with any of the parties/agencies concerned, please give reasons

What steps will be taken and who is responsible if any party/agency wants to alter these objectives and plans?

Date plan reviewed in supervision	Signature of Line Manger/Supervisor

Parents'/carer's comments

I have seen the contents of this assessment form

Parent/carer's signature ______________________ Date |___|___|___|

Parent/carer signature ______________________ Date |___|___|___|

Parents/carers comments on the assessment

Have all relevant family members been given a copy of the assessment record? Yes ☐ No ☐

If not, what arrangements have been made to ensure this happens?

Social Worker's Signature ______________________ Date |___|___|___|

Management information

Ethnicity of the young person:

Caribbean	☐	Indian	☐	White British	☐	White and Black Caribbean	☐	Chinese	☐
African	☐	Pakistani	☐	White Irish	☐	White and Black African	☐	Any other ethnic group	☐
Any other Black background	☐	Bangladeshi	☐	Any other White background	☐	White and Asian	☐	Not given	☐

Any other Asian background ☐ Any other mixed background ☐

If other, please specify ______

Immigration status if applicable:

Asylum seeking ☐ Refugee status ☐ Exceptional leave to remain ☐

Home Office registration number: ______

(H6) Details of immunisations:

Has the young person been appropriately immunised? Yes ☐ No ☐

Young people should have had the following immunisations: Heaf test and BCG (tuberculosis) and for school leavers: Diphtheria, Tetanus and Polio.

(H14) Childbirth

The girl has been/is pregnant Yes ☐ No ☐

The boy has fathered a child Yes ☐ No ☐

Child protection register:

Is the young person's name on the Child Protection Register? Yes ☐ No ☐

Category ______ Date of registration ______

Has the young person previously been on the Child Protection Register? Yes ☐ No ☐

Category	Date of registration	Date of deregistration

Education details of the young person

(E1) SATs results show young person at the end of Key Stage 4 (child of 16) performs at level 6–7 for:

English Yes ☐ No ☐

Maths Yes ☐ No ☐

Science Yes ☐ No ☐

(E2) At 16 years, number of Higher grade GCSEs ____________

(E5) Number school days missed within past year through unauthorised absence ____________

(E4) Young person is excluded from school Yes ☐ No ☐

Court Order(s)

Is the young person the subject of a court order? Yes ☐ No ☐

Was the young person previously subject of a court order? Yes ☐ No ☐

Type of Order(s)	Date Order(s) made:	Type of Order(s)	Date Order(s) made	Date Order(s) revoked/changed

(B14) Offending within the past year

Number of cautions within the past year ____________

Number of convictions within the past year ____________

Additional Management Information

Additional Notes

Additional Notes

 ISBN 0 11 322423 0

Department of Health
Department for Education and Employment
Home Office

Framework for the Assessment of Children in Need and their Families

London

TSO

TSO
information & publishing solutions

Published by TSO (The Stationery Office) and available from:

Online
www.tsoshop.co.uk

Mail, Telephone, Fax & E-mail
TSO
PO Box 29, Norwich, NR3 1GN
Telephone orders/General enquiries: 0870 600 5522
Fax orders: 0870 600 5533
E-mail: customer.services@tso.co.uk
Textphone: 0870 240 3701

TSO Shops
16 Arthur Street, Belfast BT1 4GD
028 9023 8451 Fax 028 9023 5401
71 Lothian Road, Edinburgh EH3 9AZ
0870 606 5566 Fax 0870 606 5588

TSO@Blackwell and other Accredited Agents

First published 2000
Seventh impression 2008

Published with permission of Department of Health on behalf of the Controller of Her Majesty's Stationery Office.

ISBN 9780113223107

Published by The Stationery Office Ltd

Printed in the United Kingdom for The Stationery Office
ID5913501 C2 9/08

Contents

Appendices

Foreword

We cannot begin to improve the lives of disadvantaged and vulnerable children unless we identify their needs and understand what is happening to them in order to take appropriate action.

The Government is committed to delivering better life chances to such children through a range of cross-cutting, inter-departmental initiatives. A key component of the Government's objectives for children's social services is the development of a framework for assessing children in need and their families, to ensure a timely response and the effective provision of services. This is being taken forward as part of the Quality Protects Programme.

Delivering services to children in need in our communities is a corporate responsibility. It falls on all local authority departments, health authorities and community services. Improvements in outcomes for children in need can only be achieved by close collaboration between professionals and agencies working with children and families. This Guidance reflects such collaboration and is issued jointly by the Department of Health, the Department for Education and Employment and the Home Office. It is issued under section 7 of the Local Authority Social Services Act 1970.

The Guidance draws widely on a wealth of research about the needs of children and the best of practice. Many people have contributed generously to its development and it has been substantially enriched by an extensive consultation exercise. It is intended to provide a valuable foundation for policy and practice for all those who manage and provide services to children in need and their families. This document is the cornerstone in a series of accompanying publications, materials and training resources about the assessment of children in need. The Assessment Framework has been incorporated into *Working Together to Safeguard Children.*

The value of this framework for assessing children in need and their families will be measured in future improvements in our responses to some of our most vulnerable children - children in need.

John Hutton
Minister of State for Social Services
March 2000

Preface

Securing the wellbeing of children by protecting them from all forms of harm and ensuring their developmental needs are responded to appropriately are primary aims of Government policy. Local authority social services departments working with other local authority departments and health authorities have a **duty to safeguard and promote the welfare of children in their area who are in need** and to promote the upbringing of such children, wherever possible by their families, through providing an appropriate range of services. A critical task is to ascertain with the family whether a child is in need and how that child and family might best be helped. The effectiveness with which a child's needs are assessed will be key to the effectiveness of subsequent actions and services and, ultimately, to the outcomes for the child.

A Framework for Assessing Children in Need

A framework has been developed which provides a systematic way of analysing, understanding and recording what is happening to children and young people within their families and the wider context of the community in which they live. From such an understanding of what are inevitably complex issues and inter-relationships, clear professional judgements can be made. These judgements include whether the child being assessed is in need, whether the child is suffering or likely to suffer significant harm, what actions must be taken and which services would best meet the needs of this particular child and family. The evidence based knowledge which has informed the development of the framework has been drawn from a wide range of research studies and theories across a number of disciplines and from the accumulated experience of policy and practice.

The Guidance describes the Assessment Framework and the Government's expectations of how it will be used. It reflects the principles contained within the United Nations Convention on the Rights of the Child, ratified by the UK Government in 1991 and the Human Rights Act 1998. In addition, it takes account of relevant legislation at the time of publication, but is particularly informed by the requirements of the Children Act 1989, which provides a comprehensive framework for the care and protection of children.

This document is issued under section 7 of the Local Authority Social Services Act 1970, which requires local authorities in their social services functions to act under the general guidance of the Secretary of State. As such this document does not have the full force of statute, but should be complied with unless local circumstances indicate exceptional reasons which justify a variation.

The Guidance is a key element of the Department of Health's work to support local authorities in implementing Quality Protects, the Government's programme for transforming the management and delivery of children's social services. Quality Protects aims to deliver better life chances for the most vulnerable and disadvantaged children, and good assessment lies at the heart of this work. The Government's consolidated set of objectives for children's social services published in September 1999 makes clear the importance of assessment in the work of local authority departments and health authorities. The framework has been incorporated into the Government Guidance on protecting children from harm, *Working Together to Safeguard Children* (Department of Health *et al*, 1999) and should be read in conjunction with it when there are concerns that a child may be or is suffering significant harm.

The Guidance is not a practice manual. It does not set out step-by-step procedures to be followed: rather it sets out a framework which should be adapted and used to suit individual circumstances. A range of additional publications has been produced to inform practitioners and their managers about the most up-to-date knowledge from research and practice. Practice guidance (Department of Health, 2000a) and a training pack consisting of a training video, guide and reader (NSPCC and University of Sheffield, 2000) have also been developed to accompany the Guidance and to assist the introduction and implementation of the new framework. The Department of Health will be working closely with local authorities, health services and other agencies through the Quality Protects Programme to help them put the framework into practice in the most cost effective way.

Who is the Guidance for?

The Guidance has been produced primarily for the use of professionals and other staff who will be involved in undertaking assessments of children in need and their families under the Children Act 1989. Social services departments have lead responsibility for assessments of children in need including those children who may be or are suffering significant harm but, under section 27 of the Children Act 1989, other local authority services and health authorities have a duty to assist social services in carrying out this function. These other agencies should be aware of the Assessment Framework and understand what it might mean for them.

Many agencies have contact with and responsibility for children and young people under a range of legislation. The Guidance is, therefore, also relevant to assessments concerned with the welfare of children in a number of contexts.

Health, education and youth justice services, in particular, may have already had considerable involvement with some children and families prior to referral to social services departments. They will have an important contribution to make to the assessment and, where appropriate, to the provision of services to those families. Their awareness of the Assessment Framework when contributing to assessments of children in need will facilitate communication between agencies and with children and families. It will also assist the process of referral from one agency to another and increase the likelihood of acceptance of the contents of previous assessments, thereby reducing unnecessary duplication of assessment and increasing local confidence in inter-agency work. Knowledge of the Assessment Framework can inform contributions by all agencies and disciplines when assessing children about whom there are child safety concerns (Paragraphs 5.13 and 5.33 in *Working Together to Safeguard Children*, 1999).

Effective collaborative work between staff of different disciplines and agencies assessing children in need and their families requires a common language to understand the needs of children, shared values about what is in children's best interests and a joint commitment to improving the outcomes for children. The framework for assessment provides that common language based on explicit values about children, knowledge about what children need to ensure their successful development, and the factors in their lives which may positively or negatively influence their upbringing. This increases the likelihood of parents and children experiencing consistency between professionals and themselves about what will be important for children's wellbeing and healthy development.

Government Guidance on promoting independence in adult social services, *Achieving Fairer Access to Adult Social Care Services* (Department of Health, forthcoming, a) will address how to respond to social services referrals regarding adults. With any adult referral, social services should check whether the person has parenting responsibilities for a child under 18. If so, the initial assessment should explore any parenting and child related issues in accordance with the *Framework for the Assessment of Children in Need and their Families* Guidance and provide services as appropriate. The needs of the adult should be assessed in accordance with *Achieving Fair Access to Adult Social Care Services.*

The Policy Context

The Government is committed to ending child poverty, tackling social exclusion and promoting the welfare of all children – so that they can thrive and have the opportunity to fulfil their potential as citizens throughout their lives. There are a number of programmes such as Sure Start, Connexions and Quality Protects and a range of policies to support families, promote educational attainment, reduce truancy and school exclusion and secure a future for all young people in education, employment or training. They all aim to ensure that children and families most at risk of social exclusion have every opportunity to build successful, independent lives.

At the same time, the Government is committed to improving the quality and management of those services responsible for supporting children and families particularly through the modernisation of social services, through the promotion of co-operation between all statutory agencies and through building effective partnerships with voluntary and private agencies.

Promoting the wellbeing of children to ensure optimal outcomes requires integration at both national and local levels: joined up government – in respect both of policy making and of service delivery – is central to the current extensive policy agenda. A Ministerial Group on the Family, supported by the Family Policy Unit in the Home Office, encourages this approach at Government level. Its aim is to provide a new emphasis on looking more widely at the needs of all children and families in the community and to develop a programme of measures which will strengthen family life.

Early intervention is essential to support children and families before problems, either from within the family or as a result of external factors, which have an impact on parenting capacity and family life escalate into crisis or abuse. Government departments, statutory and voluntary agencies, academics and practitioners contribute to this work. Good joint working practices and understanding at a local level are vital to the success of the early intervention agenda. Local agencies, including schools and education support services, social services departments, youth offending teams, primary and more specialist health care services and voluntary and private agencies should work together to establish agreed referral protocols which will help to ensure that early indications of a child being at risk of social exclusion receive appropriate attention.

The development of a framework for assessing children in need and their families will contribute to integrated working. The new framework was announced by the Secretary of State for Health in September 1998. Its primary purpose is to improve outcomes for children in need. It is also designed to assist local authority departments and health authorities meet one of the Government's objectives for children's social services (Department of Health, 1999e) - to ensure that referral and assessment processes discriminate effectively between different types and levels of need, and produce a timely service response.

The Contents of the Guidance

The Guidance starts by outlining the legislation, responsibilities and principles which underpin the work of local authority departments and health authorities in promoting and safeguarding children's welfare and assessing children's needs. It then describes the framework and the assessment process in more detail in Chapters 2, 3 and 4. There is reference to the needs of children in general and to children who may have specific needs and impairments throughout the Guidance. Roles and responsibilities in inter-agency assessment are described in Chapter 5. The Guidance concludes by considering the organisational arrangements which should be in place to support effective assessment of children in need.

Relationship to Previous Guidance on Assessment

This Guidance builds on and supersedes earlier Department of Health guidance on assessing children, *Protecting Children: A Guide for Social Workers undertaking a Comprehensive Assessment* (1988). That publication (often referred to as the 'Orange Book') has been widely used by social work practitioners as a guide to comprehensive assessment for long term planning in child protection cases. Its purpose was to assist social work practitioners, in consultation with other agencies, to understand the child and family's situation more fully once concerns about significant harm had been established following initial enquiries and assessment. Much of its thinking about children's development and parents' capacity to respond to children's needs has been incorporated into the Assessment Framework.

However, over the years concerns have arisen about the use made of *Protecting Children.* Inspections and research have shown that the guide was sometimes followed mechanistically and used as a check list, without any differentiation according to the child's or family's circumstances. Assessment was regarded as an event rather than as a process and services were withheld awaiting the completion of an assessment. In some authorities, an all or nothing approach was found; either very detailed comprehensive assessments were carried out or there was no record of any analysis of the child and the family's circumstances. The framework for assessing children in need and their families contained in this volume is underpinned by a set of principles which seek to remedy any misunderstandings about the task of working with children and families in order to understand what is happening to them and how they might best be helped.

Effective Implementation

A range of organisational arrangements need to be in place to ensure sound practice in using the framework for assessing children in need and their families. The effectiveness of assessment processes will be measurable over time by evidence of improving outcomes for children and families known to social services departments. The Department of Health will be working closely with all those involved in providing services to children to develop appropriate arrangements at national and local level, to learn from the experiences of children and families and to evaluate the impact this approach to assessment is having on outcomes for children in need.

1 Children in Need

Children and Families in England

1.1 There are approximately eleven million children in England. It is estimated that over four million of them are living in families with less than half the average household income. By other calculations, well over three million children are living in poverty (Utting, 1995). Where these children live is significant. 'Over the last generation, this has become a divided country. While most areas have benefited from rising living standards, the poorest neighbourhoods have tended to become more run down, more prone to crime and more cut off from the labour market' (Social Exclusion Unit, 1998). Estimates vary about how many neighbourhoods are in the poorest categories, ranging from 1,600 to 4,000 in Britain as a whole. In response to these trends, the Government is developing major strategies to tackle the root causes of poverty and social exclusion, and to respond to the serious and multi-faceted problems for children and their families which these can create, particularly in the poorest areas. These strategies also aim to encourage and promote preventive and early intervention approaches to help reduce the scale and difficulty of such problems and to tackle them before they become entrenched.

1.2 Just as the problems facing families are often interlinked, so the services provided for children and their families need to work closely together to be most effective. Everyone benefits if services are properly co-ordinated and integrated. It is the purpose of Children's Services Planning (Department of Health and Department for Education and Employment,1996) to identify the broad range and level of need in an area and to develop corporate, inter-agency, community based plans of action to provide the most effective network of services within the resources available. It is important that all those concerned with services to children and families – statutory and voluntary bodies, community groups and families – contribute to the development of these plans.

1.3 It is recognised that many families are under considerable stress, that being a parent is hard work, and families have a right to expect practical support from universal services, such as health and education. The importance of all parents having available to them good quality local resources is acknowledged. The Government is committed to supporting parenting and has set up the National Family and Parenting Institute to assess the support needs of families, to raise public awareness of the importance of parenting and the needs of children, to map and disseminate information and good practice, and to provide advice to Government and others in a way which reflects our culturally diverse society. It will work collaboratively with others to help develop parent support services and to influence the research agenda and analyse and disseminate research findings. It will draw on anonymised data from ParentLine Plus, whose freephone national telephone Helpline is available to provide a service to all parents. Steps are being taken through public service and welfare reforms to modernise the National Health Service, raise standards in local schools, provide good out of school care, reduce crime, ensure streets are safe for families and strengthen communities' capacities to respond to and support families. This forms an ambitious programme which will take many years to deliver in full and requires continuous concerted central and local government effort.

1.4 All families may experience difficulties from time to time for a whole host of reasons which may have an impact on their children. These reasons may include the death of a family member, physical or mental ill health in the family, the breakdown of marital or other significant relationships, sudden loss of employment, multiple births, or having a child with special educational needs. Not all adults are well prepared for the daily upheavals and stress of bringing up a child. Some parents may find one particular stage in their child's life especially stressful, for example adolescence. Many cope well enough with one problem but a combination of problems can have a cummulative debilitating effect.

1.5 Many families coping with extremely difficult circumstances receive sufficient support from friends, relatives and services in the community including universal services to overcome potential disadvantage. They are not likely to seek or require additional services. In this sense, parenting has been called 'a buffered system' (Belsky and Vondra, 1989). In some cases the buffers of family and community resources may not exist or be sufficient to ensure the current or future wellbeing of the child. It is in these situations that additional support or services may be necessary, some of which may be purchased by parents (such as day care) or obtained directly from other statutory or voluntary agencies (such as befriending by a volunteer). Some parents may turn to or be referred to child welfare agencies in the community and require targeted services from health, education and social services.

The Extent of Children in Need

1.6 Children may be defined as in need in many different circumstances. The information on how many children are known to social services is not available nationally, but current estimates suggest between 300,000 and 400,000 children are known at any one time. Figure 1 shows how the extent of need can be represented within the context of vulnerable[1] and all children. According to Department of Health statistics, about 53,000 children are looked after in statutory care at any one time (Department of Health, 1999b). This figure excludes those disabled children receiving respite care. Approximately 32,000 children's names are on a Child Protection Register at any one time because they require a child protection plan (Department of Health, 1999i).

1.7 The families referred to or seeking help from social services will have differing levels of need. Many will be helped by advice or practical services or short term intervention. A smaller proportion will have problems of such complexity and seriousness that they

1. Vulnerable children are those disadvantaged children who would benefit from extra help from public agencies in order to make the best of their life chances. Four million children live in families with less than half the average household income.

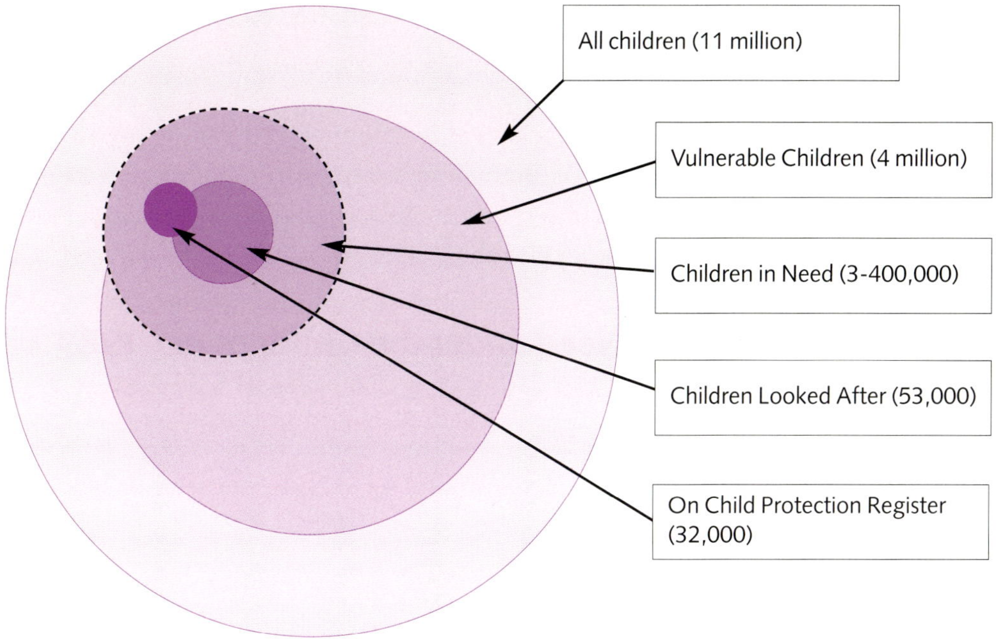

Figure 1 **Representation of Extent of Children in Need in England at any one time**

require more detailed assessment, involving other agencies in that process, leading to appropriate plans and interventions.

1.8 This can best be illustrated by examining the experience of one unitary authority, as an example:

EXAMPLE: UNITARY AUTHORITY 1997–1999

	1997/98	1998/99
Total child population under the age of 18	35,086	35,086
Children referred to social services as children in need	4.000	4,097
Child Protection s47 enquiries carried out	1,752	708
Total number of children on Child Protection Register at year end	161	96
Total number of children looked after at year end	217	202

1.9 This authority, in parallel with many others, has been working for the past three years with its community and local agencies to take a broader-based approach to helping vulnerable children and their families and has begun to find:

- a slight increase in child care referrals;
- the majority of referrals more appropriately dealt with under s17;
- proportionally fewer child protection s47 enquiries;
- fewer children's names being placed on the child protection register;
- a decrease in the numbers of children being looked after;

- a decrease in the numbers of children accommodated on an unplanned basis;
- a reduction in the anxiety levels of all staff in child and family work.

1.10 Ensuring that assessment discriminates effectively between different types and levels of need, from the point of referral onwards, is critical to the objective of improving the effectiveness of services to children and securing best value from available resources (Department of Health, 1999e).

Children in Need under the Children Act 1989

1.11 The obligations of the State to assist families who need help in bringing up their own children are laid down in legislation. Part III of the Children Act 1989 is the basis in law for the provision of local services to children in need: children in this respect are defined as under the age of 18 (s105).

It shall be the general duty of every local authority –

- *to safeguard and promote the welfare of children within their area who are in need; and*
- *so far as is consistent with that duty, to promote the upbringing of such children by their families, by providing a range and level of services appropriate to those children's needs.*

Children Act 1989 s17(1)

1.12 The Children Act 1989 places a specific duty on agencies to co-operate in the interests of children in need in section 27. Section 322 of the Education Act 1996 also places a duty on the local authority to assist the local education authority where any child who has special educational needs.

Where it appears to a local authority that any authority or other person mentioned in sub-section (3) could, by taking any specified action, help in the exercise of any of their functions under this Part, they may request the help of that other authority or persons, specifying the action in question.

An authority whose help is so requested shall comply with the request if it is compatible with their own statutory or other duties and obligations and does not unduly prejudice the discharge of any of their functions.

The persons are –

a. *any local authority;*
b. *any local education authority;*
c. *any local housing authority;*
d. *any health authority, special health authority, National Health Services Trust or Primary Care Trust; and*
e. *any person authorised by the Secretary of State for the purpose of this section.*

Children Act 1989 s27

1.13 Several key principles which underpin the Children Act 1989 are found in Part III of the Act:

- it is the duty of the State through local authorities to **both safeguard and promote the welfare of vulnerable children;**

- it is in the children's best interests to be brought up in their own families wherever possible;
- whilst it is parents' responsibility to bring up their children, they may need assistance from time to time to do so;
- they should be able to call upon services, including accommodation (under s20 of the Children Act 1989), from or with the help of the local authority when they are required.

The notion of partnership between State and families is thus also established in this Part of the Act.

1.14 In order to carry out these duties the meaning of **safeguarding** and **promoting** within the parameters of the Children Act 1989 should be appreciated, as should the contribution of these objectives to strengthening and supplementing parental capacities so that children may grow up in their families, wherever possible.

1.15 Safeguarding has two elements:

- a duty to protect children from maltreatment;
- a duty to prevent impairment.

1.16 The duty to protect children from maltreatment demands knowledge and understanding of the law and the accompanying government guidance, *Working Together to Safeguard Children* (1999).

1.17 However, safeguarding children should not be seen as a separate activity from promoting their welfare. They are two sides of the same coin. Promoting welfare has a wider, more positive, action centred approach embedded in a philosophy of creating opportunities to enable children to have optimum life chances in adulthood, as well as ensuring they are growing up in circumstances consistent with the provision of safe and effective care. A useful framework for looking at the policy context of children in need and the value of applying a twin approach of safeguarding and promoting welfare at different levels of intervention has been developed by Hardiker *et al* (1996; 1999). Their grid, reproduced in Appendix B, can be used to help the planning and appropriate provision of services.

1.18 Children who are defined as in need under the Children Act 1989 are those whose vulnerability is such that they are unlikely to reach or maintain a satisfactory level of health and development, or their health and development will be significantly impaired without the provision of services. The critical factors to be taken into account in deciding whether a child is in need under the Children Act 1989 are what will happen to a child's health and development **without services**, and the likely effect the services will have on the child's standard of health and development. Determining who is in need, what those needs are, and how services will have an effect on outcomes for children requires professional judgement by social services staff together with colleagues from other professional disciplines who are working with children and families.

1.19 The criteria for defining who is in need are spelt out above in section 17(10) of the Children Act 1989. The criteria include a child who is disabled. A child is defined as disabled *'if he is blind, deaf or dumb or suffers from mental disorder of any kind, or is substantially and permanently handicapped by illness, injury or congenital or other such disability as may be prescribed'* (s17(11)). This definition does not preclude children whose impairment may be less substantial from being defined as children in need under the other categories. Thus, where the family, educational, social or environmental circumstances may be preventing such a disabled child from achieving or maintaining a reasonable standard of health or development without the provision of services, the local authority should consider whether that child is a child in need.

A child shall be taken to be in need if –

a. he is unlikely to achieve or maintain or to have the opportunity of achieving or maintaining, a reasonable standard of health or development without the provision for him of services by a local authority ...

b. his health or development is likely to be significantly impaired, or further impaired, without the provision for him of such services; or

c. he is disabled,

And "family" in relation to such a child, includes any person who has parental responsibility for the child and any other person with whom he has been living.

Children Act 1989 s17(10)

Assessing Children in Need

1.20 The duties and powers of the local authority to assess the needs of a child and to provide services are outlined in Part III of the Children Act 1989, in particular section 17, and Schedule 2 Part I. Part III is the main part of the Act (titled *Local Authority Support for Children and Families*) about the delivery of services by social services departments. Other Parts (I, II, IV and V) outline the way in which court orders may be obtained to authorise or enforce certain actions, in relation to family proceedings, care and supervision and the protection of children.

1.21 The Act gives local authority social services the power to assess children's needs as follows:

Where it appears to a local authority that a child within their area is in need, the authority may assess his needs for the purposes of this Act at the same time as any assessment of his needs is made under:

- *the Chronically Sick and Disabled Persons Act 1970;*
- *the Education Act 1996;*
- *the Disabled Persons (Services, Consultation and Representation) Act 1986; or*
- *any other enactment.*

Children Act 1989 (Schedule 2, paragraph 3)

1.22 Professionals from a number of agencies, but in particular health and education, are a key source of referral to social services departments of children who are, or may be, in need. They may already know these children and their families well and, if so, they will be key in assisting social services departments to carry out their assessment functions under the Children Act 1989. Knowledge of the Assessment Framework will be of use to all professionals when they are contributing to assessments of children in need, including when they are undertaking or contributing to assessments as part of their responsibilities for safeguarding children under *Working Together to Safeguard Children* (1999).

1.23 The following principles should guide inter-agency, inter-disciplinary work with children in need. It is essential to be clear about:

- the purpose and anticipated outputs from the assessment;
- the legislative basis for the assessment;
- the protocols and procedures to be followed;
- which agency, team or professional has lead responsibility;
- how the child and family members will be involved in the assessment process;
- which professional has lead responsibility for analysing the assessment findings and constructing a plan;
- the respective roles of each professional involved in the assessment;
- the way in which information will be shared across professional boundaries and within agencies, and be recorded;
- which professional will have responsibility for taking forward the plan when it is agreed.

1.24 It is important to agree an assessment plan with the child and family, so that all parties understand who is doing what, when, and how the various assessments will be used to inform overall judgements about a child's needs and subsequent planning. When joint assessments are being undertaken, clarity is required about whether this means one professional will undertake an assessment on behalf of the team or whether several types of assessment are to be undertaken in parallel. In the latter situation, thought is required regarding how these can be organised to avoid duplication. Service users, in particular parents of disabled children, report that assessments are often repetitive and uninformed by previous work. The agreed process should be based on what is appropriate for the needs of the particular child and family, taking account of the purpose of the assessment, rather than what fits best with professional systems. Agreed protocols and procedures should be flexible enough to accommodate different ways of undertaking assessments within the overall Assessment Framework.

Children Who are Suffering or are Likely to Suffer Significant Harm

1.25 Some children are in need because they are suffering or likely to suffer significant harm. Concerns about maltreatment may be the reason for referral of a family to social services or concerns may arise during the course of providing services to a family. In such circumstances, the local authority is obliged to consider initiating enquiries to find out what is happening to a child and whether action should be taken to protect a child. This obligation is set out in Part V s47 of the Children Act 1989 *(Protection of Children)*:

1.26 This section of the Act requires local authorities to consider if action is necessary. To make enquiries implies the need to assess what is happening to a child. The procedures for such action to be followed are laid down in *Working Together to Safeguard Children* (1999). Where there is reasonable cause to suspect that a child may be suffering or is at risk of suffering significant harm, section 47 (9)(10)(11) places a duty on:

- any local authority;
- any local education authority;
- any housing authority;
- any health authority, special health authority, National Health Service Trust or Primary Care Trust; and
- any person authorised by the Secretary of State.

to help a local authority with its enquiries. In addition, the Police have a duty and a responsibility to investigate criminal offences committed against children.

> *Where a local authority –*
>
> *a. are informed that a child who lives, or is found in their area –*
>
> *i is the subject of an emergency protection order; or*
> *ii is in police protection; or*
>
> *b. have reasonable cause to suspect that a child who lives, or is found in their area is suffering, or is likely to suffer, significant harm,*
>
> *the authority shall make, or cause to be made, such enquiries as they consider necessary to enable them to decide whether they should take any action to safeguard or promote the child's welfare.*
>
> **Children Act 1989 s47(1)**

1.27 It is important to emphasise that the assessment should concentrate on the harm that has occurred or is likely to occur to the child as a result of child maltreatment, in order to inform future plans and the nature of services required. This is because there is substantial research evidence to suggest that the health and development of children, including their educational attainment, may be severely affected if they have been subjected to child maltreatment (Varma (ed), 1993; Adcock and White (eds), 1998; Jones and Ramchandani, 1999). It is not enough to have established the harm: action should be taken to safeguard and promote children's welfare. The duty to both safeguard and promote the child's welfare continues throughout the process of finding out whether there are grounds for concern that a child may be suffering or is at risk of suffering significant harm and deciding what action should be taken. Services may be provided to safeguard and promote the child's welfare (under Part III of the Act), while enquiries are being carried out, or, after protective action has been taken while an application is being made for a care or supervision order (under Part IV).

Providing Services

1.28 The local authority has a duty to respond to children in need in their area in the following ways:

- to provide services to children in need (s17);

- to provide such day care for children in need as appropriate (s18);
- to provide accommodation and maintenance to any child in need (s20 and s23);
- to advise, assist and befriend a child whilst he is being looked after and when he ceases to be looked after by the authority (s24);
- to provide services to minimise the effect of disabilities (Schedule 2, paragraph 6);
- to take steps to prevent neglect or ill-treatment (Schedule 2, paragraph 4);
- to take steps to encourage children not to commit criminal offences (Schedule 2, paragraph 7(b)); *and*
- to provide family centres (Schedule 2, paragraph 9).

1.29 The provision of services has a very broad meaning; the aim may be to prevent deterioration, that is to stop situations from getting worse, as well as to improve a child's health and development. Decisions about which services to provide should be based on an assessment of the child and families circumstances, in the following three domains: child's developmental needs, parenting capacity, and family and environmental factors. This framework for assessing children in need and their families is discussed fully in Chapter 2. It should be stressed that services, such as direct work with children and families, may be offered at the same time as family proceedings are in progress. The one does not preclude the other. **Furthermore, services may be provided to any members of the family in order to assist a child in need** (s17(3) of the Children Act 1989). The needs of parent carers are an integral part of an assessment. Providing services which meet the needs of parents is often the most effective means of promoting the welfare of children, in particular disabled children.

1.30 Services may include those provided by local authority children's services or by local authority adult services or by other agencies, on a single agency, inter-agency or multi-agency basis. By **inter-agency** it is meant that services are provided by individual agencies according to an agreed plan. By **multi-agency**, it is meant that services are provided by agencies acting in concert and drawing on pooled resources or a pooled budget or services defined as such in legislation, for example youth offending teams.

1.31 Services may be provided on a one off or episodic basis or over a longer period of time as determined by the child's plan (see paragraph 4.33). These provisions are often described as a **continuum of services** to support children and their families, and include care for a child in accommodation away from home. It is the function of Children's Services Planning to make sure this continuum of services is in place. Services provided in parallel with court proceedings or following on from a court order are provided under Part III of the Act.

1.32 In determining what services should be provided to a particular child and his family, social services departments are not charged with the same duty as the courts that the child's welfare shall be the 'paramount consideration' (s1(1)). Rather they have a broader duty to promote children's welfare to achieve the best possible outcomes for that particular child. Social services, in their assessment of whether a child is in need and how to respond to those needs, also have to take into consideration other children in the family and the general circumstances of that family. Social services have to identify the impact of what is happening to the child and also the likely impact of any intervention on that child and on other family members. Assessment requires careful consideration of the repercussions or consequences of providing specific types of services and the extent to which they will both safeguard and promote a particular child's welfare and development. This may be a complex equation which requires a high level of skill and professional judgement, involving all agency partners.

Principles Underpinning Assessment of Children in Need

1.33 Important principles underpin the approach to assessing children in need and their families which is outlined in this Guidance. They are important in understanding the development of the framework and in considering how an assessment should be carried out.

PRINCIPLES UNDERPINNING THE ASSESSMENT FRAMEWORK

Assessments:

- are child centred;
- are rooted in child development;
- are ecological in their approach;
- ensure equality of opportunity;
- involve working with children and families;
- build on strengths as well as identify difficulties;
- are inter-agency in their approach to assessment and the provision of services;
- are a continuing process, not a single event;
- are carried out in parallel with other action and providing services;
- are grounded in evidence based knowledge.

Child Centred

1.34 Fundamental to establishing whether a child is in need and how those needs should be best met is that the approach must be child centred. This means that the child is seen and kept in focus throughout the assessment and that account is always taken of the child's perspective. In complex situations where much is happening, attention can be diverted from the child to other issues which the family may be facing, such as a high level of conflict between adult family members, or depression being experienced by a parent or acute housing problems. This can result in the child becoming lost during assessment and the impact of the family and environmental circumstances on the child not being clearly identified and understood. The significance of seeing and observing the child throughout any assessment cannot be overstated.

1.35 The importance, therefore, of undertaking direct work with children during assessment is emphasised, including developing multiple, age, gender and culturally appropriate methods for ascertaining their wishes and feelings, and understanding the meaning of their experiences to them. Throughout the assessment process, the safety of the child should be ensured.

Rooted in Child Development

1.36 A thorough understanding of child development is critical to work with children and their families. Children have a range of different and complex developmental needs which must be met during different stages of childhood if optimal outcomes are to be achieved. Disabled children, including those with learning disabilities, may have a different rate of progress across the various developmental dimensions. Many disabled children will have quite individual patterns of development, for example a child with autism may acquire some skills ahead of the usual milestones but may never develop some communication skills. In addition, different aspects of development will have more or less weight at different stages of a child's life. For example, in the early years there is an emphasis on developing cognitive and language skills, achieving physical milestones and forming secure attachments; in middle childhood, social and educational development become more prominent; while the adolescent strives to reconcile the tensions between social and emotional dependence and independence.

1.37 Each child's development is significantly shaped by his or her particular experiences and the interaction between a series of factors. Some factors are intrinsic to individual children, such as characteristics of genetic inheritance or temperament. Other factors may include particular health problems or an impairment. Others may relate to their culture and to the physical and emotional environment in which a child is living.

1.38 Children referred for help are frequently very vulnerable and their opportunities to reach their full potential may have been or may be likely to be compromised in some way, for a variety of reasons. It is, therefore, crucial to know about the importance of developmental milestones which children need to reach, if they are to be healthy and achieve their full potential. This knowledge should recognise also that children are individuals and variations may occur in that sequence of development: such variations, however, may indicate services are necessary. Professionals should understand the consequences of variations for particular children of different ages, some of whom may have special educational needs and profound difficulties. Furthermore, they have to understand the significance of timing in a child's life. Children may not be getting what they require at a crucial stage in their development and time is passing. Plans and interventions should be based on a clear assessment of the developmental progress and difficulties a child may be experiencing and ensure that planned action is timely and appropriate in terms of the child's developmental needs.

Ecological Approach

1.39 An understanding of a child must be located within the context of the child's family (parents or caregivers and the wider family) and of the community and culture in which he or she is growing up. The significance of understanding the parent-child relationship has long been part of child welfare practice: less so the importance of the interface between environmental factors and a child's development, and the influence of these environmental factors on parents' capacities to respond to their child's needs (Jack, 1997; Stevenson, 1998 and others). The association between economic disadvantage and the chances that children will fail to thrive (Utting, 1995) and the association between a teenager's friendship group and pro-social and anti-social behaviour (Rutter *et al*, 1998) are well researched. So is the impact on parenting capacity of a supportive wider family or of struggling to bring up children in impoverished living conditions. 'Living on a low income in a run down neighbourhood does not make it impossible to be the affectionate, authoritative parent of healthy, sociable children. But it does, undeniably, make it more difficult' (Utting, 1995, p. 40).

1.40 **Assessment, therefore, should take account of three domains:**

- **the child's developmental needs;**
- **the parents' or caregivers' capacities to respond appropriately;**
- **the wider family and environmental factors.**

1.41 The interaction between the three domains and the way they influence each other must be carefully analysed in order to gain a complete picture of a child's unmet needs and how to identify the best response to them.

Ensuring Equality of Opportunity

1.42 The Children Act 1989 is built on the premise that 'children and young people and their parents should all be considered as individuals with particular needs and potentialities' (Department of Health, 1989), that differences in bringing up children due to family structures, religion, culture and ethnic origins should be respected and understood and that those children with 'specific social needs arising out of disability or a health condition' have their assessed needs met and reviewed (Department of Health, 1998a). Ensuring that all children who are assessed as in need have the opportunity to achieve optimal development, according to their circumstances and age, is an important principle. Furthermore, since discrimination of all kinds is an everyday reality in many children's lives, every effort must be made to ensure that agencies' responses do not reflect or reinforce that experience and indeed, should counteract it. Some vulnerable children may have been particularly disadvantaged in their access to important opportunities, such as those who have suffered multiple family disruptions or prolonged maltreatment by abuse or neglect and are subsequently looked by the local authority. Their health and educational needs will require particular attention in order to optimise their long term outcomes in young adulthood.

1.43 Ensuring equality of opportunity does not mean that all children are treated the same. It does mean understanding and working sensitively and knowledgeably with diversity to identify the particular issues for a child and his/her family, taking account of experiences and family context. This is further elaborated in the chapters in the accompanying practice guidance on working with disabled children and with black children.

Working with Children and their Families

1.44 The majority of parents want to do the best for their children. Whatever their circumstances or difficulties, the concept of partnership between the State and the family, in situations where families are in need of assistance in bringing up their children, lies at the heart of child care legislation. The importance of partnership has been further reinforced by a substantial number of research findings, including the child protection studies (Department of Health, 1995d) and family support studies (Butt and Box,

1998; Aldgate and Bradley, 1999; Tunstill and Aldgate, 2000). In the process of finding out what is happening to a child, it will be critical to develop a co-operative working relationship, so that parents or caregivers feel respected and informed, that staff are being open and honest with them, and that they in turn are confident about providing vital information about their child, themselves and their circumstances.

1.45 Working with family members is not an end in itself; the objective must always be to safeguard and promote the welfare of the child. The child, therefore, must be kept in focus. It requires sensitivity to and understanding of the circumstances of families and their particular needs, for example where English is not a parent's first language or where adults who are significant to a child are not living in the same household or where a parent is disabled or mentally ill. For a disabled parent reasonable adjustments will be needed, for example, it may be necessary to provide information to a blind parent in an alternative format such as Braille or on audio tape, or to communicate with a deaf parent using British Sign Language.

1.46 Parents value taking part in discussions about how and where the assessment will be carried out, as well as what they hope it will achieve. Similarly, according to the age and development of the child, listening to what children have to say and working openly and honestly is valued by them and produces more effective outcomes. This is discussed further in Chapter 3.

1.47 Developing a working relationship with children and family members will not always be easy to achieve and can be difficult especially when there have been concerns about significant harm to the child. However resistant the family or difficult the circumstances, it remains important to continue to try to find ways of engaging the family in the assessment process. Use of mediation may be helpful in assisting professionals and family members to work together. The quality of the early or initial contact will affect later working relationships and the ability of professionals to secure an agreed understanding of what is happening and to provide help. Studies have found that even in situations where child sexual abuse is alleged, despite early difficulties that may arise because of having to take immediate child protective action, it may still be possible to work with children and their parents (Cleaver and Freeman, 1995; Jones and Ramchandani, 1999). Working with children and family members, where there are concerns about a child suffering significant harm is discussed in paragraphs 7.2 to 7.12 in *Working Together to Safeguard Children* (1999).

Building on Strengths as well as Identifying Difficulties

1.48 It is important that an approach to assessment, which is based on a full understanding of what is happening to a child in the context of his or her family and the wider community, examines carefully the nature of the interactions between the child, family and environmental factors and identifies both positive and negative influences. These will vary for each child. Nothing can be assumed; the facts must be sought, the meaning attached to them explored and weighed up with the family. Sometimes assessments have been largely in terms of a child or family's difficulties or problems, or the risks seen to be attached to particular behaviours or situations. What is working well or what may be acting as positive factors for the child and family may be overlooked. For example, a single mother, in crisis over health, financial and housing problems, may still be managing to get her child up in time in the mornings, washed, dressed, breakfasted and off to school each day. An older child, living in a family periodically disrupted by domestic violence, may be provided with welcome respite care on a regular basis by a grandmother living locally. Working with a child or family's strengths may be an important part of a plan to resolve difficulties.

1.49 This is not to suggest that staff should suspend their critical professional judgement and adopt a 'rule of optimism' (Dingwall et al, 1983). It is important, however, that they not only identify the deficits in assessing a family's situation, but also make a realistic and informed appraisal of the strengths and resources in the family and the relative weight that should be given to each. These can be mobilised to safeguard and promote the child's welfare.

Inter-Agency Approach to Assessment and Provision of Services

1.50 From birth, all children will become involved with a variety of different agencies in the community, particularly in relation to their health, day care and educational development. A range of professionals, including midwives, health visitors, general practitioners, nursery staff and teachers, will have a role in assessing their general wellbeing and development. Children who are vulnerable are, therefore, likely to be identified by these professionals, who will have an important responsibility in deciding whether to refer them to social services for further assessment and help. The knowledge they already have about a child and family is an essential component of any assessment. These agencies may also be required to provide more specialist assessment for those smaller numbers of children where there are particular causes for concern. Similarly, responding to the needs of vulnerable children may require services from agencies other than social services or in combination with social services help. Inter-agency work starts as soon as there are concerns about a child's welfare, not just when there is an enquiry about significant harm. An important underlying principle of the approach to assessment in this Guidance, therefore, is that it is based on a inter-agency model in which it is not just social services departments which are the assessors and providers of services.

A Continuing Process, not a Single Event

1.51 Understanding what is happening to a vulnerable child within the context of his or her family and the local community cannot be achieved as a single event. It must necessarily be a process of gathering information from a variety of sources and making sense of it with the family and, very often, with several professionals concerned with the child's welfare.

1.52 This assessment process involves one or more of the following:

- establishing good working relationships with the child and family;
- developing a deeper understanding through multiple approaches to the assessment task;
- setting up joint or parallel assessment arrangements with other professionals and agencies, as appropriate;

- determining which types of intervention are most likely to be effective for which needs.

1.53 For many children who come to the attention of social services departments, the process will be relatively straightforward and short term. The more complex or serious a child's situation, however, the more time it may take to understand thoroughly what is happening to the child, the reasons why and the impact on the child and the more it is also likely to involve several agencies in that process. Where there are concerns about a child's safety, decisions to safeguard the child may have to be made quickly pending greater understanding of the child's circumstances. Once it has been established whether a child is in need, further questions will remain to be answered about:

- the parents' views of the child's needs and services required;
- the precise nature of these needs;
- the reasons for them;
- the priority for action and/or resources;
- the potential for change in the child and family;
- the best options to be pursued;
- the child's and family's response to intervention;
- how well the child is doing.

Assessment should continue throughout a period of intervention, and intervention may start at the beginning of an assessment.

1.54 Assessment is thus an iterative process which for some children will continue throughout work with the child and the family or caregivers. In order to achieve the best outcomes, the framework should be used also at important decision making times when reviewing the child's progress and future plans. Use of the Assessment Framework linked to the Looking After Children materials which have been used to monitor the child's progress whilst they have been looked after will enhance care planning and reviewing processes. This will provide an integrated framework for children looked after which should be used at key decision making points including return home from residential or foster care, or longer term plans for an alternative family placement such as adoption, or when leaving care.

1.55 This does not mean that assessment should be over intrusive, repeated unnecessarily or continued without any clear purpose or outcome. Effective discrimination between different types and levels of need are key considerations.

Action and Services are Provided in Parallel with Assessment

1.56 Although assessment is generally described in this Guidance as a discrete process which will result in an understanding of need, from which a plan of action and intervention can be developed, in many situations there is inevitably overlap between these different activities. Undertaking an assessment with a family can begin a process of understanding and change by key family members. A practitioner may, during the process of gathering information, be instrumental in bringing about change by the questions asked, by listening to members of the family, by validating the family's difficulties or concerns, and by providing information and advice. The process of assessment should be therapeutic in itself. This does not preclude taking timely action either to provide immediate services or to take steps to protect a child who is suffering or is likely to suffer significant harm. Action and services should be provided according to the needs of the child and family, in parallel with assessment where necessary, and not await completion of the assessment.

Grounded in Evidence

1.57 Each professional discipline derives its knowledge from a particular theoretical base, related research findings and accumulated practice wisdom and experience. Social work practice, however, differs in that it derives its knowledge from theory and research in many different disciplines. Practice is also based on policies laid down in legislation and government guidance. It is essential that practitioners and their managers ensure that practice and its supervision are grounded in the most up to date knowledge and that they make use of the resources described in the practice guidance as well as other critical materials, including:

- relevant research findings;
- national and local statistical data;
- national policy and practice guidance;
- Social Services Inspectorate Inspection Standards;
- Government and local inspection, audit and performance assessment reports;
- lessons learnt from national and local inquiries and reviews of cases of child maltreatment.

1.58 Practice is expected to be evidence based, by which it is meant that practitioners:

- use knowledge critically from research and practice about the needs of children and families and the outcomes of services and interventions to inform their assessment and planning;
- record and update information systematically, distinguishing sources of information, for example direct observation, other agency records or interviews with family members;
- learn from the views of users of services ie. children and families;
- valuate continously whether the intervention is effective in responding to the needs of an individual child and family and modifying their interventions accordingly;
- evaluate rigorously the information, processes and outcomes from the practitioner's own interventions to develop practice wisdom.

1.59 The combination of evidence based practice grounded in knowledge with finely balanced professional judgement is the foundation for effective practice with children and families.

1.60 The knowledge base from which these principles are derived and the application of the principles to the process of assessing children in need and their families are developed in subsequent chapters.

DIMENSIONS OF CHILD'S DEVELOPMENTAL NEEDS

Health

Includes growth and development as well as physical and mental wellbeing. The impact of genetic factors and of any impairment should be considered. Involves receiving appropriate health care when ill, an adequate and nutritious diet, exercise, immunisations where appropriate and developmental checks, dental and optical care and, for older children, appropriate advice and information on issues that have an impact on health, including sex education and substance misuse.

Education

Covers all areas of a child's cognitive development which begins from birth.
Includes opportunities: for play and interaction with other children; to have access to books; to acquire a range of skills and interests; to experience success and achievement. Involves an adult interested in educational activities, progress and achievements, who takes account of the child's starting point and any special educational needs.

Emotional and Behavioural Development

Concerns the appropriateness of response demonstrated in feelings and actions by a child, initially to parents and caregivers and, as the child grows older, to others beyond the family.
Includes nature and quality of early attachments, characteristics of temperament, adaptation to change, response to stress and degree of appropriate self control.

Identity

Concerns the child's growing sense of self as a separate and valued person.
Includes the child's view of self and abilities, self image and self esteem, and having a positive sense of individuality. Race, religion, age, gender, sexuality and disability may all contribute to this. Feelings of belonging and acceptance by family, peer group and wider society, including other cultural groups.

Family and Social Relationships

Development of empathy and the capacity to place self in someone else's shoes.
Includes a stable and affectionate relationship with parents or caregivers, good relationships with siblings, increasing importance of age appropriate friendships with peers and other significant persons in the child's life and response of family to these relationships.

Social Presentation

Concerns child's growing understanding of the way in which appearance, behaviour, and any impairment are perceived by the outside world and the impression being created.
Includes appropriateness of dress for age, gender, culture and religion; cleanliness and personal hygiene; and availability of advice from parents or caregivers about presentation in different settings.

Self Care Skills

Concerns the acquisition by a child of practical, emotional and communication competencies required for increasing independence. Includes early practical skills of dressing and feeding, opportunities to gain confidence and practical skills to undertake activities away from the family and independent living skills as older children.
Includes encouragement to acquire social problem solving approaches. Special attention should be given to the impact of a child's impairment and other vulnerabilities, and on social circumstances affecting these in the development of self care skills.

and the *Assessment of Family Competence, Strengths and Difficulties* developed by Bentovim and Bingley Miller (forthcoming) will be published later this year. In addition there are others which may be of use to assist the process of assessment.

2.8 Use of questionnaires and scales enables children and caregivers to express their views about their particular circumstances. They have been found also to identify areas of concern or difficulty which have not been identified previously through interviews or observations.

Dimensions of Parenting Capacity

2.9 Critically important to a child's health and development is the ability of parents or caregivers to ensure that the child's developmental needs are being appropriately and adequately responded to, and to adapt to his or her changing needs over time. The parenting tasks are described on page 21. Again, these descriptions are illustrative rather than comprehensive of all parenting tasks.

2.10 It is important that parenting capacity be considered in the context of the family's structure and functioning, and who contributes to the parental care of the child (see Family and Environmental Factors, paragraphs 2.13 to 2.25).

2.11 In family situations where there is cause for concern about what is happening to a child, it becomes even more important to gather information about how these tasks are being carried out by each parent or caregiver in terms of:

- their response to a child and his or her behaviour or circumstances;
- the manner in which they are responding to the child's needs and the areas where they are experiencing difficulties in meeting needs or failing to do so;
- the effect this child has on them;
- the quality of the parent – child relationship;
- their understanding of the child's needs and development;
- their comprehension of parenting tasks and the relevance of these to the child's developmental needs;
- the impact of any difficulties they may be experiencing themselves on their ability to carry out parental tasks and responsibilities (distinguishing realisation from aspiration);
- the impact of past experiences on their current parenting capacity;
- their ability to face and accept their difficulties;
- their ability to use support and accept help;
- their capacity for adaptation and change in their parenting response.

Observation of interactions is as critically important as the way they are described by the adults involved.

2.12 The parenting tasks undertaken by fathers or father figures should be addressed alongside those of mothers or mother figures. In some families, a single parent may be

DIMENSIONS OF PARENTING CAPACITY

Basic Care

Providing for the child's physical needs, and appropriate medical and dental care.
Includes provision of food, drink, warmth, shelter, clean and appropriate clothing and adequate personal hygiene.

Ensuring Safety

Ensuring the child is adequately protected from harm or danger.
Includes protection from significant harm or danger, and from contact with unsafe adults/other children and from self-harm. Recognition of hazards and danger both in the home and elsewhere.

Emotional Warmth

Ensuring the child's emotional needs are met and giving the child a sense of being specially valued and a positive sense of own racial and cultural identity.
Includes ensuring the child's requirements for secure, stable and affectionate relationships with significant adults, with appropriate sensitivity and responsiveness to the child's needs. Appropriate physical contact, comfort and cuddling sufficient to demonstrate warm regard, praise and encouragement.

Stimulation

Promoting child's learning and intellectual development through encouragement and cognitive stimulation and promoting social opportunities.
Includes facilitating the child's cognitive development and potential through interaction, communication, talking and responding to the child's language and questions, encouraging and joining the child's play, and promoting educational opportunities. Enabling the child to experience success and ensuring school attendance or equivalent opportunity. Facilitating child to meet challenges of life.

Guidance and Boundaries

Enabling the child to regulate their own emotions and behaviour.
The key parental tasks are *demonstrating and modelling* appropriate behaviour and control of emotions and interactions with others, and *guidance* which involves setting boundaries, so that the child is able to develop an internal model of moral values and conscience, and social behaviour appropriate for the society within which they will grow up. The aim is to enable the child to grow into an autonomous adult, holding their own values, and able to demonstrate appropriate behaviour with others rather than having to be dependent on rules outside themselves. This includes not over protecting children from exploratory and learning experiences.
Includes social problem solving, anger management, consideration for others, and effective discipline and shaping of behaviour.

Stability

Providing a sufficiently stable family environment to enable a child to develop and maintain a secure attachment to the primary caregiver(s) in order to ensure optimal development.
Includes: ensuring secure attachments are not disrupted, providing consistency of emotional warmth over time and responding in a similar manner to the same behaviour. Parental responses change and develop according to child's developmental progress. In addition, ensuring children keep in contact with important family members and significant others.

performing most or all of the parenting tasks. In others, there may be a number of important caregivers in a child's life, each playing a different part which may have positive or negative consequences. A wide range of adults, for example grandparents, step relations, child minders or baby sitters, may have a significant role in caring for a child. A distinction has to be clearly made between the contribution of each parent or caregiver to a child's wellbeing and development. Where a child has suffered significant harm, it is particularly important to distinguish between the capabilities of the abusing parent and the potentially protective parent. This information can also contribute to an understanding of the impact the parents' relationship with each other may have on their respective capacities to respond appropriately to their child's needs. The quality of the inter-parental relationship, which has an impact on the child's wellbeing will be considered more explicitly in the following section on family and environmental factors.

Family and Environmental Factors

2.13 The care and upbringing of children does not take place in a vacuum. All family members are influenced both positively and negatively by the wider family, the neighbourhood and social networks in which they live. The history of the child's family and of individual family members may have a significant impact on the child and parents. Some family members, for example, may have grown up in a completely different environment to the child, others may have had to leave their country of origin because of war or other adverse conditions, and others may have experienced abuse and neglect as children.

2.14 The narration and impact of family histories and experiences can play an important part in understanding what is happening currently to a family. An adult's capacity to parent may be crucially related to his or her childhood experiences of family life and past adult experiences prior to the current difficulties. The family may be in transition, for example refugee families.

2.15 An understanding of how the family usually functions, and how it functions when under stress can be very helpful in identifying what factors may assist parents in carrying out their parenting roles. Of particular importance is the quality and nature of the relationship between a child's parents and how this affects the child. For example, sustained conflict between parents is detrimental to children's welfare. The quality of relationships between siblings may also be of major significance to a child's welfare. Account must be taken of the diversity of family styles and structures, particularly who counts as family and who is important to the child.

2.16 The impact of multiple caregivers will need careful exploration, with an understanding of the context in which the care is being provided. As Cleaver (Department of Health and Cleaver, 2000) writes in the notes of guidance for use with the assessment records:

> Children can be protected from the adverse consequences of parenting problems when someone else meets the child's developmental needs.

She adds that it is important to record when there is evidence that no one is responding appropriately to the child. In some circumstances children who have a number of caregivers may be more vulnerable to being maltreated. Special attention should be given to the needs of disabled children who experience multiple caregivers as part of their regular routine, and to their need for reasonable continuity of caregivers.

FAMILY AND ENVIRONMENTAL FACTORS

Family History and Functioning

Family history includes both genetic and psycho-social factors.

Family functioning is influenced by who is living in the household and how they are related to the child; significant changes in family/household composition; history of childhood experiences of parents; chronology of significant life events and their meaning to family members; nature of family functioning, including sibling relationships and its impact on the child; parental strengths and difficulties, including those of an absent parent; the relationship between separated parents.

Wider Family

Who are considered to be members of the wider family by the child and the parents?

Includes related and non-related persons and absent wider family. What is their role and importance to the child and parents and in precisely what way?

Housing

Does the accommodation have basic amenities and facilities appropriate to the age and development of the child and other resident members? Is the housing accessible and suitable to the needs of disabled family members?

Includes the interior and exterior of the accommodation and immediate surroundings. Basic amenities include water, heating, sanitation, cooking facilities, sleeping arrangements and cleanliness, hygiene and safety and their impact on the child's upbringing.

Employment

Who is working in the household, their pattern of work and any changes? What impact does this have on the child? How is work or absence of work viewed by family members? How does it affect their relationship with the child?

Includes children's experience of work and its impact on them.

Income

Income available over a sustained period of time. Is the family in receipt of all its benefit entitlements? Sufficiency of income to meet the family's needs. The way resources available to the family are used. Are there financial difficulties which affect the child?

Family's Social Integration

Exploration of the wider context of the local neighbourhood and community and its impact on the child and parents.

Includes the degree of the family's integration or isolation, their peer groups, friendship and social networks and the importance attached to them.

Community Resources

Describes all facilities and services in a neighbourhood, including universal services of primary health care, day care and schools, places of worship, transport, shops and leisure activities.

Includes availability, accessibility and standard of resources and impact on the family, including disabled members.

2.17 In families where a parent is not living in the same household as the child, it is important to identify what role that parent has in the child's life and the significance to the child of the relationship with that parent. It cannot be assumed that parents who live apart are estranged. This arrangement may be by mutual agreement.

2.18 A wide range of environmental factors can either help or hinder the family's functioning. Here it is important to think broadly and creatively about the family and environmental factors described on the previous page.

2.19 Careful account should be taken of how these factors are influencing both a child's progress and the parents' responses. This can be illustrated by the following examples of the inter-relationship between such factors and a child's development:

- **Family history**
  A child may have a genetic condition or pre-disposition, such as sickle cell disorder or Huntington's Chorea, which may affect current or future physical or mental health and the need for services.

- **Family Functioning**
  Despite a recent separation, the parents co-operate regarding decisions about key events in a 10 year old boy's life such that he continues to attend the same school, maintains a strong group of friends, and is fully supported in his education by both parents. This enables him to do well in school.

- **Wider family**
  A child may have developed a close, affectionate attachment to a friend's parent who, over a number of years, compensates for chronic parental problems in the family home, giving that child a sense of belonging and selfesteem. This may become a resource to be mobilised at the time of family breakdown.

- **Housing**
  Accommodation which is damp, infested and overcrowded may be contributing to a low birth weight baby's failure to thrive and chronic ear, nose and chest problems, requiring urgent action.

- **Employment**
  The expectation that a 13 year old girl will assist regularly in the family business may result in her sudden failure to keep up with school work and difficult behaviour in class.

- **Income**
  A low income over many years and parents' inability to manage on this income may mean a young adolescent being bullied at school simply because he is wearing clothes which do not have the correct designer logo.

- **Family's social integration**
  Constant racial harassment and bullying in a neighbourhood may result in a teenager from a minority ethnic family being isolated and excluded from positive and affirming friendship group experiences at a formative stage of developing his identity.

- **Access to community resources**
  Knowledge of resources available in the community which are accessible and accommodate disabled children may enable an isolated single mother to organise

out of school care and activities for her 6 year old disabled child, thus enabling her to remain in work.

2.20 The complex interplay of factors across all three domains should be carefully understood and analysed. Parents may be experiencing their own problems which may have an impact through their behaviour on their capacity to respond to their child's needs. This could cover a variety of situations. It could include parents who are unable to read or write and are therefore unable to respond to notes sent home from school. On the other hand, it could include a child being traumatised by witnessing her mother being regularly assaulted by her father.

2.21 The publication *Children's Needs – Parenting Capacity* by Cleaver et al (1999) focuses on the impact of particular parental problems (mental illness, domestic violence, drug and alcohol misuse) on a child's development while *Crossing Bridges* (Falkov (ed) 1998) addresses parental mental illnesses in more detail. Such problems may adversely affect a parent's ability to respond to the needs of his or her child. While some children grow up apparently unscathed, others exhibit emotional and behavioural disorders as a result of these childhood experiences. This knowledge can assist professionals to be clear about the impact of a parent's difficulties on a child. In some situations, where the parents' problems are severe, such as major psychiatric illness or substance misuse, there may need to be **joint** or **concurrent assessments**; to examine the parent's problems, the impact of those problems on the child, and the effect of the child on the parent. Such assessments should be carried out within a clear focus on the needs of the child.

2.22 There is increasing knowledge about the characteristics of adults who maltreat children. Research has shown a strong association between domestic violence and child abuse. It has shown also, that not all parents who have suffered childhood abuse or deprivation go on to maltreat their children, but a significant proportion of parents who harm their children have been abused themselves (Department of Health, 1995d).

2.23 The interactions between different factors are often not straightforward which is why it is important that:

- information is gathered and recorded systematically with care and precision;
- information is checked and discussed with parents and, where appropriate, with the child;
- differences in views about information and its importance are clearly recorded;
- the strengths and difficulties **within** families are assessed and understood;
- the vulnerabilities and protective factors in the child's world are examined;
- the impact of what is happening on the child is clearly identified.

Chapter 4 elaborates on the processes of analysis, judgement and decision making which follow on from the information gathering and collation stages.

2.24 Ward (1995, p.85) in her community study of almost 400 children and their families concludes:

It is likely to be the interaction between a number of factors rather than any specific characteristic that leads to parenting difficulties. Thus most families are able to overcome adversities and provide their children with a sufficiently nurturing environment, although they may fall down in one or two areas. Only a very small proportion are unable to provide a sufficiently consistent standard of care across all seven (child development) dimensions, but it is they who form the group whose children are most likely to be admitted to care or accommodation.

2.25 The framework for assessment is, therefore, a conceptual map which can be used to understand what is happening to all children in whatever circumstances they may be growing up. For most children referred or whose families seek help, the issues of concern will be relatively straightforward, parents will be clear about requiring assistance and the impact on the child will not be difficult to identify. For a smaller number of children, the causes for concern will be serious and complex and the relationship between their needs, their parents' responses and the circumstances in which they are living, less straightforward. In these situations, further, more detailed and, in some cases, specialist assessment will be required. These issues are considered in the next chapter on the process of assessment.

Inclusive Practice

2.26 The Assessment Framework is predicated on the principle that children are children first, whatever may distinguish some children from others. This poses a challenge for staff - how to develop inclusive practice which recognises that all children share the same developmental needs to reach their optimal potential but that the rate or pattern of progress of individual children may vary because of factors associated with health and impairment. At the same time, due weight needs to be given to other important influences on children's development. Prominent amongst these are genetic factors, the quality of attachment to primary caregivers and the quality of everyday life experiences.

2.27 When assessing a child's needs and circumstances, care has to be taken to ensure that issues which fundamentally shape children's identity and wellbeing, their progress and outcomes are fully understood and incorporated into the framework for assessment. Dutt and Phillips (Department of Health, 2000a) write:

> Issues of race and culture cannot be added to a list for separate consideration during an assessment, they are integral to the assessment process. From referral through to core assessment, intervention and planning, race and culture have to be taken account of using an holistic framework for assessment.

2.28 In assessing the needs of children, practitioners have to take account of diversity in children, understand its origins and pay careful attention to its impact on a child's development and the interaction with parental responses and wider family and environmental factors.

2.29 Use of the framework requires that children and families' differences must be approached with knowledge and sensitivity in a non-judgemental way. Ignorance can result in stereotyping and in inappropriate or even damaging assumptions being made, resulting in a lack of accuracy and balance in analysing children's needs. To achieve sensitive and inclusive practice, staff should **avoid:**

- using one set of cultural assumptions and stereotypes to understand the child and family's circumstances;
- insensitivity to racial and cultural variations within groups and between individuals;
- making unreasoned assumptions without evidence;
- failing to take account of experiences of any discrimination in an individual's response to public services;
- failing to take account of the barriers which prevent the social integration of families with disabled members;
- attaching meaning to information without confirming the interpretation with the child and family members.

2.30 The use of the framework, derived from children's developmental needs and which also takes account of the context in which they are growing up, takes on more significance in relation to children for whom discrimination is likely to be part of their life experience. Such children and their families may suffer subsequent disadvantage and a failure of access to appropriate services. It is for this reason that chapters have been included in the practice guidance which consider in more detail issues of race and culture and of disability in assessing the needs of children in the context of their family and their environment.

Disability Discrimination Act 1995

2.31 Under Part III of the Disability Discrimination Act 1995 (rights of access to goods, facilities and services) service providers, including social services departments and health but not as yet education, must not discriminate against disabled people (including children) by refusing to provide any service which is provided to members of the public, by providing a lower standard of service or offering a service on less favourable terms. These requirements came into force on 2 December 1996.

2.32 Since October 1999, service providers have had to take reasonable steps to:

- change any policy, practice or procedure which makes it impossible or unreasonably difficult for disabled people to make use of services;
- provide an auxiliary aid or service if it would enable (or make easier for) disabled people to make use of services; and
- provide a reasonable alternative method of making services available to disabled people where a physical feature makes it impossible or unreasonably difficult for disabled people to make use of them.

2.33 From 2004 service providers will have to take reasonable steps to remove, alter or provide reasonable means of avoiding physical features that make it impossible or unreasonably difficult for disabled people to use the services.

3

The Process of Assessing Children in Need

Process of Assessment and Timing

3.1 Assessment is the first stage in helping a vulnerable child and his or her family, its purpose being 'to contribute to the understanding necessary for appropriate planning' (Compton and Galaway, 1989) and action. Assessment has several phases which overlap and lead into planning, action and review:

- clarification of source of referral and reason;
- acquisition of information;
- exploring facts and feelings;
- giving meaning to the situation which distinguishes the child and family's understanding and feelings from those of the professionals;
- reaching an understanding of what is happening, problems, strengths and difficulties, and the impact on the child (with the family wherever possible);
- drawing up an analysis of the needs of the child and parenting capacity within their family and community context as a basis for formulating a plan.

3.2 Prior to social services departments becoming involved with a child and family, a number of other agencies and community based groups may have had contact with the family. For some children, assessments will have already been carried out for purposes other than determining whether they are a child in need. In particular, health and education will have undertaken routine assessments as part of monitoring children's developmental progress. The familiarity of other agencies with the Assessment Framework will assist when making a referral to a social services department or contributing to an assessment of a child in need, thereby facilitating a common understanding of the child's needs within their family context.

3.3 The response from social services departments to an initial contact or a referral requesting help is critically important. At that point the foundation is laid for future work with the child or family. Children and families may have contact with social services staff in a wide range of settings. These may be as diverse as a family or day centre, a social services area office, an accident and emergency, adult or paediatric unit in a hospital, an education setting, an adolescent drop-in service or specialist services for adults. Not all staff in these settings will be professionals or qualified in work with children and families. This will apply particularly to those who work predominantly with adults. Whoever has first contact with a child or family member, however, has a vital role in influencing the course of future work. It is quite clear from research that the quality of the early or initial contact affects later working relationships with professionals. Furthermore, recording of information about the initial contact or referral contributes to the first phase of assessment. It is essential, therefore, that all staff responding to families or to referrers are familiar with the principles which underpin the Assessment Framework and are aware of the importance of the information collected and recorded at this stage.

3.4 For unqualified or inexperienced staff, the NSPCC chart *Referrals Involving A Child* (Cleaver *et al*, 1998) may act as a useful aide memoire to ensure that important information, which will assist later decision making, is not overlooked. It should not be treated as a check list but, used alongside local agency referral forms, it can serve as a reminder of:

- issues which may need to be covered in a response to the referrer;
- matters raised by the referrer that should be recorded.

The chart is included in Appendix C.

3.5 Arrangements for managing the reception of initial contacts or referrals vary widely according to local circumstances. It is important that social services for adults are aware of their responsibilities to children of adults who have parenting responsibilities and ensure that an initial assessment takes place to ascertain whether the children are children in need under s17 of the Children Act 1989 (Department of Health, forthcoming, a).

3.6 It is important also that each social services department has structures and systems in place to ensure an effective, accessible and speedy response to children and families. Some local authorities are developing innovative approaches to referrals and initial assessment. These include local telephone help lines, help desks, multi-agency information and advice centres and drop-in services. An example of this is the help desk service established in a rural county below (Figure 3). When there are such arrangements, it becomes imperative that reception staff are carefully selected and

FEATURES:

- one accessible, responsive point of contact in a district for child and family referrals.
- staffed by a team of specially selected and trained unqualified referral and information co-ordinators, administrative reception staff, qualified social workers (to undertake assessments of children whose welfare may need safeguarding and promoting) and a team manager.
- priority to provide a safe short term service at the front end through:
  – advice and advocacy eg. welfare benefits
  – information
  – help eg. by signposting
  – referral taking by telephone and personal interview
  – initial and core assessments of children in need
  – direct access to practical services

Figure 3 **Helpdesk for Children's Services in a Rural County**

trained for their tasks. Reception staff will also need the support of qualified practitioners and managers to ensure that situations of serious or immediate concern about a child receive prompt and expert professional attention.

3.7 Time, as discussed in Chapter 1, is critical in a child's life. A timely response to responding to a child's needs means that the process of assessment cannot continue unchecked over a prolonged period without an analysis being made of what is happening and what action is needed, however difficult or complex the child's circumstances. Prior to the publication of the Government's Objectives for children's social services (Department of Health, 1999e), no timescales had been set for completing assessments of children in need, although there had been timescales for action to be taken to protect children where there were concerns that a child was suffering or likely to suffer significant harm. This has now been remedied and timescales have been specified in the objectives for children's social services.

3.8 There is an expectation that **within one working day** of a referral being received or new information coming to or from within a social services department about an open case, there will be a decision about what response is required. A referral is defined as a request for services to be provided by the social services department. The response may include no action, but that is itself a decision and should be made promptly and recorded. The referrer should be informed of the decision and its rationale, as well as the parents or caregivers and the child, if appropriate.

3.9 A decision to gather more information constitutes an initial assessment. An initial assessment is defined as a brief assessment of each child referred to social services with a request for services to be provided. This should be undertaken **within a maximum of 7 working days** but could be very brief depending on the child's circumstances. It should address the dimensions of the Assessment Framework, determining whether the child is in need, the nature of any services required, from where and within what timescales, and whether a further, more detailed core assessment should be undertaken. An initial assessment is deemed to have commenced at the point of referral to the social services department or when new information on an open case indicates an initial assessment should be repeated. All staff responding to referrals and undertaking initial assessments should address the dimensions which constitute the Assessment Framework. There is more detailed discussion about the contribution of respective agencies in Chapter 5.

3.10 Depending on the child's circumstances, an initial assessment may include some or all of the following:

- interviews with child and family members, as appropriate;
- involvement of other agencies in gathering and providing information, as appropriate;
- consultation with supervisor/manager;
- record of initial analysis;
- decisions on further action/no action;
- record of decisions/rationale with family/agencies;
- informing other agencies of the decisions;

- statement to the family of decisions made and, if a child is in need, the plan for providing support.

As part of any initial assessment, the child should be seen. This includes observation and talking with the child in an age appropriate manner. This is further discussed in paragraphs 3.41 to 3.43.

3.11 **A core assessment** is defined as an in-depth assessment which addresses the central or most important aspects of the needs of a child and the capacity of his or her parents or caregivers to respond appropriately to these needs within the wider family and community context. While this assessment is led by social services, it will invariably involve other agencies or independent professionals, who will either provide information they hold about the child or parents, contribute specialist knowledge or advice to social services or undertake specialist assessments. Specific assessments of the child and/or family members may have already been undertaken prior to referral to the social services department. The findings from these should inform this assessment. At the conclusion of this phase of assessment, there should be an analysis of the findings which will provide an understanding of the child's circumstances and inform planning, case objectives and the nature of service provision. The timescale for completion of the core assessment is a **maximum of 35 working days**. A core assessment is deemed to have commenced at the point the initial assessment ended, or a strategy discussion decided to initiate enquiries under s47, or new information obtained on an open case indicates a core assessment should be undertaken. Where specialist assessments have been commissioned by social services from other agencies or independent professionals, it is recognised that they will not necessarily be completed within the 35 working day period. Appropriate services should be provided whilst awaiting the completion of the specialist assessment.

3.12 The Department of Health has published an **Initial Assessment Record**, which has been developed for all staff to record salient information about a child's needs, the parents' capacity and the family's circumstances, to assist in determining the social services' response and whether a core assessment should be considered. This record is consistent with the **Core Assessment Record**. These have been developed to assist in assessing the child's developmental needs in an age appropriate manner for the following age bands: 0–2 years, 3–4 years, 5–9 years, 10–14 years and 15 and upwards. These age bands are the same as those used in **Looking After Children Assessment and Action Records** (Department of Health, 1995b). The initial and core assessment recording forms have been designed to assist in the analysis of a child and family's circumstances (Department of Health and Cleaver, 2000) and in the development and reviewing of a plan of action.

3.13 At the conclusion of either an initial or core assessment, the parent(s) and child, if appropriate, should be informed in writing, and/or in another more appropriate medium, of the decisions made and be offered the opportunity to record their views, disagreements and to ask for corrections to recorded information. Agencies and individuals involved in the assessment should also be informed of the decisions, with reasons for these made clear. This sharing of information is important to assist agencies' own practice in their work with the child and family. Local authorities are required by section 26 of the Children Act 1989 to establish complaints procedures, and children and parents should be provided with information about these. Parents

Figure 4 **Maximum Timescales for Analysing the Needs of Child and Parenting Capacity**

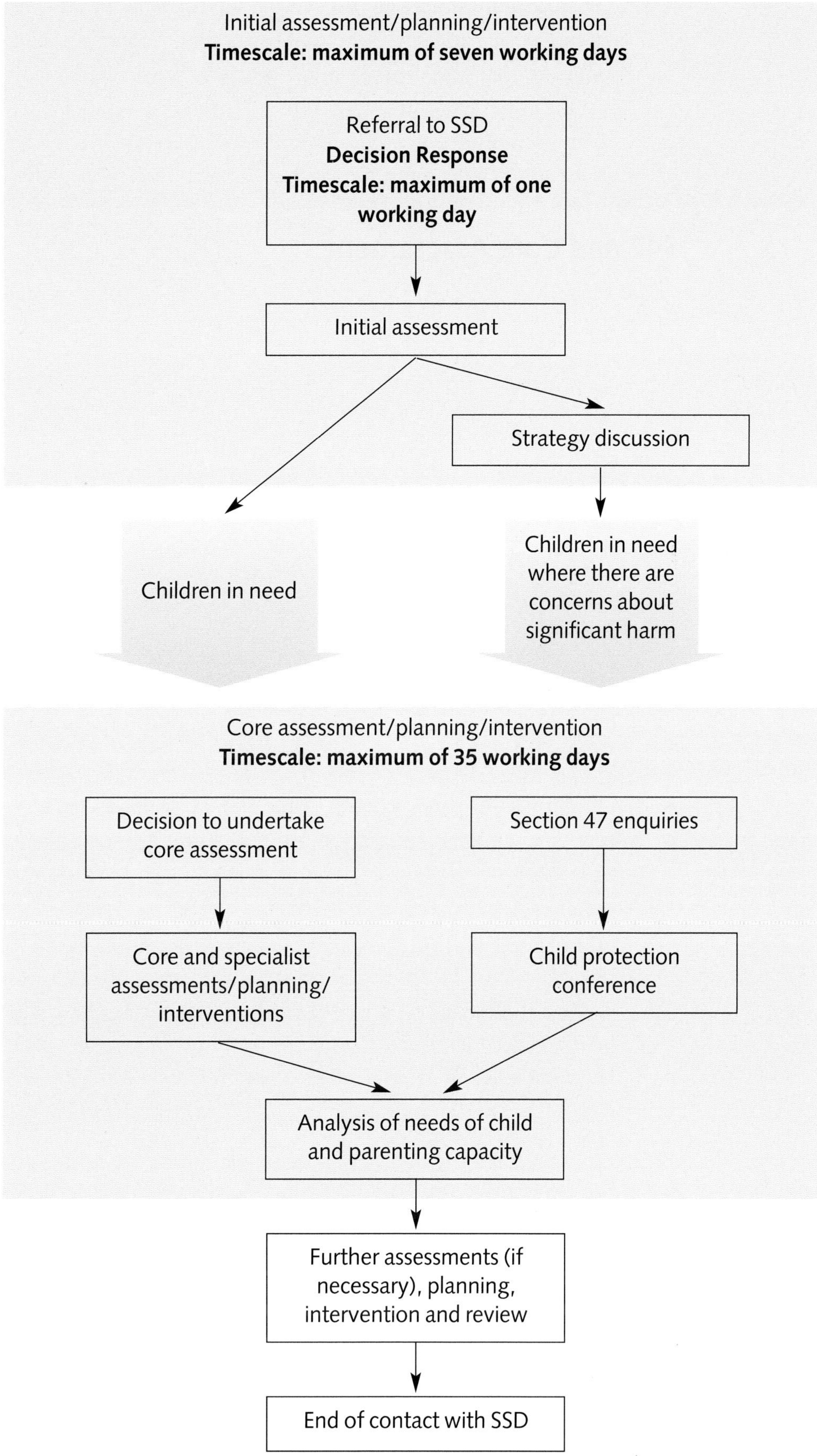

who have a complaint about a particular agency's services should take it up with the agency concerned.

3.14 The **maximum timescales** for completing an analysis of the needs of children and the parenting capacity to respond to those needs are represented in Figure 4. The needs of some children, in particular those who require emergency intervention, may mean that the initial assessment stage is brief. It may also be brief where the needs of the child can be determined in a period of less than seven working days. The same considerations apply to the minimum and maximum timescales for the core assessment.

S47 and Core Assessment

3.15 At any stage, should there be suspicions or allegations about child maltreatment and concern that the child may be or is likely to suffer significant harm, there must be strategy discussions and inter-agency action in accordance with the guidance in *Working Together to Safeguard Children* (1999). Assessment of what is happening to a child in these circumstances is not a separate or different activity but continues the same process, although the pace and scope of assessment may well have changed (see paragraphs 5.33 to 5.38 in *Working Together to Safeguard Children* (1999)). A key part of the assessment will be to establish whether there is reasonable cause to suspect that this child is suffering or is likely to suffer significant harm and whether any emergency action is required to secure the safety of the child.

3.15 The way in which the initial and core assessments have been integrated into the processes for children who are considered to be, or likely to be suffering significant harm are set out in Figure 5. This flow chart concerning individual cases is reproduced from *Working Together to Safeguard Children* (1999, p.116).

3.16 As indicated in paragraphs 5.39 to 5.41 of *Working Together to Safeguard Children* (1999) sometimes it will be appropriate to undertake an investigative interview of a child who may have been a victim to a crime or a witness, with a view to gathering evidence for criminal proceedings. These interviews should take account of information known from any previous assessments. A child should never be interviewed in the presence of an alleged or suspected perpetrator of abuse, or somebody who may be colluding with a perpetrator. The guidance (which is currently being revised) in the *Memorandum of Good Practice on video recorded interviews for child witnesses for criminal proceedings* (Home Office and Department of Health, 1992) should be followed for all video-recorded investigative interviews with children.

3.17 All such interviews with children should be conducted by those with specialist training and experience in interviewing children. Additional specialist help may be necessary if the child's first language is not English; the child appears to have a degree of psychiatric disturbance but is deemed competent; the child has an impairment; or where interviewers do not have adequate knowledge and understanding of the child's racial, religious or cultural background. Consideration should also be given to the gender of interviewers particularly in cases of alleged sexual abuse.

3.18 Following the publication of *Speaking Up For Justice* (Home Office, 1998), the report of the Working Group on Vulnerable or Intimidated Witnesses, Part II of the Youth

Figure 5 **Working Together to Safeguard Children (Individual Cases Flowchart)**

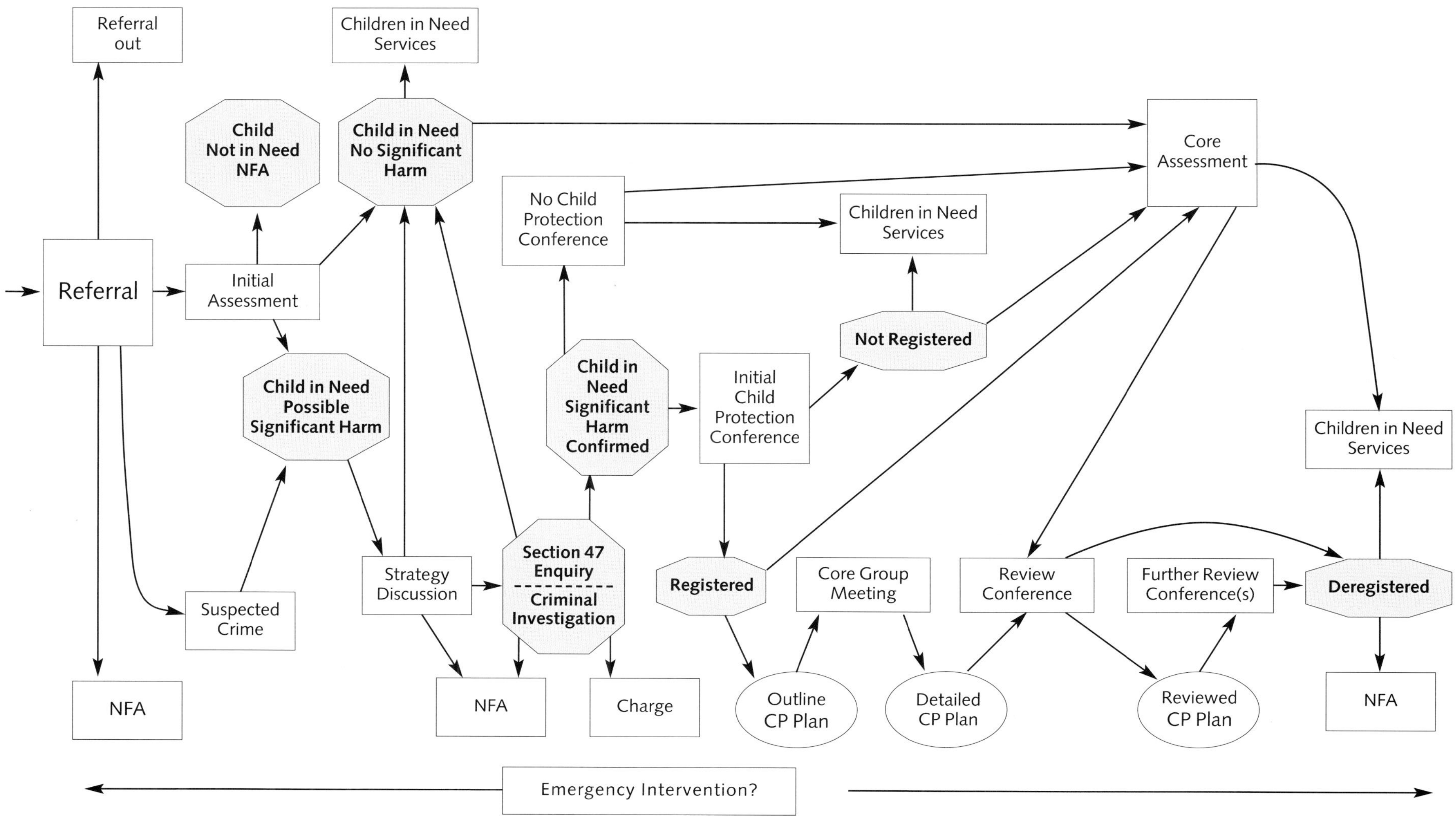

Justice and Criminal Evidence Act 1999 extends the range of measures available to assist child witnesses.

The Act provides different levels of protection for three groups of child witnesses according to the nature of assistance each group is considered to need. These are:

- All children in need of special protection – because they are giving evidence in a case that involves a sexual and/or violent offence – will give video-recorded evidence-in-chief unless this would not be in the interests of justice.
- Children under 17 who are giving evidence in a case involving violence, neglect, abduction or false imprisonment will be cross-examined via a live link at the trial.
- When facilities are available, children under 17 who are giving evidence in a sexual offence case will be cross-examined at a video-recorded pre-trial hearing unless the child informs the court that he would prefer to be cross-examined at trial (on live link or in court).

There is a presumption that all children who are giving evidence in cases involving other offences will give evidence-in-chief by means of a video recording, and will be cross-examined on live link at the trial.

3.19 The Act also provides a range of other measures to assist child witnesses including:

- assistance with communication;
- the use of an intermediary to assist with the questioning;
- screening the witness from the accused in court;
- the removal by judges of their wigs and gowns;
- clearing the public gallery in sexual offence cases.

The majority of these measures will be available to the Crown Court and youth courts by the end of 2000.

Use of Assessments in Family Proceedings

3.20 It may be appropriate to use evidence gathered during the assessment process for family proceedings. This may arise where an assessment has been completed **before** the commencing of proceedings or because it is necessary to undertake an assessment **during** the proceedings. The following paragraphs set out some issues around the interface between the assessment processes and reporting in writing in family proceedings.

3.21 The term **family proceedings** is one that is defined statutorily in section 8 of the Children Act 1989. It includes all public law applications (care, adoption, emergency protection, contact) and a large range of private law matters concerning divorce and separation, including those within applications under section 8 for contact, residence, specific issue and prohibited steps.

Care Applications and Assessment

3.22 In court proceedings involving the local authority, such as an application for a care or supervision order, the local authority's main evidence will be set out by way of one or more formal statements. These include the relevant history and the facts to support the **threshold criteria** (ie. significant harm) for an order under section 31. Information concerning the **welfare checklist** (section 1(3)) to which the court must have regard will also be included in the application.

3.23 Before making any order, the court must also consider the **no order principle** (section 1(5)). The court will look to the detail of the local authority's care plan for evidence as to how the care order, if made, would be implemented. Guidance about the structure and contents of care plans was issued in 1999 (*Care Plans and Care Proceedings under the Children Act 1989* LAC (99(29)).

3.24 Evidence arising from assessments may be used within the proceedings in one or more of the following ways by providing evidence:

- in support of the threshold criteria;
- around issues in the welfare checklist;
- about the rationale for the overall aim of the care plan or specific details within it (such as contact arrangements).

Disclosure

3.25 In family proceedings, documents produced by parties are normally shared among all parties – typically, the local authority, the parents and the guardian ad litem. It should be remembered that an assessment undertaken for the purpose of the proceedings will generate information for the **court** and this cannot, save exceptionally with the court's agreement, be withheld in full or in part because aspects may be unfavourable to one of the parties.

3.26 Assessments may be commissioned before the commencement of court proceedings or where such proceedings have not been anticipated. Where such an assessment includes information, opinions and recommendations from professionals not employed by the local authority (such as specialists in child and adolescent mental health), those persons should be advised that their contribution may be used in family proceedings.

3.27 Appendix D sets out a number of practice issues to be considered when using information gathered during assessment for family proceedings.

Court Sanctioned Assessments

3.28 A range of assessments may be made without legal restriction in respect of a child who is **not** the subject of care or related court applications.

3.29 Section 38(6) provides that where the Court makes an interim care order or interim supervision order it may give such directions (if any) as it considers appropriate with regard to the medical or psychiatric examination or other assessment of the child. By subsection (7) a direction may be to the effect that there is to be **no** such examination or assessment **unless** the Court directs otherwise.

3.30 Rule 18 of the Family Proceedings Courts (Children Act 1989) Rules 1991 provides that no person may without leave of the Justice's Clerk or the Court cause the child to be medically or psychiatrically examined, or otherwise assessed, for the purpose of the preparation of expert evidence for use in the proceedings. (See also paragraphs 3.61 to 3.62 in *An Introduction to the Children Act 1989* (1989) which deal with assessments in the context of care proceedings.) There are corresponding Rules for the County and High Court. Where care proceedings are underway, the nature and scope of any specialist assessment to be commissioned should be discussed in advance with legal advisers. Legal advisers will also help ensure that the implications of relevant case law, Practice Directions, Human Rights Act 1998, European Court of Human Rights judgments and other authoritative guidance are brought to the attention of those preparing assessments and subsequent reports for courts.

Oral Evidence

3.31 The assessment provides the basis for formal written evidence for use in the proceedings. However, it may be necessary for the professional(s) undertaking the assessment to give additional evidence orally. In family proceedings, there is less emphasis on restrictions such as hearsay and generally the proceedings are considered to be less adversarial than non-family cases. The key worker should liaise closely with the local authority legal department in anticipating those issues likely to be raised.

Working with Children and Families

3.32 Gathering information and making sense of a family's situation are key phases in the process of assessment. It is not possible to do this without the knowledge and involvement of the family. It requires direct work with children and with family members, explaining what is happening, why an assessment is being undertaken, what will be the process and what is likely to be the outcome. Gaining the family's co-operation and commitment to the work is crucially important. Families often have a number of fears and anxieties about approaching social services departments for help or about being referred to them by other agencies. Parents are fearful, for instance, that they will be perceived as failing in some way (Cleaver and Freeman, 1995; Aldgate and Bradley, 1999). They are also very clear about what they value from the professionals they meet, even in the most difficult circumstances. In particular, parents ask for clear explanations, openness and honesty, and to be treated with respect and dignity. Children's needs for explanations of what is happening may sometimes be overlooked. They should be informed clearly and sensitively even when they do not communicate through speech and where professionals may be unclear how much of what is being said is understood. They do not want to be kept in the dark or patronised. Studies have found that 'children are particularly sensitive to professionals who treat them personally, with care, and above all respect' (Jones and Ramchandani, 1999). It is especially important to help children handle uncertainty while plans are being formulated.

3.33 Different ways of providing explanations to families have been developed, some in written form accompanying the use of local authority records or materials for gathering information, which are shared with family members. An example of one such approach developed by a local authority is included above (Figure 6). Other local authorities have produced leaflets for families or use materials published by specialist

Figure 6 **Explaining Assessment to Family Members: An Example Accompanying a Written Record**

What is an assessment?

- Either you, or someone else on your behalf, has asked the social services departments for help with some difficulty you are having which affects your child (or children).
- Before we can help you, we need to know more about you and your family. This will involve collecting information, talking this through with you and agreeing what might be done. We call this an assessment.

Why is an assessment being carried out?

- Through making an assessment of your situation, it should be possible to see what help and support you and your family might need, and who could best give that help.
- Information will be gathered and written down. Although social workers and other professionals will normally take the lead in completing the assessment, this should always be done in a way which helps you to have your say, and encourages you to take part.
- Any information you give to us will be held in confidence within the social services department. If there is a need to discuss this information with anyone else, we will normally ask for your permission. The only exception to this is if information comes to light which, in the social worker's view, may indicate a serious threat to the welfare of your child. If this is the case, you will be told what your rights are in this new situation.

What will happen?

- Completing an assessment usually means the social worker will meet with you and members of your family a number of times.
- When children are old enough to take part in the assessment, the social worker will encourage and help them to do so.
- The assessment will take into consideration your ethnic and cultural background. If required, help will be provided in your first language.
- When other people are already helping you and your family, it is likely the social worker will talk to them too. We shall discuss this with you.
- If you do not agree with what the social worker says in the assessment, there will be an opportunity for you to record your point of view on the assessment record.
- The purpose of assessment is to draw up a plan of action to address the needs of your child (or children) and how you might need help to respond to these. You will be given a copy of the plan.

What will be expected of you?

- We know that almost all parents want to do their best for their children, and completing the assessment will help the social workers recognise the strengths you and your family have, as well as your difficulties.
- We can help you best if you tell us about what you do well in your family and your difficulties. We will keep you informed about what we are doing and thinking.
- An assessment is an important part of our working with you. In a very small number of cases, there are serious concerns about a child's safety. Making sure the child is safe will be our first concern. Please ask your social worker to explain this to you. You have a right to know.

What can you expect of us?

- We will listen carefully to what you have to say, offer advice and, if necessary, support to help you bring up your children and resolve your difficulties.
- We know that with a little help most families can sort out their own problems, and our aim is to help you do that.
- We will try our best to offer you any services you need as soon as possible. But there are often many more people needing services than there are services to give. This means that sometimes although everyone is agreed that you need a service, it might not be available at the time. If this happens we will always look to find an alternative, but we cannot guarantee to provide a particular service.

groups such as Family Rights Group, NSPCC or Who Cares? Trust. Key to the use of written materials is that they must be accompanied by direct communication and involvement by practitioners with family members and that repeated explanations may be necessary.

3.34 The issues of working with children and families where there are concerns that a child is being maltreated are explored in *The Challenge of Partnership in Child Protection* (Department of Health, 1995a). That publication provides detailed practice guidance about how to work with families throughout the process of enquiries being made and action taken to protect a child. It warns that 'those under the stress associated with allegations of child abuse may drift away from a working method which is sensitive to families' needs and which encourages their participation in the process' (p.46).

3.35 There will be situations where family members do not wish to work co-operatively with statutory agencies. This may be for a variety of reasons; they are too afraid or they believe they or their child have no problem or they are generally hostile to public welfare agencies. They may be resistant because of the nature of their own difficulties, such as psychiatric illness or problems of alcohol and drug misuse, or because of allegations being made against them. Whatever the reasons for their resistance, the door to co-operation should be kept open. At the very least, family members should be informed of what is happening and how they could participate more fully. Ways should be explored to engage some family members in the assessment process. The experience of research and practice confirms that, even after initial difficulties, the prospect of working in partnership with one or more family members may not be lost for ever, and that to do so will have long term beneficial outcomes for the child and family. The desirability of working with family members, however, must not override the importance of ensuring that children are safe.

3.36 Where there is resistance, 'a determination not to be overwhelmed, distracted or immobilised by the parents' initial response is essential' (Department of Health, 1995a). However, in a small number of instances, resistance to co-operation by a parent is accompanied by overtly aggressive, abusive or threatening behaviour or by more subtle underlying menace. Staff may be aware of the threat and in response either avoid family contact or unwisely place themselves in situations of danger (Cleaver *et al*, 1998). It is in these circumstances that access to available, skilled, expert supervision is essential so that the nature of the threat can be understood, the implications for the child and other family members identified and strategies found for maintaining work with the family. These may include co-working with experienced staff within or across agencies, changing times and venue for meetings with the family and other measures. Concerns about such matters should always be taken seriously and acted upon. It may be necessary to involve the expertise of professionals from a number of agencies to arrive at an understanding of the risks a particular individual may pose to the safety of staff, as well as to family members.

Planning Assessment

3.37 Gathering information requires careful planning. However difficult the circumstances, the **purpose** of assessing the particular child and the family should always be kept in mind and the impact of the process on the child and family considered. It has to be remembered that:

- the aim is to clarify and identity the needs of the child;
- the process of assessment should be helpful and as unintrusive to the child and family as possible;
- families do not want to be subjected to repeated assessments by different agencies;
- if, during the assessment, the child's safety is or becomes a concern, it must be secured before proceeding with the assessment.

3.38 It is essential, therefore, that the process of assessment should be carefully planned, whatever the pressure to begin work. 'Preparation, process and outcome are inextricably linked' (Adcock, 2000). This planning should take place in discussion with the child and family members unless to do so would place the child at increased risk of significant harm (*Working Together to Safeguard Children*, 1999, paragraph 5.6). As part of the preparation, key questions should be considered:

- Who will undertake the assessment and what resources will be needed?
- Who in the family will be included and how will they be involved (remembering absent or live-out family members, wider family and others significant to the child)?
- In what groupings will the child and family members be seen and in what order?
- Are there communication issues? If so, what are the specific communication needs and how will they be met?
- What methods of collecting information will be used? Which questionnaires and scales will be used?
- What information is already available?
- What other sources of knowledge about the child and family are available and how will other agencies and professionals who know the family be informed and involved? How will family members consent be gained?
- Where will assessment take place?
- What will be the timescale?
- How will information be recorded?
- How will it be analysed and who will be involved?

3.39 The nature of concerns about a child's needs will determine how the process is carried out and the extent of detail collected. The greater the concern, the greater the need for specificity, for use of specialist knowledge and judgement in the process and, therefore, the need for careful co-ordination and management of work with the family and other agencies. The more complex or difficult the child's situation, the more important it will be that multiple sources of information are used. These may include:

- **Direct work with the child** through shared activities, interviews, questionnaires, scales and play, which are age and culturally appropriate to the child's age, development and culture.
- **Direct work with the parents** through interviews with one or more parental members; parental discussions; taking parental histories; using scales, questionnaires and other resources to gain a shared view of parental issues and parental functioning.
- **Direct work with the family** through interviews with the family in appropriate groupings of family members; taking family histories; using scales, questionnaires and other resources to gain a shared view of family issues and family functioning.
- **Direct work with the child and current caregivers**, if the child is not living with parents.
- **Observation** of the child alone and of the child/parent(s)/caregiver(s) interaction. Consideration should be given to doing this in the home, in school (both classroom and play areas) and with friends as well as family members.
- **Other sources of knowledge**, including those who have known the child over time, such as the midwife, health visitor, general practitioner, nursery staff or school teachers, and others who know the family such as staff from voluntary agencies, housing departments and adult health and social services. Other professionals may have become involved with the child or other children in the family for a specific purpose, for example educational psychologists, speech therapists, youth offending team members. Police and probation may also be important sources of information where there are concerns about a child or family members' safety.
- **Other information held on files and records and from previous assessments.** These should always be carefully checked as far as possible.
- **Specialist assessments** from a range of professionals may be commissioned to provide specific understanding about an aspect of the child's development, parental strengths and difficulties or the family's functioning. The timing of these and their particular contribution to the analysis of the child's needs and the plan of intervention will require careful consideration.

3.40 As a general principle, any records of assessments, plans or reports should be routinely shared with family members and children as appropriate, in addition to being shared with relevant professionals. These may require explanation and re-explanation to family members. Copies of assessments and plans, in their first language, should be given to family members wherever possible. Care should be taken to ensure that the meaning and implications of assessments are understood by the child and family members, as far as is possible.

Communicating with Children

3.41 In responding to a request for help or a referral, the importance of working with family members has been emphasised. However, if the process of assessment is to be child centred, an understanding of what is happening to the child cannot only be gained from information contributed by family members or other professionals who know the child. Direct work with children is an essential part of assessment, as well as recognising their rights to be involved and consulted about matters which affect their lives. This applies to all children, including disabled children. Communicating with some disabled children requires more preparation, sometimes more time and on occasions specialist expertise, and consultation with those closest to the child. For example, for children with communication difficulties it may be necessary to use alternatives to speech such as signs, symbols, facial expression, eye pointing, objects of reference or drawing. Communicating with a child with very complex difficulties may benefit from help of a third party who knows the child well and is familiar with the child's communication methods (see Chapter 3 in Department of Health, 2000a). Children whose first language is not English should have the opportunity to speak to a professional in their first language, wherever possible. It is particularly important at turning points in their lives that 'children are enabled to express their wishes and feelings; make sense of their circumstances and contribute to decisions that affect them' (NSPCC *et al*, 1997).

3.42 It is essential that a child's safety is addressed, if appropriate, during the course of undertaking direct work with him or her. There are five critical components in direct work with children: seeing, observing, talking, doing and engaging:

- **Seeing children**: an assessment cannot be made without seeing the child, however young and whatever the circumstances. The more complex or unclear a situation or the greater the level of concern, the more important it will be to see the child regularly and to take note of appearance, physical condition, emotional wellbeing, behaviour and any changes which are occurring.

- **Observing children:** the child's responses and interactions in different situations should be carefully observed wherever possible, alone, with siblings, with parents and/or caregivers or in school or other settings. Children may hide or suppress their feelings in situations which are difficult or unsafe for them, so it is important that general conclusions are not reached from only limited observations.

- **Engaging children:** this involves developing a relationship with children so that they can be enabled to express their thoughts, concerns and opinions as part of the process of helping them make real choices, in a way that is age and developmentally appropriate. Children should clearly understand the parameters within which they can exercise choice. In offering children such options, adults must not abdicate their responsibilities for taking decisions about a child's welfare.

- **Talking to children:** although this may seem an obvious part of communicating with children, it is clear from research that this is often not done at all or not done well. It requires time, skill, confidence and careful preparation by practitioners. Issues of geographical distance, culture, language or communication needs because of impairments may require specific consideration before deciding how best to communicate with the child. Children themselves are particularly sensitive to how and when professionals talk to them and consult them. Their views must be sought before key meetings. Again, a range of opportunities for talking to children may be needed, appropriate to the child's circumstances, age and stage of development, which may include talking to the child on their own, in a family meeting or accompanied by or with the assistance of a trusted person.

- **Activities with children**: undertaking activities with children can have a number of purposes and beneficial effects. It is important that they are activities which the child understands and enjoys, in which trust with the worker can develop and which give the child an experience of safety. They can allow positive interaction between the worker and the child to grow and enable the professional to gain a better understanding of the child's responses and needs.

3.43 Children have been asked what they consider to be good professional practice. They value social workers who:

- **Listen** – carefully and without trivialising or being dismissive of the issues raised;
- are **available and accessible** – regular and predictable contact;
- are **non-judgemental and non-directive** – accepting, explaining and suggesting options and choices;
- have a sense of **humour** – it helps to build a rapport;
- are **straight-talking** – with realism and reliability; no 'false promises';
- can be **trusted** – maintain **confidentiality** and consult with children before taking matters forward.

Butler and Williamson (1994) reproduced from *Turning Points: A Resource Pack for Communicating with Children*. Introduction. pp. 1–2. (1997)

3.44 The exercise of professional judgement will be important in deciding when and how to communicate with children during the assessment process and how to interpret their communication in the context of the circumstances. Consideration should be given as to how children are informed and involved at each stage of the process, so that they have the opportunity to agree what the key issues are, what they would like to happen and to discuss what is possible and not possible. 'Children need to trust that they will be understood as individuals in their own right; usually they will want reassurance about what their parent/carer will be told about what they say' (Brandon, 1999).

3.45 Consideration of when and how to involve specific professionals with expertise and experience in assessing children's development will also be important throughout the assessment process. Professionals in a variety of child welfare agencies may be able to assist social services staff through discussion or advice based on their understanding and interpretation of information and views gathered from children. There may, however, be aspects of children's development and behaviour which require specialist assessment, either by joint work or referral to specific agencies. For example, assessing the strength of a child's attachment to a parent in circumstances of maltreatment or the educational potential of a school leaver who is living rough on the streets and seeking help. Children will require careful and straightforward explanations about why new professionals are being involved.

Consent and Confidentiality

3.46 When a family approaches social services for help or is referred, the family is generally the first and most important source of information about the child and the family's circumstances. However, in establishing whether this is a child in need and how best those needs may be met, it is likely to be important to gather information from a number of professionals who have contact with and knowledge of the child and family.

3.47 Personal information about children and families held by professionals and agencies is subject to a legal duty of confidence and should not normally be disclosed without the consent of the subject. However, the law permits the disclosure of confidential information if it is necessary to safeguard a child or children in the public interest: that is, the public interest in child protection may override the public interest in maintaining confidentiality. Disclosure should be justifiable in each case, according to the particular facts of the case, and legal advice should be sought in cases of doubt.

3.48 Children are entitled to the same duty of confidence as adults, provided that, in the case of those under 16 years of age, they have the ability to understand the choices and their consequences relating to any treatment. In exceptional circumstances, it may be believed that a child seeking advice, for example on sexual matters, is being exploited or abused. In such cases, confidentiality may be breached, following discussion with the child.

3.49 All agencies working with children and families should make their policies about sharing personal information available to users of their services and other agencies. This includes ensuring that such information is accessible and appropriate to children and families. Individual professionals should always make sure their agency's policies are known to the family with whom they are working. There will be variations in policy between agencies in accordance with their roles and responsibilities. Personal information about a child and family should always be respected but, in order to achieve good outcomes for the child, it may be appropriate to share it between professionals and teams within the same agency. Sensitive and careful judgements are required in the child's best interests.

3.50 In obtaining consent to seek information from other parties or to disclose information about the child or other individuals under the Data Protection Act 1998 it is important that explanations include:

- clarity about the purpose of approaching other individuals or agencies;
- reasons for disclosure of any information, for example about the referral or details about the child or family members;
- details of the individuals or agencies being contacted;
- what information will be sought or shared;
- why the information is important;
- what it is hoped to achieve.

3.51 The **Data Protection Act 1998** allows for disclosure without the consent of the subject in certain conditions, including for the purposes of the prevention or detection of crime, or the apprehension or prosecution of offenders, and where failure to disclose would be likely to prejudice those objectives in a particular case.

3.52 Article 8 of the **European Convention on Human Rights** states that:

(1) Everyone has the right to respect for his private and family life, his home and his correspondence.

(2) There shall be no interference by a public authority with the exercise of this right except such as in accordance with the law and is necessary in a democratic society in the interests of national security, public safety or the economic wellbeing of the country, for the prevention of disorder or crime, for the protection of health or morals, or for the protection of the rights and freedoms of others.

3.53 Disclosure of information without consent might give rise to an issue under Article 8. Disclosure of information to safeguard children will usually be for the protection of health or morals, for the protection of the rights and freedoms of others, and for the prevention of disorder or crime. Disclosure should be appropriate for the purpose and only to the extent necessary to achieve that purpose.

3.54 Obtaining consent and respecting confidentiality may not always be straightforward, particularly in situations of family conflict or dispute, or where a number of parental figures including absent parents are involved or where there are allegations of abuse about which enquiries are being made. The consent of any one parent acting alone, rather than all those with parental responsibility, is required to disclose information about a child (section 2(7) of the Children Act 1989).

3.55 Where there are concerns that a child may be suffering or is likely to suffer significant harm, it is essential that professionals and other people share information for it is often 'only when information from a number of sources has been shared and is then put together that it becomes clear that a child is at risk of or is suffering harm' (*Working Together to Safeguard Children*, 1999, paragraph 7.27). Unless to do so would place the child or children at increased risk of significant harm the nature of the child protection concerns should be explained to family members and to children, where appropriate, and their consent to contact other agencies sought. This requires careful explanation in plain language. It may be helpful to have written as well as verbal explanations (an example of this is the statement for family members on pages 39 and 40). For some families under stress or coping in difficult circumstances, explanations may need to be repeated several times. In all cases where the police are involved the decision about when to inform the parents will have a bearing on the conduct of police investigations and should inform part of the strategy discussion.

3.56 In any potential conflict between the responsibilities of professionals towards children and towards other family members, the needs of the child must come first. Where there are concerns that a child is or may be at risk of suffering significant harm, the overriding principle must be to safeguard the child. In such cases, when it is considered that a child may be in danger or that a crime is being or has been committed, the duty of confidence can be overridden. However, it will be important that the respective duties and powers of different agencies are clearly understood by all parties.

3.57 These matters are fully discussed in paragraphs 7.27 to 7.46 of *Working Together to*

Safeguard Children (1999) in the context of the legal framework and professional guidelines for different agencies. In this publication, Appendix E reproduces an abridged version of the Data Protection Registrar's checklist for setting up information sharing arrangements.

Assessment of Children in Special Circumstances

3.58 Some of the children referred for help because of the nature of their problems or circumstances, will require particular care and attention during assessment. These are children who may become lost to the statutory agencies, whose wellbeing or need for immediate services may be overlooked and for whom subsequent planning and intervention may be less than satisfactory. This may be for a number of reasons including the following:

- They are **children in transition**. For example, their families may be moving from one geographical location to another; they may be moving schools, leaving school or leaving care, or moving into young adulthood and into the remit of adult rather than children's services. They may be disabled young people and their families, moving from child to adult services (Morris, 1999). They may be part of a travelling community or in families based periodically overseas, such as the armed forces.
- They are **children in hospital** for long periods of time. Under section 85 of the Children Act 1989 the social services department has a duty to assess the welfare of a child in hospital for longer than three months consecutively. This assessment is to ascertain whether the child's welfare is being adequately safeguarded and promoted and whether the child and their family require services.
- They (or their parents) have specific **communication needs**, for example they do not use English as a first language, or they do not communicate through speech.
- They (or their families, including siblings) have **a long history of contact with social services** and other child welfare agencies. Their circumstances may be chaotic; files numerous; many staff may have been involved; they may not currently have an allocated worker. Any of these circumstances may result in the need for assessment or reassessment at this point in time not being recognised.
- They are children whose problems or those of their parents are **not sufficiently serious to receive services** under social services priorities. These children's health or development may not be considered to be being impaired, but an analysis of the risk factors and stressors in their lives would suggest they are likely to suffer impairment in the future. What is required is recognition of the interaction of child and/or parental problems on a child's health and development and the cumulative effect of such problems over time. For example, a mother with a mild learning disability may not reach the criteria for help from an adult services team and her child's standard of care may not be sufficiently poor to meet the criteria for children's services intervention. However, the failure to recognise the need for early intervention to provide support to the child and family on a planned basis from both children's and adult's services may result in the child's current and future development being impaired.
- They are **children and young people involved in the use of drugs** where the level

and nature of their drug use is unknown to their parents and/or any professionals to whom they are known, for example, teachers, although their general health or behaviour may be a cause for concern. These children may be fearful of asking for help from statutory agencies and may be more receptive to approaches from voluntary agencies or specialist drug services.

- They are young people about whom there are concerns that they are becoming or might be **involved in prostitution**. Draft government *Guidance on Children Involved in Prostitution,* issued for consultation in December 1998, sets out an inter-agency approach to helping this group of young people. The emphasis is on both preventing these vulnerable children from becoming involved in prostitution and safeguarding and promoting the welfare of those who are being abused through prostitution. These situations may require careful assessment of the young person's needs and consideration of how best to help him or her.

- They are children **separated from their country of origin** who are without the care and protection of their parents or legal guardian, often referred to as **unaccompanied asylum seeking children**. Their status, age and circumstances may all be uncertain, in addition to their having experienced or witnessed traumatic events, and they may be suffering the most extreme forms of loss. The situations in which they are accommodated, albeit on a temporary basis, may be less than adequate, for example, where an 18 year old Eritrean young woman is caring for her 10 year old brother in bed and breakfast accommodation for homeless people. There is a helpful *Statement of Good Practice* (Separated Children in Europe Programme, 1999) which provides a straightforward account of the policies and practice required to act to protect the rights of such children.

- They are **children of asylum seeking families** who may have extensive unmet needs while the focus of activity is on resolving the adults' asylum applications, accommodation or other pressing issues.

- They have **a parent in prison**. It is estimated that 125,000 children have a parent in prison at any one time (Ramsden, 1998). In 1997, approximately 8,000 women were received into the prison system (either untried and/or following custodial sentences). A survey by the Home Office (Caddle and Crisp, 1997) suggests that over 60% have children under the age of 18 and over half the women have had their first or only child as teenagers. At the very least, children in these circumstances experience disruptions in their care, but for some the consequences are much more severe and long lasting. Furthermore, social services departments may be asked by the Prison Service to contribute to assessments when there are children involved (See paragraph 5.82).

3.59 There are common features which apply to the assessment of children in all these and other similar situations:

- they require a high degree of co-operation and co-ordination between staff in different agencies, in planning or preparing for assessments, in undertaking and completing them;

- extra care must be taken to ensure that there is an holistic view of the child and that the child does not become lost between the agencies involved and their different systems and procedures;

- as most children are registered with a GP, this route could be used for locating lost children and obtaining information about their past histories;
- particular attention should be given to health and education assessments of these children. The older the child, the more these may be overlooked or found difficult to arrange;
- consideration must be given to the means by which information will be analysed and action planned, how the outcome of assessment is communicated and to whom;
- responsibility for action and providing services must be clearly identified and recorded, with specific timescales;
- overall responsibility for ensuring the welfare of the child in need must be clearly allocated.

3.60 It is significant that, where adolescents are the subject of assessment, studies emphasise the importance of staff finding time to engage in direct work with young people and getting to know them well, although it may be difficult sometimes 'to get below the surface' (Sinclair *et al*, 1995). Sadly, such studies reveal that all too often assessments with older children fail to be completed, especially where specialist professional assessments are required. Even greater efforts are necessary to co-ordinate and achieve co-operation from all parties in these situations.

Assessing the Needs of Young Carers

3.61 A group of children whose needs are increasingly more clearly recognised are young carers for example those who assume important caring responsibilities for parents and siblings. Some children care for parents who are disabled, physically or mentally ill, others for parents dependent on alcohol or involved in drug misuse. For further information and guidance refer to the *Carers (Recognition and Services) Act 1995: Policy Guidance and Practice Guide* (Department of Health, 1996a) and *Young Carers: Making a Start* (Department of Health, 1998a).

3.62 An assessment of family circumstances is essential. Young carers should not be expected to carry inappropriate levels of caring which have an adverse impact on their development and life chances. It should not be assumed that children should take on similar levels of caring responsibilities as adults. Services should be provided to parents to enhance their ability to fulfil their parenting responsibilities. There may be differences of view between children and parents about appropriate levels of care. Such differences may be out in the open or concealed. The resolution of such tensions will require good quality joint work between adult and children's social services as well as co-operation from schools and health care workers. This work should include direct work with the young carer to understand his or her perspective and opinions. The young person who is a primary carer of his or her parent or sibling may have a good understanding of the family's functioning and needs which should be incorporated into the assessment.

3.63 Young carers can receive help from both local and health authorities. Where a child is providing a substantial amount of care on a regular basis for a parent, the child will be entitled to an assessment of their ability to care under section 1(1) of the *Carers (Recognition and Services) Act 1995* and the local authority must take that assessment into account in deciding what community care services to provide for the parent. Many young carers are not aware that they can ask for such an assessment. In addition, consideration must be given as to whether a young carer is a child in need under the Children Act 1989. The central issue is whether a child's welfare or development might suffer if support is not provided to the child or family. As part of the *National Strategy for Carers* (1999a), local authorities should take steps to identify children with additional family burdens. Services should be provided to promote the health and development of young carers while not undermining the parent.

The Assessment Framework and Children Looked After

3.64 The Assessment Framework has been designed to assess children's needs across the same developmental dimensions as the Looking After Children materials (Parker (eds), 1991; Department of Health, 1995b). This will enable the Looking After Children system to be revised during 1999–2001 in a way which will result in an integrated model for assessing and providing services to the wider group of children in need and their families than looked after children. Most children who come into contact with social services departments do not enter the care system. However, should a child need to be looked after, congruence in the system will ensure that good quality baseline information is available about the child's developmental and wider needs at the point of entry to the looked after system. This will support improved assessment of the child's needs which will enable better placement matching in foster and residential care. The parenting capacity domain within the Assessment Framework can also be used with foster carers in assessing suitability for a particular child. It will also inform the provision of services to children and birth and foster families during the care episode. When children return home, or are placed with a permanent substitute family, using the same Assessment Framework will ensure continuity of planning to secure the best outcomes for the child.

3.65 The parenting capacity dimensions in the Assessment Framework will be particularly useful for evaluating improvements in parenting capacities as part of any decision making processes and, where appropriate, a reunification programme. This information will also be important in planning and managing contact. Once baseline information on parenting capacity has been collected during the core assessment, it will be possible to identify key areas for change and target social work and other resources more effectively whilst the child is looked after and reunification plans are being implemented. It should also enable social workers to decide when family reunification will not be possible and an alternative placement is required.

Children Being Placed for Adoption

3.66 In circumstances where there are children for whom adoption is planned, the Assessment Framework may be used as part of the assessment of the capacities of potential adopters, matching children with approved adopters, and planning what kinds of services a child and adopting parents might benefit from post placement and post adoption. These services might include help to understand any specific needs the child has and how best to respond to them. Some needs may require time limited interventions whereas others may exist on a continuing basis. The medical adviser to the social services department has a critical role to play in offering advice and information from the point at which a child is being considered for adoption and throughout the adoption process. A holistic approach to the consideration of what are likely to be complex needs of the child requires good inter-disciplinary co-operation and co-ordination.

Children Leaving Care

3.67 Where children leave care and live independently of their families, family links often remain very important. Research has pointed to the considerable potential of working in partnership with the child and their family during this transition period (Marsh and Peel, 1999).

3.68 The Children (Leaving Care) Bill which has been introduced in the 1999/2000 Parliamentary Session will, subject to Royal Assent, provide for every looked after child to have a personal adviser and a pathway plan by their sixteenth birthday. The pathway plan will be informed by an assessment of need based on the Assessment Framework and will, in effect, extend existing assessment and planning requirements to cover the child's transition to adulthood. The plan will be subject to regular review irrespective of whether the child remains looked after or has left care and the Bill provides for the continuation of the plan and contact by the personal adviser until the young person reaches the age of 21 and, where supported in higher education and training, up to the age of 24.

4

Analysis, Judgement and Decision Making

> Treatment itself is intimately bound up with assessment, relying on it as a house relies on its foundation. Consequently, assessment continues throughout the treatment process, despite a change in focus during its course (Jones, 1997).

4.1 The Guidance has emphasised that assessment is not an end in itself but a process which will lead to an improvement in the wellbeing or outcomes for a child or young person. The conclusion of an assessment should result in:

- an analysis of the needs of the child and the parenting capacity to respond appropriately to those needs within their family context;
- identification of whether and, if so, where intervention will be required to secure the wellbeing of the child or young person;
- a realistic plan of action (including services to be provided), detailing who has responsibility for action, a timetable and a process for review.

4.2 Generally, all these phases of the assessment process should be undertaken in partnership with the child and key family members, and with their agreement. This includes finalising the plan of action. There may be exceptions when there are concerns that a child is suffering or may be suffering significant harm.

4.3 In many approaches or referrals to social services departments, families are clear about their problems but may not be sure where to turn or how to obtain services. With advice and information, they are able to take appropriate action. This action may be all that is required by a social services department. Where there is a question about whether a child is in need and therefore services are necessary an assessment is required. For some families, the process of assessment is in itself a therapeutic intervention. Being able to look at problems in a constructive manner with a professional who is willing to listen and who helps family members to reflect on what is happening, is enough to help them find solutions. During the assessment process, it may emerge that families will best be helped by agencies other than social services. Armed with this information, families may wish to seek solutions themselves; others may wish to have help in gaining access to other agencies or practical services.

4.4 A significant proportion of families who seek help from social services are unable to resolve stresses or problems solely from within their own emotional or practical resources or from their own support network. It is for these families that assessment may be important in order to identify the nature of their children's needs and, simultaneously, may be the first stage in a longer process of positive intervention. Ultimately, careful judgements must be made about balancing the needs of children and parents.

4.5 In most situations, meeting children's needs will almost always involve responding also to the needs of family members. The two are closely connected and it is rarely possible to promote the welfare of children without promoting the welfare of significant adults in their lives. In some cases, meeting the children's needs may mean giving others either parenting responsibility or legal parental responsibility for the child, either for short periods or on a longer term basis. Where consideration is being given to meeting parents' needs, as part of the plan of intervention, this must be because it is in the best interests of the child and will assist in securing better outcomes for the child. Parents may also require help in their own right as adults who have specific needs.

Analysis

4.6 In Chapter 3 it was emphasised that gathering information is a crucial phase in the assessment process, which requires careful planning about how best to undertake it. Information may be gathered from a variety of sources, using methods which will be determined by the purpose of the assessment and the particular circumstances of each child and family (see paragraph 3.38). Some of the information may have been gathered through the use of questionnaires and scales, such as those published in the accompanying materials (Department of Health, Cox and Bentovim, 2000). The **Home Inventory** (Caldwell and Bradley, 1984) and the **Assessment of Family Competence, Strengths and Difficulties** (Bentovim and Bingley Miller, forthcoming), due for publication later in 2000 will also provide important information about the child's world and family functioning respectively.

4.7 The information should be organised according to the dimensions of the Assessment Framework as a necessary beginning to the next phase of analysis. Information should be summarised under each of the three domains ie. children's developmental needs, parents' or caregivers' capacities to respond, and wider family and environmental factors. The Department of Health has developed assessment recording forms to assist practitioners and their managers in this phase of work (Department of Health and Cleaver, 2000).

4.8 In organising the information, there may be different perspectives to be explored, recorded and taken into account, for example, the child may have a different understanding and interpretation of what is happening from that of either parent or of a professional. These differences are important when developing an understanding of the child's needs within the family context. Different family members may attach different meanings to the same information, for example, the significance of past family history or events. The same information may vary in its salience for different family members, for example, the impact of a bereavement in a family. Sometimes these differences in perception can lead to conflicts in the family or between family members and professionals. In reaching a shared understanding of what is happening in a family, it is important to keep the focus on the needs of the child. This enables family members and professionals to agree a plan of action, even in the context of some differences or tensions, that will address the identified needs of the child with the aim of improving outcomes for the child.

4.9 By this point, there should be clear summaries which identify from the information gathered the child's developmental needs, parenting capacity and family and environmental factors. In each of these domains, both strengths and difficulties should be identified. Children's needs do not exist in a vacuum (Jones, 2000) and, therefore, the inter-relationships between the child, family and environment must be understood. Some factors will work positively to support children's growing up while others will militate against or undermine their healthy development. In weighing up the impact that various factors have on a child, it has to be borne in mind that not all factors will have equal significance and the cumulative effect of some relatively minor factors may be considerable. Thus the analysis of a child's needs is a complex activity drawing on knowledge from research and practice combined with an understanding of the child's needs within his or her family.

4.10 The elements of parenting capacity can be described, and minimum parenting standards or requirements assessed by the practitioner and related to their child. However, it is not possible to ascribe numerical values to each element because parenting capabilities and behaviours are complex and subject to influences from within and outside the family (Jones, 2000). Parenting capacity can only be understood within the overall context in which children are being brought up. The analysis should identify the family and environmental factors which have an impact on the different aspects of the child's development and on the parent(s) capacity in order to explore the relationship between the three domains (Department of Health and Cleaver, 2000). At some points in time judgements may be made (based on the analysis of their parental functioning) that the parent is unable to respond to their child's needs.

4.11 To summarise the analysis stage:

- A child's needs must be based on knowledge of what would be expected of this child's development;
- Parenting capacity should draw on knowledge about what would be reasonable to expect of parental care given to a similar child;
- Family and environmental factors should draw on knowledge about the impact these will have on both parenting capacity and directly on a child's development.

Judgements

4.12 Professionals will be drawing on their respective knowledge bases to inform the judgements they come to about a child's circumstances, whether the child is in need and whether their health and development is likely to be impaired without the provision of services. For some children, decisions will also have been made about whether they are suffering or are likely to suffer significant harm. The knowledge base will include information about the factors which are intrinsic to all children such as temperament, genetic make-up and race, and other factors which may be intrinsic to some children, such as physical or sensory impairments.

4.13 Critical to an understanding of what is happening to a child is the knowledge of the way in which children need to achieve certain tasks at particular ages and stages of development. Bentovim (1998) summarises current views on child development which 'emphasise that what matters for development is that the various systems – biological and psychological – should be well integrated. Development is about progression, change and re-organisation throughout life' (p.66). This normal pattern of development may not be achieved for some children either because of unavoidable factors such as impairments or because they are suffering significant harm (Bentovim, 1998).

4.14 There is a considerable literature to assist professionals when making a judgement about a parent's capacity and assessing what is a reasonable standard of care (Jones, 2000; Cleaver *et al*, 1999) 'even though research cannot provide the kind of numerical accuracy which is often sought' (Jones, 2000).

4.15 Critical at this phase will be judgements about a number of key issues (Jones, 1998):

- determining what has been happening and whether this is a child in need or is suffering significant harm;
- understanding the child and family context sufficiently to be able to secure the child's wellbeing or safety;
- assessing the likelihood of change;

and later

- reviewing whether such change is being achieved.

4.16 It is important to identify strengths in the child's family system and to use these areas as the basis on which the child's development can be promoted. The more complex the family's problems, the more these will involve sophisticated inter-disciplinary and inter-agency co-operation in order to reach judgements about these issues. Stevenson (1998) provides a cautionary note in such circumstances. 'The families themselves may seem overwhelmed to the point of powerlessness, so the workers may experience similar feelings' (p.18). The reflective process for professionals working with children and families may be stressful, particularly in difficult circumstances. Some children's lives are such that profound, sensitive judgements may be required. This could include judgements about medical treatment in life threatening situations; judgements about whether to separate a child from his or her parents or caregivers; judgements about whether to place children with permanent substitute families. However, careful and systematic gathering of information, and its summary and analysis according to the framework can assist professionals in making sound evidence based judgements. The practice guidance has been developed to assist this process (Department of Health, 2000a).

4.17 Sometimes, where there are multi-faceted problems, assessments can become stuck and little progress made. Reder and Duncan (1999) talk about the danger of **assessment paralysis** which they describe as 'an impasse in the professional network where the issue of whether the parent has a psychiatric diagnosis becomes the context for deciding about all interventions'. Assessment paralysis can apply in other situations, where the focus of attention becomes stuck on a particular diagnostic issue and decision making is driven by this consideration rather than the child's needs. It requires vigilance and careful management by those staff who hold responsibility for the child's welfare to ensure that progress continues to be made to help the child.

Use of Consultation

4.18 Social services departments have lead responsibility for undertaking assessments of children in need. In order to arrive at well balanced judgements about the needs of children, practitioners and their managers may benefit from the expertise and experience of professionals in other disciplines. These professionals can act as consultants or advisers to assist and contribute to the assessment processes, which includes analysis of information gathered. This type of input may be as useful to the assessment as the commissioning of specialist assessments.

4.19 In some situations, where the available evidence requires careful analysis by those with particular expertise, sufficient information about a child and the family may already be available. Therefore, the specialist task is to assist in the analysis of available material, drawing on knowledge in particular areas about likely outcomes of certain courses of action. This expert knowledge can assist the practitioner and his or her manager when constructing a plan and deciding how to implement it.

Decision Making

4.20 In drawing up a plan of intervention, careful distinction should to be made between **judgements** about the child's developmental needs and parenting capacity and **decisions** about how best to address these at different points in time. These decisions will have to take account of a number of factors including:

- how existing good relationships and experiences can be nurtured and enhanced;
- what type of interventions are known to have the best outcomes for the particular circumstances of the child who has been assessed as in need;
- what the child and family can cope with at each stage. Complicated arrangements regarding the provision of services and interventions might well overwhelm the child or individual family members;
- how the necessary resources can be mobilised within the family's network and within professional agencies, including social services;
- what alternative interventions are available if the resources of choice cannot be secured;
- ensuring interventions achieve early success and have a beneficial impact. The self-esteem of children and parents is critical to the outcome of longer term intervention. Good experiences are important when many other aspects of family life may be in chaos or problems feel insurmountable;
- there may be an optimal hierarchy of interventions which will require distinguishing between what is achievable in the short term, what will have maximum impact on the child and family's wellbeing and what are the long term goals;
- identifying what the child regards as highest priority, for example, learning to ride a

bicycle may be far higher on a child's list of wants than therapy, and such practical wishes should be taken account of because they may result in changes which will enable the child to make use of therapeutic help.

- It will be essential to achieve some parts of a proposed intervention within a predetermined timescale, in order to meet the child's needs. Other components of a plan will be less pressing and although desirable to achieve, not considered necessary for the prevention of future significant harm.

4.21 Underlying these critical considerations is the importance of keeping the child at the centre of the planning processes. Three key aspects of a child's health and development must inform the content and timing of the plan:

- ensuring the child's safety;
- remembering that a child cannot wait indefinitely;
- maintaining a child's learning.

4.22 The development of secure parent-child attachments is critical to a child's healthy development. The quality and nature of the attachment will be a key issue to be considered in decision making, especially if decisions are being made about moving a child from one setting to another, or re-uniting a child with his or her birth family. (For further discussion of attachment see Crittenden and Ainsworth, 1989; Schofield, 1998; Howe, 2000).

4.23 In complex situations, it may be helpful for those involved in the assessment process to meet to discuss the findings and formulate the plan. This should involve the parents and, as appropriate, the child. Family Group Conferences or multi-disciplinary meetings may provide for the construction of plans for children in need. *Working Together to Safeguard Children* (1999) sets out the processes to be followed for children about whom there are concerns that they are suffering or likely to suffer significant harm. The role of the key worker appointed when a child's name has been placed on a child protection register, the role of the group of professionals responsible for developing and implementing the child protection plan and the aims, content and processes for constructing such a plan are set out in paragraphs 5.75 to 5.84 of *Working Together to Safeguard Children* (1999).

4.24 For some families, the findings from the core assessment will indicate that the parents are responding appropriately to their child's needs, but in order to maximise the child's health and developmental outcomes, specific services are required to assist the parents and/or the child. In the absence of particular stress factors, such as those resulting from having a chronically ill child, the parents would be able to bring up their children without external help. However, the presence of these stressors require parents and families to develop new ways of functioning, as well as to accept support from outside their family and friendship networks. In these families, siblings may be affected significantly and services should address their needs.

4.25 It has to be recognised that in families where a child has been maltreated there are some parents who will not be able to change sufficiently within the child's timescales in order to ensure their children do not continue to suffer significant harm (Jones, 1998). In these situations, decisions may need to be made to separate permanently the child and parent or parents. In these circumstances decisions about the nature and form of any contact will also need to be made, in the light of all that is known about the child and the family, and reviewed throughout childhood. Key in these considerations is what is in the child's best interests, informed by the child's views (Cleaver, 2000).

4.26 The following criteria have been identified as suggesting a poor outcome for reuniting children who have been maltreated with their parents (Bentovim *et al*, 1987; Silvester *et al*, 1995):

- the abusing parent completely or significantly denies any responsibility for the child's developmental state or abuse;
- the child is rejected or blamed outright;
- the child's needs are not recognised by their parents who put their own needs first;
- parents have frequently failed to show concern, or acknowledge, long-standing difficulties such as alcoholism or psychiatric problems;
- during therapeutic interventions, the relationships within the family and with professionals remain at breaking point.

4.27 However, most parents are capable of change, and following appropriate interventions, able to provide a safe family context for their child. At times, children may need to be separated temporarily from their parent or parents. This enables change to take place while the child is living away from home in a safe environment. During this time, it will be important to address the changes required in the parent(s) as well as meeting any therapeutic needs of the child and other family members by active programmes of intervention, appropriate deployment of resources and careful review of progress. If a child is separated from their parent(s), it is essential that parents are able to sustain any improvements made whilst the child is living away from home, when the child returns to live with them. Careful thought should be given to the nature of services required by the parents and child during this transition phase, to ensure that earlier achievements are able to be maintained and continue to be improved upon. For some families continued intervention may be necessary for a considerable length of time until the child is no longer vulnerable.

4.28 Jones (1998, p.108) summarising relevant child maltreatment research findings reports the following features as having been identified in those cases where there are better prospects of achieving good outcomes for children:

- Those infants and children who despite abuse do not have residual disability, developmental delay or special educational needs;
- Those children subjected to less severe abuse or neglect;
- Children who have had the benefit of non-abusive or corrective relationships with peers, siblings and/or a supportive adult;
- Children who have developed more healthy and appropriate attributions about the maltreatment which they had suffered;
- Children and families who are able and willing to co-operate with helping agencies;
- Children and families who have been able to engage in therapeutic work;

- Situations where successful partnerships between professionals and family members have occurred;
- Children and families where the psychological abuse component of the maltreatment experience has been amenable to change.

4.29 When an analysis of a child's needs and parenting capacity within their family context is completed, there is then a baseline from which further assessment and re-assessment, using the Assessment Framework, can be undertaken to review progress as services are provided.

4.30 In a number of family situations where there is concern about a child's safety and future wellbeing whilst living in his or her family, the findings from a core assessment may provide an uncertain picture of the family's capacity to change. These families are characterised by one or more of the following (Bentovim *et al*, 1987; Silvester *et al*, 1995):

- uncertainty as to whether the parents are taking full responsibility for either the abuse or the child's developmental state;
- whereas the child's needs may sometimes be viewed as primary, the parents put their own needs as dominant;
- the child may be scape-goated and parent-child attachments are ambivalent or anxious;
- family patterns are rigid rather than healthily flexible;
- relationships with professionals are ambivalent.

4.31 These families often cause professionals considerable concern. It is important that services are provided to give the family the best chance of achieving the required changes. It is equally important that in circumstances where the family situation is not improving or changing fast enough to respond to the child's needs, decisions are made about the longterm future of the child. Delay or drift can result in the child not receiving the help she or he requires and having their health and development impaired.

Plans for Children in Need

4.32 The details of the plan are bench marks against which the progress of the family and the commitment of workers are measured, and therefore it is important that they should be realistic and not vague statements of good intent (Department of Health, 1995).

4.33 The analysis, judgement and decisions made will form the basis of a plan of work with a child in need and his or her family. The complexity or severity of the child's needs will determine the scope and detail of the plan. The different circumstances under which the assessment has been carried out will also determine the form in which it is recorded and the status of the plan:

- **Children in Need Plan** at the conclusion of a core assessment, which will involve the child and family members as appropriate and the contributions of all agencies.

A format for the plan is contained in assessment records (Department of Health and Cleaver, 2000).

- **Child Protection Plan** as a decision of an inter-agency child protection conference, following enquiries and assessment under s47. The expectations of a child protection plan are outlined in paragraphs 5.81 to 5.84 of *Working Together to Safeguard Children* (1999).
- **Care Plan for a Child Looked After** as a result of an assessment that a child will need to be looked after by the local authority either in the short term or long term and placed in foster or residential care. The requirements for a care plan in these circumstances are laid out in Volume 3 of the Children Act 1989, Guidance and Regulations (paragraphs 2.59 to 2.62). A format for the care plan is an integral part of the Department of Health's Looking After Children materials (Department of Health, 1995b).
- **Care Plans** for a child who is the subject of a care or supervision order or for whom the plan is adoption (see paragraphs 3.22 to 3.24).
- **Pathway Plan for a young person who is in care or leaving care** as outlined in the Government's intentions for young people living in and leaving care (Department of Health, 1999f; Children (Leaving Care) Bill, 1999).

4.34 There are some general principles about plans for working with children and families, whatever the circumstances in which they have been drawn up. First that, wherever possible, they should be drawn up in agreement with the child/young person and key family members and their commitment to the plan should have been secured. There are two caveats which the professionals responsible for the plan need to bear in mind:

- objectives should be reasonable and timescales not too short or unachievable;
- plans should not be dependent on resources which are known to be scarce or unavailable.

Failure to address these issues can be damaging to families and jeopardise the overall aim of securing the child's wellbeing. Second, the plan must maintain a focus on the child, even though help may be provided to a number of family members as part of the plan. As Jones *et al* (1987) write 'It is never acceptable to sacrifice the interests of the child for the therapeutic benefit of the parents'.

4.35 Department of Health practice guidance (1995a) recommended that professional workers and relevant family members should be clear about the following aspects of the plan which have general application (an abridged list is in Figure 7). With clarity about these matters, it is possible for both professionals and the family to take issue with the other when their expectations are not met or when perceptions and objectives begin to differ.

4.36 Fundamental to the plan, from the beginning, is the commitment of all the parties involved and the signatures to the plan of those who have lead responsibility for ensuring it is carried forward (in social services, this should include the team manager/supervisor as well as the practitioners). There should also be a clear recorded statement on the plan about when and how it will be reviewed. Reviewing the child's progress and the effectiveness of services and other interventions is a continuous part

Figure 7 AREAS IN WHICH CLARITY IS REQUIRED IN CHILD CARE PLANNING

- the objective of the plan, for example to provide and evaluate the efficacy of therapeutic interventions
- what services will be provided by which professional group or designated agency
- the timing and nature of contact between the professional workers and the family
- the purpose of services and professional contact
- specific commitments to be met by the family, for example attendance at a family centre
- specific commitments to be met by the professional workers, for example the provision of culturally sensitive services or special assistance for those with disabilities
- which components of the plan are negotiable in the light of experience and which are not
- what needs to change and the goals to be achieved, for example the child's weight to increase by a specific amount in a particular period, regular and appropriate stimulation for the child in keeping with her or his development and age
- what is unacceptable care of the child
- what sanctions will be used if the child is placed in danger or in renewed danger
- what preparation and support the child and adults will receive if she or he appears in court as a witness in criminal proceedings.

of the process of work with children and families. The timescales and procedures for reviewing plans for children in need which are also part of other guidance, regulations and legislation (child protection plans, care plans for children looked after and pathway plans) are already prescribed. For children in need plans, where work is being undertaken to support children and families in the community, it is good practice to review the plan with family members **at least every six months**, and to formally record it. Key professionals should also be involved in the review process and in constructing the revised plan.

4.37 The purpose of an assessment is to identify the child's needs within their family context and to use this understanding to decide how best to address these needs. It is essential that the plan is constructed on the basis of the findings from the assessment and that this plan is reviewed and refined over time to ensure the agreed case objectives are achieved. Specific outcomes for the child, expressed in terms of their health and development can be measured. These provide objective evidence against which to evaluate whether the child and family have been provided with appropriate services and ultimately whether the child's wellbeing is optimal.

5

Roles and Resposibilities in Inter-Agency Assessment of Children in Need

Principles of Inter-Disciplinary and Inter-Agency Assessment

5.1 A key principle of the Assessment Framework is that children's needs and their families circumstances will require inter-agency collaboration to ensure full understanding of what is happening and to ensure an effective service response. This chapter elaborates further on the roles and responsibilities of different disciplines and agencies when assessing whether a child is in need under the Children Act 1989. Some children in need may be being assessed concurrently under legislation other than the Children Act 1989. Other children may have already been assessed under different legislation and may be in receipt of services from agencies but not from social services. A further group of children may have parents or other significant family members or caregivers who are in receipt of social services.

5.2 In order to ensure optimal outcomes for children, whilst at the same time avoiding duplication of services or children receiving no service at all, it is important for all disciplines and agencies to work in a co-ordinated way to an agreed plan. Increasingly, there are service developments designed on a multi-agency basis, where teams operate with a pooled budget and shared objectives. An example is Youth Offending Teams.

5.3 There may be a number of voluntary and private organisations and community based groups, whose staff and volunteers have knowledge of a child and their family. In undertaking an assessment, it is important to find appropriate ways of using their understanding of the family to inform the overall analysis of the child's needs and how best to help the family. Communication with staff and volunteers from other agencies and groups should be based on the principles of confidentiality and consent set out in paragraphs 3.46 to 3.57.

5.4 Inter-agency, inter-disciplinary assessment practice requires an additional set of knowledge and skills to that required for working within a single agency or independently. It requires that all staff understand the roles and responsibilities of staff working in contexts different to their own. Having an understanding of the perspectives, language and culture of other professionals can inform how communication is conducted. This prevents professionals from misunderstanding one another because they use different language to describe similar concepts or because they are influenced by stereotypical perceptions of the other discipline. The use of the Assessment Framework for assessing children in need provides a language which is common to children and their family members, as well as to professionals and other staff.

Corporate Responsibilities for Children in Need

5.5 Under s17 of the Children Act 1989, social services departments carry lead responsibility for establishing whether a child is in need and for ensuring services are provided to that child as appropriate. This may not require social services to provide the service itself. Following a child in need assessment, for example, a child with communication impairment may require the help of a NHS speech therapist and additional classroom support at school rather than any specialist services of the social services department. The voluntary sector may have an important role to play in contributing to an assessment and providing services to a family.

5.6 This inter-agency responsibility is spelt out in s17(5) of the Children Act 1989.

> *Every local authority –*
>
> a *shall facilitate the provision by others (including in particular voluntary organisations) of services which the authority have power to provide by virtue of this section, or section 18, 20, 23 or 24; and*
>
> b *may make such arrangements as they see fit for any person to act on their behalf in the provision of any such service.*
>
> Children Act 1989 s17(5)

5.7 The corporate responsibilities for working with children in need and their families have been emphasised in the Government's objectives for children's social services (Department of Health, 1999e).

> The Government believes that local authorities corporately have a responsibility to address the needs of such children and young people. There should be effective joint working by education, housing and leisure in partnership with social services and health. Social services alone cannot promote the social inclusion and development of these children and families. However, in partnership with others, social services can play a vital role (p.4).

Inter-Agency Responsibilities for Assessments of Children in Need

5.8 The next section sets out the responsibilities of local authority departments and health authorities for assessing children in need and their families and the basis on which professionals working in statutory agencies and independent settings work with social services staff who have lead responsibility for this task. This section should be read in conjunction with Chapter 3 in *Working Together to Safeguard Children* (1999) which addresses the primary roles and responsibilities of statutory agencies, professionals, the voluntary and private sector and the wider community in respect of children, and in particular children about whom there is concern that they may be suffering or are suffering significant harm. The following sections address specifically some of the key issues about agency roles and responsibilities when assessing children in need or contributing to other assessments of children and their families. It includes most of the major agencies but is not comprehensive.

Social Services Departments

5.9 The social services department has the lead role for ensuring initial and core assessments are carried out according to the *Framework for the Assessment of Children in Need and their Families.* In practice this means, planning, preparation, co-ordination and communication with professionals in other agencies, in accordance with the principles set out in paragraph 1.23. This is where inter-agency protocols (and intra-agency where adults services are concerned) can be an effective means of providing a structure for collaboration and lines of communication.

5.10 With any child or family referral, social services should check whether the person with parenting responsibility has needs independent of the child's needs, which may call for the provision of adult community care services. If so, those needs should be further assessed in accordance with *Achieving Fairer Access to Adult Social Care Services* (Department of Health, forthcoming, a). The assessment of the child's needs and the capacity of their parent(s) to respond appropriately to those needs within their family context, should follow the *Framework for the Assessment of Children in Need and their Families.*

5.11 With any adult referral, social services should check whether the person has parenting responsibility for a child under 18. If so, the initial assessment should explore any parenting and child related issues in accordance with the *Framework for the Assessment of Children in Need and their Families.* This will determine if the child is in need, and the nature of services required to support his or her family, under Section 17 of the Children Act 1989. Further assessment should be undertaken and services provided as appropriate, following this Guidance. The assessment of adult needs should follow the *Achieving Fairer Access to Adult Social Care Services Guidance.*

5.12 Where the child is looked after or there is concern about significant harm, the responsibilities of local authorities are clearly laid out in *Children Act 1989 Guidance and Regulations* (1991) and in *Working Together to Safeguard Children* (1999). Although social services will continue to work closely with other agencies in such circumstances, it is social services which has a statutory duty to safeguard and promote the welfare of children and to ensure that this is effectively carried out.

5.13 The role of the key worker for a child whose name has been placed on a Child Protection Register is set out in paragraph 5.76 of *Working Together to Safeguard Children* (1999). It states that the key worker has responsibility for completing the core assessment of the child and family and securing contributions from core group members and others as necessary.

5.14 For children looked after and children whose names have been placed on the child protection register and who are subject to a child protection plan, the responsibilities for monitoring and reviewing the children's progress (including safety) are set out in the same *Regulations and Guidance* (Department of Health 1991; Department of Health *et al*, 1999). Social services departments have lead responsibility for ensuring these reviews take place within the prescribed time scales. As stated in Chapter 4, there are no such regulations governing the review of welfare of other children in need. However, it is essential that agreements are reached on an inter-agency basis about how best to monitor and review children in need plans. The lead agency for this activity may not necessarily be the social services department, as another agency may be better placed to undertake this responsibility.

5.15 In the process of all relevant agencies working collaboratively to construct and agree the child in need plan, decisions will have been made about which agencies will provide the necessary services. Careful thought should be given to which professional would be best placed to have lead responsibility for co-ordinating the review of the child in need plan. Amongst the considerations will be the respective roles and responsibilities of the various agencies.

Voluntary and Independent Agencies

5.16 Voluntary and independent agencies are key providers of a number of different types of services for children and families. They may be undertaking or contributing to assessments for a range of purposes: under the terms of a service agreement with a social services department, in partnership with other agencies or organisations or as part of the service they provide in response to direct referrals from children and families. Their staff's knowledge and use of the Assessment Framework when undertaking an assessment will enable information to be organised within a common framework, using a common language. This will be particularly important where the assessment has been commissioned by a social services department.

Health Authority

5.17 Every Health Authority is required to work with local agencies and trusts to consider the health needs of their residents and then determine local priorities and ways to address those needs. In particular Health Authorities and Primary Care Groups and Trusts should ensure that they participate in inter-agency planning and co-operation through Children's Services Plans and Quality Protects Management Action Plans, and that there are clear cross references in the Health Improvement Programmes.

5.18 The Health Improvement Programme is a jointly agreed health strategy which has the support of the local authority, NHS Trusts and Primary Care Groups. Services for healthcare for vulnerable children should be described and the health authority should ensure that local services and professionals contribute fully and effectively to local inter-agency working to safeguard children and promote their welfare.

5.19 The Health Authority should agree with Primary Care Groups and Trusts (PCG/Ts) how the local health service obligation to contribute to assessments involving inter-agency working should be discharged locally. Service specifications drawn up by PCG/Ts should include clear service standards for assessments of children in need. For children where there are grounds for concern that they are suffering significant harm these must be consistent with local Area Child Protection Committee protocols.

5.20 NHS Trusts and PCG/Ts are responsible for providing acute and community health services in hospital and community settings, and a wide range of staff will come into contact with children and parents in the course of their normal duties. Staff should be alert to concerns about a child's health and development and should know how to act upon these concerns in line with local protocols. Conversely, they should also be aware of how adult patients with, for example, physical or mental illness may require help to carry out their parent roles successfully.

5.21 Most health professionals, in the NHS, private sector, and other agencies play an important part in the lives of children and their parents. Because of the universal nature of health provision, health professionals are often the first to become aware of the needs of children or that some families are experiencing difficulties looking after their children. They should consider what help would benefit those families. Social services departments can assist health professionals by providing information about help that is available in the community and through their own departments.

The General Practitioner and the Primary Health Care Team

5.22 The General Practitioner (GP) and other members of the primary health care team (PHCT) are well placed to recognise when a child is potentially in need of extra support or services to promote health and development, or may be at risk of suffering significant harm. Primary care team members should know when it is appropriate to refer a child, as a potential child in need, to social services for help and support, and how to act on concerns that a child may be at risk of harm through abuse or neglect. When other members of the primary care team become concerned about the welfare of a child, the GP should be involved in discussing these concerns. The GP and primary health care team will have an important contribution to make to initial and core assessments of children in need.

5.23 The GP and the primary health care team are also well placed to recognise when a parent or other adult has problems which may affect their capacity as a parent or carer, or which may mean that they pose a risk of harm to a child. While GPs have responsibilities to all their patients, the child is particularly vulnerable and the welfare of the child of paramount importance. If they have concerns that an adult's problems or behaviour may be causing, or putting a child at risk of harm, they should follow the procedures set out in *Working Together to Safeguard Children* (1999).

Nurses, Midwives, Health Visitors and School Nurses

5.24 Nurses work in a variety of settings where they are likely to meet vulnerable children and their families. They will consider the circumstances in which it would be appropriate to refer them to social services departments for further assessment. They will then continue to work in partnership with social workers, general practitioners and others to contribute to integrated assessments, through sharing facts and professional opinions and by helping children and families identify and address their own needs.

5.25 The midwife and health visitor are uniquely placed to identify risk factors to a child during pregnancy, birth and the child's early care. Health visitors and school nurses monitor child health, growth and physical, emotional and social development. In addition, health visitors are aware of the health of the parents and may identify particular difficulties, for example, postnatal depression in mothers. The regular contact health visitors and school nurses have with children and families gives them an important role to play in the promotion of children's health and development and the protection of children from harm. Many of these staff provide parental support services or parenting sessions and programmes. Some also offer leadership to local schemes which support parents.

Paediatric Services

5.26 If, in the course of a social services department assessments of children in need, an opinion from a specialist paediatric service (including child development teams which are multi-disciplinary and may include a social worker) is required, the service should be requested by or after consultation with the appropriate member of the Primary Health Care Team. Where an urgent opinion is required, because there are grounds for concern that a child is suffering significant harm, this should be sought in line with local child protection procedures.

5.27 A paediatrician and/or a child development team may already know a child who is being assessed by a social services department. This will certainly be the case for children with chronic or recurrent significant illnesses and for disabled children. Social workers based in child development teams should be guided by the Assessment Framework when preparing their contribution to a multi-disciplinary assessment of a disabled child and family. Health professionals seeing such a child will have a contribution to make both to an assessment of need and in advising on medical and child development services that would be of benefit to the child and family. Information should be shared with the informed consent of the parents and of the child (obtained in a way appropriate to the child's age and understanding).

5.28 Many paediatric services have an identified lead Community Paediatrician for children in need who can advise social workers and parents on how to gain access to services. Within the health services, community paediatricians can raise awareness of the difficulties faced by vulnerable and disadvantaged families. Innovations are being proposed (eg. within Health Action Zone schemes) for the introduction of one stop shops where social services and health staff can work together to provide supportive and therapeutic services for children and their families.

Professionals Allied to Health

5.29 Other professionals allied to health, for example audiologists, physiotherapists, occupational therapists and speech therapists will also have important roles to play in the lives of some disabled and developmentally delayed children. Of these professionals, speech therapists are the most likely to be involved in the assessment of children in need. This is because the language development of children is most often affected by adverse environmental and family circumstances. Speech and language therapists can also provide expertise to facilitate communication with a child during an assessment.

Mental Health Services

5.30 Mental health problems are relatively common in children. Preliminary results of a recent survey found that around 10 per cent of 5–15 year olds in England, Scotland and Wales has some type of mental disorder sufficient to cause considerable distress and substantial interference with personal functioning in most cases (Office for National Statistics, 1999). Children of families in Social Class V (unskilled occupations) were about three times as likely to have a mental health problem compared with those in Social Class I (professionals). There are strong associations between family income and the mental health of children.

5.31 The evident increased likelihood of children in need having a significant mental health problem indicates the importance of specific consideration being given to their mental health needs. Not all children and young people, however, will require the help of specialists and, for many, effective and straightforward interventions at an early stage may prevent more serious problems developing later.

5.32 Those children and young people with more severe and complex disorders will require both specialist services and community based support to ensure the best possible outcomes. Social workers and other staff working within such services, whether in hospital or community child and family mental health service settings, should draw on knowledge of the Assessment Framework to inform their contributions.

5.33 An assessment of the mental health of a child or young person will attempt to unravel the various factors that have played a part in the causation of any particular problem or difficulty. This will include an assessment of those factors that are protective as well as those that constitute a risk to the child. As understanding about the aetiology of mental disorders in children increases, it is clear that attention must be given as much to intrinsic factors in the child, such as inherited temperamental characteristics, as to the external social and family influences. This is particularly relevant for children with hyperkeinetic disorder, for instance, whose parents otherwise might feel totally responsible for their child's difficult, demanding and hyperactive behaviour.

5.34 Child and adolescent mental health services provide a range of psychiatric and psychological assessment and treatment services for children and families. There may be very specific reasons why a specialist child mental health professional may become involved. The possibility of a psychotic illness (eg. schizophrenia), suicide or risk of self harm, the consideration of medical or psychological treatment for hyperkeinetic disorder or attention deficit hyperactivity disorder (ADHD), attachment disorders and an assessment of post traumatic stress following severe trauma are all clear cut examples. A referral may also be made for an assessment of individual family factors which contribute to a child's disorder and to ascertaining the therapeutic needs of the child and family members. Many requests, however, are less specific and these often relate to the complexity and chronicity of problems experienced by children who have suffered from a variety of disadvantages and adversities. Assessments of aggressive and oppositional behaviour of a child, family functioning, parenting capacity, and attachment between parent and child are other examples of important mental health tasks where child and mental health services might usefully contribute. In these circumstances a consultation or planning session may help clarify who is best able to undertake which task and what types of intervention may be most appropriate to help the child and family.

5.35 Some children and young people may require admission to hospital for psychiatric treatment. The legal framework governing the admission to hospital and treatment of children is complex. The use and relevance of the Mental Health Act 1983 or the Children Act 1989 should be considered particularly where consent is an issue. Professionals charged with responsibility for helping the child will use the statutory framework which reflects the predominant needs of the child. *The Mental Health Act 1983 Code of Practice* (Department of Health and the Welsh Office, 1999) contains essential guidance (see in particular chapter 31) which should inform the assessment and treatment of children who are either formal or informal patients.

5.36 Adult mental health services, including those providing general adult and community, forensic, psychotherapy, alcohol and substance misuse and learning disability services, have a key role to play in the assessment process when parental problems in these areas have an impact on their capacity to respond appropriately to their children's needs (see paragraphs 6.18 to 6.22 on commissioning specialist services). *Crossing Bridges* (Falkov (ed), 1998) was developed to help staff working with mentally ill parents and their children. It provides a rich source of training material for both adult and children's services staff.

5.37 There are two specific pieces of guidance regarding children visiting parents, other family members and close friends in psychiatric settings where social services departments may be asked to assess whether it is in the best interests of a child to visit a named patient.

5.38 *The Visits by Children to Ashworth, Broadmoor and Rampton Hospital Authorities Directions* (HSC 1999/160) and the *Guidance to Local Authority Social Services Departments on Visits by Children to Special Hospitals* (LAC(99)23) sets out the assessment process to be followed when deciding whether a child can visit a named patient in these hospitals. When a social services department considers it has powers under the Children Act 1989 to undertake the necessary assessment, it is required to assist the hospital by assessing whether it is in the interests of a particular child to visit a named patient and providing the special hospital with this information.

5.39 The Circular *Mental Health Act 1983 Code of Practice: Guidance on the visiting of psychiatric patients by children* (HSC1999/222 LAC(99)32) sets out principles to underpin child-visiting policies in respect of children visiting patients in other psychiatric units. This guidance emphasises the importance of facilitating a child's contact especially with their parents or other key family members, wherever possible. Where there are child welfare concerns, the Trust may ask the social services department where the child is resident to assess whether it is in the best interests of a child to visit a named patient.

Psychologists

5.40 Psychologists – clinical, counselling, educational, forensic – who work with children and families are well placed to contribute to core assessments and to offer a range of services to support children in need and their families. In particular, educational psychologists working with children, their parents, schools and other agencies to promote children's social, emotional and intellectual development will have a significant contribution to make.

Education Services

5.41 A major protective factor in a child's life is having good relationships and succeeding in school. Education staff, through their day to day contact with pupils, have a crucial role to play enabling children to have positive experiences in school – academically and through good relationships – as well as ensuring and observing their wellbeing. Education Welfare Officers and Educational psychologists may, through their work with schools, have knowledge of a particular child. If a child is thought to be in need, social services departments may be able to assist. With parental agreement, these concerns may be discussed with the local social services department and a way forward agreed on identified matters.

5.42 Schools and colleges may on occasions be asked by a social services department for information about a child for whom there are concerns about their health or development, abuse or neglect. The education service itself does not have a direct investigative responsibility in child protection work, but schools and other maintained establishments have a role in assisting the social services department by referring concerns and providing information for s47 child protection enquiries. The role of the independent schools in relation to child protection is the same as that of any other school (Paragraphs 3.12 and 3.15 in *Working Together to Safeguard Children,* 1999).

5.43 When a child has special educational needs, or is disabled, schools and educational psychologists will have important information about the child's development, their level of understanding and the most effective means of communicating with the child. This information should be sought before beginning an assessment. The school and the educational psychologist will also be well placed to give a view on the impact of different types of treatment or intervention on the child's care or behaviour.

5.44 *Social Inclusion: Pupil Support* (Department for Education and Employment,1999a) sets out government guidance on pupil attendance, behaviour, exclusion and re-integration of children at school. It takes a multi-agency approach to supporting schools and enabling them to help pupils with behavioural difficulties, including poor attendance. Where a pupil may be at serious risk of permanent exclusion from school or engaging in criminal activity, a **Pastoral Support Programme** should be set up to plan interventions to help the pupil remain in school. The social services department should as appropriate be involved in the programme (see paragraph 5.5 of Circular 10/99). In addition to contributing to work undertaken with pupils by staff from other agencies, social services departments can assist directly by working with individual children and their families who are experiencing difficulties which impact on the child's educational progress. This could include work with children who are caring for a sick or disabled adult, or where there are relationship difficulties within the family, or where a child has suffered abuse or neglect. In such situations where a child and family is referred to a social services department for help with difficulties identified at school, an initial assessment will be undertaken using the dimensions in the Assessment Framework to ascertain if the child is in need and what help could be offered to respond to the particular needs of the child and their family.

5.45 **Children looked after** can experience a range of problems at school due to the disruptions experienced prior to and during care. These disruptions often include breaks in education. Good liaison with **schools** is important, both to ascertain the school's assessment of these young people and their current needs and to plan with the school how these needs can best be met. *Guidance on the Education of Children and Young People in Public Care* (Department for Education and Employment and Department of Health, forthcoming) sets out the importance of education to young people in public care and the action that local authorities (education and social services departments) must take to safeguard the education and thus the future of these young people.

5.46 **Learning Mentors** are a new resource, being introduced in secondary schools in major cities as part of the Government's Excellence in Cities initiative. They will work closely with pupils to help them to overcome barriers to learning. They will provide intensive counselling and support to a small number of pupils facing significant problems, and will perform a 'signposting' function for others, helping them to access other agencies and local systems of support, such as business and community mentoring schemes and social services. It will be important for learning mentors to work closely with local social services departments in supporting the pupils in their charge.

5.47 Part of the learning mentor function is to participate in progress checks for pupils in year 7 and year 9. They will also draw up individual targets for the pupil to achieve at school. Each school will have its own assessment arrangements in place for progress checks, but all learning mentors will be informed about the Assessment Framework, and encouraged to use a consistent format in order to facilitate effective information sharing.

5.48 The Connexions strategy (Department for Education and Employment, 2000) will introduce a universal network of Personal Advisers for young people. The **Connexions Service** will seek to develop a common assessment tool, with a common core and sections related to specific problems a young person might face, that can be used by all Personal Advisers to assess a young person's needs. Its use will allow different agencies to agree on how a young person's needs can be met either directly or through referral, and encourage a co-ordinated response to a young person's needs. The development of this assessment tool will take full account of this framework for assessing children in need.

5.49 For most young people, the end of compulsory education (at around the age of 16) marks a significant decision and transition point in their development towards adulthood. Government maintained schools have a legal duty to prepare children for this decision and transition by providing a programme of careers education and guidance during the last three years of their compulsory education. Various assessment methods are used to help children identify their occupational interests and potential. The methods include self-assessment questionnaires, standardised tests and practical tasks which are formally assessed.

5.50 In 1999 the Department for Education and Employment established a new form of provision for young people who had failed to make a successful transition from compulsory education. This programme – known as the Learning Gateway – is run jointly by careers services and Training and Enterprise Councils. Personal advisers help 16 and 17 year olds who are struggling to find their way to identify realistic career goals and to obtain a suitable learning or employment opportunity. This often involves some remedial education/preparatory training in basic skills and personal effectiveness before the young person is ready for mainstream provision. The Department for Education and Employment has provided comprehensive *Guidance on Assessment in the Learning Gateway* (Department for Education and Employment, 1999b). This covers both vocational assessment and the assessment of pre-vocational learning and development needs such as personal effectiveness and social skills.

5.51 **Youth and Community Workers** have close contact with young people. They should be alert to any concerns about a young person's welfare and know how to refer to the social services department if they consider a child would benefit from its help. They will also be well placed to assist in a child in need assessment. In some instances joint working may be appropriate.

Special Educational Needs Code of Practice

5.52 Education legislation does not distinguish between disability and special educational needs. Not all children with special educational needs have a disability. Equally some disabled children do not have special educational needs. In January 1999, schools in England identified 20% (1.52 million) of their pupils as having some form of special educational needs, and 3% (248,000) of pupils had statements of Special Educational Needs.

5.53 Special educational needs cover a wide spectrum of needs/difficulties including emotional and behavioural difficulties which are described within the code as:

- Emotional and behavioural difficulties may result, for example, from abuse or neglect; physical or mental illness; sensory or physical impairment; or psychological trauma. In some cases emotional and behavioural difficulties may arise from, or be exacerbated by, circumstances within the school environment. They may also be associated with other learning difficulties.
- Emotional and behavioural difficulties may become apparent in a wide variety of forms – including withdrawal, depressive or suicidal attitudes; obsessional pre-occupations with eating habits; school phobia; substance misuse; disruptive, antisocial and unco-operative behaviour; and frustration, anger and threat of actual violence (*Special Educational Needs Code of Practice*, paragraphs 3.65 and 3.66).

5.54 Under the Education Act 1996, local education authorities have a duty to identify and make a statutory assessment of those children for whom they are responsible who have special educational needs and who probably require a statement of their special educational needs. A child is said to have **special educational needs** if (s)he has:

A learning difficulty which calls for special educational provision to be made for him

5.55 A child has a learning difficulty if:

a. *he has a significantly greater difficulty in learning than the majority of children his age;*

b. *he has a disability which either prevents or hinders him from making use of educational facilities of a kind generally provided for children of his age in schools within the area of the LEA, or*

c. *he is under the age of five and is, or would be if special educational provision were not made for him, likely to fall within paragraph (a) or (b) when over that age.*

5.56 Having decided that a statutory assessment should be made, the local education authority must seek parental, educational, medical, psychological and the social services department's advice. Where a child is known to a social services department, the social worker should draw on information which has already been gathered and is on the child's file. At the same time, the social services department may decide to undertake a child in need assessment under s17 of the Children Act 1989, to ascertain whether social services would benefit the child and family.

5.57 The *Code of Practice on the Identification and Assessment of Special Educational Practice* (1994) sets out the duties of health authorities and social services departments in respect of children who may have special educational needs as follows:

> All those bodies to which the Code applies must, of course, fulfil their duties. But it is up to them to decide how to do so, in the light of the guidance in the Code of Practice. All those to whom the Code applies have a statutory duty to have regard to it; they must not ignore it. Whenever the health services and social services help schools and LEAs take action on behalf of such children those bodies must consider what the Code says.

5.58 When a statement of special educational needs has been completed, the social services department will be provided with a copy of the statement and the accompanying advice from professionals. This information can assist social services in current or future work with the child and family.

Day Care Services

5.59 Day care services – family centres, early years centres, nurseries (including workplace nurseries), childminders, playgroups and holiday and out of school schemes – play an increasingly important part in the lives of growing numbers of children. Many services will be offering a range of support to children and families experiencing problems and stress. This makes them well placed to intervene early and resolve difficulties before they become more serious or entrenched.

5.60 Day care services may identify children where there are concerns about their developmental progress or wellbeing, or alternatively parents who may have difficulties in responding to their child's needs sufficiently or appropriately. Day care services may contribute by:

- identifying and referring families to social services departments;
- contributing to the assessment of children and their parents or caregivers, sometimes providing a specialist assessment of family relationships;
- providing services which support the child's development and strengthen the parents' capacity to respond, through routine work or as part of a child care plan which is monitored and reviewed.

Sure Start

5.61 **Sure Start** is an area based programme providing universal services for children under four and their families in some of the most disadvantaged communities. Sure Start aims to improve the health and wellbeing of children and families before and from birth, so children are ready to thrive and succeed when they go to school.

5.62 Local programmes work with parents and parents-to-be to improve the life chances of young children through better access to:

- family support;

- advice on nurturing;
- health services;
- early learning.

5.63 Sure Start programmes provide a range of co-ordinated services, locally determined, to meet national objectives and targets and local priorities. These are likely to include:

- outreach and home visiting;
- support for families and parents;
- support for good quality play, learning and childcare experiences for children;
- primary and community health care, including advice about family health and child health and development;
- support for children and parents with special needs, including help accessing specialised services.

5.64 Sure Start programmes are run by local partnerships bringing together people from statutory agencies, voluntary and community organisations and local parents to plan and organise local services. The involvement of local parents in Sure Start partnerships ensures that services are responsive to local needs and will strengthen local communities, and build capacity and confidence.

5.65 Sure Start provides an opportunity for early support and intervention and to ensure that health, education and social services are actively engaged in supporting the most vulnerable pre-school children. Some children and families using Sure Start services may be referred to or known to social services departments as children in need. Co-ordinated assessments will therefore be essential as part of providing effective services to secure optimal outcomes.

Youth Offending Teams

5.66 The principal aim of the youth justice system, to prevent offending by children and young people, is set out in the Crime and Disorder Act 1998. Under this Act, the Local Authority, acting in co-operation with every chief officer of police and police authority and every probation committee and health authority in the local authority's area, has a duty to *'secure that, to such extent as is appropriate for their area, all youth justice services are available there'* (s38) and that a Youth Offending Team is in place (s40) comprising police and probation officers, social workers and education and health staff. The Youth Offending Teams (YOTs), which are multi-agency, have responsibility for co-ordinating or delivering the provision of local youth justice services and helping to implement the Youth Justice Plan (s41).

5.67 The Youth Justice Board for England and Wales has developed an assessment profile, ASSET, for use with all youth offenders who enter and leave the youth justice system. ASSET provides YOTs with a consistent means of assessing the needs of individual young people and the risks of their re-offending, causing harm to themselves or to others. The profile covers the areas of a young person's life most linked to offending behaviour including living arrangements, family and personal relationships, education, employment and training, lifestyle, substance use, physical health, emotional and mental health, personal identity and cognitive and behavioural development. In addition, there is a detailed risk of harm assessment for use when the profile suggests that the young offender has the potential to commit serious harm to others. The profile will assist practitioners plan a programme of interventions to meet the identified needs of the young person and reduce the factors associated with risks of re-offending, causing harm to themselves or to others.

5.68 It will be important for YOTs completing ASSET to liaise within social services departments about young people with whom social services have had or have contact. Prior assessments of need undertaken by social services departments can inform the work of YOTs. Similarly, assessments undertaken by YOTs will be an important source of knowledge if the young person continues to be worked with as a child in need under the Children Act 1989 or is re-referred to the social services department for help following their involvement with the youth justice system. The dimensions of the Assessment Framework in this Guidance are consistent with those of the youth offending assessment profile. The key difference is that ASSET concentrates in depth on areas of a young person's life most likely to be associated with offending behaviour.

Housing

5.69 Housing Authority staff, through their day to day contact with members of the public, may become aware of concerns about the welfare of particular children and should refer to one of the statutory agencies as appropriate.

5.70 Equally, Housing Authorities may have important information about families which could be helpful to social services departments carrying out assessments under s17 or s47 of the Children Act 1989. In accordance with their duty to assist under s27 of the Children Act 1989, they should be prepared to share relevant information verbally or in writing, including attending child protection conferences when requested to do so.

5.71 The provision of appropriate housing can make an important contribution to meeting the health and developmental needs of children. Housing Authorities should be prepared to assist in the provision of accommodation, either directly, through their links with other housing providers or by the provision of advice.

5.72 Social services departments have a duty under section 20(3) of the Children Act 1989 to accommodate any child in need aged 16 and 17 whose welfare is likely to be seriously prejudiced without the provision of accommodation. At the same time, Housing Authorities are required under the Housing Act 1996 to secure accommodation for people who are homeless, eligible for assistance and in priority need. Homeless young people may frequently come to the notice of both housing and social services and will need to be assessed to establish whether they should be provided with accommodation. There is a danger that in these circumstances young people may be passed from one agency to another and it is important therefore that joint protocols are agreed between housing and social services in the matter of how and by whom they are to be assessed.

Police

5.73 The role of members of the Police Force can be seen quite broadly in terms of the overall wellbeing and welfare of children and their families. They have a key role in their knowledge of local communities. Information may be available from the police either generally about local environmental factors or specifically about family or household members. Their contribution in referring children and families to social services departments and in providing information and advice should be considered when undertaking a child in need assessment. The role of the police in relation to safeguarding children is set out in paragraphs 3.57 to 3.64 of *Working Together to Safeguard Children* (1999).

5.74 Protecting life and preventing crime are primary tasks of the police. Children are citizens who have the right to the protection offered by the criminal law. The police have a duty and responsibility to investigate criminal offences committed against children, and such investigations should be carried out sensitively, thoroughly and professionally. The police should be notified as soon as possible where a criminal offence has been committed, or is suspected of being committed, against a child.

5.75 The police have a responsibility to co-ordinate and lead the risk assessment and management process for the exchange of information about all those who have been convicted of, cautioned for, or otherwise dealt with by the courts for a sexual offence; and those who are considered to present a risk to children and others (see paragraphs 7.37 and 7.38 of *Working Together to Safeguard Children* (1999)).

Probation Services

5.76 Probation Services have a statutory duty to supervise offenders effectively in order to reduce offending and protect the public. In the execution of that duty, probation services will be in contact with, or supervising, a number of men (and, to a far lesser extent, women) who have convictions for offences against children. When undertaking assessments of children in need social services staff should draw on the knowledge probation services have about family members or other adults in contact with a child and family, who may have committed offences against children.

5.77 The Probation Service has an important role in working with men and women in prison who may be parents of children under the age of 18. Probation should be informed by social services if an assessment of a child whose parent is in prison is being undertaken and should be asked to contribute. There may be a range of issues when a parent is in prison which will need careful assessment and planning, for example, contact between parent and child; reunification and release arrangements; resettlement in the community. Joint working between probation and social services may be essential to securing the wellbeing of the child.

5.78 In addition, specialist probation officers working in the family courts may be alerted to child care concerns through their investigations as court welfare officers, for example, through work with families under Family Assistance Orders (s16 of the Children Act 1989).

The Prison Service

5.79 The Prison Service works closely with other agencies to identify any prisoner who may represent a risk to the public on release. Regular risk assessment takes account of progress made during the sentence, and informs decisions on sentence planning for individual prisoners, including sex offender treatment programmes. Governors are required to notify social services departments and the probation service of plans to release prisoners convicted of offences against children and young people so that appropriate action can be taken by agencies in the community to minimise any risk to children or young people (Instruction to Governors 54/1994).

5.80 The Prison Service has a duty to safeguard the welfare of those children aged under 18 in its custody. From 1 April 2000, all Prison Service Establishments in the new under 18 estate are required to appoint a child protection co-ordinator; and to establish, in consultation with local ACPCs, arrangements for acting on allegations or concerns that a young person may have suffered, or is at risk of suffering significant harm (HM Prison Service, 2000). A s47 enquiry and core assessment is undertaken concurrently drawing on knowledge of the Assessment Framework.

5.81 When a young person is entering or leaving a Young Offender Institution or prison, it will be important for there to be close liaison between staff in the prison service and the social services department, regarding children already known to a social services department or who are considered likely to benefit from the provision of social services assistance on their release.

5.82 The Prison Service may ask a social services department to carry out an assessment regarding a baby whose mother is in prison (HM Prison Service, 1999). This may be to assist the Service decide whether it is in the best interests of a baby to live with his or her mother in a mother and baby unit. In rare instances, it may be as part of the process of making s47 enquiries where there are concerns about the safety of a child who is living with his or her mother in a mother and baby unit. Mother and baby units are not a place of safety. A prison governor may refer children to a social services department if she or he believe the baby is at risk with the identified carer or other adults.

Armed Services

5.83 In England, social services departments have statutory responsibility for safeguarding and promoting the welfare of children of Services families. When Services families (or civilians working with the Armed Forces) are based overseas, the responsibility for their welfare is vested with the Ministry of Defence. All three Services provide professional welfare support and in some cases, medical support, to augment those provided by local authorities.

5.84 When social services departments are undertaking assessments of children in need, contact should be made with the welfare service appropriate to the particular Service. Appendix 2 of *Working Together to Safeguard Children* (1999) gives details of these Services and contact numbers. The roles and responsibilities of the Armed Forces in respect of safeguarding children of Services families or of ex-Services families are set out in paragraphs 3.89 to 3.96 of *Working Together to Safeguard Children* (1999).

Summary

5.85 This chapter has elaborated the roles and responsibilities of a range of agencies, organisations and disciplines that work with children and families. Understanding these roles and responsibilities is a cornerstone of effective inter-agency, inter-disciplinary working. Individual practitioners will use their professional relationships and networks to assist them achieve good outcomes for children and their families. Quality collaboration at an inter-personal level requires effective organisational arrangements to support these informal processes and ensure good inter-agency working is not solely dependent on the commitment of dedicated individuals.

6

Organisational Arrangements to Support Effective Assessment of Children in Need

6.1 This chapter considers the organisational arrangements which should be in place to support effective practice in assessing children in need and their families. A key longer term measure of success of the Assessment Framework will be evidence of improving outcomes for children as described in the Government's Objectives for Children's Social Services (Department of Health, 1999e). Another measure is whether the timescales set out in the objectives for undertaking initial and core assessments and responding to referrals are met. Chief Executives of local authorities have overall responsibility for ensuring that all departments of their authority play their part in achieving these objectives (Department of Health and Department for Education and Employment, 1999).

Government's Objectives for Children's Social Services

6.2 The *White Paper Modernising Social Services* (Department of Health, 1998e) set out the Government's objectives for both children's and adults' social services, together with objectives common to both on user involvement and training. A consolidated version of the Government's objectives for children's social services, incorporating more detailed sub-objectives, targets and performance indicators was published in September 1999. They outline the social services role, and what they are expected to achieve together with other agencies in the community for some of society's most disadvantaged families and most vulnerable children. This and other work has made clear that targeted help is required to ensure that disadvantaged children and young people are able to take maximum advantage of universal services – in particular education and health – as well as any specialist services.

6.3 In addition to working with children requiring support from social services, the Government believes that local authorities have a corporate responsibility to address the needs of a wider group of disadvantaged children, defined as children at risk of social exclusion. These are children who would benefit from extra help from public agencies in order to make the best of their life chances. To this end, there should be effective joint working by education, social services, housing, leisure and health. Social services alone cannot promote the social inclusion and development of these children and families. However, as part of a corporate endeavour, in partnership with others, social services can play a vital role.

6.4 Local authorities have to work closely with the NHS to ensure that shared objectives for children's services – particularly in areas such as services for disabled children and child and adolescent mental health services – are delivered effectively. The targets for child welfare in *Modernising Health and Social Services : National Priorities Guidance* (Department of Health, 1999j) are incorporated into the Government's objectives for children's social services.

6.5 A comprehensive performance assessment system based on the Best Value regime has been put into place to monitor the delivery of all social services and progress towards the objectives, priorities and targets set out by the Government. This includes in-year monitoring information, end-year performance data and in-depth evaluation through inspections and Joint Reviews. A set of 50 performance indicators were confirmed in July 1999 after a wide-ranging consultation exercise and 13 of these were designated statutory Best Value performance indicators in December 1999. Baseline data for 35 of the indicators were published in *Social Services Performance in 1998–99* (Department of Health, 1999k).

6.6 Elected members have a vital role in ensuring that the corporate responsibilities of local authorities are carried out. This was emphasised in a joint Department of Health/Local Government Association communication to local government councillors:

> As a councillor, you need to be involved in setting strategic objectives for children's services and monitoring how health care, education and life chances are improving for children who are looked after by your council, or who are in need of support in your community (Department of Health and the Local Government Association, 1999).

6.7 Good partnerships with the voluntary and private sector are also important to the delivery of the Government's objectives. In children's services, voluntary and private organisations are important providers of services. In addition to the family based services they already provide, they have a role in representing the voice of service users and carers, and in developing new and flexible approaches to service delivery. Local authorities should make sure that such organisations are fully involved in implementing the Assessment Framework.

6.8 Good assessment of the needs of children and families plays an important part in meeting the Government's children's social services objectives, by enabling needs to be identified at an early stage, so that services and support can be provided before problems escalate. *The Framework for the Assessment of Children in Need and their Families* will assist all agencies in making judgements about which children are in need and how best to help them.

Children's Services Planning

6.9 Children's Services Planning should provide the local vehicle for determining how the contributions of all the relevant agencies fit together and support each other in delivering shared objectives for vulnerable children and, in particular, children in need (Children's Services Planning Order, 1996). It is the Department of Health's intention to issue new guidance on planning for children's services which will address joint working towards these objectives.

6.10 A prime purpose of the children's services planning process is to ensure co-ordination and coherence across local planning arrangements for children and to improve the outcomes and efficiency of the services provided. Planning for children's services should ensure that local objectives in different plans are consistent and support each other. It is important to reduce duplication of planning effort. A balance has to be struck between ensuring that the separate policy intentions behind each set of plans are preserved and that planning is not carried out in separate compartments.

6.11 Fundamental to this will be effective information systems which identify the needs of local children and the nature of services required to meet those needs. Social services departments have an important contribution to make in this respect, in line with their responsibilities under the Children Act 1989:

Every local authority shall take reasonable steps to identify the extent to which there are children in need within their area.
Children Act 1989, Schedule 2, Part 1, paragraph 1 (1).

6.12 Record keeping and the aggregation of data from case records is a critical part of providing an information base for planning purposes. The assessment recording forms (Department of Health and Cleaver, 2000) have been designed to provide the means by which good quality data can be collected and aggregated by social services departments. They can be adapted for use by other agencies working with children, often the same children in need. A common recording system not only ensures data are collected in a consistent manner across agencies, but also facilitates communication about the particular needs of a child and about the needs of all children in an area.

6.13 These records will also provide a means by which supervisors and managers can monitor the quality of practitioners' work with children and families. They will enable them to monitor compliance in implementing the Assessment Framework. This monitoring is an integral part of the overall quality assurance process which departments should have in place.

Departmental Structures and Processes

6.14 The way in which a social service department is structured and the processes it uses to process requests for advice or information, referrals and further work with children and families should be organised to support staff responding to these requests and undertaking assessments of children in need within the required timescales. One example of how a department has organised itself was described in paragraph 3.6.

6.15 The formats for recording information about individual children and their families and the systems by which this information will be used for management and planning purposes will also make a significant contribution both to the effectiveness by which assessments of children in need can be undertaken and to the processes by which the appropriate services are planned and delivered in a local authority area, regionally and nationally.

Departmental Protocols and Procedures

6.16 Departmental procedures, and intra- and inter-agency protocols between adult's and children's services and between agencies involved in work with children and families respectively, which are consistent with the Assessment Framework, will facilitate working within social services departments and across agency boundaries. These should assist in reducing the amount of time spent on duplicated or unfocused work. These should not only benefit children and families but also achieve efficiency in this area and to contribute to **Best Value** in local government services.

6.17 It will be important to be explicit about expectations regarding staff having knowledge of and using the Assessment Framework when partnership arrangements, which include undertaking assessments, are being agreed between agencies. Similarly, when service level agreements are being drawn up, it will be essential for the social services department to be clear about it's expectations regarding the use of the Assessment Framework when, for example, a voluntary or independent agency is undertaking a specific type of assessment with a child and family.

Commissioning Specialist Assessments

6.18 There will be circumstances, where a specialist assessment will be necessary to provide information to social services departments when they are undertaking a core assessment. This is in addition to information that would normally be available about a child from other agencies in the community or information that is known as a result of a previous or current assessment.

6.19 In deciding who to commission to undertake a particular specialist assessment, social services should be clear about what type of assessment is required, for what purpose, within what timescale and who or what agency/professional is best placed to undertake it. This careful planning of specialist assessments not only contributes to the quality of the individual child in need assessment but also to the effective use of available resources. Local inter-agency protocols should provide guidance about how to commission specialist assessments, and who will implement the decision(s).

6.20 When commissioning a specialist assessment, it is important to ask questions which are within the remit of the particular professional to answer. For example, when a parent is being treated for alcohol addiction, it is appropriate for a social services practitioner to ask for an adult psychiatric opinion on the likelihood of the parent being able to stop or reduce his or her drinking, and the impact of the parent's addiction on behaviour, but not necessarily to ask whether that parent is capable of responding appropriately to the child's needs. The adult psychiatrist may also be able to offer an opinion on whether the parent is likely to both engage in and benefit from treatment. This could include treatment for personality disorders or mental health problems, as well as alcohol addiction.

6.21 Another example may occur where there are issues of sex offending; a practitioner who is involved in assessing a child's situation may need to know how effective a treatment programme has been for a particular sex offender, and how that information will assist the assessment of the child in need. It will be essential to check out with the professional who undertook the therapeutic work, the areas in which they consider they have expertise, and what questions the professionals they consider they are qualified to answer. Some may have an excellent understanding of child and family work; others may conceive of their role solely within an adult context.

6.22 When an agency is commissioned to undertake a specialist assessment, this should be undertaken as part of the overall assessment. The findings should be integrated into an analysis of the needs of the child and family. There should be clarity about who has responsibility for analysing these findings and taking action forward, as spelt out in Chapter 4.

A Competent Work Force

6.23 Effective delivery of the Assessment Framework is dependent on the capacity of the workforce to implement it and having the appropriate resources to support the work force. This capacity relates to having sufficient staff in place, who have the requisite knowledge, skills and confidence to undertake assessments. They must be able to make sound judgements about the needs of each child and how best to enable those caring for them to respond appropriately to their needs.

6.24 Staff using the Assessment Framework should continue to update their knowledge about the needs of children and the effectiveness of interventions. This is a continuing process but one which is essential to ensure that members of the workforce are able to deliver good quality practice.

6.25 Knowledge of the wider context of national policy and research should be supplemented by information about the needs of the local population. Feedback from the analysis of locally collected information about what is happening to children and the impact of each agency's contribution should inform future plans and methods of intervention. There will always be debate about how best to help children and their families. These debates and consequent decisions should be continually informed by local and national information on what works in producing the best possible outcomes for children.

Supervision of Practice

6.26 Staff who are in the front line of practice must be well supported by effective supervision. The concepts of practice supervision varies from discipline to discipline. However, the underlying importance of supervision applies to all disciplines and should include consideration of the impact of working with children and families under stress. As Bentovim and Bingley Miller (forthcoming) point out:

> Supervision of workers carrying out family assessment is essential, as the assessment can have far reaching effects on the planning of care and whether families can respond to children's needs within their time frames.

6.27 It is important that supervision addresses:

- the process of assessment;
- the timing and relevance of making a child and family assessment;
- practice which recognises the diversity of family lives, traditions and behaviours;

- information about the children and the parents or caregivers, and its analysis;
- what further information is needed and how it will be obtained;
- the need for any immediate action or services;
- the plan for work with the child and family, and allocation of resources;
- the provision of services or intervention and their likely impact on child and family members;
- involvement/contact with staff in other agencies;
- the review of progress, of earlier understanding of the child and family's situation and of the action/intervention plan.

6.28 Agencies should consider carefully, therefore, the expertise, experience, knowledge and professional confidence of those who undertake the critical task of supervision. Their learning needs will be of equal importance to those of the practitioners who carry out assessments.

Staff as Members of Learning Organisations

6.29 This Guidance has an expectation that staff who work directly with children and families and those who supervise and manage this work are knowledgeable, confident and able to exercise professional judgement. This includes senior managers who carry important responsibilities for determining policy and practice at local level, for developing appropriate inter-agency relationships, and for securing and allocating resources.

6.30 An evidence based approach to practice requires front line staff to reflect on what they are doing during assessment and planning, and to examine the impact of their interventions and services on outcomes for children and families. To keep up to date, therefore, continuing learning is essential. It is critical that staff are provided with opportunities for developing appropriate competencies commensurate with their responsibilities and for staff development, including further and post qualifying training.

6.31 A culture of individual staff learning can only exist successfully within an organisational context which values this activity. Individual staff are being required to adapt and respond to changing expectations. This has repercussions for the way in which agencies direct and support their staff. Research in related areas suggests the importance of:

- **coherence** throughout the organisation about the objectives of policy and practice changes being implemented, exemplified in departmental arrangements, systems and procedures;
- commitment to the changes being reflected in the **values and behaviour** of staff throughout the organisation;
- acknowledgement that new policy expectations require adaptation and change, and involve the whole organisation in a **learning process**.

6.32 In this respect, Pearn *et al* (1995) write:

> In a world that changes at an ever accelerating rate, some organisations survive and thrive and others stagnate and die. With ever faster change as a permanent fact of life for all kinds of organisations, there is a growing need to make intentional use of learning processes to help ensure that they continue not only to survive but also to thrive, by reacting effectively to whatever the future may bring, but also helping to shape that future. In this sense all organisations need to be learning organisations. Organisations which are not learning as fast as they could or should, and have not ensured that they continue to learn, risk becoming less effective, becoming unhealthy, and eventually ceasing to exist.

6.33 These considerations, if firmly embedded in the organisation arrangements will contribute to ensuring effective assessments of children in need.

Preparing the Ground for Training and Continuing Staff Development

6.34 The Department of Health commissioned training materials, *The Child's World: Assessing Children in Need* (NSPCC and University of Sheffield, 2000), to assist the understanding and use of the Assessment Framework. The materials were funded from the Training Support Programme and therefore were intended primarily for a social services audience but can be used in inter-agency training on assessing children in need. These training materials were also designed to be used as part of a continuing programme of staff development. They should be used in qualifying and post qualifying social work training especially in the programmes leading to the Post Qualifying Child Care Award. They should also be of relevance to candidates for the Level 3 NVQ 'Caring for Children and Young People'. The occupational standards for child care at post qualifying level, should enable managers in performance appraisal to identify the current competences of staff and their learning needs.

6.35 The full range of resources commissioned by the Department of Health to support the Assessment Framework has been described in Chapter 4 in the accompanying practice guidance (Department of Health, 2000a).

6.36 Agencies should ensure that all practitioners, managers and administrative staff involved with children, are familiar with and keep up to date with developments in relation to the Assessment Framework. This will involve a range of training and briefing methods as a continuing programme of action.

6.37 A list of training and staff development issues which should be regularly considered and reviewed is listed on page 88 (Figure 8).

6.38 Once introduced, use of the Assessment Framework should be monitored and evaluated. The messages of initial training may be ignored or forgotten as staff become preoccupied with more pressing concerns; some will need additional advice about how the various materials should be used and the recording forms completed. Supervisors and managers have a key role in checking that the framework is being used appropriately and effectively, and that findings from individual assessments are informing planning and service provision of children's services.

Figure 8 TRAINING AND STAFF DEVELOPMENT ISSUES

Training Issues

A training strategy team, in consultation with senior managers, should consider and review:

- who needs training
- what will be single agency/inter-agency
- how much training
- who will do it
- how it will be resourced

The purpose of training would be to ensure that key staff know:

- why they are using the Assessment Framework
- the knowledge which underpins it
- what to use
- when to use it
- how to use it
- how to evaluate their practice (or work)

Staff Development Issues

A training strategy team could also consider:

- what are the continuing staff development needs
- how can these best be addressed.

Summary

6.39 In summary, the following organisational arrangements should be in place to support the effective assessments of children in need:

- policies, intra- and inter-agency protocols and procedures;
- assessment processes;
- structures and other processes for referral, planning and provision of services;
- recording and management information systems;
- training and staff development opportunities for professional staff, trainers, carers and others including administrative staff;
- inter-agency training programmes;
- quality control/quality assurance systems;
- child and family involvement and feedback on the assessment processes;
- systems for obtaining feedback on the implementation programme and then on the training programmes established on a continuing basis.

6.40 These arrangements will need to be monitored and reviewed from time to time to ensure they reflect the most up to date legislation, policies, procedures and evidence based knowledge. In this way, use of the Assessment Framework will be dynamic and continue to draw on developments in a rapidly changing world.

Appendix

A

The Assessment Framework

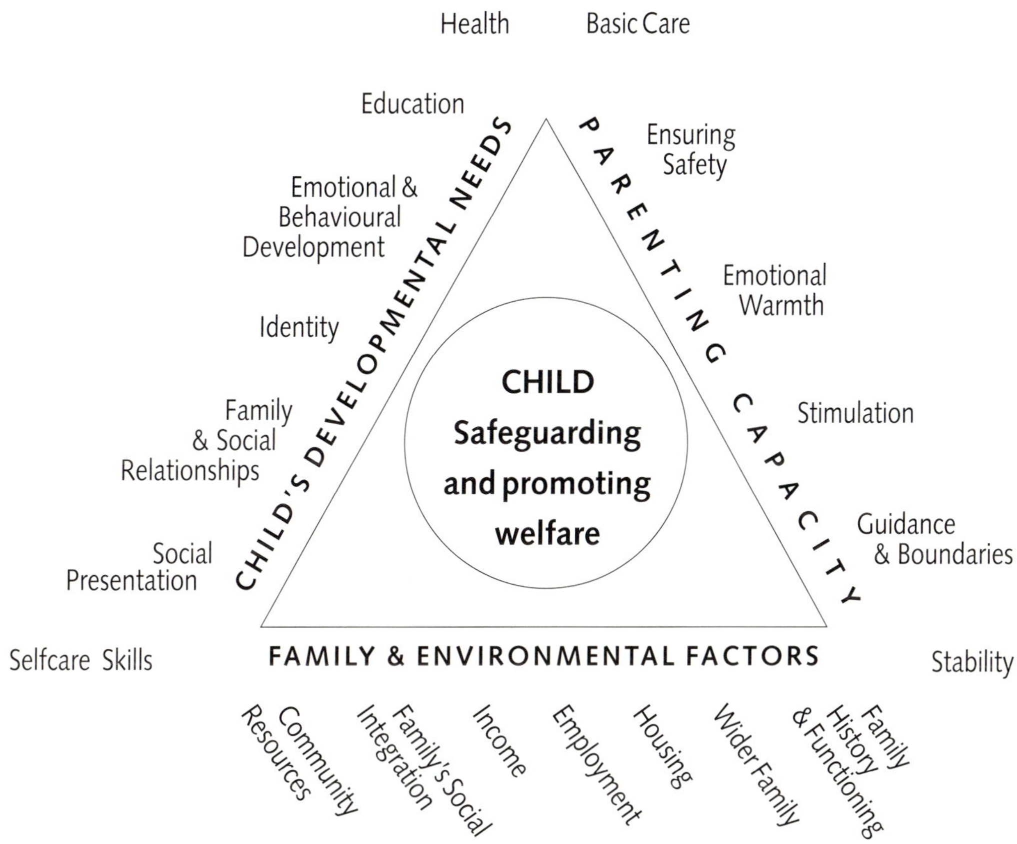

Appendix

B A Framework for Analysing Services

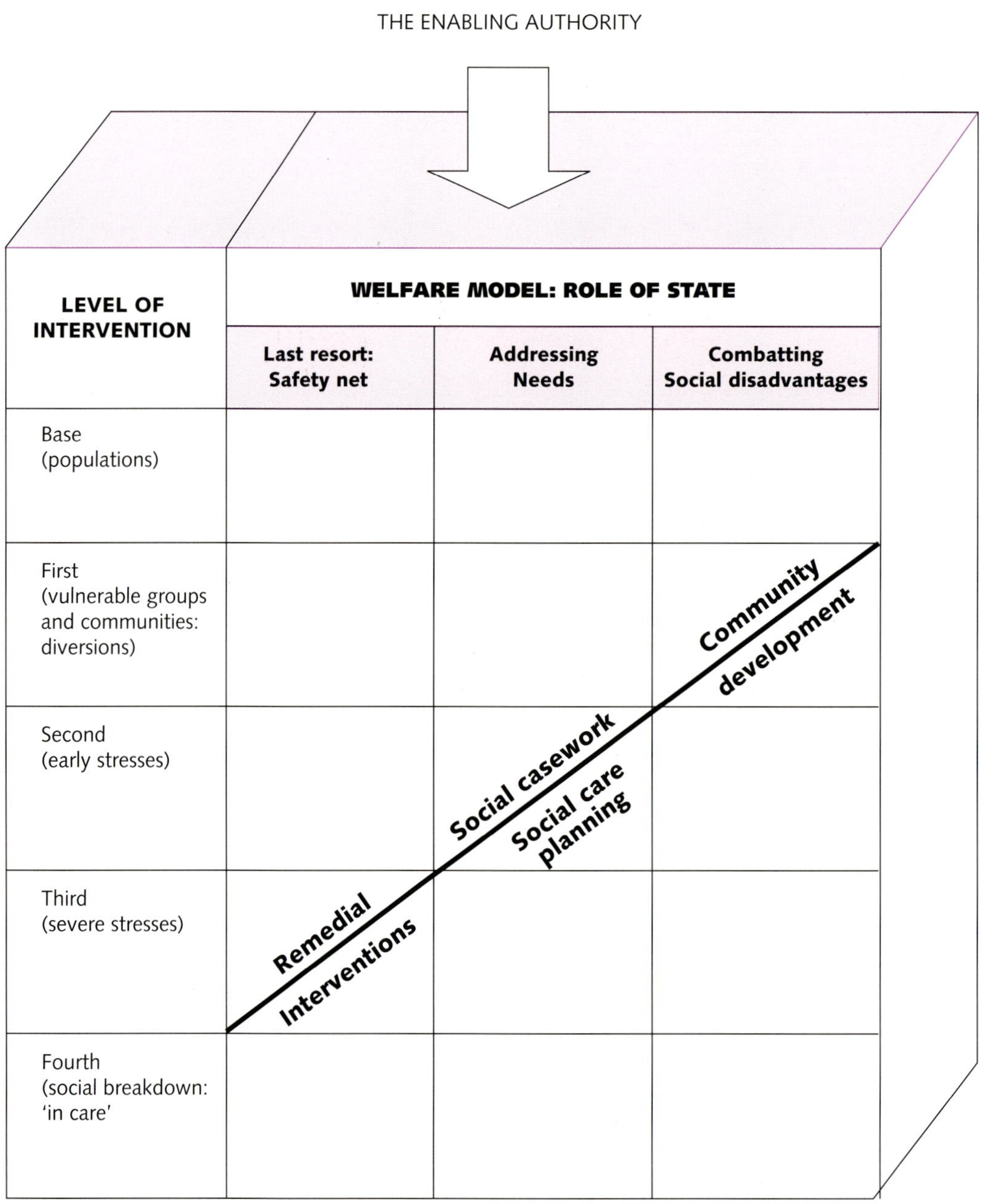

Reproduced with kind permission of the authors. From: Hardiker *et al* (1999) Children Still In Need, Indeed: prevention across five decades. In Stevenson O (1999) *Childhood Welfare in the UK*, p.43, Blackwell Science Ltd, Oxford.

Referrals Involving a Child (Referral Chart)

Guide for use

This chart is designed to help you gather information at the initial referral stage. It is not exhaustive and should not be treated as a checklist.

Please use the chart alongside the usual referral forms as a reminder of:

A. issues which may need to be checked

B. matters raised by the referrer that should be recorded.

What help is requested?

Material resources
Housing, beds, clothing, money, other

Practical help for parent/carer
Respite care, other

Support for parent/carer
Someone to talk to, advice/information, other

Support for referrer
Advice/information, discussion of current concern, other

Practical help for child
Accommodation, school place, specialist equipment, other

Support for child
Befriending, counselling, youth scheme, other

Protection for child
Home visit, immediate shelter, other

Is there a child in danger?

Source of information
- Problem observed by referrer
- Child talked to referrer
- Someone else told referrer of their concern – who?
- Referral has general concerns –why refer now?

Why is the referrer worried?
- Is there a need for immediate medical treatment?
- Is there a physical injury – size, colour, shape and location?
- Is the child neglected – appearance, clothing, home conditions?
- Is there a lack of supervision – whereabouts and situation of child?
- Is child a victim of sexual assault – child's account or behaviour?
- Is the child emotionally abused – observed behaviour?
- Is there a person present who has been convicted of an offence against a child?
- Is there an explanation?

Details of:
- Child's current whereabouts?
- Date child was last seen
- Any previous concerns
- Background to current concern
- Any specific injury or event causing concern
- When did it happen
- Child's, parent's/carer's account
- Identity of alleged abuser – personal details assist police checks
- Alleged abuser's current whereabouts
- Any supporting medical or forensic evidence

Is there any other possible explanation the referrer can offer for their concern?

Additional information
- Willingness of referrer to be interviewed
- Discrepancies or inconsis-tencies in the report

Family/household details

Child
Name, age, gender, ethnic origin, address and telephone number

Referrer
Name, address and telephone number

Referrer's Relationship to the child

Parent/carer
Name, address, telephone number and age if under 18 years

Access to parent/carer
Is an appointment necessary?

Alternative carer(s)
Name, address and telephone number

Other children in the household
Age and gender

Primary language of family

Ethnic origin of family

Religion of family

Disability of parent or child

Other professionals involved with the family

School/nursery
Address, telephone number and name of head teacher

Health visitor
Name, address and telephone number

General Practitioner
Name, address and telephone number

Probation Service
Name, address and telephone number

Any other

Is any other help needed?

Remember this is not a checklist. Record anything the referrer tells you about these or similar matters:
- Bereavement
- Child/parent conflict
- Drug/alcohol/ substance misuse
- Housing/homelessness
- Learning disability
- Non school attendance
- Physical disability
- Police involvement
- Racial harassment
- Violence
- Bullying
- Child behaviour
- Family/marital conflict
- Financial crisis
- Mental ill health
- Parenting
- Physical ill health
- Poverty
- Unemployment

Consider
- Is this the correct agency? – if not, refer elsewhere and tell referrer
- Have you sufficient information – if not where could you get more?
- Is the service available?
- Does the referrer want a visit immediately?
- Will an interpreter/sign language facilitator be needed?
- Are there mobility/access considerations?
- Are there any assurances you need to give? i.e. referrer's identity must be protected
- Feedback to the referrer about the action you will take
- How will you close the conversation – does anything else need saying, do they have any questions?
- Do you need to consult someone about the action to take?

Check
- Is the child/parent aware of the referral?
- Is the family/child known to the department?
- Is the family/child currently receiving services?
- If suspected child abuse – the Child Protection Register.

Useful telephone numbers
Record your most used telephone numbers here:

First published 1998 by NSPCC, 42 Curtain Road, London, EC2A 3NH

Published as part of a pack in the NSPCC Policy Practice Research Series: Assessing Risk in Child Protection, by Hedy Cleaver, Corinne Wattam, Pat Cawson (ISBN 0 902498 81 9).

Registered charity number 21640

Appendix

D

Using Assessments in Family Proceedings: Practice Issues

1. There are a number of practice issues to which attention should be given in order to ensure that any information derived from assessment that is to be used in court proceedings conforms with court practice. These are set out below. Addressing these issues will assist legal practitioners, including the judiciary, and other professionals who may be involved in the case in giving proper weight to the conclusions reached during assessment.

2. When preparing a report summarising evidence from the assessment, each page should be typed/word processed on one side of A4. The first page should be headed **Front Sheet** and include the following information:

   - full name of child;
   - date of birth;
   - court case number;
   - name of court hearing application;
   - date of the court hearing;
   - type of hearing (ie. directions, interim or final hearing);
   - name of local authority;
   - date of the report summarising the assessment.

   Subsequent pages should also be singled sided. Headings and paragraph numbers will aid communication in court.

3. It should be noted that the document submitted to court will usually be a summary of the key assessment issues rather than the full record concerning the assessment, as the latter will not usually be in a format or language suitable for court.

4. Where during proceedings several assessments have been produced, the report to the court should identify each by a separate number to avoid confusion.

5. Initial assessments, although incomplete, may sometimes be needed at an interim stage in the care proceedings. Reports to court on these initial assessments will not necessarily represent the local authority's comprehensive view that will be brought to the final hearing. It is therefore important that the front page of such an initial report, under **type of hearing**, should clearly distinguish between those for interim court

hearings and the report of the complete or core assessment prepared for the final hearing.

6. The last and separate page of the report of the assessment should include the following information:

- full name and professional position of the person who has prepared the report;
- this should normally be the social worker allocated to the case, although a range of other people within the authority and from other agencies may have contributed to aspects of the assessment;
- signature;
- date;
- work address and telephone number;

  Followed by

- local authority making the application;
- signature(s);
- date (s);
- work address(es) and telephone number(s).

7. The endorsement of the report of the assessment by the local authority raises similar issues to the approach commended in paragraphs 20–22 of LAC 99(29) *Care Plans and Care Proceedings Under the Children Act* 1989. The key point is that the report of the assessment is a statement by the local authority which is likely to be a crucial part of the authority's evidence in the care proceedings. However, it does not itself imply the commitment of resources across the local authority in the way care plans may do and, for this reason, endorsement at the level of a team manager may well be sufficient.

Appendix

E

Data Protection Registrar's Checklist

Data Protection Registrar's Checklist for Setting up Information Sharing Arrangements (abridged version)

(i) What is the purpose of the information sharing arrangement?

1. It is important in data protection terms that the purpose of any information sharing arrangement is clearly defined. This is because if *personal* information is to be disclosed, then disclosures must be registered with the Data Protection Registrar and the data protection principles will take effect. These principles themselves relate directly to the purpose or purposes for which personal information is held. For example, information must be adequate, relevant, and not excessive in relation to the purpose for which it is held, and must not be held longer than is necessary for that purpose.

2. Parties to any arrangement should be aware that under the Data Protection Act 1998 they will need to have a 'legitimate basis' for disclosing sensitive personal data. The introduction of special controls on the processing of sensitive data (including holding and disclosing them) is one of the major innovations of the new Act. Under section 2, 'sensitive data' include information as to the commission, or alleged commission, by the data subject of any offence; and criminal proceedings involving the data subject as the accused, and their disposal. The definition of 'sensitive data' also includes information about the data subject's sexual life. It should also be made clear to all parties that information received under the arrangement is to be used only for the specified purpose(s). Thus, there should be a restriction on secondary use of personal data received under any information sharing arrangement *unless* the consent of the disclosing party to that secondary use is sought and granted.

(ii) Will it be necessary to share *personal* information in order to fulfil that purpose?

3. Depersonalised information is information presented in such a way that individuals cannot be identified. If depersonalised information can be used to achieve the purpose, then there will be no data protection implications. Consideration should therefore always be given to whether the purpose can be achieved using depersonalised information; 'would failure to share personal information mean that the objectives of the arrangement could not be achieved?'

(iii) Do the parties to the arrangement have the *power* to disclose personal information for that purpose?

4. If the purpose cannot be achieved without sharing *personal* information, then each party to the arrangement will need to consider whether they have the power to disclose information for this purpose. This is particularly significant for public sector bodies or agencies whose powers and responsibilities are defined by statute or administrative law. If a public body acts *ultra vires* or outside its powers, then it may, at the same time, breach the lawfulness requirement of the first data protection principle. Section 115 of the Crime and Disorder Act 1998 may provide the parties with the lawful power they need provided the requirements of that section are met. This provides that any person can lawfully disclose information, where necessary or expedient for the purposes of any provision of the (1998) Act, to a chief officer of police, a police authority, local authorities, Probation Service or health authority, even if they do not otherwise have this power. This power also covers disclosure to people acting on behalf of any of the above named bodies. The 'purposes' of the Act referred to in Section 115 include a range of measures such as local crime audits, youth offending teams, anti-social behaviour orders, sex offender orders, and local child curfew schemes. It should also be noted that Section 17 of the Act places a statutory duty on every local authority to *exercise its various functions . . . with due regard to . . . the need to do all that it reasonably can to prevent . . . crime and disorder in its area.*

(iv) How *much* personal information will need to be shared in order to achieve the objectives of the arrangement?

5. Consideration must be given to the extent of any personal information disclosed. Some agencies may hold a lot of personal information on individuals but not all of this may be relevant to the purpose of the information sharing arrangement, so it may not be right to disclose it all. This is a matter for consideration by the agency holding the information.

(v) Should the *consent* of the individual be sought before disclosure is made?

6. When disclosing personal information, many of the data protection issues surrounding disclosure can be avoided if the consent of the individual has been sought and obtained. This is particularly significant if the personal information to be shared identified victims or witnesses where consideration should be given to any effects of disclosure of their personal data on third parties.

(vi) What if the consent of the individual is *not* sought, or is sought but *withheld*?

7. Consideration must be given to whether the personal information can be disclosed lawfully and fairly. In terms of *lawfulness*, an agency will need to consider whether personal information is held under a *duty of confidence*. If it is, then it may only be disclosed:

(a) with the individual's consent; or

(b) where there is an overriding public interest or justification for doing so.

It will not *always* be the case that the prevention and detection of crime or public safety constitutes an overriding public interest for the exchange of personal information.

8. As regards *fairness*, even if the personal information held is not subject to a duty of confidence, the agency will still need to consider how the disclosure can be made fairly. In data protection terms, in order to obtain and process personal data fairly, the individual should be informed of any non-obvious uses (including disclosure) of their personal data, and be given the opportunity to consent to those uses. If consent is therefore not obtained, consideration will have to be given to how the disclosure can be made fairly. This might involve arguments of public interest, but these would have to be balanced against any potential resulting prejudice to the interests of the individual concerned.

(vii) How does the non-disclosure *exemption* apply?

9. The Data Protection Acts 1984 and 1998 contain general 'non-disclosure provisions', but allow a number of specific exemptions. There is an exemption in both Acts which states that personal information may be disclosed for the purposes of the prevention or detection of crime, or the apprehension or prosecution of offenders, in cases where failure to disclose would be likely to prejudice those objectives. A party seeking to rely on this exemption needs to make a judgement as to whether, in the particular circumstances of an individual case, there would be a substantial chance that one or both of those objectives would be noticeably damaged if the personal information was withheld.

(viii) How do you ensure compliance with the *other data protection principles*?

10. Any information sharing arrangement should also address the following issues:

- how will it be ensured that only the *minimum personal information necessary* is shared and held for the purpose(s) of the arrangement?
- how will the *accuracy* of the personal information be maintained? One party to the arrangement may know that there has been a change in personal information which they have disclosed: how does that party ensure that all recipients of that personal information are kept informed of developments, so that they can keep their records up to date?
- *for how long* will personal information be retained? It would be anomalous if the disclosing agency were to remove the personal information from its systems, but the other parties continued to hold it.
- how will individuals be given *access* to personal information held about them? Under data protection legislation, individuals have a right of access to any information held about them. This right may be denied in certain limited circumstances, which include where access would prejudice the prevention or detection of crime. This could be significant, if, for example, a police force wished to disclose personal data to another party, but for operational reasons did not want the individual concerned to know the disclosure had been made. On the other hand, it is not sufficient to deny subject access merely because the information is held for

crime prevention purposes. Mechanisms must therefore be in place to ensure that the wishes of the disclosing party are considered.

- how will the personal data be *stored*? The more sensitive the personal data shared, the more security measures should be taken by each party receiving that personal data. This is not limited to physical security of the equipment on which it is held, but extends to technological security (for example, limited staff access, appropriate levels of staff access) and to staff security (staff with authorised access should be aware of its purpose and extent).

Appendix F

Acknowledgements

Many people have helped in the development of the Assessment Framework and in shaping the Guidance in this volume and the associated materials. They have given generously of their time and expertise. Members of the Steering and Advisory Groups and critical readers have contributed their professional experience and management wisdom. A considerable debt is also owed to consultants from different disciplines who have worked closely with the Department of Health, especially Arnon Bentovim, Tony Cox and Steve Walker. Throughout there has been a strong collaborative effort involving Government Departments, the Open University, Royal Holloway College, the Universities of Sheffield and East Anglia, REU, Triangle, NSPCC, and many others. The development work has been marked by a collective commitment to improving outcomes for children and to assisting those critically important staff who daily work with children in need and their families.

In the chair of the Steering and Advisory Groups

Jenny Gray	Social Services Inspector, Department of Health

Consultant to the Project

Wendy Rose	Senior Research Fellow, The Open University

Members of the Steering Group

Sarah Bateman*	Section Head (Child Protection), Department of Health (until August 1999)
Bruce Clark*	Director of Central Children's Services, National Council for the Prevention of Cruelty to Children (until August 1999) Section Head(Child Protection), Department of Health (from September 1999)
Jonathan Corbett*	Social Services Inspector, National Assembly For Wales (from October 1999)
Chris Corrigan*	Section Head (Family Support and Children in Need), Department of Health
Ann Gross*	Section Head (Quality Protects), Department of Health (until September 1999)

Steve Hart*	Social Services Inspector, Department of Health
Gillian Harrison	Head of Evidence and Procedures Section, Home Office
David Hill	Local Government Association and Head of Services (Children and Families), London Borough of Havering Social Services Department
Tom Jeffery	Branch Head, Children's Services, Department of Health
Dr Robert Jezzard*	Senior Policy Adviser, Department of Health
David Johnston*	Social Services Inspector, National Assembly For Wales (until September 1999)
Dr David Jones	Consultant Child and Family Psychiatrist, The Park Hospital, Oxford
Helen Jones*	Social Services Inspector, Department of Health
Dorothy Lewis	Regional Development Worker, Department of Health (from September 1999)
Margaret Lynch	Senior Policy Advisor, Department of Health (from September 1999)
Katrina McNamara*	Nursing Officer, Department of Health
Jeremy Oppenheim	Association of the Directors of Social Services and Director of Social Services, London Borough of Hackney (until August 1999)
Neil Remsbery	Team Leader (Special Educational Schools), Department for Education and Employment
Jennifer Ruddick*	Social Services Inspector, Department of Health
Kim Sibley *	Team Leader, Special Educational Needs Strategy Team, Department of Education and Employment
Gail Treml *	Professional Adviser, Special Educational Needs,Department of Education and Employment
Peter Smith*	Social Services Inspector, Department of Health
Andrew Webb	Association of the Directors of Social Services and Head of Children's Services, Cheshire County Council
Elizabeth Wulff-Cochrane	Development and Promotions Department, Central Council for the Education and Training of Social Workers

*also members of Advisory Group

Members of the Advisory Group

Jane Aldgate	Professor of Social Care, The Open University
Hedy Cleaver	Senior Research Fellow, Royal Holloway, University of London

Ratna Dutt OBE	Director, REU
Amanda Farr	Children's Services Manager, Milton Keynes County Council
Enid Hendry	Head of Child Protection Training, National Society for the Prevention of Cruelty to Children
Jan Horwath	Lecturer in Social Work, Department of Sociological Studies, University of Sheffield
Hugh McLaughlin	Assistant Director (Children and Families), Wigan Social Services Department
Jill Pedley	Assistant Director (Children and Families), Nottinghamshire Social Services Department
Melanie Phillips	Freelance Trainer, Researcher, Consultant to REU
Nigel Richardson	Assistant Director (Children and Families), Directorate of Social and Housing Services, North Lincolnshire Council
David Roberts	Team Leader, Health Services (Child Health), Department of Health
David Simpkins	Child Care Policy Officer, Devon Social Services Department
Ruth Sinclair	Director of Research, National Children's Bureau
June Thoburn	Professor of Social Work, University of East Anglia

Secretariat to the Project

Jim Brown	Policy Administrator, Department of Health
Dawn Tharpe	Secretary to Jenny Gray, Department of Health

Appendix

G

Bibliography

Adcock M (2000) *The Core Assessment: How to synthesise information and make judgements.* In Horwath J (ed) (2000) *The Child's World: Assessing Children in Need. The Reader.* The NSPCC, London.

Adcock M and White R (eds) (1998) *Significant Harm: its Management and Outcome.* Significant Publications, Croydon.

Aldgate J and Bradley M (1999) *Supporting Families Through Short Term Fostering.* The Stationery Office, London.

Belsky Y J and Vondra J (1989) *Lessons from child abuse: The determinants of parenting.* In Acchetti D and Carlson V (eds) (1989) *Child Maltreatment: Theory and Research on the Causes and Consequences of Child Abuse and Neglect.* Cambridge University Press, New York.

Bentovim A (1998) *Significant Harm in Context.* In Adcock M and White R (eds) (1998) *Significant Harm: its Management and Outcome.* pp. 57–89. Significant Publications, Croydon.

Bentovim A and Bingley Miller L (forthcoming) *Assessment of Family Competence, Strengths and Difficulties.*

Bentovim A, Elton A and Tranter M (1987) Prognosis for rehabilitation after abuse. *Adoption and Fostering.* **34**: 821–826.

Birleson P (1980) The validity of depressive disorder in childhood and the development of a self-rating scale: A research report. *Journal of Child Psychology and Psychiatry.* **22**: 73–88.

Bradley R and Caldwell B (1977) Home observation for measurement of the environment: A validation study of screening efficiency. *American Journal of Mental Deficiency.* **81**: 417-420.

Brandon M (1999) *Communicating with Children and Ascertaining their Wishes and Feelings.* In Shemmings D (1999) *In on the Act – A training programme for relevant professionals.* University of East Anglia, Norwich.

Brugha T, Bebington P, Tennant C and Hurry J (1985) The list of threatening experiences: A subset of 12 life event categories with considerable long-term contextual threat. *Psychological Medicine.* **15**: 189–194.

Butler I and Williamson H (1994) In NSPCC in association with Chailey Heritage and Department of Health (1997) *Turning Points: A Resource Pack for Communicating with Children. Introduction.* pp.1–2. The NSPCC, London.

Butt J and Box C (1998) *Family Centred. A study of the use of family centres by black families.* REU, London.

Caddle D and Crisp D (1997) *Imprisoned women and mothers.* Home Office Research Study 162. Home Office, London.

Caldwell B M and Bradley R H (1984) *Home Observation for Measurement of the Environment – Administration Manual (revised edition).* University of Arkansas, Arkansas.

Carers (Recognition and Services) Act 1995 (1995) HMSO, London.

Carers and Disabled Children Bill (2000) The Stationery Office, London.

Children Act 1989 (1989) HMSO, London.

Children Act 1989 (Amendment) Children's Services Planning Order 1996. Statutory Instrument 1996 No. 785. HMSO, London.

Children (Leaving Care) Bill (1999). The Stationery Office, London.

Cleaver H (2000) Fostering Family Contact: a study of children, parents and foster carers. The Stationery Office, London.

Cleaver H and Freeman P (1995) *Parental Perspectives in Cases of Suspected Child Abuse.* HMSO, London.

Cleaver H, Unell I and Aldgate J (1999) *Children's Needs – Parenting Capacity: The impact of parental mental illness, problem alcohol and drug use, and domestic violence on children's development.* The Stationery Office, London.

Cleaver H, Wattam C and Cawson P (1998) *Assessing Risk in Child Protection.* The NSPCC, London.

Compton B R and Galaway B (1989) *Social Work Processes.* Brookes Cole, Pacific Grove.

Connolly J and Shemmings D (1998) *Undertaking Assessments of Children and Families: A directory of training materials, courses and key texts.* University of East Anglia, Norwich.

Crime and Disorder Act 1998 (1998) The Stationery Office, London.

Crittenden P and Ainsworth MDS (1989) *Child Maltreatment and Attachment.* In Cicchetti D and Carlson V (eds) *Handbook of Child Maltreatment: Clinical and Theorectical Perspectives.* pp. 432–463. Cambridge, New York.

Crnic K A and Booth C L (1991) Mothers' and fathers' perceptions of daily hassles of parenting across early childhood. *Journal of Marriage and the Family.* **53**: 1043–1050.

Crnic K A and Greenberg M T (1990) Minor parenting stresses with young children. *Child Development.* **61**: 1628–1637.

Data Protection Act 1998 (1998) The Stationery Office, London.

Davie C E, Hutt S J, Vincent E and Mason M (1984) *The young child at home*. NFER-Nelson, Windsor.

Department for Education and Employment (1994) *Code of Practice on the Identification and Assessment of Special Educational Needs*. HMSO, London.

Department for Education and Employment (1999a) *School Inclusion: Pupil Support. The Secretary of State's guidance on pupil attendance, behaviour, exclusion and re-integration*. Circular No 10/99.

Department for Education and Employment (1999b) *Guidance on Assessment in the Learning Gateway for 16 and 17 year olds*. DfEE Publications (Ref: RDT/LG/9901).

Department for Education and Employment (2000) *Connexions: The best start in life for every young person*. DfEE Publications (Ref: CX2).

Department for Education and Employment and Department of Health (forth-coming) *Guidance on the Education of Children and Young People in Public Care*.

Department of Health (1988) *Protecting Children: A Guide for Social Workers Undertaking a Comprehensive Assessment*. HMSO, London.

Department of Health (1989) *An Introduction to the Children Act 1989*. HMSO, London.

Department of Health (1991) *The Children Act (1989) Guidance and Regulations. Volumes 1–10*. HMSO, London.

Department of Health, Social Services Inspectorate (1995a) *The Challenge of Partnership in Child Protection: Practice Guide*. HMSO, London.

Department of Health (1995b) *Looking After Children: Trial Pack of Planning and Review Forms and Assessment and Action Records (Revised)*. HMSO, London.

Department of Health (1995c) *Looking After Children: Good Parenting, Good Outcomes. Training Guide*. HMSO, London.

Department of Health (1995d) *Child Protection: Messages from Research*. HMSO, London.

Department of Health, Social Services Inspectorate (1995e) *Growing up and moving on – transition services for disabled young people*. (CI(95)27). Department of Health, London.

Department of Health, Social Services Inspectorate (1995f) *Young Carers. Something to Think About*. (CI(96)38). Department of Health, London.

Department of Health (1996a) *Carers (Recognition and Services) Act 1995: Policy Guidance and Practice Guide*. Local Authority Circular LAC(97)7 and Health Services Guidelines HSG(96)8). Department of Health, London.

Department of Health, Social Services Inspectorate (1996b) *Standards Used by the Social Services Inspectorate, Volume 2: Children's Services, plus supplement to Vol 2. Children's Services* (CI(96)23). Department of Health, London.

Department of Health, Social Services Inspectorate (1996c) *Standards Used by the Social Services Inspectorate, Volume 3: Children's Residential Care, Secure Accommodation and Juvenile Justice.* (CI(96)23). Department of Health, London.

Department of Health, Social Services Inspectorate (1998a) *Young Carers: Making a Start.* Department of Health, London.

Department of Health (1998b) *National Priorities Guidance: A commitment to improve modern social services.* Department of Health, London.

Department of Health (1998c) *Adoption: Achieving the right balance.* Local Authority Circular LAC(98)20.

Department of Health (1998d) *Quality Protects Circular: Transforming Children's Services.* Local Authority Circular (LAC(98)28).

Department of Health (1998e) *Modernising social services: Promoting independence, Improving protection, Raising standards.* Department of Health, London.

Department of Health (1999a) *Caring about Carers: A National Strategy for Carers.* Department of Health, London.

Department of Health (1999b) *Children Looked After by Local Authorities. Year Ending 31 March 1998. England.* Government Statistical Services, London.

Department of Health (1999c) *Guidance to Local Authority Social Services Departments on Visits by Children to Special Hospitals.* Local Authority Circular (LAC(99)23).

Department of Health (1999d) *Care Plans and Care Proceedings under the Children Act 1989.* Local Authority Circular (LAC(99)29). Department of Health, London.

Department of Health (1999e) *The Government's Objectives for Children's Social Services.* Department of Health, London.

Department of Health (1999f) *Me, survive, out there?: new arrangements for young people living in and leaving care.* Department of Health, London.

Department of Health (1999g) *Adoption Now: Messages from Research.* Wiley, Chichester.

Department of Health (1999h) *Mental Health Act 1983 Code of Practice: Guidance on the visiting of psychiatric patients by children* (HSC1999/222 LAC(99)32). Department of Health, London.

Department of Health (1999i) *Children and Young People on Child Protection Registers. Year Ending 31 March 1999.* England. Government Statistical Service, London.

Department of Health (1999j) *Modernising Health and Social Services: National Priorities Guidance.* Department of Health, London.

Department of Health (1999k) *Social Services Performance in 1998–99. The Personal Social Services Performance Assessment Framework.* Local Authority Social Services LASSL(99)24. Department of Health, London.

Department of Health (2000a) *towards safer care. Training and Resource Pack.* Department of Health, London.

Department of Health (2000b) *Assessing Children in Need and their Families: Practice Guidance.* The Stationery Office, London.

Department of Health (2000c) *Studies which inform the development of the Framework for the Assessment of Children in Need and their Families.* The Stationery Office, London.

Department of Health (forthcoming, a) *Achieving Fair Access to Adult Social Care Services.*

Department of Health (forthcoming, b) *The Children Act 1989 Now: Messages from Research.* The Stationery Office, London.

Department of Health and Cleaver H (2000) *Assessment Recording Forms.* The Stationery Office, London.

Department of Health, Cox A and Bentovim A (2000) *The Family Assessment Pack of Questionnaires and Scales.* The Stationery Office, London.

Department of Health and Department for Education and Employment (1996) *Children's Services Planning Guidance.* Department of Health, London.

Department of Health and Department for Education and Employment (1999) *The Quality Protects Programme: Transforming Children's Services 2000/01.* Health Service Circular (HSC(99)237), Local Authority Circular (LAC(99)33) and DfEE Circular No. 18/99. Department of Health, London.

Department of Health, Dutt R and Phillips M (2000) *Improving identity and self-esteem for looked after children.* REU, London.

Department of Health, Home Office, Department for Education and Employment (1999) *Working Together to Safeguard Children: A guide to inter-agency working to safeguard and promote the welfare of children.* The Stationery Office, London.

Department of Health and The Local Government Association (1999) *Think Child! The councillor's guide to Quality Protects.* The Department of Health and the Local Government Assication, London.

Department of Health, University of Bristol, The NSPCC and Barnardos (1998) *Making an Impact: Children and Domestic Violence: Training Resource.* Barnardos, London.

Department of Health and The Welsh Office (1999) *Code of Practice Mental Health Act 1983.* The Stationery Office, London.

Dingwall R, Eekelaar J and Murray T (1983) *The protection of children: state intervention and family life.* Basil Blackwell, Oxford.

Disability Discrimination Act 1995 (1995) The Stationery Office, London.

Dutt R and Phillips M (2000) *The Assessment of Black Children in Need and their Families.* In Department of Health (2000b) *Assessing Children in Need and their Families: Practice Guidance.* The Stationery Office, London.

Education Act 1996 (1996) The Stationery Office, London.

Falkov A, Mayes K, Diggins M, Silverdale N and Cox A (1998) *Crossing Bridges – Training resources for working with mentally ill parents and their children.* Pavilion Publishing, Brighton.

The Family Proceedings Courts (Children Act 1989) Rules 1991 (SI 1395/1991 for Magistrates Courts and SI 1247/1991 for Higher Courts).

General Assembly of the United Nations (1989) *The Convention on the Rights of the Child.* Adopted by the General Assembly of the United Nations on 20 November 1989.

Goodman R (1997) The Strengths and Difficulties Questionnaire: A Research Note. *Journal of Child Psychology and Psychiatry.* **38**: 581-586.

Goodman R, Meltzer H and Bailey V (1998) The strengths and difficulties questionnaire: A pilot study on the validity of the self-report version. *European Child and Adolescent Psychiatry.* 7: 125–130.

Hardiker P, Exton K and Baker M (1996) The prevention of Child Abuse: a framework for analysing services. In *Childhood Matters: Report of the National Commission of Inquiry into the Prevention Of Child Abuse. Vol 2.* HMSO, London.

Hardiker P, Exton K and Barker M (1999) Children Still in Need, Indeed: prevention across five decades. In Stevenson O (1999) *Childhood Welfare in the UK.* Blackwell Science Ltd, Oxford

HM Prison Service (1994) *Release of Prisoners Convicted of Offences Against Children or Young Persons Under the Age of 18.* Instructions to Governors 54/1994.

HM Prison Service (1999) *Report of a review of principles, polices and procedures on mothers and babies/children in prison.* Women's Policy Unit, London.

HM Prison Service (2000) *Protocol: Additional Child Protection Arrangements for Under 18 years olds in Prison Service Establishments.* HM Prison Service, London.

Home Office (1998) *Speaking up for Justice Report of the Interdepartmental Working Group on the treatment of Vulnerable or Intimidated Witnesses in the Criminal Justice System.* The Stationery Office, London.

Home Office and Department of Health (1992) *Memorandum of Good Practice on Interviewing of Child Witnesses.* HMSO, London.

Home Office and Department of Health (1998) *Draft Guidance on Children Involved in Prostitution.* The Home Office, London.

Home Office and Department of Health (forthcoming) *Guidance on Children Involved in Prostitution.*

Horwath J (ed) (2000) *The Child's World: Assessing Children in Need. The Reader.* The NSPCC, London.

Human Rights Act 1998 (1998) The Stationery Office, London.

Howe D (2000) Attachment. In Horwath J (ed) (2000) *The Child's World: Assessing Children in Need. The Reader.* The NSPCC, London.

International Save the Children Alliance and United Nations High Commissioner for Refugees (1999) *Separated Children in Europe Programme, Statement of Good Practice.*

Jack G (1997) An Ecological Approach to Social Work with Children and Families. *Child and Family Social Work.* **2**: 109–120.

Jones D P H (1997) *Treatment of the child and the family where child abuse or neglect has occurred.* In Helfer R, Kempe R and Krugman R (eds) *The Battered Child, 5th edition.* pp.521–542. University of Chicago Press, Chicago.

Jones D P H (1998) *The effectiveness of intervention.* In Adcock M and White R (eds) (1998) *Significant Harm: its Management and Outcome.* pp. 91-119. Significant Publications, Croydon.

Jones D P H (2000) The Assessment of Parental Capacity. In Horwath J (ed) (2000) *The Child's World: Assessing Children in Need. The Reader.* The NSPCC, London.

Jones D P H (forthcoming) *Communicating with Children who may have been traumatised or maltreated.*

Jones D and Ramchandani P (1999) *Child Sexual Abuse: Informing Practice from Research.* Radcliffe Medical Press. Abingdon.

Kinston W and Loader P (1988) The Family Task Interview: A tool for clinical research infamily interaction. *Journal of Marital and Family Therapy.* **14**: 67–87.

Local Government Bill (1999) The Stationery Office, London.

Marsh P and Peel M (1999) *Leaving Care in Partnership: family involvement with care leavers.* The Stationery Office, London.

Morris J (1999) *Move on Up: Supporting Young Disabled People in the Transition to Adulthood.* Barnardos, London.

Morris K, Marsh P and Wiffin J (1998) *Family Group Conferences – A Training Pack.* The Family Rights Group, London.

NHS (1999a) *The Visits by Children to Ashworth, Boradmoor and Rampton Hospitals Directions.* Health Service Circular (HSC1999/160).

NHS (1999b) *Mental Health Act 1983 Code of Practice: Guidance on the visiting of psychiatric patients by children.* Health Service Circular (HSC1999/222) and Local Authority Circular (LAC 99(32)).

The NSPCC in association with Chailey Heritage and Department of Health (1997) *Turning Points: A Resource Pack for Communicating with Children.* The NSPCC, London.

The NSPCC and the University of Sheffield (2000) *The Child's World: Assessing Children in Need. Training and Development Pack.* The NSPCC, London.

Office for National Statistics (1999) *Mental Health of Children and Adolescents.* Monograph series (99)409. Office for National Statistics, London.

Office for National Statistics (2000) *The development and well-being of children and adolescents in Great Britiain.* Office for National Statistics, London.

Parker R M, Ward H, Jackson S, Aldgate J and Wedge P (eds) (1991) *Looking After Children: Assessing Outcomes in Children Care.* HMSO, London.

Pearn M, Roderick C and Mulrooney C (1995) *Learning Organisations in Practice.* McGraw-Hill, Maidenhead.

Piccinelli M, Tessari E, Bortolomasi M, Piasere O, Semenzin M, Garzotto N and Tansella M (1997) Efficacy of the alcohol use disorders identification test as a screening tool for hazardous alcohol intake and related disorders in primary care: A validity study. *British Medical Journal.* **514**: 420–424.

Ramsden S (1998) *Working with Children of Prisoners: A Resource for Teachers.* Save the Children, London.

Reder P and Duncan S (1999) *Lost Innocents.* Routledge, London.

Rutter M, Tizard J and Whitmore K (eds) (1970) *Education, Health and Behaviour.* Longmans, London.

Rutter M, Giller H and Hagell A (1998) *Anti-social Behaviour by Young People.* Cambridge University Press, Cambridge.

Ryan M (2000) *Working with Fathers.* Radcliffe Medical Press, Abingdon.

Schofield G (1998) Inner and outer worlds: a psychosocial framework for child and family social work. *Child and Family Social Work.* **3**, pp. 57–67.

Shemmings D (1999) *In on the Act – A Training Programme for Relevant Professionals. School of Social Work,* University of East Anglia, Norwich.

Silvester J, Bentovim A, Stratton P and Hanks H (1995) Using spoken attributions to classify abusive families. *Child Abuse and Neglect.* **19(10)**:1221–1232.

Sinclair R, Garnett l and Berridge D (1995) *Social Work and Assessment with Adolescents.* National Children's Bureau, London.

Smith M A (1985) *The Effects of Low Levels of Lead on Urban Children: The relevance of social factors.* Ph.D. Psychology, University of London.

Snaith R P, Constantopoulos A A, Jardine M Y and McGuffin P (1978) A clinical scale for the self-assessment of irritability. *British Journal of Psychiatry.* **132**: 164–171.

Social Exclusion Unit (1998) *Bringing Britain Together: A National Strategy for Neighbourhood Renewal.* The Stationery Office, London.

Social Exclusion Unit (1999) *Bridging the Gap: New opportunities for 16–18 year olds not in education, employment or training.* The Stationery Office, London.

Social Services Inspectorate and Surrey County Council (1995) *Unaccompanied Asylum-Seeking Children: A Training Pack.* Department of Health, London.

Stevenson O (1998) *Neglected Children: Issues and Dilemmas.* Blackwell Science, Oxford.

Thomas T and Beckford V (1999) *Adopted Children Speaking.* BAAF, London.

Tunstill J and Aldgate J (2000) *From Policy to Practice: Services for Children in Need.* The Stationery Office, London.

Utting D (1995) *Family and Parenthood: Supporting Families, Preventing Breakdown.* Joseph Rowntree Foundation, York.

Varma V (ed) (1993) *How and Why Children Fail.* Cassell, London.

Ward H (ed) (1995) *Looking After Children: Research into Practice: The Second Report of the Department of Health on Assessing Outcomes in Child Care.* HMSO, London.

Youth Justice and Criminal Evidence Act 1999 (1999). The Stationery Office, London